ISBN 978-1-330-21634-7
PIBN 10055027

Forgotten Books is a registered trademark of FB &c Ltd.
Copyright © 2018 FB &c Ltd.
FB &c Ltd, Dalton House, 60 Windsor Avenue, London, SW19 2RR.
Company number 08720141. Registered in England and Wales.

For support please visit www.forgottenbooks.com

1 MONTH OF
FREE
READING

at

www.ForgottenBooks.com

By purchasing this book you are eligible for one month membership to ForgottenBooks.com, giving you unlimited access to our entire collection of over 1,000,000 titles via our web site and mobile apps.

To claim your free month visit: www.forgottenbooks.com/free55027

HISTORY OF
ELEMENTARY EDUCATION

OF

ELEMENTARY EDUCATION

IN ENGLAND AND WALES

FROM 1800 TO THE PRESENT DAY

BY

C. BIRCHENOUGH, M.A.

LECTURER IN EDUCATION AT THE UNIVERSITY OF SHEFFIELD

LONDON: W. B. CLIVE

University Tutorial Press Lᵈ

HIGH ST., NEW OXFORD ST., W.C.

PREFACE.

THE aim of this book is primarily to present a concise and accurate account of the evolution of the system of elementary schooling in England and Wales as we know it to-day. It covers on broad lines the history of Elementary Education in this country since 1800, and meets the requirements of, for instance, the Syllabus of the Board of Education for teachers in training.

The need for such a book is widely admitted. The development of our educational system during the last fifty years, and particularly during the last decade, has been wide and rapid. The result is that all who are closely concerned with education, and especially teachers, are finding a knowledge of the history of elementary education in England and Wales in the nineteenth century to be almost essential to their work. Witness the inclusion of the subject in the syllabus for Training Colleges and for the Higher Froebel Certificate, and in the education course of almost every University in the country. The time therefore seems ripe for taking stock of what has been achieved, and seeing in what directions further progress is tending.

The treatment and the choice of subject-matter, which differ considerably from those adopted in other books dealing with the period, are the fruits of a number of years' experience in lecturing to University students. Thus while due regard has been paid to tracing the increasing demand for popular education, the movements that have

contributed to this, the gradual growth of State interference, and the building up of a great system of administrative machinery, equal attention has been given to the
development of the school itself, its planning, staffing,
curriculum, and method.

Accordingly, with a view to simplicity, the book has
been divided into two parts. Part I. deals with the
growth of the elementary school system as viewed, so to
speak, from *without*. Part II. follows the changes that
have taken place *within* the four walls of the school.
The last Chapter—called for convenience Part III.—
is concerned with the changes in the status and in the
training of the teacher. The arrangement is clearly one
of expedience, and if the plan appears on occasion to be
somewhat artificial, it is nevertheless hoped that the total
gain in clearness will more than compensate for this.
Cross references have been given, and an effort has been
made to avoid unnecessary repetition.

In using the book students may follow the order of the
chapters, concentrating first on the development of the
system of popular instruction, and afterwards re-studying
the period from the standpoint of the class-room. Or they
may prefer to study the two aspects together, in which
case they will read Chapters I. and VI.; II. and VII.;
III., IV., and VIII.; V. and IX. together. Some may
choose to study the second part of the book first.

In this attempt to trace the history of elementary
schooling I have derived considerable help from two books
by Kirkman Grey, *A History of English Philanthropy* and
Philanthropy and the State. I have also found useful such
well-known writings on the period as those of Sir Henry
Craik, Mr. Graham Balfour, Mr. de Montmorency, Dean
Gregory, and Dr. Michael Sadler. But in the main I have

depended on a first-hand study of the mass of source material available. Numerous references have been given to enable the student to pursue any topic at greater length for himself.

It is impossible to acknowledge in detail the help which I have received in connection with the book. To Professor Welton of the University of Leeds my thanks are specially due for his careful reading of the whole book in proof, for his valuable suggestions, and for placing unreservedly at my disposal his wide experience, his ripe judgment and rich historical scholarship. To Professor Green I am indebted for reading part of the book in manuscript. I have to acknowledge many kindnesses in lending me scarce books and pamphlets. In particular I have to thank Canon Symonds for the loan of the whole of the Reports, etc., so far as they are still available, of the Sunday Schools at Stockport since their foundation in 1785, together with the Accounts, Minutes, and Reports of the National Day and Sunday Schools. My thanks are also due to Mr. A. J. Mundella, Monsignor Pennington, Professor W. J. Roberts, and Mr. Holman, as well as to many friends both in England and Wales among inspectors of schools, professors and teachers of all grades who have so kindly given of their knowledge and advice.

As the danger of error in writing briefly on a variety of topics is very great, I ought to add that I alone am responsible for the contents of the book.

C. B.

The University,
Sheffield.
August 1914.

CONTENTS.

PART I.

THE EVOLUTION OF THE MODERN STATE SYSTEM OF ELEMENTARY EDUCATION.

CHAPTER   PAGE

I. GENERAL EDUCATION, BEFORE 1800 1

II. THE PHILANTHROPIC PERIOD, 1800-1833 . . . 28

III. PERIOD OF INCIPIENT STATE ACTION.—I. SUPERVISION OR ANNEXATION? 1833-1847 62

IV. II. PERIOD OF SUPERVISION, 1847-1870 . . . 102

V. PARTITION AND ANNEXATION—

I. PERIOD OF PARTITION 130

II. PERIOD OF ANNEXATION 169

PART II.

THE EVOLUTION OF THE CURRICULUM AND THE INTERNAL ORGANISATION OF THE PRIMARY SCHOOL.

VI. THE ELEMENTARY SCHOOL AT THE CLOSE OF THE EIGHTEENTH CENTURY 183

VII. TEACHING BY MACHINERY 210

VIII. TRANSITION AND REACTION 250

IX. THE NEW SPIRIT IN EDUCATION 285

PART III.

X. THE TEACHER 324

INDEX 374

PART I.

THE EVOLUTION OF THE MODERN STATE SYSTEM OF ELEMENTARY EDUCATION.

CHAPTER I.

GENERAL INTRODUCTION.

BEFORE 1800.

"It is manifest that a Christian and Useful Education of the Children of the Poor is absolutely necessary to their Piety, Virtue and honest Livelihood . . . to their Happiness here and hereafter . . . as well as to the Ease and Security of all other People whatsoever."—*An Account of Charity Schools*, 1708.

"The poor man has no need of education."
—ROUSSEAU : *Emile*, Bk. I.

"The education of the common people requires, perhaps, in a civilised and commercial society the attention of the public more than that of people of some rank and fortune."
—ADAM SMITH : *Wealth of Nations.*

"A nation under a well-regulated government should permit none to be uninstructed. It is a monarchial and aristocratical government only that requires ignorance for its support."
—THOMAS PAINE : *Rights of Man.*

THE history of elementary education[1] in this country during the nineteenth century is the record of a persistent attack against privilege. What was once a question of charity is now a matter of right, and equality of educa-

---

[1] The term "elementary education" is somewhat ambiguous. As used in legislation and politics it has reference to provision for definite needs of the community, and is equivalent to *schooling*. It is in this sense that it is used here.

H. ED.

1

tional opportunity is taking the place of a system of education graded according to the social position of the individual. National elementary education as it now exists is the result of a slow process of evolution characterised by experiment, by successes and failures, by opportunism and compromise. Here, as always, reform has been the outcome of long and sometimes blind struggle towards better things. There has therefore been no sudden reform, no attempt to implant a new or foreign system on the country as a whole. There have been of course periods of rapid educational advance when the vitality and force of a new faith have carried the nation forward, just as there have been periods when criticism rather than constructive ideas have predominated. Some epochs stand · out with especial significance, for example 1808, 1811, 1833, 1839, 1843, 1870, 1902—great landmarks in the history of popular education.

What is true of the development of the present system of national education is no less true of the school itself, its curriculum, its motive. As it has passed by almost imperceptible stages from the school of the poor to the school of the people its breadth of outlook, the liberality of its curriculum, its effectiveness and its dignity have shown a corresponding advance. No institution has more effectually resisted foreign influence or shown greater capacity for assimilation and for compromise. Indeed the most characteristic feature of English elementary education whether viewed from without or from within is the way in which it has responded to and interpreted the conflicting social, religious, and educational aspirations of the times. We shall understand these better and see more clearly how they affected elementary education if we look first of all at the eighteenth century.

Elementary education in England and Wales in the eighteenth century was a matter of indi-

Eighteenth Century Private Schools.

vidual enterprise or dependent upon charity. All the existing agencies may be roughly grouped under three heads—private, domestic (home), and charitable. Of these the private schools were by far the most numerous and were the recognised means of educating all but the poorest children. They were fee-paying schools, conducted by individuals at their own risk and for their own profit. Their number we have no means of knowing; they depended entirely upon local circumstances and the demand for education that changing economic conditions would create. There was probably much truth in what Shenstone wrote in 1742 :—

> " In every village mark'd with little spire,
>   Embower'd in trees, and hardly known to fame,
> There dwells, in lowly shed and mean attire,
>   A matron old, whom we schoolmistress name,
> Who boasts unruly brats with birch to tame." [1]

These private schools covered the whole field of educational activity. Some were dame schools and provided only for children up to about seven years of age. They sought in a very imperfect way to meet the demand for a crèche and for an infant school. Others under various names gave an elementary education. Some were day schools, others were boarding schools, others again were held in the evening. It was at one of these evening schools, William Cobbett tells us,[2] that his father got his education (c. 1740) while working as a plough boy at twopence a day. Some schools offered a definite cur-

---

[1] *The Schoolmistress.*
[2] *William Cobbett : a Biography*, Edward Smith, Vol. I., p. 6.

riculum at a fixed charge, but in others pupils might take one or more subjects as they pleased and according to the fees they were prepared to pay. There was in fact endless variety. Some schools prided themselves on giving a commercial education, some specialised in penmanship and called themselves Writing Schools, some laid stress on mathematics ; some merely taught reading, others taught nothing at all. As might be expected this class of school showed every degree of excellence and incompetency. Some were well housed, others were mere hovels. In these private schools we find as masters the refuse of every other profession, the lazy, the economic misfit, the decrepit, and the unemployed, as well as others who combined the office of teacher with such occupations as cobbling, tinkering, engraving, and in the case of women washing and shop-keeping. Such schools existed and indeed flourished in great numbers down to the introduction of a State system of elementary education in 1870.

But not all private schools were inefficient. On the contrary, many were uncommonly efficient even when judged by the standards of to-day. Some of these schools, as for example in Sheffield,[1] were in charge of men who showed no mean acquaintance with the history of education, who were thoroughly alive to the importance of making school work meaningful and of stimulating their pupils to self-help, who bestowed much thought on the organisation and the grading of their schools, and composed special books for the use of their scholars. It was

---

[1] See for example the volume of *Juvenile Essays*, to which is prefixed a " Brief History of Education and a Table of the System " pursued in the Milk Street Academy, Sheffield.—J. H. Abraham, 1805.

The writer has before him three other books by Sheffield private-school masters, two on arithmetic and one on the use of the globes, dated respectively 1766, 1794, and 1787.

in a private school attended by poor children that Lancaster worked out his plan of a monitorial system. Again, we have only to recall the excellent work done by Mrs. Barbauld at Palgrave and to reflect that the best elementary text-books of the day were the product of this class of school, to realise that at their best they were unequalled by any of their contemporaries in the freshness and reality of the education they provided.

Home education was common among the middle classes during the period, and calls for some attention in any attempt to present a picture of elementary practice in this country at the close of the eighteenth century, when, as Crabbe tells us,—

> "To every class we have a school assign'd,
> Rules for all ranks and food for every mind." [1]

It will be treated under the development of educational practice in the second half of the book.[2]

But without exception the agencies for providing a free schooling called themselves educational **Charity Education.** charities. They embraced a variety of parochial, ward, and other "charity" schools, schools of industry, workhouse and hospital schools, Sunday schools, evening schools, circulating schools (Wales), etc. These were institutions that provided for the education of the poor. There was of course an important body of endowed grammar and allied writing schools scattered unevenly up and down the country, but these were in the main secondary schools, they were not and never had been intended for the masses. They were essentially a middle class provision thoroughly aristocratic in conception, offering to the poorest boy of ability the avenue to a liberal education. There was nothing in the

---

[1] *The Borough*, Letter xxiv.   [2] See p. 198 f.

nature of public elementary school provision such as we are accustomed to to-day.[1]

The explanation of this seems to be found not in any distrust of State interference in domestic matters, but in the prevailing class view of society and in the tendency to regard education, in so far as it had any public significance, as an ecclesiastical affair.[2]

In a highly stratified society, where the station of each individual was regarded as fixed by Divine or other dispensation at birth, where great numbers of hewers of wood and drawers of water were essential,—a broad basis of poverty on which an aristocracy might rest—there was little hope for popular

Education and Society.

---

[1] It is interesting however to note that in the Commonwealth Parliament 1649, in view of the neglected religious condition of many parts of Wales, an Act was passed appointing Commissioners to examine the religious and educational needs of the several counties and to appoint preachers and schoolmasters applying to their support various ecclesiastical funds. In Scotland a Parochial Schools Act 1646 provided for the establishment of an elementary school in every parish, but it remained inoperative until it was amended in 1696. Even so, it was not until the nineteenth century that every parish had its school. A similar Massachusetts Act 1692 provided for the compulsory establishment of a school for reading and writing, and maintained by local rates in every village of fifty householders.

[2] In England, as well as in Germany, the Reformation had done much to destroy existing means of education (see De Montmorency: *State Intervention in English Education*). Public instruction, however, was necessary to check the growth of superstition, and it was under this influence that we find both Edward VI. and Elizabeth ordering the clergy to teach their parishioners reading and writing. The injunction seems, however, to have been poorly carried out and must soon have been ignored, for the Canon of 1604 only enjoined catechising. This, too, never became universal. It left too much to the interest and initiative of individual clergy, many of whom seem to have considered it beneath their dignity. It was, however, a well recognised practice previous to the eighteenth century, for it was to the decay of catechising that many earnest men of that period attributed the spread of ignorance and irreligion.

Thus we find the Bishop of Norwich insisting upon the practice of catechising throughout his diocese. Bishop Ken is said to have set up a education save from a humanitarian or religious impulse. This was equally the case whether the social grades were supposedly determined by wealth or, as with the men of the Enlightenment, by brains. Mandeville was only expressing a well recognised sentiment when he wrote:[1] " Reading and writing I would not hinder them, nor force them upon society: as long as there was anything to be got by them, there would be masters enough to teach them: but nothing should be taught for nothing but at church : . . . for if parents are so miserably poor that they cannot afford their children these first elements of learning, it is impudence of them to aspire any further." Even Rousseau, with all his sympathy for the poor, makes no provision in the *Emile* for giving them any other education beyond what they can get in ordinary intercourse with their fellows, through their daily occupations, and in contact with nature. The poor man has no need of schooling, he tells us,—a position from which he retreats, however, when face to face with the practical problem of framing a scheme of education for Poland.

parochial school in every parish of his diocese, and to have been actively engaged in founding village and Sunday schools. Again, we find the Rev. Abraham Colfe, Vicar of Lewisham, by his will dated 1656 providing for catechising, for the purchase of Bibles, for the founding of almshouses and two schools—one a reading school for poor and destitute children, the other a grammar school for the sons of needy clergy and the children of poor tradesmen, etc. (Cf. Kirkman Grey : *History of Philanthropy*, pp. 47-49.)

In 1663 Marchamont Needham, the journalist and pamphleteer, in advocating the exclusion of schismatic schoolmasters from the teaching profession, was urging the employment of parish clerks for teaching the children of the poor and preparing them for public catechising in church on Sundays. It was in reviving and taking steps to make permanent the old practice of catechising that much of the educational activity of the eighteenth century was expended.

[1] *Fable of the Bees*, 1772 Edition, p. 224.

In short it is to a religious motive, or to some pressing social problem such as pauperism, that we **The Religious Motive in Education.** must look for any interest in the education of the poor previous to the rise of a new school of social thinkers in the latter half of the century. It was the men who believed that charity was a duty before God—that "the delivery of the talent was the injunction of the duty"—the men who sought to check irreligion by spreading broadcast the great principles of Christianity who were the pioneers of popular education. Their charity was catholic in its range. Beside endeavouring to bring the means of instruction within the reach of the poor they were variously employed providing for the sick, finding work for the unemployed, supporting the aged, subscribing to funds for the release of prisoners, and so on. To be rich in good works was held to be one of "the surest and safest ways of thriving." It was thrice blessed, not only did it bring such immediate relief to the poor, but it was conducive to a better understanding and attachment between classes, and it gave hope through improvement in the children for a better state of society in the future.[1]

These ideas were of course not peculiar to the eighteenth

---

[1] Cf. Gouge: *Collected Works*, 1706, *passim*; Robert Nelson: *An Address to Persons of Quality and Estate*, 1715; Sir Thos. Bernard: *A Digest of the Reports of the Society for Bettering the Condition of the Poor (Education)*, 1809; also Kirkman Grey: *History of Philanthropy*.

How deeply significant this two-grade view of society was in determining the outlook of even the philanthropically minded towards "the inferior part of mankind" may be seen from the wording of a typical charity school prayer for daily use: "Give me Grace I beseech thee, O my God, to live this day as in thy Sight, and to do always such Things as please thee. Make me dutiful and obedient to my Benefactors and charitable to my Enemies. Make me temperate and chaste, meek and patient, just and true in all my dealings, content and industrious in my station."—*The Poor Girl's Primer. For the Use of the Charity School in Sheffield*. 1789.

century. It is, however, in this period that we see the first concerted attempt to provide an elementary education for all the children in the country. Of the circumstances that contributed to this the most important was the application to philanthropy of the joint stock principle that had astonished the commercial world in the previous century. It was the subscription list and the resources of associative philanthropy that made organised movement possible. The first venture of this kind was probably the founding of a society in London in 1674 by Thomas Gouge in conjunction with Dean (afterwards Archbishop) Tillotson, Richard Baxter, Thomas Firmin, and others, for the purpose of establishing catechetical schools for "teaching the poorest Welsh children to read English and the boys to write and cast accounts, whereby they will be enabled to read our English Bibles and treatises," and for circulating throughout the Principality religious books both in English and Welsh.[1] It was followed by three great ventures in popular education :—

(1) the Parochial Charity School movement, which was especially vigorous during the first thirty years of the eighteenth century and may be dated from the founding of the Society for Promoting Christian Knowledge, 1698;

(2) the Circulating School movement under Griffith Jones and later Madam Bevan, 1737-1777, which was confined exclusively to Wales;

(3) the Sunday School movement, which spread rapidly after 1784.

In each of these movements a religious and humanitarian motive predominated. The first was principally within the confines of the Church, and was designed to counteract the vice and degradation into which the poor

---

[1] A copy of the engagement is given in *The Sunday Schools of Wales*, D. Evans, p. 87; also in Phillips : *Wales*.

had been allowed to fall through the decline of religious enthusiasm that had accompanied the rationalising influence of the age. "It must needs pity any Christian heart to see the little dirty infantry which swarms up and down the alleys and lanes with curses and ribaldry in their mouths and other rude behaviour as if they were intended to put off their humanity and degenerate into brutes."[1] The Sunday schools were an outcome of the Methodist movement, and the Circulating Schools of an earlier revival under Griffith Jones in Wales. In a very real sense they may be regarded as so many attempts to evangelise the masses by reviving and making permanent the old practice of catechising.

> " Happy's the child whose youngest years
>   Receive instruction well ;
> Who hates the sinner's path and fears
>   The road that leads to hell.
>
> .   .   .   .
>
> 'Tis easier work if we begin
>   To fear the Lord betimes
> While sinners that grow old in sin
>   Are hardened in their crimes."[2]

But they had in view much more than religious instruction. Rather they aimed at spreading abroad a practical piety, at helping the poor to lead industrious, upright lives in the sphere in which they were placed. Their ideal might with little exaggeration be summed up as training the poor to poverty. They offered one means of attacking the problem of pauperism that was eating like a canker into the life of the nation. The causes of pauperism were little understood, but men were inclined to attribute it to laziness, to a want of robustness of character, to an

Aim of Charity School Education.

---

[1] *Discourse concerning Schools and Schoolmasters*, Marchamont Needham, 1663.   [2] *Divine Songs for Children*, I. Watts.

absence of self-respect, and to regard it as largely or entirely dependent upon the individual. There was some difference of opinion, however, as to the best methods of treating the disease. Those that believed that laziness lay at the root of the trouble were in favour of inuring children from an early age to habits of industry, giving them a trade and providing them with religious instruction. Others looked rather to the 3 R's, to the growth of self-respect, and the moral uplift that came from religious teaching that touched the heart and the conscience. But the ideal education undoubtedly provided a training in industry " which is no unprofitable Piece of Learning, considering that an early Habit of Idleness is the common Bane of those who cannot hope to support life otherwise than by their Labour."[1] Each of these opinions found expression in a special type of curriculum.

Here it is necessary to emphasise the fact that the question of child labour is inextricably bound up

Working Schools and Child Labour.

with the development of elementary education during the eighteenth and nineteenth centuries. Child labour was of course nothing new,[2] but owing to industrial competition abroad and low wages at home it had come to be regarded by parents as a regular means of augmenting the family income, especially at a time when the spinning of linen yarn opened up avenues of labour well within the capabilities of young children. The practice of setting poor children to work was viewed with favour by middle class opinion and became a recognised philanthropic device in attacking social and educational problems. Thus John Locke, in a memorandum on Poor Law Reform, 1697, written while Commissioner of Trade and Plantations, advocated the general

---

[1] *Charity Sermon* (St. Sepulchre's). Robert Moss, D.D., 1708.
[2] Cf. Macaulay on child labour in the seventeenth century, *History of England*, Vol. I., p. 417. (Library Edition.)

adoption in every parish of a workhouse school. To these
"working schools" were to be sent all pauper children
between 3 and 14 years of age, to be there taught " spinning
or knitting or some other woollen manufacture, unless in
countries (districts) where the place shall furnish other
material fitter for the employment of children." Each child
was to have an allowance of bread and in winter a little
gruel. Provision was to be made for religious instruction,
but apparently not for learning to read. The proceeds of
a child's labour were estimated ultimately to cover the cost
of his teaching and partial maintenance.[1]

In this way it was hoped that children would be kept
"in much better order, be better provided for and from
infancy be inured to work, which is of no small consequence
to the making of them sober and industrious all their lives
after." Workhouse schools on these lines were opened at
Bristol, Hull, and elsewhere, and were maintained by donations and local rates.[2] There was little difference during
the first quarter of the century between these schools and
charity schools with an industrial bias—" schools of industry " as they were called.[3]

Ordinary day school education was decidedly unpopular:
employers objected to it on the ground of its diminishing
the supply of labour and producing disaffection[4]; the well-

---

[1] *Life of John Locke*, Fox Bourne, Vol. II., pp. 383-5.

[2] Cf. *Considerations on the Increase of the Poor-rates and on the
State of the Workhouse in Kingston-upon-Hull*, 1799.

[3] For a typical school of industry cf. that of Thomas Firmin in Little
Britain, 1675. It was partly a school, partly a factory, and was conducted
for the joint purpose of teaching children to read and providing them with
employment, the money so earned being carried home at week end. Children
were admitted when 3 years old, and until 4 years of age were taught the
elements of reading. At 5 to 6 years of age the children, we are told, could
earn 2d., and when rather older 3d. per day. A woman was engaged at
5s. a week to teach spinning and reading. (Cf. *History of Philanthropy*,
Kirkman Grey.)   [4] See *Essay on Charity Schools*, I. Watts.

to-do complained that it was producing a race of idlers; the poor opposed it because it involved a loss of income. As the eighteenth century advanced and the demand for child labour increased with the coming of the industrial revolution, we find that one of the main claims urged in favour of Sunday schools was that they provided an elementary education without interfering with the work of the week.[1] At the same time the " school of industry " acquired a new popularity.

We may now trace briefly by way of illustration the history of the three charity school movements.

9

The Parochial Charity School Movement. The S.P.C.K. had its origin in one of the devotional societies that were common at the close of the seventeenth century. Among its objects were the founding of Catechetical schools for the education of poor children in the principles of the Established Church, and the establishment of circulating lending libraries, together with the distribution of Bibles and other suitable literature. These schools were copied from others already in existence,[2] and directions as to their constitution and management were carefully laid down by the central body. They were generally supported by subscription, and were designed for the benefit of such poor children between 7 and 12 years of age whose parents or friends were unable ",to give them learning." The schools spread rapidly. By 1734 there were 132 schools in London and 1,329 in the country, providing for 5,123 and 19,506 children respectively.[3]

---

[1] Cf. for example the Reports of the Sunday Schools at Stockport.

[2] In this connection see *Charity Schools*, by De Montmorency, *Cyclopedia of Education*, Paul Munro.

[3] Some of the mine-owners in Wales supported schools for the children of their workpeople. At Winlaton in Durham the employees of an ironworks, assisted by the owner, made a weekly contribution for the education of their children.

Sometimes the schools were endowed, and many were the recipients of bequests and donations from time to time. Some were boarding schools, which maintained, clothed, and educated the children until they were of age to be apprenticed or put to service. Many adopted a distinctive dress, blue, green, orange, etc., after the fashion of earlier hospital schools.[1]

Some establishments made provision for but a few boarders; others were day schools only. Of these some merely educated the children, others clothed them as well, others again provided the children with a free meal a day. A number of similar institutions were founded and supported by Dissenters and Roman Catholics.[2] In all alike religion and dogma constituted the most important part of the curriculum, but they also provided reading and writing, and in boys' schools arithmetic as well. From the outset some schools introduced such industrial occupations as spinning wool, mending and making shoes, sewing, knitting, etc., and in 1712 the S.P.C.K. recommended a half-time system, devoting only alternate days to ordinary school work. The object was to fit boys for apprenticeship and girls for domestic service. In some schools special apprenticeship funds were available.

As early as 1700 an Inspector of Charity Schools in and about London was appointed, and in 1710 a plan for a Training School for Masters and Mistresses was discussed. The teachers were generally of inferior merit, as might be expected when the annual expense of a school[3] for 50 boys, including master's salary, room, firing, books, clothing, and all expenses, required only £75, and a corresponding school

---

[1] *Account of Charity Schools. Two Hundred Years : a History of the S.P.C.K.*, Allen and McClure. *Elementary Education*, Gregory.

[2] See *The Education of the Poor in the Eighteenth Century*, David Salmon, pp. 23-28; "An Essay towards the Encouragement of Charity Schools," I. Watts, *Collected Works*, Vol. IV.   [3] In London.

for girls £60. According to the early regulations of the S.P.C.K. the master of a charity school was required to be a member of the Church of England, to be not under 25 years of age, to be able to pass an examination in the principles of the Christian religion, to be equilibrated and a good disciplinarian, to have aptitude for teaching, to write a good hand and to understand arithmetic.[1]

By the middle of the century the Charity School movement had reached its height and was providing for the educational needs of some 30,000 children. After that, although charity schools continued to be founded, interest in the work flagged, and the latter half of the century furnishes many records of disappointment, lowered ideals, and partial failure. Funds were mismanaged, schools were left in charge of masters too old for the work, and some establishments practically ceased to exist. We have it on Bernard's[2] authority that in a number of schools only a single scholar was on the foundation at the close of the century. With the rise of the National schools at the beginning of the nineteenth century the *raison d'être* of a number of these schools disappeared, and they were merged into the new establishments.[3]

In spite of their narrow curriculum and limited outlook these schools did a great work in the cause of popular education, and the legacies and endowments they received from old boys who had prospered in after life are the best evidence of the gratitude they evoked. Nor did they exist in England alone. A similar movement began in Scotland in 1705 for establishing charity schools in parishes that had failed to carry out the provisions of the Act of 1696, while abroad the great charity school movement that arose

---

[1] *Account of Charity Schools.*

[2] Sir Thomas Bernard : *Digest of Reports (Education) S.B.C.P.,* pp. 98-9 ; see on p. 39.   [3] *E.g.* at Barnsley.

under the stimulus of pietism had its origin in the pioneer work of Francke at Halle, 1695-1727, work that was closely followed by the Central Committee of the S.P.C.K.[1]

Meanwhile a new educational movement had been begun in Wales by the Rev. Griffith Jones, vicar of Llanddowror, a corresponding member of the S.P.C.K. Impressed by the ignorance of many of his congregation of the Scriptures, he had established catechising classes for adults. The success of the plan over many years inspired him with a desire to extend his system over the whole country and provide schools for old and young. This he was enabled to do through the liberality of philanthropic individuals in England and Wales, backed up by large donations of Bibles and other books from the S.P.C.K. The existing English Charity Schools in Wales were quite inadequate in numbers and were failures educationally, for after three, four, or five years all the children were able to do, according to Griffith Jones,[2] was " to read very badly some early parts of the Bible without knowing the Welsh of it or the meaning of what they said when they repeated the catechism." In 1737 he began to establish his " Schools of Piety," variously named Catechetical Charity Schools, Circulating Schools, and subsequently Madam Bevan's Schools, the names emphasising special characteristics of these institutions. They were free schools for teaching the poor to read the Bible in the vernacular, and for instructing them in the principles of religion by way of question and answer. They were established in any sort of building that came to hand, church, chapel, or

Welsh Circulating Schools.

---

[1] It is worth noting that Francke's account of the schools at Halle, *Pietas Hallensis*, was included in the list of books recommended for Masters of Charity Schools, 1713. There is no mention of La Salle.

[2] *Welch Piety*, 1738.

untenanted house, and were conducted by travelling school-masters who continued in the place for three months, and for a further three months if needful, before moving on elsewhere. In this way they were extended over the whole of Wales. They were opened day and evening to people of all ages, and careful records of the numbers attending during the day time were kept.[1] This movement is credited by Griffith Jones with stimulating a new interest in charity education in England.[2]

By Griffith Jones' death in 1761, 3,495 schools had been established at different times and in various places, attended by 158,237 scholars not counting more than twice the number who were instructed in the evening. The work was continued by Madam Bevan until her death in 1777, by which time the numbers had risen to 6,465 schools and 314,051 scholars. After this, through the misdirection of trust funds, the schools soon ceased to exist. Nothing however could better express the spiritual forces at work, or the appeal these schools made to the affections of the Welsh people, than the fact that they flourished during the very years when disillusionment and loss of faith were paralysing the spread of popular education in England.[3] In 1785 the establishment of circulating schools was again begun by the Rev. Thomas Charles, of Bala.[4] Instruction in reading and in the Scriptures was now given on Sunday as well as during the week. In spite of early opposition Sunday Schools soon sprang up, under the stimulus of the Revival movement, wherever the ground had been prepared

---

[1] A summary of the method of organising these schools is given by Griffith Jones in *Welch Piety*, 1743.

[2] *Welch Piety*, 1740.

[3] For a detailed account of the Circulating Schools see the volumes of *Welch Piety* or *The Life and Times of Griffith Jones of Llanddowror*. David Jones.

[4] In some districts of North Wales only 1 in 20 could read.

by Griffith Jones' schools. Thus arose the Welsh Sunday
School movement,[1] thereby making permanent the work that
had begun half a century before of bringing the elements
of education within the reach of all the people regardless
of age. In this it differed from the English Sunday
School movement, which in the early stages made no provision for adults.

Though isolated Sunday schools had existed in England
certainly as far back as the middle of the
**The
Sunday School
Movement.** seventeenth century, the concerted movement
for the establishment of these institutions
dates from the opening of a Dame Sunday
school for the ragged and turbulent boys in one of the
poorest districts of Gloucester in 1780 by Robert Raikes.
A similar work was begun about the same time by the Rev.
Thomas Stock, a local curate. Raikes was a typical middle
class business man, the editor of the *Gloucester Journal*,
and a regular attendant at Church. The coarse, undisci-
plined, illiterate state of the children in the poorer districts
of the city suggested to him the desirability of a school
where they might learn self-control and the elements of
reading, and be brought up under Christian influences.
After some experimenting the plan of Sunday schools in
charge of paid teachers, where children were taught reading
and a knowledge of the Bible, was widely advertised through
the medium of his journal. The leading magazines of the
day[2] were also used for propagandist purposes and the
idea succeeded in capturing popular imagination. This is
Raikes' title to fame—that he made universal a practice
that until then had been local and practically unheard of.
Though meeting with opposition in some quarters schools
sprang up rapidly everywhere, in manufacturing towns

[1] *The Sunday Schools of Wales*, D. Evans.
[2] See e.g. *The Gentleman's Magazine*.

and in country villages, sometimes as the outcome of individual initiative, sometimes in connection with particular
churches and chapels. At the outset the movement was
undenominational in character, as witness the founding in
1785 of " The Society for the Establishment and Support
of Sunday Schools throughout the Kingdom of Great
Britain," with local committees half Churchmen and half
Dissenters. Two years later it was estimated that a
quarter of a million children were attending these schools,
and the numbers increased rapidly. By 1801 the London
Society alone had connected with it 1,516 schools and
156,490 children.[1]

The explanation of the rapid spread of Sunday Schools
is to be found in the religious, social, and
economic forces at work in society. The
endeavour to establish the reasonableness of
Christianity, to harmonise reason and revela-
tion, had resulted in a cold unemotional religion that failed
to touch the hearts of a great section of the community.
To win men back from the indifference into which they had
fallen, learned discourses had to be put aside and attention
once more directed to the simple truths set out in the
Gospel. To preach this evangel to eighteenth-century
England was the work of the two Wesleys and George
Whitefield. In Wales the same message was preached by
Howell Harris, Daniel Rowlands, and others. In each
country the result was a great religious revival, a stirring
of dry bones, and the infusion of a new spirit into the
Established Church that found expression in the Evangelical movement. Along with it, as in the earlier revival
of Griffith Jones, went a new interest in popular education.

The Methodist Movement.

[1] *Robert Raikes: a History of the Origin of Sunday Schools*, A.
Gregory. *Robert Raikes, the Man and his Work*, J. H. Harris.
History of Philanthropy, Kirkman Grey.

Through the work of men like Henry Venn and William Wilberforce and the writings of Hannah More, many among the middle and upper classes of society acquired a new sense of responsibility towards social and educational reform. To it is due a large share of the credit for the rise of the new voluntary movement in the sphere of elementary education at the beginning of the nineteenth century.

But other factors were contributing to direct attention to popular education—(1) the rapid growth of population in towns, and (2) revolutionary thought.

Both before and after the Revolution of 1789 French revolutionary thought exerted a great influence on public opinion in this country. **Influence of Revolutionary Thought.** Briefly, it represented an attack on over-interference, vested interests, superstition, and tyranny in every form. It showed a marked propensity to ignore history and judge everything by its immediate reasonableness. It pictured a society free from all laws and coercion, freed from all clerical influence and ruled by universal benevolence, a society in which all men had equal rights and were able to attain the fullest self-realisation. In its strictly educational aspects, it demanded the withdrawal of education from the Church and the setting up of a State system of secular instruction. La Chalotais put the position concisely in these words: " I do not presume to exclude ecclesiastics, but I protest against the exclusion of laymen. I dare claim for the nation an education which depends only on the State, because it belongs essentially to the State; because every State has an inalienable and indefensible right to instruct its members; because, finally, the children of the State ought to be educated by the members of the State." [1]

[1] *Essai d'éducation nationale.* See Compayré: *Histoire critique des doctrines de l'éducation en France,* Vol. II.

Among those who believed that public instruction was a civil affair, a "government undertaking," we find three schools of thought. First, there were those who, like Voltaire, had no sympathy with popular schooling, and who regarded education as essentially aristocratic. Secondly, there were men like Rousseau and La Chalotais, who exhibited strong prejudice against popular instruction and especially against such instruction badly conceived, but who were not consistent in their opposition. Thus, La Chalotais taught that "the peasantry . . . . ought not to be neglected in the system of instruction, ... there should be instructed and competent generals, magistrates, and ecclesiastics, and skilful artists and citizens all in fit proportion. It is for the Government to make each citizen so pleased with his condition that he may not be forced to withdraw from it." Finally, in Turgot and the physiocrats on the one hand, and many Parliamentarians on the other, we have men deliberately working for the cause of popular education and urging the doctrine of equality of educational opportunity. " Each one ought to have the opportunity to receive the education which is adapted to his need," said Rolland, the President of the Parliament of Paris, in 1768. " Education cannot be too widely diffused." Similarly Turgot, seven years later in a memorial to the King on local government and national education, pleaded the cause of popular schooling as the best means of ensuring the public good and attaching the affections of the people to the throne.[1]

At the same time the theoretical justification of popular instruction was being unwittingly provided by Helvetius and others, who taught that mental life was simply the product of sense impression, and that education in its widest sense was the sole cause of the difference between

[1] *Life and Writings of Turgot*, Stephens, pp. 269-272.

individuals. From such a theory, imperfectly apprehended, it was easy to deduce an exaggerated view of the value of mere schooling as a means of social betterment, which inevitably resulted at a later period in disappointment and disillusionment.

All this had far-reaching results. On the one hand it confirmed many of the middle and upper classes in their opposition to popular education in the hope of safeguarding the masses from the disturbing influences of revolutionary thought and checking the spread of socialism, deism, and atheism. On the other hand it provided men of more liberal outlook with a convincing argument for enlightening the people, so as to render them a less easy prey to inflammatory writings and the declamation of interested and ambitious demagogues.[1] This was the more necessary in view of the distress that had accompanied the change in agricultural and industrial conditions. It was especially important now that the grouping of large numbers of men in the factory towns had made discussion of social conditions inevitable, but had made no corresponding provision for their general enlightenment.

At the same time there gradually grew up a body of opinion in favour of State action in popular education, of separating secular from religious teaching, and of making school attendance compulsory. Adam Smith, Malthus, and Thomas Paine exerted a profound influence in this connection. The first two approached the question from an economic, the last from a political standpoint. On the

Importance of Popular Education.

---

[1] Thus Sir T. Bernard looked to a "general system of EDUCATION, regulated according to the rites and doctrines of the Church of England" to preserve the poor "against the taint of sedition and the poison of infidelity." —*Digest of Reports* (*Education*) *S.B.C.P.*, 1809. Cf. the sets of *Cheap Repository Tracts* published with a similar object.

other hand Godwin, the philosopher and oracle of the revolutionary party in England, is a representative of those who looked with extreme distrust on State interference in any form in educational affairs.

Adam Smith (1776) argues that in all highly organised societies, unless special steps are taken to check it, the labouring poor inevitably de-generate both physically and mentally. In a ruder con-dition of society more varied demands are made upon the individual, inventiveness is constantly being called for, and the mind has no opportunity to stagnate. This is no longer the case when the individual is confined to a narrow routine occupation day after day. Such an individual degenerates and may well become a danger to society, the victim of all sorts of prejudice and a prey to every kind of superstition.

Adam Smith.

" A man without the proper use of the intellectual faculties of a man, is, if possible, more contemptible than even a coward, and seems to be mutilated and deformed in a still more essential part of the character of human nature. Though the State was to derive no advantage from the instruction of the inferior ranks of the people, it would still deserve its attention that they should not be altogether uninstructed. The State, however, derives no inconsiderable ad-vantage from their instruction. The more they are instructed the less liable they are to the delusions of enthusiasm and superstition, which, among ignorant nations, frequently occasion the most dread-ful disorders. An instructed and intelligent people, besides, are always more decent and orderly than a stupid one. They feel themselves, each individually, more respectable and more likely to obtain the respect of their lawful superiors, and they are therefore more disposed to respect those superiors. They are more disposed to examine, and are more capable of seeing through, the interested complaints of faction and sedition, and they are, upon that account, less apt to be misled into any wanton or unnecessary opposition to the measures of government. In free countries, where the safety of government depends very much upon the favourable judgment which the people may form of its conduct, it must surely be of the highest importance that they should not be disposed to judge rashly or capriciously concerning it." [1]

Accordingly the State has every right to make elementary education compulsory and to make it a public charge, though for the sake of efficiency he recommends leaving provision for the payment of school fees and for voluntary contributions. At the same time he advocates a cautious introduction of military training to keep up the standard of national physique and to check any loss of martial spirit likely to result from confined employment.

Thomas Paine. Thomas Paine was the pamphleteer of the revolutionary party, a deist and a man of unbounded faith in the efficacy of argument. His *Rights of Man* [2] was intended as a reply to Burke's *Essay on the French Revolution.* He saw a sharp antithesis between society and government. Government was an evil, yet as things were it had great powers for good if only they were properly exercised. In his scheme of social reform he proposed to substitute for poor relief a grant of £4 a year for each child of the very poor under 14 years of age, and to compel the parents to send their children to school to learn reading, writing, and arithmetic. The provision of education he proposed to leave to individual interest. The school fees of children above the very poor were also to be paid, for many of this class find it difficult to afford the necessary money for education. In a nation under a well regulated government none should be permitted to go uninstructed. [3]

William Godwin. Godwin, on the other hand, expressed his abhorrence of any kind of State interference. Government he believed to be an evil in any case and especially in such a matter as education, where human

---

[1] *Wealth of Nations*, Bk. V., Chap. I., Part III., Art. II.
[2] 1791-2.　　　　　　[3] *Rights of Man*, Part II., Chap. V,

perfectibility was determined partly by environment and partly by the growth of opinion. A State system would check the growth of free opinion, it would induce over-veneration for things as they were, it would tend to check free enquiry and replace it by dogma. Moreover its very element of permanence was a vital objection; so was its tendency to produce a dull uniformity and to spread ideas favourable to the party in power. To trust the State with the management of education he considered far more pernicious than leaving it under ecclesiastical control.[1]

In Malthus arose an influential advocate of State interference in education. His contribution was **Malthus.** embodied in his *Essay on Population* first published in 1798, which was avowedly a reply to Godwin's *Political Justice* and its assertion of the doctrine of human equality. Malthus' object was to show that inequality was a necessary result of the working of a natural law, viz. that population constantly tends to outstrip the means of subsistence, and that it is only prevented from so doing by the operation of checks of various kinds that involve a great amount of misery and vice. Here the roots of pauperism lay revealed. Indiscriminate charity was worse than useless. Pauperism could only be checked by each individual playing his part, and exercising moral restraint and foresight. To this end a widespread system of public instruction was necessary.

" We have lavished immense sums on the poor, which we have every reason to think have constantly tended to aggravate their misery. But in their education and in the circulation of those important political truths that most nearly concern them, which are perhaps the only means in our power of really raising their condition, and of making them happier men and more peaceful subjects, we

---

[1] *Enquiry concerning Political Justice*, 1st edition, 1793, *passim*. See also *Shelley, Godwin, and their Circle*, H. N. Brailsford.

have been miserably deficient. It is surely a great national disgrace, that the education of the lowest classes of people in England should be left entirely to a few Sunday Schools, supported by a subscription from individuals, who can give to the course of instruction in them any kind of bias which they please." [1]

Malthus, in fact, would remove much of the onus of dealing with the most pressing of social problems from society as a whole to the individual. He would have nothing to do with those who feared the results of schooling on the common people, rather he expressed his whole-hearted agreement with Adam Smith, that knowledge was the surest means of guarding men against the " false declamation of interested and ambitious demagogues." And he urged that the elements of political economy might very well be taught in the common schools so as to enable the poor to live to greater advantage in a society governed by competition.

The further discussion of this question of State education was carried on by Robert Owen and the Benthamites in the nineteenth century, and will be considered in the following chapter.

Malthus' influence was seen immediately, and was already very important when Mr. Whitbread introduced his Poor Law Reform Bill in 1807. It was in accord with Adam Smith's teaching that elementary education developed during the first half of the century. Godwin soon suffered eclipse, though his teaching was welcomed by a section of both Liberals and Conservatives. Paine's influence was important both because of the fear of popular education that he aroused among conservative people, and the popularity of his teaching among working men.[2]

To sum up, the educational ideal of the century at its

---

[1] *Essay on Population*, Bk. IV., Chap. IX.
[2] The popularity of the *Rights of Man* may be judged from the fact that Paine made a profit of over £1000 on the book.

best was the training of the poor to poverty, an honest, upright, grateful, industrious poverty. But, as we have seen, the change had already begun through the gradual interfusion of revolutionary thought and the new conditions that had inevitably followed the grouping of large numbers of men in towns as a result of the industrial revolution. Working men were now demanding not only political rights but political enlightenment, and ideas for democratising education were already at work.

CHAPTER II.

THE PHILANTHROPIC PERIOD, 1800-1833.

"Schools for all."—Motto of the West London Lancasterian Association.

"Whereas the greater part of persons had hitherto been content to take no heed of passing circumstances, and to allow abuses to continue scarcely recognising their existence, the time was come when the rights of humanity would make themselves heard. Men of reflection had begun to investigate the causes, and the probable results, of the facts around them. Enormous errors were committed, incalculable mistakes made, . . . ; yet the good preponderated . . ., undeniable truths were proclaimed."—*Memoir of Elizabeth Fry*, Vol. I., p. 401.

This period begins with the publication (1797) of Dr. Andrew Bell's account of his educational experiment at Madras, and ends with the first Parliamentary grant for education (1833). In its main characteristics it belongs rather to the eighteenth than to the nineteenth century. Movements that belong to the preceding century continue for a time with renewed vigour and then flicker out. Social ills are still a matter for philanthropic rather than State action, but a new spirit is evident from the outset.

General Survey.

The period is one of great social and political unrest, of extraordinary philanthropic and educational activity. To realise a need was sufficient warrant for private individuals to rush in to alleviate it without pausing to examine too closely either the attendant circumstances or the extent of

28

their own resources. It was accordingly a time of cheapness, superficiality, and variety of endeavour rather than of thoroughness. Nevertheless an impulse was given to popular education that has never died out.

At the back of much philanthropy the idea of a "beautiful order providentially arranged" between diverse ranks and positions was as deeply trenched as in the preceding century. Numerous projects for alleviating the social and educational condition of the masses appeared, but they were in the main middle class schemes, devised and run by the middle class with no thought of training the people to manage their own affairs. Infant schools arose and became popular largely because they were demonstrably "safe" institutions. Savings banks and mechanics' institutes, on the other hand, occasioned some suspicion. As for elementary schools for the poor, religious instruction still formed the backbone of the curriculum. They "were to be as little as possible scholastic. They were to be kept down to the lowest level of the workshop, excepting perhaps in one particular—that of working hard : for the scholars were to throw time away rather than be occupied with anything beyond the merest rudiments."[1]

Between Churchmen and Dissenters there was nothing to choose in this respect, and, as a contemporary writer[2] says, it was necessary in order to obtain contributions "to avow and plead how little it was that they (the schools) pretended or presumed to teach."[3] Mental cultivation, enlarged knowledge, the elements of science, a habit of thinking, exercise of judgment, free and enlightened opinion, were ideas that had to be handled very carefully at the

---

[1] *An Essay on the Evils of Popular Ignorance*, John Foster, Sec. VI., p. 259.

[2] John Foster.   [3] *Ibid.*, p. 259.

beginning of the century.   A more liberal view that
gathered strength and attracted to it all that was best in
the new working class movement was, however, not wanting.   It was represented by men like Robert Owen, Wordsworth, and James Mill, the latter of whom summed up
the new liberalism when he wrote: "As we strive for an
equal degree of justice, an equal degree of temperance,
an equal degree of veracity, in the poor as in the rich, so
ought we to strive for an equal degree of intelligence."[1]

It was an age feeling the full effects of the machine
industries, prone to a doctrine of *laissez faire*, and to a
want of imagination.   It is characteristic of the mechanical
spirit of the age that the quality that appeared especially
to justify the monitorial system to posterity, the feature
that evoked the highest admiration, was that it brought
into action in the province of education "a new expedient,
parallel and rival to the most modern inventions in the
mechanical departments."[2]

Only slowly did the view prevail that society is something more than the summation of individuals, that men
are in fact members one of another.   This is seen, for
example, in the slow alleviation of glaring social abuses
like the exploitation of children in factories.   But that
a new spirit was at work is evident from the application
of statistical methods to the investigation of social and
educational problems, the object being first to obtain accurate information of things as they were and then to use
the data so gained as a means of propaganda and of
stimulating social consciousness.   The first census dates
from 1801 and is typical of a new social attitude.[3]   Educa-

[1] Reprint of *Article on Education*, 1818 : *Encyclopaedia Britannica*,
p. 39.
[2] *An Essay on the Evils of Popular Ignorance*, John Foster, Sec. II.,
p. 87.   [3] See *History of Philanthropy*, Kirkman Grey.

tional statistics were used with effect before the various commissions and committees of enquiry during this period, and in the thirties statistical societies had, come to be regarded as the most effective means of furthering reform.

In the marked growth of public interest in education during the first thirty years of the nineteenth century three motives can be seen at work—

Educational Forces at Work. religious, political, and socialistic respectively. The first predominates in the spread of Sunday Schools, " Schools of Industry," in the work of the Society for Bettering the Condition of the Poor, and in the development of the monitorial system. The second is seen in the teaching of the Radicals that gathered round Bentham—men like James Mill, Brougham, and Francis Place. The third had a worthy exponent in Robert Owen. Associated with each and standing out with greater or less clearness are, of course, other motives; but these we may ignore. The important point is that from the outset of the century we find influences prominently at work antagonistic to ecclesiastical monopoly in the field of popular education.

The spirit of the Radical party is not unappropriately expressed in Bentham's dictum " The way to be comfortable is to make others com-

The Benthamites. fortable. The way to make others comfortable is to appear to love them. The way to appear to love them is to love them in reality." These benevolent aspirations found expression in the well-known formula " the greatest happiness," where, it is important to note, every individual should count as one and one only. Benthamism was an attack on monopoly, vested interest, class prestige, " sinister interests " of all kinds. Instead of a society in which one half existed by plundering the other half, it would establish a universal brotherhood and distribute

broadcast the elements of well-being.¹   Selfish interest
would give way before an all-sufficing conception of public
good, and each man would have within his reach the
elements that make for individual and general happiness;
and of these education would be one. Education was necessary for the growth of intelligence and in order that each
might take his part in the life of a democratic community. "The question whether the people should be
educated, is the same with the question whether they
should be happy or miserable. The question whether
they should have more or less of intelligence, is merely the
question whether they should have more or less misery
when happiness might be given in its stead."² Accordingly
alike on individual and on social grounds education for
all was essential, an education as liberal as circumstances
would permit.³

The whole outlook on life was profoundly optimistic
and profoundly mechanical. Man was a rational animal:
teach him to reason, give him in other words the power to
read and write, and social ills would vanish before instructed intelligence. Of the affections no account was
taken whatever. As Sydney Smith put it, "if everything
is to be sacrificed to utility, why do you bury your grand-
mother? Why don't you cut her into small pieces at
once, and make portable soup of her?"

It needed the leavening influence of Wordsworth,
Coleridge, Carlyle, and the new Anglican revival in the

¹ See Essay on Bentham in *Six Radical Thinkers*, John MacCunn;
Autobiography, J. S. Mill, Chap. IV.; *Life of Francis Place*, Graham
Wallas, Chap. III.; *James Mill: a Biography*, Bain; *Rise of Demo-
cracy*, Rose.

² Mill: *Article on Education*, p. 38.

³ Through his distrust of government Bentham himself looked to the
supply of education mainly by voluntary agencies.

thirties to reassert the spiritual character of man, to insist that

> " We live by admiration, hope, and love ;
> And e'en as these are well and wisely fixed
> In dignity of being we ascend."

For the time being, however, liberals were satisfied that spiritual influences were unnecessary.[1]

Few men were more zealous in the cause of popular education, both in Parliament and outside, than the Benthamites.   Naturally they magnified the value of useful knowledge; but their interest in education was catholic in its range, and in general they showed a liberalism much in advance of the thought of their day.   They included among them staunch supporters of the British and Foreign School Society, and men who were actively interested in the spread of adult education, in the Society for Diffusing Useful Knowledge, in the infant school movement, and in the proposed Chrestomathic secondary school.[2] Bentham himself was for some years one of Owen's partners at New Lanark.   It was largely to the teaching of men of this party that we owe the gradual growth of a demand for popular education on purely democratic grounds, popularly managed and freed from clerical interference. In this connection two names, Brougham and Roebuck, stand out with special prominence in Parliamentary activity during this period.

Robert Owen's influence was of a different order.   He was the founder of the English socialist movement, and is one of the most important figures in the social history of the century. He was a self-educated man and a philanthropist, who for a quarter of a century (1799-1824) managed with cor-

Teaching of Robert Owen.

---

[1] *A History of Philosophy*, Windleband, pp. 662-667.

[2] *Chrestomathia*, 1815.   Also in Bentham's Collected Works.

spicuous success the New Lanark Cotton Spinning Mills in which he had a large monetary interest. For some years previous to this he had shown considerable interest in social questions from being daily brought into contact with the evils existing in the factory towns, and in Manchester in particular. He seems to have been well acquainted with revolutionary literature, and he used his position at New Lanark to carry out a series of social experiments, the results of which he embodied in four essays—*A New View of Society, or Essays on the Formation of the Human Character*—written between 1813 and 1816.

Briefly, Owen's aim was to establish a new social order. Social misery he traces to the absence of right character in man, the result of upbringing and environment. All the agencies in society, all its punitive measures, are based on a false assumption, viz. that man is responsible for his own character, whereas in fact this is the one thing over which the individual has absolutely no control. " The character of a man is, without a single exception, always formed for him ; . . . it may be and is chiefly created by his predecessors ; . . . they give him, or may give him, his ideas and habits, which are the powers that govern his conduct. Man, therefore, never did, nor is it possible he ever can, form his own character." [1] The criminal is the criminal and the judge the judge, entirely as the result of their early environment and upbringing. Moreover, not only has the individual no control over his own character, his very opinions are not his own. " The will of man has no power whatever over his opinions ; he must, and ever did, and ever will believe what has been, is, and may be impressed on his mind by his predecessors and the circumstances that surround him." [2]

[1] *Ibid.*, Essay Third, p. 46 (Heywood's Reprint, 1837).
[2] *Ibid.*, III., p. 43.

It is because of this that ignorance, hatred, and error are generated and perpetuated from one generation to another. But the very ease with which external circumstances determine the individual proves a source of hope to the social reformer, for it means that if the environment can be controlled and right habits and opinions implanted, the millennium will be in sight. This plasticity of human nature, and of child nature in particular, makes the office of teacher one of first-rate importance. "Children are, without exception, passive and wonderfully contrived compounds; which by an accurate previous and subsequent attention, founded on a correct knowledge of the subject, may be formed collectively to have any human character. And although the compounds, like all other works of nature, possess endless varieties, yet they partake of that plastic quality, which by perseverance under judicious management, may be ultimately moulded into the very image of rational wishes and desires."[1] Nay more, "the infants of any one class in the world may be readily formed into men of any other class."[2] And it must be laid down as a maxim so self-evident as to win the assent of all rational beings, that "any general character, from the best to the worst, from the most ignorant to the most enlightened, may be given to any community, even to the world at large, by the application of proper means; which means are to a great extent at the command and under the control of those who have influence in the affairs of men."[3]

By adopting the proper means, men may by degrees be trained to live in any part of the world without poverty, without crime, and without punishment;[4] for all these are the results of error in the various systems of training and

[1] *Ibid.*, II., pp. 11-12.   [2] *Ibid.*, IV., p. 60.   [3] *Ibid.*, I., p. 5.
[4] *Ibid.*, II., p. 25.

government, which proceeds from gross ignorance of human nature.

The end of government is to make the governed and the governors happy.[1] The one and only criterion of good government is that it should effect the greatest possible happiness. Each individual will systematically pursue his own happiness, but from the nature of things this will only be attained by conduct that promotes the happiness of the community as a whole. This, however, requires "true knowledge."[2]

Accordingly Owen proposes first to reform the environment and to make the fullest use of public education. In his plan of national reform which he based on his social experiments at New Lanark he proposed (1) that the national church, as the first step to removing the grounds of envy and strife, should lay aside all formularies and declarations of belief, (2) the checking of the drink traffic and gambling, (3) the amendment of the Poor Law on rational and humanitarian lines, (4) a universal system of elementary education from infancy, (5) a labour bureau, and (6) national work for the unemployed.

"The best governed State will be that which possesses the best national system of education."[3] The State should provide a Department of Education and empower it to establish training colleges, to build schools, to draft the curriculum, and to appoint teachers—the office of teacher being, as with Herbert Spencer, the most important in the State.[4] Great stress was laid on the importance of early education, equality of opportunity, and an education that should train the whole being. The object of all this is to establish habits and sentiments, a social consciousness and an open-mindedness such as are calculated to make the

[1] *Ibid.*, IV., p. 52.   [2] *Ibid.*, IV., p. 54.   [3] *Ibid.*, IV., p. 62.
[4] *Ibid.*, IV., pp. 70-71.

individual and the community lead full, happy, and vigorous lives, sanctified by a spirit of social service.

The defects in Owen's treatment call for little comment. He altogether misconceived the meaning of environment, he gave no thought to heredity, and was unable to free himself from the mechanical view of the educative process prevalent at the time. Nevertheless his influence both on working men and on middle class opinion was very great. The Infant School movement in this country was an outcome of his teaching, and he exerted great influence on the Chartists and on factory reform.

The social misery, the pauperism, and the unrest that were rampant in this country at the begin-
The Religious and Humanitarian Motive. ning of the century offered a worthy field for the exercise of that new religious and philanthropic zeal, the rise of which has been mentioned in the previous chapter. On all hands it was felt that something must be done to check the ruinous expenditure on poor relief that was going up by leaps and bounds, and charity and prudence alike emphasised the necessity for improving, in some measure, the well-being of the poor.

> " The discipline of slavery is unknown
> Among us,—hence the more do we require
> The discipline of virtue ; order else
> Cannot subsist, nor confidence, nor peace.
> Thus, duties rising out of good possest
> And prudent caution needful to avert
> Impending evil, equally require
> That the whole people should be taught and trained.
> So shall licentiousness and black resolve
> Be rooted out, and virtuous habits take
> Their place ; and genuine piety descend,
> Like an inheritance, from age to age." [1]

---

[1] Wordsworth : *The Excursion*, Bk. IX., lines 350-361.

Numerous ameliorative schemes were proposed, all centring round one or other of three propositions—to open up new avenues of employment, to encourage thrift, and to spread widely the elements of a religious education, with the object of training the poor to self-help and to the formation of " inveterate habits."   Of the many associations that arose it will suffice to mention four—The Society for Bettering the Condition and increasing the Comforts of the Poor (1796) ; the Sunday School Union (1803) ; the Royal Lancasterian Institution (1808) ; and the National Society (1811).

The Society for Bettering the Condition of the Poor was founded by Sir Thomas Bernard in conjunc-
The Society for Bettering the Condition of the Poor. tion with Dr. Barrington, Bishop of Durham, Wilberforce, and others.[1]   Nothing that concerned the happiness of the poor was foreign to its purpose.   Its aim was to educate public opinion, to break down prejudice, and to reduce all that concerned the poor and their happiness to a science. Branches were established all over the country ; friendly societies of various kinds were started ; village shops and soup kitchens for the supply of cheap food were opened ; savings banks were started in connection with schools ; and so on.   From the outset it took a great interest in the question of popular education, and with experience increasing attention was given to this aspect of its work.   Briefly, it directed its activities to extending Sunday schools, increasing the usefulness of charity schools, promoting schools of industry, and establishing monitorial schools [2]

It is interesting as showing the alertness of the Society

[1] An excellent account of the non-scholastic work of this Society is given in easily accessible form in *Self-Help a Hundred Years Ago*, by J. Holyoake.

[2] For details see the *Digest of Reports* (*Education*), 1809,

that in January 1804 it asked for a Parliamentary Return from all charity[1] schools in the kingdom, with certain exceptions, with a view to investigating the abuse of endowments and getting accurate information as to the educational needs of different localities : a proposal which, had it succeeded, would have anticipated the work of Brougham's Commission by twelve years.[2]   The returns were to show the date of the foundation ; a copy of the trust deed ; the nature and the amount of income ; the average number of children educated during the previous five years ; the number of children clothed, and the number boarded in addition.   Information was also to be given as to the practicability of improving or extending the usefulness of the school.   It was felt that all the children of the poor could be properly educated granted the following conditions : (1) The adequate carrying out by schools of the intention of their founders.   (2) The admission to these schools of poor children as day scholars at a small fee, viz. 3d. a week.   (3) The opening of parochial schools, where needed, on similar terms.   (4) The enabling of magistrates in certain cases, where parents were too poor, to order the payment of the children's schooling.   (5) The institution of legal process by the Crown in case of the uncorrected abuse of funds.[3]

---

[1] *I.e.* all *endowed* schools "with the exception of the great classical schools." *Ibid.*, No. xxvii., pp. 306-9.

[2] In 1788 a Committee of the House of Commons had called attention to the loss and mismanagement of charitable funds as a matter demanding the "serious and speedy" consideration of Parliament, but nothing had come of it. *Ibid.*, pp. 44-5.

[3] It is worth noting that William Lovett, a man of very different social views, had a similar robust faith in the capability of all, save a small minority, to pay for the education of their children. See *Chartism, a New Organisation of the People*, by William Lovett and John Collins, Second Edition, 1841, pp. 49, 52.

The founding of the Sunday School Union gave a new impulse to the spread of Sunday schools.

Sunday Schools. There seems to have been great diversity in the proportions of Sunday scholars in different parts of the country, the proportion being highest in Wales and in the manufacturing districts in the North of England. The popularity of these institutions was due to the fact that in a very special way they met the sentiment of the times. They were cheap—many were conducted by purely voluntary teachers—they reached a wide audience—they did not teach too much, and they had the further merit of not interfering with the work of the week. Connected with many of these schools were week-day evening classes. Others following the plan recommended by Mrs. Trimmer,[1] opened " schools of industry." Many of these were little more than sewing classes, where girls were trained to make and mend their own clothes, and to undertake at a fixed rate of payment the plain sewing of private individuals resident in the neighbourhood.[2]

At no period do we find a greater faith in the efficiency of " Schools of Industry." They were

Schools of Industry. capable of infinite adaptation to meet every need, from the checking of chronic pauperism to providing a universal system of popular education. Thus Pitt, in his proposed scheme of Poor Law reform (1796), provided for the compulsory establishment of such schools for children whose parents were in receipt of poor

---

[1] See *Œconomy of Charity*, 1787.

[2] Cf. the Society of Industry at Caistor. Here the children went to school on Sundays. During the rest of the week they might go to the " Settlement of Industry," thereby earning 1s. 6d. a week, which they carried home, in addition to 1s. a week that was put to their credit in the savings bank. They might also win a premium of 1½d. a month by regularity and good work at the Sunday School.[3]

[3] *Reports*, Vols. I. and II., 1821,

relief. The value of their labour was to be applied to lessening the burden of the ratepayer.[1]

In 1808 Bell published a plan of a national system of education for the poor that contemplated the establishment of schools to teach nothing but reading and religion, and to give a training in industry, arguing that "Parents will always be found to educate, at their own expense, children enow to fill the stations which require higher qualifications."[2] This plan was made good use of by Bell's detractors as an example of his lack of sympathy with the poor. It is worth noting, however, that the more democratic Lancaster was of opinion that the "school of industry" was more fitted than the ordinary school for children whose parents were too poor to pay, or to keep the children at school until their education was "finished." "One proper object of such schools is to enable children to earn as much money as will remove the difficulty occasioned by the poverty of their parents. . . . By this means they are enabled to keep their children at school till their education is finished, until they have acquired habits of industry which will follow them into future life."[3] Indeed, to combine industry with schooling was one way of getting hold of a class of children who would otherwise be left outside educational influence altogether. This can readily be understood when at some of these schools the children, beside learning the three R's, earned sufficient to take home at the week end 1s. 8d. each, and

---

[1] According to the Parliamentary Returns (1803) comprising nearly the whole of England and Wales, the numbers of children out of the workhouse between 5 and 14 years of age who had been in receipt of parish relief was 188,794 ; whereas the number of those who were receiving, or had received, a training in "schools of industry" was only 20,336. The population was under 9 millions, and the poor rate for 1803 exceeded £5,000,000.

[2] *The Madras School*, p. 292.

[3] *Improvements in Education*, 1806, p. 120.

to provide themselves with a new outfit of clothes once a year ; sometimes a good midday meal was provided in addition.[1] There were enormous difficulties, however, in the way of carrying on these establishments successfully.[2] They started from a false economic and educational stand-point, and by 1834 they did not number 1 per cent. of the schools then in existence.[3]

But though this narrow vocational training was a mistake, it represented an attempt to embody in practical shape the belief that the only cure for existing social ills was " by exalting the character of the labouring classes." Education was the key to the situation, and men were looking to some cheap yet efficient means that would bring the elements of instruction within the reach of the masses. What the real effect of this would be it was difficult to forecast, but "keeping clear of the vain extravagances of expectation, . . . it is, at the very lowest, self-evident," writes a contemporary, " that there is at any rate such an efficiency in cultivation, as to give a certainty that a well-cultivated people cannot remain on the same degraded moral level as a neglected ignorant one—or anywhere near it."[4] In illustration of this it is customary to point to Scotland and elsewhere, countries which had enjoyed the benefits of popular education over a long period.

To supply this need the monitorial method, rediscovered independently by Dr. Andrew Bell and Joseph Lancaster, and worked up by each into a system, seemed providentially devised. The essence of the method consists in setting children to teach

The Monitorial Systems.

---

[1] *E.g.* at Oakham. *Digest of Reports (Education) S.B.C.P.*, p. 179.

[2] For a description of typical schools see *infra*, pp. 191-2.

[3] Trimmer's evidence before the Select Committee. For accounts of attempts to encourage industrial work in connection with schools in 1830 see *The Quarterly Journal of Education*, vol. II., p. 79; vol. VII., p. 185; vol. IX., p. 39.   [4] *Essay on Popular Ignorance*, John Foster, pp. 254-5.

children.   Mutual instruction is, of course, a common feature of all family education, and belongs to no age or people.   A classical example is afforded in the education of the Edgeworth family.   But even here it is very liable to abuse.   John Stuart Mill, for example, as soon as he was seven years old, was made responsible for instructing his younger brothers and sisters, and in after years recorded his opinion of the broad merits and defects of the system in no uncertain terms.   " It was a part which I greatly disliked.   I, however, derived from this discipline the great advantage of learning more thoroughly and retaining more lastingly the things which I was set to teach ;   perhaps, too, the practice it afforded in explaining difficulties to others, may even at that age have been useful.   In other respects, the experience of my boyhood is not favourable to the plan of teaching children by means of one another.   The teaching, I am sure, is very inefficient as teaching, and I well know that the relation between teacher and taught is not a good moral discipline to either."[1]   As a device of school organisation the employment of senior boys to superintend the work of juniors had been used in William of Wykeham's time.[2]   Robert Raikes made use of the method in his early efforts at organising Sunday schools.   Bell and Lancaster, however, both believed firmly that they had made a discovery that would revolutionise teaching for all time.

Both men had hit upon the device by accident.   Bell **Andrew Bell.** was a graduate of St. Andrews and a clergyman of the Established Church.   Along with other posts he occupied for a time the Headship of

---

[1] *Autobiography*, pp. 9-10.

[2] For a full account of the use of monitors in the seventeenth century see *A New Discovery of the Old Art of Teaching Schools*, Charles Hoole, 1660.   (Liverpool University Press reprint.)

the Male Orphan Asylum at Madras. While there he was confronted with the difficulty of carrying on the school during a strike of the staff. In face of such an emergency and being a man of resource it occurred to him to put the different classes in charge of a few selected senior boys. Thanks to his own organising ability, the experiment succeeded so well that he dispensed with the services of the regular staff and set himself to perfect a plan that permitted one master to instruct twenty times as many boys as had been possible hitherto, and to do it much more effectively. An account of the experiment[1] was published on his return to England in 1797, and the system was successfully introduced into St. Botolph's Charity School, Aldgate, the Kendal Schools, and elsewhere.

Lancaster was a man of little school education and a Quaker in humble circumstances. He began his career as a private adventure school-master in a poor district in London in 1798.

Joseph Lancaster.

He was a man with a real sympathy for children, and was possessed of considerable organising ability. From an early period his thoughts were turned to ways and means of increasing the efficiency and extending the usefulness of the school. As was customary in such institutions he taught reading, writing, and cyphering, and as the number of scholars increased he employed an usher to assist him in his work. His numbers continuing to grow, it occurred to him to make use of monitors as a means of keeping all the children occupied and at the same time extending the numbers it was possible for one adult to look after. In working out the idea he derived assistance from the published account of Bell's experiment at Madras.

[1] *An Experiment in Education made at the Male Asylum at Madras, suggesting a System by which a School or Family may teach itself under the Superintendence of the Master or the Parent.*

Through the co-operation of Mrs. Fry and other members of the Society of Friends, he was able to admit to his school an increasing number of free scholars who were too poor to pay the fee of 4d. a week. The schoolroom was enlarged to provide for the steady influx of new children, but such were the improvements in method and organisation that the quality of the work showed no falling off. Ultimately the establishment was advertised as a Free School for the poor of the locality. Visitors were attracted, and by 1803, when an account of the experiment was published under the title *Improvements in Education*, the annual cost of schooling was only 7s. 6d. per head, a sum still further reduced to between 4s. and 5s. as the school was increased to accommodate 1,000 children.

When we recall the mechanical spirit of the age and remember that the average cost of educating a
Popularity of Lancaster's Plan. child in a charity school was 15 guineas[1] a year, it is little to be wondered at that the friends of popular education welcomed the system with open arms. The school in the Borough Road included . in its list of subscribers many distinguished individuals, both Churchmen and Dissenters, and chief among them the King. So well had Lancaster succeeded in convincing himself and others of the possibility of educating children at 5s. a head that Mr. Whitbread, in introducing his Parochial Schools Bill[2] in 1807, used this fact as an argument why Parliament should take up the work of popular education.

Education, he was convinced, was "the incipient principle and grand foundation" of any plan of
Mr. Whitbread's Bill. Poor Law legislation. The times were particularly favourable to the establishment of a system of

---

[1] This includes feeding, lodging, and clothing. *Digest of Reports (Education)* S.B.C.P., p. 17.   [2] The Parochial Schools Bill was introduced as part of a more comprehensive Poor Law Reform Bill.

rate-aided parochial schools, " because within a few years
there has been discovered a plan for the instruction of
youth which is now brought to a state of great perfection ; happily combining rules, by which the object of
learning must be infallibly attained with expedition and
cheapness." The scheme provided for two years' free
schooling for all poor children between 7 and 14 years
of age in reading, writing, and arithmetic, and for girls,
in addition, needlework, knitting, etc. ; schools were to be
established by vestries, or failing these by the magistrates,
with power to levy a local rate not exceeding 1s. for maintenance; the clergy and parish officers were to be the
managers. The Bill raised for the first time in Parliament the question " whether it was proper that education
should be diffused among the lower classes." In introducing the measure its promoter anticipated the usual
objections that education would make the poor despise
their lot, that it would make them indolent and refractory,
and would set a premium on seditious books. He pointed
out that if schools were not to educate, the gutter would.
But in vain. The Bill was unpopular in the country.
Many petitions were presented against it and not a
single one for it. Parliament as a body did not believe
in popular education, and though the Bill passed the Commons it was rejected by the Upper House. There the
matter remained for nine years until the end of the war.

Meantime important events were happening in the
country at large. Lancaster's experiment
**Controversy
round
Lancaster's
System.**
and the publicity that had been given to it
had done good service in stimulating interest
in popular education, and schools on the
Lancasterian model were being established. Lancaster's
plan of education was avowedly non-sectarian. The very
fact of this, while it won the approval of some, was calcu-

lated to arouse the suspicion of still more. This was evident from the moment Lancaster's book appeared. Mrs. Trimmer, who by her writings and good works had won for herself a position of some authority in matters that concerned the education of the poor, while commending the system, disapproved of anything in the nature of unsectarianism. Nothing seemed more likely to lead men to Deism, the thing above all others that smacked of revolution and the destruction of the Church. Accordingly attention was directed to Bell's Madras school. Criticism along these lines gained strength and developed from other quarters as time went on and as the system showed signs of spreading. Lancaster was denounced as a deist, an atheist, an infidel, but for a time the attack does not seem to have hurt him financially, for he continued to flourish. By 1808, however, subscriptions had begun to fall off. Many Churchmen withdrew their support, though this was in some measure compensated for by winning new adherents from the rationalist party and by receiving the support of many Nonconformists. Controversy grew apace, and hard things were said on both sides. It was continued for years and developed into a party quarrel with the Whigs and *The Edinburgh Review* on the one hand, and the Tories, the Church, and *The Quarterly Review* on the other.[1]

Here we find already at work the same forces that later contrived to produce the so-called "religious difficulty"—the difficulty of getting a body of men to agree to conduct

---

[1] An account of this controversy has been written by Principal Salmon in *The Educational Record*, Vol. XVIII., Nos. 43-45; Vol. XIX., No. 47. The student will find a great deal of very valuable material dealing with the history of this period in the recent volumes of the above journal, under the respective signatures of Principal Salmon and W. See also *Joseph Lancaster*, Salmon; *Andrew Bell*, Meiklejohn; and *A Century of Education, 1808-1908*, H. B. Binns.

a system of religious education in a wholly disinterested way, without any suspicion of either sectarian aggrandisement or sectarian aggression. But it is more than this. It is the difficulty of harmonising deep-rooted differences of religious and social ideals. In the present instance we have a party of men who regarded the widespread dissemination of the three R's and simple Bible reading, without note or comment, as a matter of urgency. On the other side, we see many individuals no less honest, pinning their faith to the spiritual uplift of religious formularies and observances, and less convinced of the importance and urgency of mere secular instruction. In addition they were firmly persuaded that if any universal system of education was to be established, the Church was the only organisation with the power and the sanction to carry on the work.

But to return. Lancaster's worst enemy was himself. With growing success he extended his opera-**The Royal Lancasterian Institution.** tions. Schools on his plan were springing up, and he must needs provide for them. He established a free residential school for monitors, set up a printing press, began a slate manufactory, and in various ways proved himself extravagant and unbusiness-like. He was soon involved in serious difficulties, from which he was extricated by two supporters, Fox[1] and Corston.[2] In 1808 very few schools had been established, and with the decline of subscriptions more money had to be found if the work was to continue. Allen Fox, Corston, and others rose to the occasion, advanced

---

[1] Jos. Fox, a surgeon-dentist at Guy's Hospital, a Baptist, and the Secretary of the British and Foreign School Society.

[2] Wm. Corston, a hat manufacturer of Ludgate Hill; founder of a school of industry at Fincham for teaching children to make straw plait; a Moravian, see *infra*, pp. 191-2.

money, and constituted themselves trustees to manage the business part of the work, leaving Lancaster free to lecture up and down the country on his "truly British" system of education. In this way he was instrumental in establishing within two years 95 Lancasterian schools. More money being needed, the Royal Lancasterian Association (Institution) was formally instituted (1810),[1] and on the Committee were Brougham, Whitbread, and James Mill.

Such activity stimulated the heads of the Church to do their duty. Soon after Bell's return to England he received preferment to the Rectory of Swanage. Here he set to work to establish day and Sunday schools in his parish, and generally became a source of good works in the neighbourhood. Since 1805 his name had not suffered from want of public attention. He was appealed to for advice by correspondents in various parts of the country, among whom we find R. L. Edgeworth, at that time one of the Commissioners concerned with the establishment of a system of popular education in Ireland. Old schools were being reorganised on the Madras model and new ones opened. Among them was the charity school at Whitechapel that was used as a training school for teachers. In 1808 Bell published his Sketch of a National Institution for training the children of the poor in the elements of letters, morality, and religion, in conjunction with industry. The Barrington school[2] was founded by the Bishop of Durham for training monitors on the Madras plan, and generally the system was making steady progress, for Lancaster declined to admit the catechism into a Lancasterian school.

Bell in England.

---

[1] It had existed in a more or less nebulous shape since 1808.
[2] *The Barrington School*, by Sir Thomas Bernard, 1815.

The time was ripe for more extended operations. An event of first importance was the founding in 1811 of "The National Society for Promoting the Education of the Poor in the Principles of the Established Church throughout England and Wales." The credit for this seems to be primarily due to Joshua Watson and two friends, all three High Churchmen and active members of the Society for Promoting Christian Knowledge. Their object seems to have been a frank attempt to capture the new movement in popular education at the critical moment for the Church. Intimately connected with them was Dr. Marsh, well known for his Charity School sermon at St. Paul's, and many leading clergy. The Archbishop of Canterbury was President, and he was supported by a distinguished body of Church dignitaries, peers, and others. It was adopted as a fundamental principle "that the national religion should be made the foundation of national education, and should be the first and chief thing taught to the poor, according to the excellent liturgy and catechism provided by our Church for that purpose." It followed that Bell's system, "which made religious instruction an essential and necessary part of the plan," was adopted in preference to Lancaster's, "which confined itself to the mechanical part alone." [1]

Within a month of the founding of the society £15,000 was subscribed, and this was soon followed by a contribution of £500 from each of the Universities of Oxford and Cambridge. A school to accommodate 600 boys and 400 girls was opened at Baldwin's Gardens to serve as a training school for teachers. District Societies were founded in various parts of the country, and grants were made towards the building, enlarging, etc., of affiliated

[1] *Memoir of Joshua Watson*, Churton, Chap. V.

schools.   Between 1813 and 1816 £13,792 was distributed
in 167 grants, 121 of which were towards the building of
new schools.   As a condition of grant it was necessary to
follow the mechanism of the National (*i.e.* Bell) system;
children were to be instructed in the liturgy and catechism
of the Church of England and to attend church regularly
on Sundays; moreover, no religious tract was to be admitted into the school unless it was contained in the catalogue of the Society for Promoting Christian Knowledge.

The cost per child in a school of 500, exclusive of building charges, was estimated in 1816 at 4s. 2d.   Children
were admitted to the school at Baldwin's Gardens at 7 years
of age and might remain until 14, though it was considered
that an attendance of two years was " abundantly sufficient
for any boy."   By this date 336 masters and 86 mistresses
had been trained, and a special staff was kept for the
purpose of organising schools as occasion required.[1]

The total number of children receiving instruction in
Church schools in 1831 was, according to the returns of
the National Society, 900,412.[2]

At the outset these schools were generally free, though a
few made a charge of 1d. per week, the cost of maintenance
being met by donations, local subscriptions, church collec-
tions, and occasional grants from the National Society.
In 1823, the funds of the society being exhausted, a Royal
appeal for further support was addressed to congregations

---

[1] The following table, which unfortunately includes Sunday schools, shows
the spread of the movement:—

1812	52 affiliated schools	8,620	children
1813	230 ,, ,,	40,484	,,
1817	725 ,, ,,	117,000	
1820	1,614 ,, ,,	(over) 200,000	,,
1830	3,670 ,, ,,	(about) 346,000	,,

[2] *Report of the Select Committee*, 1834: Minutes of Evidence, 1877,
pp. 138, 139.

through the parochial clergy.   A similar appeal was made nine years later.[1]   Owing to the quality of the work in some schools having fallen, and in order to improve the regularity of attendance, Bell suggested a system of payment by results, whereby the teacher's emolument would in some measure depend upon the number and the improvement of the scholars.   To effect this, and at the same time to open up a new source of revenue, the institution of small weekly fees was recommended by the society (1824).[2]

The Royal Lancasterian Association had not long been formed before Lancaster quarrelled with his trustees.   Against their will he had set up a middle class boarding school for his own profit at Tooting (1812), a piece of recklessness that resulted for the second time in bankruptcy.   His affairs were now taken over by the trustees, and the Royal Lancasterian Association became the British and Foreign School Society in 1814; Lancaster was paid a fixed salary as Superintendent, but excluded from any share in the management of the society.   Further difficulties followed, and Lancaster left the country a disappointed man four years later to end his days in America.

The British and Foreign School Society.

The rules of the society provided for the maintenance of the central school at Borough Road as a model school and training establishment for teachers.   All schools supplied with teachers at the expense of the society were to be open to children of all denominations; the subjects of instruction were to be reading, writing, arithmetic, and needlework; the reading lessons were to consist of extracts

---

[1] A further Royal appeal was made in 1837, after which it was continued triennially.   See *National Society Directory*.

[2] In 1832 the central school of the society was removed to Westminster, and children were admitted at 6 years of age.   An infant school was established somewhat later.

from the Bible; no catechism or distinctive teaching of any denomination was to be admitted into the schools; and children were required to attend regularly some place of worship on Sundays.

Francis Place had been a staunch supporter of the Lancasterian system for the past nine years.

Lancasterian Secondary Schools. He now became a member of committee, and along with Brougham and James Mill conceived the idea of a complete system of primary and secondary schools at any rate for London. Their first venture was the founding of the West London Lancasterian Association[1] (1813) to investigate educational needs in the west half of London north of the Thames, and to invite penny a week subscriptions by house to house canvass for the purpose of establishing schools. It was hoped that similar associations[2] would be started over the country, but only two are mentioned two years later, viz. at Bristol and at Southwark. By this time, however, the West London Association had been killed through difficulties that had arisen between it and the parent body. Had the plan succeeded, Place had in mind the establishment of higher primary or secondary schools giving a modern education. The association is worthy of notice, as it was indirectly the means of inducing Bentham to invent his Chrestomathic scheme for giving to boys and girls between 7 and 14 years an encyclopaedic secondary education on Lancasterian lines.[3]

By 1816 nearly 300 schools had been established, 205 for boys and 74 for girls, many of which had circulating

[1] Cf. The City of London Auxiliary School Association, in which Joshua Watson took a special interest.

[2] Numerous Foreign associations were founded in Europe, America, and the Dependencies, but with these we are not concerned. See *Educational Record*, Vol. XXVII.

[3] *Life of Francis Place*, Graham Wallas, Chap. IV.

libraries connected with them. The average length of time necessary to complete a boy's schooling was one and a half to two years. As in the case of the National schools no fees were charged at the outset, but after 1816 small weekly fees became customary, and exerted a salutary influence on both attendance and discipline. At the central schools fees were not charged until ten years later.

With so much attention being given to improving and extending elementary instruction it is not surprising to find special interest being taken in the question of infant education.

Infant Education.

The schools of industry at Kendal admitted children from three years of age (1799), and six years later Lancaster was calling special attention to the need for improving *initiatory schools*, schools, that is to say, frequented by boys and girls rarely more than seven years of age, conducted oftentimes by the wife of some working man in order to increase the family income, and providing tuition in reading and needlework. Oftentimes they taught nothing at all, and disorder and noise were their most characteristic features.[1] Efficient establishments combining the function of school and nursery were necessary in order to provide, while the children were yet too young for other employment, the only education many of them would ever obtain. Moreover, by keeping the children off the streets something would be done towards implanting good habits, and a foundation would be laid for the work of the monitorial schools. The school element was, however, to be prominent, for time was valuable and learning could not be begun too young.[2]

---

[1] Cf. *infra*, p. 232.

[2] As an example of this sentiment cf. Bentham's Chrestomathic School, where none could enter at seven years of age unless they had already mastered the elements of the three R's.

To Robert Owen, however, belongs the credit of having awakened public opinion to the importance **The London Infant School Society.** of an efficient system of infant schools. Believing as he did that man is entirely the creature of circumstance, he held that it was impossible to begin too early to implant right habits and to evoke feelings of brotherliness one towards another, arguing that "as the twig is bent, the tree's inclined." Accordingly children were admitted to his infant school at New Lanark as soon as they could walk, and there taken care of while their parents were at work. Their time was occupied in free play, games, and hearing stories. Later they were taught to read and write and were instructed in certain parts of natural history, geography, etc. At six years of age they were promoted to the upper school. Brougham conceived such a favourable opinion of the plan that in 1818 a school on similar lines, financed by a small committee, was opened in London under the superintendence of Buchanan, the master of the New Lanark Infant School, who had been borrowed for the purpose. On the committee were James Mill and Joseph Wilson. The latter, thinking well of the plan, opened a second school at his own expense in the following year and put it in charge of Wilderspin.

So well did the experiment prosper that other schools were opened, and in 1824 the Infant School Society was founded for promoting the establishment of schools, " or rather asylums for the children of the poor " between two and six years of age, to replace the inefficient Dame schools. The schools were designed to accommodate a maximum of from 200 to 300 children; great stress was laid on the necessity of playgrounds as a means of training the scholars to good habits and incidentally leading them "to the acquisition of useful knowledge." For the time being

Wilderspin's school at Spitalfields was to be the model school of the new society. The first Church Infant School was opened in the same year at Walthamstow by the Rev. William Wilson (brother of Joseph Wilson) and quickly won a reputation at least equal to that of Wilderspin. The spread of these schools was largely due to the exertions of Wilderspin, who travelled up and down the country lecturing, demonstrating, and founding schools at the request of local committees.[1] In 1836 the Home and Colonial Infant School Society was founded with the special object of training efficient teachers for infant schools in accord with the spirit of Pestalozzi.

The first instance of State interference in education during the nineteenth century was the passing of the Health and Morals of Apprentices Act in 1802. For some years the Manchester Literary and Philosophical Society had been conducting a campaign against the evils that attended the system of apprenticeship in factories and the reckless exploitation of children five years old and upwards, drawn from workhouses and elsewhere. This was the first of a series of measures directed against establishments

Education of Factory Children.

> "where is offered up
> To Gain, the master-idol of the realm,
> Perpetual sacrifice."

The Act limited the working hours of apprentices to 12 hours a day; forbade night work; required provision to be made for instruction during the day in reading, writing, and arithmetic, together with attendance at church at least once a month; provided for the registering and inspection of factories, and imposed fines for non-compliance. The Act was, however, imperfectly enforced, and made no provision for the large number of unapprenticed

[1] *Early Discipline*, Wilderspin.

children. Its value lay in the fact that it established useful precedents, and was a sign of an enlarged conception
on the part of the State of its social responsibilities.[1]

It has been seen[2] how, at the beginning of the century,
the attention of philanthropists was already
directed to educational charities as likely to
afford, if properly administered, a sufficient
income for a wide extension of the means of
popular education. With the rejection of
the plan for a national system of rate-aided
schools (1807), it was in the adapting of the resources of
these charities for elementary education that the hopes of
reformers lay.

Brougham:
Educational
Commissions
and Par-
liamentary
Activity.

With the close of the French war distress increased apace
among the masses of the people, and laid the foundations,
with very little help on the part of agitators, of two working-class movements—Trades Unionism and Chartism.
The time seemed ripe for re-opening the question of
national education. In 1816 Brougham, who with the
death of Whitbread (1815) now became the main support
of the cause of popular education in Parliament, moved as
a preliminary measure the appointment of a Select Committee of the House of Commons "to inquire into the
education of the lower orders of the Metropolis, . . . and
to consider what may be fit to be done with respect to the
children of paupers who shall be found begging . . . and

---

[1] Some of the more humane manufacturers already provided education for
their apprentices. Thus David Dale employed at New Lanark (1797) three
regular day schoolmasters for the younger children. The older children
were taught between seven and nine in the evening. For these, if additional
teachers were employed, one of them was a writing master. A woman was
appointed to teach the girls sewing, and another master occasionally gave
lessons in Church music. There were 500 children in all. See *Self Help a
Hundred Years Ago*, G. J. Holyoake.

[2] *Ante*, p. 39.

whose parents . . . have not sent " them to school.   Subsequently the investigation was extended to the whole country.

Under the none too tactful chairmanship of Brougham
the scope of inquiry was laxly interpreted to cover all available means of supplying existing deficiencies in education.
The committee sat for two years, gathered together a wealth
of valuable information, and raised a storm of criticism
and abuse.   It reported that a large number of poor
children were wholly without the means of instruction,
although parents generally seemed desirous of it[1]; it commended the good work done by the various charitable
institutions; indicated the existence of many abuses in the
administration of charity trusts for education, and urged
the appointment of a Parliamentary Commission to investigate the application of such funds throughout England
and Wales; recommended for necessitous districts a system
of rate-aided parochial schools, and elsewhere a grant for
building purposes, care being taken not to dry up the
sources of voluntary contributions; suggestions were also
made for introducing a conscience clause.   It was anticipated that a proper application of charitable funds would
leave no considerable burden on the taxpayer.[2]   It is interesting to note that the idea of building grants was
adopted in 1833, but rate aid was postponed until 1870.

In 1818 Brougham succeeded in getting through a
measure after much mutilation for the appointment of a
Royal Commission to inquire into educational charities
throughout the country.   This work occupied the Commissioners until 1837.

[1] Cf. the statement of a speaker on Mr. Whitbread's Bill, who said that
in Reading, with a population of 10,000, three-quarters of whom were poor,
there was hardly a child who had not learned to read " at some of the
threepenny schools kept by the poor old people."

[2] *Third Report of the Select Committee on the Education of the Lower
Orders.*

Two years later Brougham introduced a Bill "for the better education of the poor in England and Wales." It provided for the erection of parochial schools, authority for the establishing of which was to rest with the Quarter Sessions, application having been made by the Grand Jury, two magistrates, the local clergyman, or five resident householders. The cost of building was to fall on the manufacturers, the cost of maintenance on the local rates. School fees of from 2d. to 4d. a week were to be charged to foster a spirit of independence among parents, special provision however being made for poor children. Schoolmasters were to be appointed by the Vestry; they were to be Churchmen, and the right of vetoing their appointment was vested in the local clergyman. Their salary was to be from £20 to £30 a year, with the addition of a house, though this sum might be increased at the option of the local ratepayers, the object being to ensure that every master should have a real interest in developing his school to the utmost. The curriculum was to be decided by the clergyman at the time of each new appointment, and in all cases simple Bible teaching was to be included. Provision was made for teaching the Catechism on Sunday evenings to all who did not object. Part of the expenses of the system was to be borne by the application of educational endowments.

Brougham tells us that his reason for introducing the Bill was a fear that, instead of continuing to expand, the voluntary impulse might die. He paid tribute to the work that the local clergy had done in the matter of popular education, estimating that of some 650,000 boys and girls being educated in endowed and unendowed schools one-third were in monitorial schools. In addition, about 50,000 were being educated at home, and another 100,000 exclusively in Sunday schools. Some 53,000 in Dame schools he neglected. From these data he argued that on the average 1 in 15 of the population was attending some sort of school in England. In Wales the proportion was only 1 in 20. In 1803 the proportion for England and Wales he estimated to have been 1 in 21. Assuming about one-tenth of the population to be of school age, he calculated that one in five was still unprovided for. School provision varied greatly in different parts of the country. London was by far the worst off in this respect, for accommodation existed for only 1 in 24, or, if Dame schools were deducted, for 1 in 46. Lancashire came next. It was to remedy this state of affairs that the Bill was intended. At the same time he advanced a strong plea for the support of Infant schools as rescue institutions.

Striking as these figures are, they afford no real idea of the actual state of education at the time. Brougham's calculations were based on the assumption that children between 7 and 13 ought to be in school. In other words, he based his estimate on a school life spreading over five or six years. At the time, however, $1\frac{1}{2}$ to 2 years was the extent of the ordinary day school course,—a time "abundantly sufficient" for learning all that the poor boy needed in the way of reading and writing. Hence the proportion of children who were attending school was probably much larger than Brougham gave credit for.

The Bill called forth the strongest opposition from Roman Catholics, Dissenters, and the British and Foreign School Society, as a measure dangerous to religious liberty and as accentuating the privileges of the Church in contrast to the other denominations. Nor did it please the Church party. It was accordingly withdrawn, and no further attempt at legislative action was made for the next ten years.

During this period, however, a great change had come over the general attitude towards popular education, a direct result of the forces mentioned earlier in the chapter. The voluntary movement spread rapidly. According to returns obtained by Brougham in 1828 the number of children attending day schools had doubled since 1818. Education as a measure of protective and preventive police had never been more popular. It was during this period that the great movement in adult education began [1] and the Society for Diffusing Useful Knowledge came into existence.

In 1832 the Reform Bill was passed, thereby fulfilling Cobbett's prediction at the close of the French War that the legacy of debt must inevitably bring about a reform in popular representation. The balance of power now passed to the newly enfranchised middle classes, and popular education became more than ever a matter of expediency. In 1833 Parliament made its first grant in aid of elementary education.

---

[1] Some idea of the interest in the subject may be gained from the fact that Brougham's pamphlet on *Popular Education* (1825), setting out a scheme of working-class education by means of reading rooms, libraries, and evening institutes, and by the institution of cheap literature, went through twenty editions in the year.

CHAPTER III.

PERIOD OF INCIPIENT STATE ACTION.

I.—Supervision or Annexation ? 1833-1847.

> "O for the coming of that glorious time
> When, prizing knowledge as her noblest wealth
> And best protection, this imperial Realm,
> While she exacts allegiance, shall admit
> An obligation, on her part, to *teach*
> Them who are born to serve her and obey ;
> Binding herself by statute to secure
> For all the children whom her soil maintains
> The rudiments of letters, and inform
> The mind with moral and religious truth."
>
> —WORDSWORTH.

"Civil government is no fit agency for the training of families or of souls. . . . Throw the people on their own resources in education as you did in industry ; and be assured, that, in a nation, so full of intelligence and spirit, Freedom and Competition will give the same stimulus to improvement in our schools, as they have done in our manufactures, our husbandry, our shipping, and our commerce."

—EDWARD BAINES.

With the first Parliamentary grant for elementary education (1833) a new era begins. Among all ranks there was still a great deal of ignorance and apathy towards popular education, but a new note is evident from the outset. The forces of progress were abroad. Education gradually ceased to be given to the poor as a charity. It became a

General Survey.

62

right of the people.   To educate men to this larger view was the work, among others, of Carlyle, Dickens, and J. S. Mill.   After 1837 education began to take a prominent place in the programmes of the working-class movement through the influence of William Lovett.[1]

There was a growing hatred of shams, monopoly, and vested interests—a desire to liberalise education at all costs. Existing agencies were either to be stimulated into action or to disappear.   The Central Society of Education arose in 1836 with the avowed object of doing what the two existing societies seemed unable or refused to do, viz. to take an enlarged view of the situation, to set aside sectarian rivalry, to endeavour to raise educational practice from dogmatism and rule of thumb to the plane of a science, to cease counting heads, and to remove the reproach of being content with giving to the people an education that was a disgrace to the age.

Rigidity and inelasticity of view, intolerance and a disposition not to compromise were the dominant features of the greater part of the period.   They were peculiar to no one party, but the characteristic of all.   With the abolition of the Test Acts and the advent of Catholic Emancipation the previously "inferior" sects showed a determination to use their newly-acquired liberty to the full.   Dissenters and Churchmen alike made grievous mistakes, and were not above sacrificing future good to an immediate advantage.   Occasionally they combined to present a united front to the common enemy—the growing rationalist party.

The period between the first Parliamentary grant and the advent of School Boards divides into two parts—

(1) 1833-1847.   (2) 1847-1870.

---

[1] Leader of the Moral Force Chartists, compiler of the People's Charter, organiser of the National Union of the Working Classes, etc.

During the first period we see the prospect of a State
system of education which should bring the
1833-1847.
means of instruction within the reach of all
endangered and finally destroyed for the time being by
the controversies that centred round the " religious difficulty." A Liberal Government had burnt its fingers in
1839, and a like fate attended a Conservative Government
in 1843. In 1847 the Government, through the Committee
of Council, resigned itself to the inevitable, and definitely
entrusted the spread of education as far as might be to
voluntary agencies.

The country was divided into five parties: (1) those who
would have State-aided denominational schools under
private management, (2) denominationalists who would
admit a conscience clause, (3) undenominationalists, (4)
those who would exclude religious instruction altogether
from State-aided schools, (5) those who would have
nothing to do with State aid in any form.

The second period saw successive Parliaments acquiescing[1]
in the spread of a great denominational
1847-1870.
system, and in the growth of a great depart-
ment of State that distributed in the course of thirty years
some £10,000,000 and gradually regulated the education
of half the children in the country, without the control or
guidance of a single Act of Parliament.

Meantime the struggle between the rival parties continued. The extremists of all parties gradually abandoned
their position. Voluntary agencies had proved themselves
unequal to the task of reaching all the children in the
country. Accordingly Liberal opinion set strongly in favour
of a State system, rate-aided and locally managed. In
other words many desired to see the State annex elementary
education instead of continuing merely to aid and supervise

---

[1] Cf. *Public Education*, Kay-Shuttleworth, Chap. I. .

the work of voluntary associations.   Conservatives, on the other hand, were for retaining the *status quo* but making education compulsory and opening up other sources of revenue.   Between the two came a third party who favoured a partition of the work between the State and the voluntary associations.   That is to say, the State was to undertake the responsibility of supplementing the already existing provision, but to allow freedom for private individuals to continue their work—a policy calculated to attract the support of those who distrusted any undue interference or predominance of the State in social affairs, who saw progress not in the narrow individualism of "Hands off," nor in paternalism, but rather in a fuller and richer individualism such as found expression in the teaching of John Stuart Mill.   The Act of 1870 realised in some measure this third view.

The demand of the Benthamites for popular education has already been noted.[1]   In the thirties

Growing Demand for Popular Education. reformers were demanding the establishment of a State system with a persistence that seriously alarmed the Church party.   Propaganda on these lines was the *raison d'être* of the Central Society.   In 1831 the labour movement may be said to have begun with the founding of the National Union of the Working Classes.   Six years later Lovett, in an address to working men,[2] was claiming

William Lovett. popular education as a right derivable from society itself—an education that should offer to each the means of developing his capacities to the utmost.   For this he proposed a system of State education under a Committee of Public Instruction appointed by

[1] See *ante*, pp. 31-3.

[2] *An Address to the Working Classes on the Subject of Education*, 1837, reprinted in *The Life and Struggles of William Lovett*, pp. 135-146.

Parliament, with the building of schools a State charge, and their maintenance dependent upon local rates. In 1839, however, he changed his position and repudiated State control.[1] Education was too important to be left to any Government to take in hand, especially " an irresponsible one." Accordingly he advocated a plan by which the working classes could educate themselves on free co-operative lines.

Carlyle, writing in 1840, saw in education and emigration the two means of curing the social evils of the day. "Who would suppose," he says, "that education were a thing which had to be advocated on the ground of local expediency, or indeed on any ground? As if it stood not on the basis of everlasting duty as a prime necessity of man."[2] To impart the gift of thinking seemed to him the first function of government. Yet, in spite of this, education was being shelved through sectarian controversy. Religious teaching he admitted was essential, but until the sects could agree to sink their differences he prayed for the strong man to come and impose a secular system on the whole country.

Carlyle.

Dickens' influence came through his writings and his readiness to speak to popular audiences on the subject of education. No one of his generation had a greater belief in the masses or greater sympathy with the poor. No aspect of educational work escaped his notice. He was among the first to expound Froebel's teaching in this country,[3] and was one of the greatest influences of the day in improving the school education and making it more meaningful. He favoured

Dickens.

[1] *Chartism*, Lovett and Collins.
[2] *Chartism*, Chap. X.
[3] See *Household Words*, 1855. The article is reprinted in *Dickens as an Educator*, Hughes.

a compulsory State education, comprehensive and unsectarian in kind, that should lead individuals to self-improvement and make them generous, self-respecting, intelligent men and women.

J. S. Mill set out with an unlimited faith in the ordinary individual, and he demanded as the end and aim of government—as the end of man himself—the fullest opportunity for each to develop his capabilities to the utmost. His " grand leading principle " was the absolute and essential importance of human development in its richest diversity. It was education that was to bridge the gulf that separates men as they are from men as they might become. It was, however, much more than mere schooling. It included education in and through social duties. But popular education was necessary from another standpoint. According to him the ideally best form of government was that in which the sovereignty was vested in the entire aggregate of the community, and where every citizen was called upon occasionally to take his share in the actual work of government by discharging some local or general public office. Universal education was an essential condition to this, and he went so far as to say that it was wholly inadmissible for any person to have a vote who was ignorant of at any rate the three R's. While, however, he was prepared to justify State assistance and compulsory education,[1] he was opposed to the State monopolising education, on the ground that it would be dangerous to the life of a free community.

"An education established and controlled by the State should only exist, if it exist at all, as one among many

J. S. Mill.

---

[1] " Is it not almost a self-evident axiom that the State should require and compel the education of every human being who is born a citizen ? "—*On Liberty*, Chap. IV.

competing experiments, carried on for the purpose of example and stimulus, to keep the others up to a certain standard of excellence." [1]

We may now examine the period in detail.

The struggle for a State system of popular education in place of the existing voluntary agencies began with the passing of the Reform Bill. The new Government contained a number of men notoriously sympathetic to the cause, but they lacked adequate backing in the country.

Brougham was now in the Upper House, his place in the Commons being taken by Mr. Roebuck **Mr. Roebuck's Proposed Bill.** and Mr. Wyse. For some years the success of voluntaryism had been leading him to modify his views as to the expediency of compulsory educational provision. A declaration to this effect in the first session of the new Parliament provoked Mr. Roebuck to move that in the following session the House would " proceed to devise a means for the universal and national education of the whole people," pointing to the critical state of the times, and urging that education was essential to the production of a virtuous, industrious, happy, enlightened democracy, and that it was a duty incumbent on a State to undertake and enforce it. The education, however, must be real : no mere mechanical drilling in the three R's would do. He had in view the compulsory attendance at school of all children between six and twelve years of age; the establishing in every village of at least one infant school and one school of industry, a provision to be supplemented in towns by evening schools for all over fourteen years of age; and, finally, the opening of normal schools for schoolmasters. For administrative purposes the

---

[1] *On Liberty*, Chap. IV. See Essay on Mill in *Six Radical Thinkers*, MacCunn.

country was to be divided up into school districts under the control of locally-elected committees.

The school of industry had two functions to perform, first, to impart scholarship and to teach a trade, and second, to lay the foundation of taste and to educate for leisure. Hence the curriculum was to be "as liberal as prudence would permit." Besides the three R's it was proposed to provide for instruction in art, music, and singing, in natural history, elementary science, hygiene and civics—the latter to include "a general knowledge of our government and other institutions, with such portions of political economy" as were appropriate. The control of the system was to be vested in a Cabinet Minister; equal rights were to be given to all denominations; and the cost of education was to be met partly by school pence, but mainly by taxes and the income from existing endowments.

The speech is interesting because of its grasp of the meaning of education, for its liberal handling **The First Parliamentary Grant.** of the whole question of popular education, and as typifying the educational position of the advanced reformers. To have accepted such a motion, however, would have seriously embarrassed the Government, and it was not pressed. As an earnest that they were not passive in the matter a grant of £20,000 for the erection of school houses was proposed and passed after a struggle in a thin House, thereby carrying out an idea suggested in the Report of 1818.[1]

---

[1] See *ante*, p. 58. The vote ran, "That a sum, not exceeding twenty thousand pounds, be granted to His Majesty, to be issued in aid of private subscriptions for the erection of school houses for the education of the children of the poorer classes in Great Britain, to the 31st day of March, 1834: and that the said sum be issued and paid without any deduction whatever."

No special machinery was set up to distribute the money. It was administered by the Treasury under a special Minute (1833), according to which grants were to be applied exclusively to the erection of schools: no grants would be made unless at least half the cost were met by voluntary contributions; grants would only be made through the National or the British and Foreign School Society; applicants were to be prepared to submit the school accounts to audit and to make reports; populous places would be given preference in the allocation of grants. The result was an immediate stimulus to local effort, and before the end of the year the grant was inadequate to meet the demands made upon it. The result was a further discrimination in favour of large schools accommodating upwards of 400 children, and in which two school places were provided for each £1 of grant asked for. In other words, the grant was applied to assist the erection of schools in comparatively well-to-do populous neighbourhoods, rather than in poor and relatively more necessitous districts. On these terms the grant was renewed annually for the next six years. During this time the State was merely the contributor to two voluntary societies, laying down no standards to which buildings should conform, and eliciting no security for the maintenance of the fabric when erected nor for the efficiency of the instruction—a condition of affairs that is accounted for by the tentative nature of the experiment.[1]

---

[1] Within a few months of the passing of the grant sixty-two schools, forty-four of which belonged to the Church of England, providing in all for 12,191 children had been aided. By the end of the year applications had been made from 236 projected schools. Of these 185 were not assisted owing to the exhaustion of the grant. By 1838 714 National schools accommodating 140,591 children, and 181 British and Foreign School Society schools had been helped.

It is noteworthy that a similar method of distributing grants had been

Meantime the question of State interference with education was not allowed to drop, and reformers set themselves the task of educating public opinion. The full extent of the deficiency in school accommodation was not known, no authoritative data being available. To obtain this information a good deal of effort was expended both by Parliamentary agencies and local associations, for it was felt that "facts, numerous and well attested," were the only ground on which conclusions with regard to the state of the country could be safely based.

Educational Returns and Statistics.

In 1833 a Parliamentary Return was called for by Lord Kerry, showing the number of Infant, Day, and Sunday schools in every town, parish, and chapelry, together with the number and sex of the children in attendance, the average age of entering and leaving school, the nature of the school funds, etc. This was followed by the investigations of three Select Committees, the most important being that appointed in 1837 to consider the best means of providing useful education for the children of the poorer classes in the large towns of England and Wales.

Further information of the social, moral, physical, and educational conditions of particular districts was obtained by the inquiries of various local agencies, statistical societies and private individuals. Foremost in importance of these was the work done by the Manchester Statistical Society, founded in 1833, and the London Statistical Society, established in the following year, which proved the

---

tried in Ireland since 1816. The medium in this case was the Kildare Place Society. After the passing of the Catholic Emancipation Act, 1831, a Board of unpaid Commissioners was set up to administer the Government grants, to appoint inspectors, to establish training schools, to publish suitable school books, etc.

data of the Kerry Parliamentary Return to be untrustworthy.[1]

These enquiries revealed not only a good deal of educational destitution, particularly in large
The Demand towns, but also emphasised the deplorable
for a State condition of much so-called schooling. The
System of
Education. demand for a State system was again taken
up by Brougham, who in 1835 introduced a
Bill for establishing a Board of Education similar to that
existing in France, with powers to extend education
throughout the country, to plant schools, to bestow
Parliamentary grants, and to superintend the distribution
of such other funds as might be raised by local taxation.
The Board was to consist of paid commissioners holding
their posts on conditions similar to judges, but with a
Cabinet Minister at the head. A similar Bill was introduced in 1837 and re-introduced in 1838, when in
answer to a question Brougham stated his position
with regard to religious instruction by saying that every
plan of national education should embrace religious
instruction, but owing to the conscientious scruples of
Roman Catholics and Jews he would not compel these to
be present either when the Scriptures were read or when
the Catechism and Thirty-nine Articles were expounded.[2]

Meantime the Central Society, to which belonged Lord
John Russell, Mr. Wyse, Mr. Slaney, and others, was engaged in propagandist work. "A Board of Education
for England, another for Scotland, a third for Ireland,
all acting under the Minister of Public Instruction here,
with large powers over new and old endowments, and
with adequate funds, composed fairly (representing, that

---

[1] A similar society sprang up in Bristol in 1836, another at Birmingham.
The Central Society of Education began work the same year.

[2] *Hansard, 3rd Series*, Vol. xliv., col. 1174.

is, the various parties and feelings in the country in due proportion), and acting under constant Parliamentary and Government inspection ; but, above all, under the universal public eye : a wise share of co-operation granted, and required from the people, in parishes, towns, counties, and provinces, through the public bodies most appropriate to each " [1]—such was regarded as preliminary to all real reform.

In summing up the educational condition in towns in 1838 the Select Committee reported that, however defective the existing system of instruction for the poorer classes might be, it was impossible not to recognise the great service that had been rendered to the country by the persevering efforts of benevolent individuals in the cause of education. In large towns 1 in 12 of the population were on the average in receipt of some sort of schooling, but only 1 in 24 were getting an education likely to be useful. In some places the proportion was as low as 1 in 41,[2] whereas it was considered that provision ought to exist for 1 in 8. To meet this deficiency further Government assistance was urgently needed. In view of existing difficulties the Committee could not see its way to recommend the establishment of a National Board of Education, and suggested a continuance of the present system whereby grants should be distributed through the National and the British and Foreign School Societies. Some modifications in the terms of grant ought, however, to be made in favour of poor districts. In short, vested interests and fear of

The State of Education, 1838.

---

[1] *Central Society of Education*, First Publication, p. 63.

[2] Cf. Leeds. See *Report of the Select Committee on Education of the Poorer Classes*, 1838, p. viii. The data used were those obtained by the Statistical Societies, and only take into account day schools. See however *ante*, p. 60, for the note as to the average length of school life.

civil interference appeared to the Committee too strong to warrant the State in departing from its position as the contributor to two societies that were far from commanding the confidence or representing the opinion of the country as a whole.   In Parliament in 1838 a motion by Mr. Wyse for the establishment of a Board of Commissioners only just failed to pass, and the same year the British and Foreign Society petitioned for the same object.

The Government now took up the matter.   There were three parties to propitiate.   The Church under the stimulus of the Anglican Revival was vigorously pressing its claims to dominate popular education.   The Dissenters were disputing the claim with no less perseverance. Apart from both, Liberal opinion as expressed by the Central Society looked to the separation of secular and religious education under the control of a centrally elected body.   By its emphasis on secular instruction it had drawn upon itself the dislike and distrust of Churchman and Dissenter alike—and to this party belonged Lord Melbourne, Lord Lansdowne, and Lord John Russell.   The state of affairs was clearly unpropitious to establishing a Board of Commissioners to supervise education.   The claim of the Church that education was essentially an ecclesiastical matter was also regarded as untenable.   At the same time to look upon it exclusively as a civil function, and to attempt to set up a purely State system as in Prussia or the United States, would be to ignore history and existing conditions.   Accordingly a compromise was effected, tentative and opportunist in character.   The Queen, on the advice of her Ministers, appointed by Order in Council a Special Committee of the Privy Council, analogous to the Committee of Council on Trade, " for the consideration of all matters affecting the education of the

The Establishment of the Committee of Council.

people," and to determine " in what manner the grants of money made from time to time " by Parliament should be distributed. The step was important, for it asserted the claim of the civil authority to a dominant position in national education, and if the measure was not as comprehensive as the Government would have liked, it was at any rate " a beginning." [1]

The Committee was appointed on April 10th, 1839, and a Minute, dated the following day, provided for the establishment and constitution of a State Training College with Model Schools attached ; for the appointment of two inspectors for the inspection of aided schools ; and for granting aid to teachers and to schools not necessarily confined to the two Societies. It proposed to throw the College and Model Schools open to all regardless of sect, to provide general, non-distinctive religious instruction for all, and to give opportunities for definite doctrinal instruction at stated times during the week by specially appointed ministers. [2]

The First Minute.

A storm of opposition greeted the publication of the Minute. It was characterised as a piece of legerdemain, designed by a stroke of the pen to bring into operation schemes identical in all essentials with the projects of Roebuck, Brougham, and others, that had been consistently opposed. [3]

Church Opposition.

---

[1] The Marquis of Lansdowne, *Hansard, 3rd Series*, Vol. xlv., col. 351.

[2] A full account of the doings of this period, told from the official point of view, is given in *Four Periods of Public Education*, Kay-Shuttleworth.

[3] For an account of the history of this period, written from the Church standpoint, see *The History and Present State of the Education Question*, printed for the Metropolitan Church Union, 1850. See also the pamphlet, *The Church and Education prior to 1870*, published by the Church Committee for Church Defence and Church Instruction; also *Elementary Education*, Gregory. For an account written from the civil point of view see Adams' *History of the Elementary School Contest.*

The main opposition came from the Church, the Wesleyans, and the National Society, and was directed against the plan of a State Training College. The policy of the Government was to acknowledge equal rights to all denominations, or, in the words of Lord John Russell, to give "a temperate attention to the fair claims of the Established Church, and the religious freedom sanctioned by law." The application of this policy to religious instruction in the proposed College and affiliated Model Schools aroused the gravest distrust. Many saw in it the first step towards a compulsory State scheme of religious conformity. Religion was henceforth to be a mere "subject" like Arithmetic. Petitions poured in against it from all over the country. Religious controversy— the mark of deep-rooted differences of principle—was never higher. The Government was in low water at the time, so the Training College scheme was dropped, and the money—a sum of £10,000—handed over to the National and the British and Foreign School Societies.

But the opposition did not end here. Distrust had been aroused, and the Committee of Council itself was attacked on all manner of grounds. Some objected to it on the ground of its exclusively political character and its necessarily fluctuating and uncertain composition, so that it was regarded as incapable of pursuing any fixed policy. Many saw in it an instrument of political tyranny. Others were opposed to it as an instrument of instruction and not of education, alleging that it worshipped machinery and neglected sympathy. Others, again, objected to any form of State interference, on the ground that education is essentially spiritual in character, no mere matter of restraint, of disciplining the faculties, of facts and opinions. The State might add new elements of information in the effort to improve national education, but it was powerless to evoke the spiritual forces that give stability and unity to national life.[1]

An address to the Crown, protesting against the establishment of the Committee of Council, was defeated by 280 to 275 votes, and the education grant for the year—£30,000 for Great Britain—passed by two votes. In the Upper House a similar address was carried by 229 to 118 votes without result.

The Government adhered to its plan so far as the Committee of Council, the right of inspection, and the extension of building grants to other bodies were concerned. Dr. Kay (afterwards Sir James Kay-Shuttleworth), an assistant Poor Law Commissioner, was appointed Secretary of the Committee, but in view of the general feeling in the country at the time a common school system was impossible.

To understand the heat engendered and the bitterness of the conflict it is necessary to remember that this momentous change in the attitude of the State towards popular education came at the very climax of the Anglican Revival, when the Church was awakening to a new sense of its dignity and an enlarged faith in its destiny. At the same time the coming of Catholic Emancipation and the abolition of the Test Acts left no doubt that the Church of England could no longer claim, as it could with some justice at the beginning of the century, to represent the religious aspirations of the whole community. Frederick Denison

The Religious Difficulty.

---

[1] Mr. Gladstone saw in State interference, divorced from orthodox religious instruction, the ultimate destruction of national religion and national character. Mr. Disraeli was equally opposed to it, though he had no fear of the growth of national infidelity.

Maurice, writing as a Broad Churchman, put the position admirably in these words :—

" No cowardice, putting on the face of modesty, shall prevent us from declaring that we have a commission, and authority, and ability, to educate the whole mind of the country ; a power of forming the nation, which those who would take upon themselves our duties do not, and cannot possess. No shame for past misuse of the trust which has been committed to us, shall tempt us to the further sin of denying that we retain it. But at the same time, we are bound, by the most solemn obligations, to make our pretensions good, to prove that they are not put forth rashly or proudly for the sake of self display, or that we may retain selfish honours, but in the firm belief that the tenure by which we hold our gifts is not one that makes them dependent upon our individual merits any more than upon State patronage, but one that ensures a continual renewal of the only strength in which we are able to exercise them for good to this age, or to posterity." [1]

" You have always a vague notion that we want you to do something for us—in some way or other to help us against the sects. We ask no such thing.[2] . . . We are born in an age in which men are trying to find a bond of union for themselves, and cannot find it—in which they are abusing one another for not being conciliatory, and are ready to tear one another in pieces for the sake of establishing charity. We are born in an age of parties—it is God's will that it should be so ; we cannot make it otherwise by not believing it. We (Churchmen) have an Education which assumes men to be members of one family—of one nation.   (A ' family we declare to be universal, limited by no conditions of time or country ; to belong to it is our great human privilege. This principle underlies all our education, and is the very meaning of it ! Only on such a foundation can a united nation be built. We have learned, therefore, to reverence our own function more, because it is the function of proclaiming truth to men ; and we have come to think less and less of your State machinery, because it carries with it no such power.') If any persons like to be educated on that ground, we will educate them ; if they do not like it, they must educate themselves upon what other principle they

[1] Has the Church or the State the Power to Educate the Nation ?   A Course of Lectures, 1839, p. 129.   [2] Ibid., p. 163.

may, for we know of no other. The State rushes in and says, 'But we can. We will make you members of one family, whether you like it or no. You shall love by Act of Parliament, and embrace by an Order in Council. You have paid for our protection; of course, therefore, we are bound in honour to make you wise and charitable.' This is their scheme; I believe that it will work in this way. It will teach those who are indifferent to be more indifferent, . . . more intolerant, . . . (and result in) the nation growing . . . more divided and broken." [1]

There is no mistaking the sincerity of the sentiments set out here. Any system of education that was not based on orthodox Church teaching was unthinkable. It was a frank declaration in favour of a rigid denominational system where each sect should educate its own children. Similar sentiments were held with equal conviction by the Wesleyans, the Roman Catholics, and the Jews. There is no doubt that Lord John Russell, the leader of the Government in the House of Commons, had greatly miscalculated the situation when he asserted: "In the midst of these conflicting opinions there is not practically that exclusiveness among the Church Societies, nor that indifference to Religion among those who exclude dogmatic instruction from the school which their mutual accusations would lead bystanders to suppose." [2] Moreover, in judging of the attitude of the sects towards religious instruction it is well to remember that popular education owed its spread mainly to a religious impulse, and that the various agencies that came into existence were frankly sectarian in character and that dogmatic religious teaching was their *raison d'être*, "nothing else being comparable to it in formative influence."

[1] *Ibid.*, pp. 172-3.

[2] *Parliamentary Papers: Letter to the Marquis of Lansdowne*, Feb. 4th, 1839.

A difficulty arises whenever children of any particular
sect have no school of their own to attend
Rival
Schemes.
and accordingly may have to submit to
teaching to which their parents object. With
the application of public funds to the support of schools
various schemes were put forward and terms were invented to describe them. By a *denominational system* was
meant a system under the control of a particular sect that
made no provision for any but those of its own persuasion.
The plan of giving public aid in such cases was described
as "concurrent endowment" of the denomination. A
comprehensive system was one in which schools were connected with some particular religious body and definite
religious instruction given, but the rights of conscience
were respected. In a *combined system* secular instruction was given by the teacher, and distinctive religious instruction left to the ministers of the denomination. All
the efforts at compromise centre round one or other of
these plans.

State interference having definitely begun, the question
confronting statesmen of both parties was,
Second
Attempt to
Establish a
State System.
how far and by what means it was politic to
press forward.[1] With the change of Government Sir James Graham, the Conservative
Home Secretary, was fully alive to the importance of education—State education if possible, but in
any case religious education—as the chief means of sub-
duing the strong and general tendencies to acts of vio-
lence—intimidation, rioting, and insurrection. Brougham
urged him to press forward a Government measure, favour-

---

[1] In Parliament a small group of men, among them Mr. Slaney and Mr.
Roebuck, constantly pressed for a larger measure of Government interest,
urging larger grants, the appointment of a Minister of Public Instruction,
and school rates for the maintenance of schools in rural parishes.

ing the Church if need be, as the matter was so urgent to the social welfare of the country. "All real friends of education," he believed would accept it, "with the exception of those who hate the Established Church and love their sects more than they love education—a class of most worthy and most conscientious men, who have done incalculable service hitherto, but whose honest scruples and prejudices prevent them from doing more now."[1]

Graham's reply dealt frankly with the issues involved. Could national education work well without religion? He thought not. At the same time he was clear that the State could not teach "the established creed" with the aid of rates and taxes without provoking the resistance of Dissenters. He was also frankly of opinion that as far as England was concerned an "agreement on the fundamental articles of the Christian faith as the basis of a mixed scheme of general instruction" was delusive. Such a scheme in Ireland had failed. That it had succeeded in Scotland was because the churches had a common creed and catechism, however much they might differ on points of discipline. The situation was such that the Prime Minister—Sir Robert Peel—believed the times altogether unfavourable to Government action, and thought the best service would be rendered "by the cautious and gradual extension of the power and the pecuniary means of the Committee of the Privy Council"—a view that turned out to be correct.[2]

An opportunity to test the feeling of the country on the question arose in 1843. In that year Lord Ashley, better known as Earl Shaftsbury, moved an address to the Queen praying for "instant and serious consideration of the best means for promoting the blessings of a moral and religious

---

[1] *Life and Letters of Sir James Graham, 1792-1861*, Parker, Vol. I., p. 337.   [2] *Ibid.*, pp. 337-340.

education among the working classes." For half a century reformers have been pleading for shortening the hours of labour and improving the educational condition of children employed in factories. The Health and Morals of Apprentices Act (1802) has already been referred to. Factory Acts had been passed: that of 1833 made two hours' daily schooling compulsory and inspectors were appointed to see that the regulations were not evaded; yet the reports of the Factory and School Inspectors, the Children's Employment Commission, and the Statistical Societies served to emphasise their failure, the vast amount of educational destitution, and the results of ignorance.

Sir James Graham complied by bringing in a Factory Bill. He expressed the wish that all party feeling and religious differences should be laid aside, and that they should endeavour "to find some neutral ground on which they could build something approaching to a scheme of national education with a due regard to the wishes of the Established Church on the one hand, and studious attention to the honest scruples of Dissenters on the other."

Sir James Graham's Bill, 1843.

The Bill was a small measure providing for the compulsory education of children in workhouses and those employed in woollen, flax, silk and cotton factories, for at least three hours per day, at the same time limiting the working day of children between eight and thirteen years of age to six and a half hours. Government loans were to be offered for the erection of schools, their maintenance being a charge on the local poor rate. The management of each school was to be vested in seven trustees, composed of the clergymen and churchwardens *ex officio*, two trustees appointed by the magistrates, and two millowners. The schoolmaster was to be a member of the Church of England, and his appointment was subject to the approval of the Bishop. The right of inspection was reserved to the clerical trustees and to the Committee of Council. Attendance at Church on Sunday was compulsory, and religious instruction during the week day was to conform to the doctrines of the Establishment. Provision was, however, made for the children of parents who objected to the teaching of the Catechism and attendance at Church. The introduction of this conscience clause, together with the constitution of the trust would, it was hoped, satisfy Dissenters.

The measure quickly evoked the opposition of Nonconformists, on the ground that it rated all **Nonconformist Opposition.** classes and gave the management to one, that it was an attempt to recruit the Church at the expense of Dissent under the guise of education, and that its influence would be mainly felt in populous districts where Dissenters were in a majority. Meetings were held all over the country; resolutions pledged the people to resist the measure; and a great mass of petitions poured into Parliament against it. In the face of such opposition Sir James Graham proposed a series of amendments, making denominational teaching separate and voluntary, and assigning set hours when the Ministers of different denominations might instruct their own children. Bible reading and the Lord's Prayer were the only compulsory religious observances. At the same time it was proposed that four of the trustees should be elected by the ratepayers, each ratepayer being allowed to vote for two trustees. In short, the Government was prepared to adopt the "Combined" plan of education favoured by the majority of Dissenters, and at the same time to grant the principle of local management by trustees elected *ad hoc*. "I am aware," said Sir James Graham in introducing these concessions, " that the waters of strife have overflowed, and now cover the land—this is my olive-branch."

It was of no avail. Nonconformists might have found ample ground for agreement at this stage, but they distrusted the Government and, elated with the success of their agitation in the country, were determined to sacrifice all to party advantage. Thus for the second time within four years the hope of establishing a universal system of national education disappeared. The Government had no option but to drop the Bill (1843).

The following year the non-controversial clauses were embodied in a new Factory Act. Increased powers were given to Factory Inspectors to inspect schools and to disqualify inefficient masters. Half-time employment began at eight years of age, and parents as well as employers were made responsible for the attendance of their children at school on three full days or for three hours on six half-days in each week. No mention was made of religious instruction, and the total deduction from the child's wages for school pence was 2d. a week.[1]

The outcome of the controversy was the rise of a body of Dissenters whose object was to resist the **The Rise of the "Voluntaryists."** intervention of the State in matters of education. Dissenters of all parties had supported by petition and active exertion the Government scheme in 1839, which embodied the principle of State interference in the education of the people, and they had not hesitated to accept Government assistance. As late as 1842 the *Leeds Mercury* was advocating two schools in every district—one for the Church, one for Dissent— each equally supported by the Government. It was only as alarm spread among Nonconformists, and especially among Congregationalists, through the introduction of Sir

---

[1] These regulations were extended to non-textile factories and workshops in 1864 and 1867.

James Graham's Bill that a party arose—the "Voluntaryists"—who embraced the doctrine of educational free trade and the immorality of State action. The objections were first formulated at a meeting of the Congregational Union held at Leeds in 1843, and were developed as time went on. Briefly, they adopted as their platform three principles: (1) All education must have a religious basis; (2) The State cannot educate, and State interference is necessarily pernicious; (3) The spread of education depends upon self-help and free competition. The leaders of the movement were Edward Baines and Edward Miall. One of the first steps was the founding of the "Congregational Board of Education to promote the advancement of Popular Education, upon strictly religious principles, free from all magisterial authority."[1] It was connected with the Congregational Union and was composed of subscribers, its object being to aid the erection of school buildings, to establish and support day and Sunday schools, to promote the training of teachers, to supply books and other school requisites, to improve education generally, and to disseminate voluntary principles.[2]

Education, they held, was not a department of State law and administration—"Government interference in any form with the education of mind" they repudiated on the ground that it could only retard if not positively injure, for from its nature it tended "to abuse, to stereotyped forms,

Their Educational Position.

---

[1] The Baptist Voluntary Education Society was founded at the same time.

[2] By 1859 £180,000 had been raised for school buildings. Homerton Training College was opened in 1846, and by 1851 364 schools had been erected and were wholly supported by subscriptions and school pence. The *Crosby Hall Lectures*, the series of Congregational tracts, the quarterly journal *The Educator*, and Edward Baines' *Letters to Lord John Russell*, *A Letter to the Marquis of Lansdowne*, etc., give the authoritative exposition of the principles.

to perfunctory discharge of duties." It was not in harmony with the principle of free trade. It contained no incentive to improvement. " Government can build schools, advance money, employ masters, commission inspectors, and distribute books ; and it can so cover the land with the means and the aspect of education, but it cannot educate. Soon all this will be found obstructive machinery, cumbering the ground. Change will be impossible. School books will be as unchangeable as Church books, and for the same reason—their fixed use and immense numbers. A vast interest will be created, and stand as an insurmountable obstacle to spontaneous effort and improvement." [1] Besides, taxation which is applied to teach doctrines objected to by great numbers is unjust. Only by adopting the voluntary principle will universal spontaneous effort and interest in education be evoked, parents freely seeking it for their children and freely making sacrifices to secure their training, instructors free under competition for every effort and every improvement, and all men of religion, philanthropy, and patriotism concurring in voluntary effort. [2]

No labour was spared in canvassing these principles. In their enthusiasm " Voluntaryists " were led to over-rate seriously the efficiency of existing means, [3] they depreciated the amount of education needed, and had supreme faith in the ability of all parents to pay fees adequate to make the schools practically self-supporting. Moreover, they overlooked the large area where they could not work at all, and they disregarded or denied the great truth that the " voluntary principle is inapplicable in education because

---

[1] *The Connection of Religion with Popular Education*, Algernon Wells, pp. 6-7. See series of *Tracts on Popular Education*, Congregational Board of Education.   [2] *Ibid.*, p. 11.

[3] See, for example, Ed. Baines' *Letter to the Rt. Hon. Lord John Russell on the History and Progress of Education in Wales*, 1848.

it is precisely those who need education most that are least capable of demanding it, desiring it, or even conceiving it."

In 1847 the Minutes authorising the apprenticing of pupil teachers, providing Queen's Scholarships to Normal Schools and allocating grants and pensions to teachers and to schools of industry were laid before Parliament. "Voluntaryists" saw here a means of strengthening the hands of the Church, and the vote of £100,000 for Education was strongly opposed. Macaulay, as a member of the Committee of Council, made a strong speech in favour of the State principle. " I appeal with still more confidence to a future age which, while enjoying all the blessings of State education, will look back with astonishment to the opposition which the introduction of that system encountered, and which will be still more astonished that such resistance was offered in the name of civil and religious freedom." [1]

Opposition to State Action.

Moderate men felt that such extreme " voluntaryism " was a mistake, and many Dissenters and Congregationalists gradually joined the number of those who favoured either a " combined," or a " comprehensive," system of State education. Indeed, had it not been for sectarian rivalry and party zeal, it is inconceivable that such a theory could have been seriously supported for a moment. The facts of history were against it, and the law of supply and demand were clearly not applicable. Moreover, whatever it might do as a middle class scheme it made little provision for the poor districts most in need of education. By 1858 the number of persons having conscientious objections to the acceptance of State aid had greatly diminished, and all denominations were then in receipt

Voluntaryism a Mistake.

---

[1] *Speeches.* The whole of this speech, April 18th, 1847, is worth reading.

of grants. Meantime the Committee of Council had perforce to work cautiously and tentatively.

Its policy was to favour a religious, as opposed to a secular, education, to work through existing **Work of the** agencies, and to conciliate as far as possible **Committee** **of Council.** the various denominations. At the same time the main abuses that attended the distribution of money under the Treasury Minute of 1833 came to an end. Buildings were required to conform to definite conditions; adequate security for the continuance of the school had to be given; the property had to be vested in trustees; and the school had to submit to inspection. The work of the inspectors to begin with was mainly to inquire into the needs of districts applying for aid, to investigate the actual educational conditions of the various parts of the country, to obtain trustworthy information as to the work being done in schools, to help in spreading a truer view of the meaning of education, and of more efficient methods of school organisation and instruction, and generally to place their knowledge and experience at the disposal of such managers and others as invited it, whether in aided or non-aided schools.[1] In reporting on a school they were asked to note such points as the following : the suitability of the site; the condition of the fabric; the size of the chief schoolroom; whether there was a gallery, a cloak-room, a playground; the heating and ventilating of the school; the teaching apparatus; the school books in use (reading, arithmetic, geography, English history, grammar, etymology, singing, drawing, land-surveying); whether physical exercises were an integral part of the work; the nature of any gymnastic appliances in the playground; the method of school organisa-

---

[1] *Minutes of the Committee of Council*, 1839-40, pp. 25-45.

tion in vogue; the attendance; school fees, salaries, income; etc.

In this way valuable suggestions for guiding the policy of the central authority were obtained. The reports are interesting as giving a detailed picture of elementary education at the time. They tell a tale oftentimes of extraordinary sacrifice and self-denial on the part of clergy and others to bring the elements of education within the reach of the poor. Yet in spite of the most valiant efforts little progress was being made. Managers were without the means to make the schools really efficient: books and apparatus were too meagre, salaries were too low, teachers were in charge of far too many children, the attendance was bad, and the methods of teaching were far too mechanical.[1] In short, the official reports merely confirmed the impression that a good deal of education existed merely in name, and that if schools were to be efficiently conducted money would have to be found somewhere. Building grants were all very well, but it was impossible for the matter to rest there.

This machinery was not established without arousing much misgiving. The religious basis of education had been recognised by the Committee of Council as being in accord with the sentiment of the nation, but the idea of an inspection that confined itself to secular subjects occasioned great suspicion. In view of the attitude of the Government towards religious instruction the Church of England took alarm, seeing in it an insidious means of introducing a religious conformity repugnant to Church principles.[2] Grants were declined and a deadlock ensued.

---

[1] The Managers' Reports of individual schools during this period fully confirm the official account. See *infra*, pp. 256-7.

[2] Lord John Russell was of course a staunch supporter of the cause of unsectarian religious instruction. Brougham in 1839 had introduced still

Accordingly, in order to conciliate the Church, a concordat was entered into whereby inspectors of schools under either the Church of England or the Church of Scotland should be approved by the archbishops previous to appointment, they should be required to give special attention to the religious teaching in the school, and a copy of the reports on such schools should be lodged with the bishop of the diocese. In order to meet the views of the British and Foreign School Society, a similar concession was granted to them four years later, and to the Roman Catholic Poor School Committee in 1847. It was to these arrangements that the clerical element among Government inspectors until comparatively recent times was due.[1]

In 1846 the Committee of Council definitely took in hand the task of improving school staffing and providing a succession of professional teachers. This it did by instituting the pupil teacher system. At the same time it took steps to make the profession of teacher more attractive by paying grants in augmentation of salaries and providing a pension scheme.[2] The following year special grants were made in aid of apparatus, maps, books, etc.

At this point a most important step was taken by the **The Management Clauses.** Government. Any thought of the State annexing popular education was abandoned, and instead the Government resigned itself, at any rate for the time being, to handing over the work of

another Bill proposing a system of rate-aided schools under local management, to be conducted on the "combined" plan. Anything that savoured of making religion a "subject" was abhorrent to Churchmen. Had Kay-Shuttleworth—a Nonconformist—and the Committee of Council failed to recognise this, there can be little doubt that the establishment of a State system would have been indefinitely postponed.

[1] *Four Periods*, Kay-Shuttleworth, Period Three, Chap. II. The Ven. Archdeacon Sinclaire's *Charge to the Clergy of the Archdeaconry of Middlesex*, 1845. [2] See *infra*, pp. 347-8.

popular education to such voluntary agencies as could be induced to undertake it, and it contented itself merely with supervision. The occasion was the issue of the Management Clauses for schools in connection with the Church, Wesleyans, Roman Catholics, and the British and Foreign Society. These clauses defined the conditions to which managers must conform for purposes of grant.

Hitherto only schools connected with the National and British and Foreign School Societies and a few others belonging to neither body had participated in the Parliamentary grants. Now they were thrown open, subject to provision being made for religious instruction.

The Minutes provided for four forms of management. In the case of Church schools, the superintendence of moral and religious instruction was vested in the hands of the clergyman of the parish, with power to use the premises for a Sunday school. In case of dispute appeal was allowed to the bishop. In all other respects the government of the school, the management of the funds, and the appointment and dismissal of teachers were vested either in a committee consisting of the clergyman, his curates, and certain representatives of the subscribers being members of the Church of England, or, where the population was small, in the clergyman alone. Disputes had to be referred to the Committee of Council. For Wesleyan schools similar provisions were made, the circuit ministers being substituted for the clergy. In the case of Roman Catholic schools the priest acted under faculties from his bishop, and the members of the committee were nominated by the priest and not elected by the subscribers. In British and other undenominational schools the whole committee was elected. The purpose of these clauses was to safeguard any undue clerical influence, and to put the management of the school as far as possible into the hands of the laity.

The clauses were the subject of a long controversy between the Committee of Council and the National Society. The chief points of objection were that the " obnoxious distinction between secular and religious instruction was covertly and by implication reintroduced," that no guarantee was afforded that the Committee would be composed of " *bona fide* members of the Church of England, that is to ·say Communicant members," and that in both respects the clauses constituted " a plain violation of the limits of State interference settled by the Archbishop and the Committee of Council, and affirmed by Order in Council in 1840." The opposition of the Church was fed through the intense distrust of many of its members of the educational policy of Lord John Russell, who was again back in power. The lay committee savoured too much of the plan of local government of each school by bodies elected *ad hoc*, without any religious test. Compromise in detail was effected, but the Committee of Council succeeded in carrying its main points.[1]

[1] *Minutes of Committee of Council. Correspondence*, 1848, 1849. *History and Present State of the Education Question*, Metropolitan Church Union, 1850. For Jewish schools see *Minutes*, 1852-3.

Progress up to 1851 *as given in the Census Returns* of the chief classes of schools.

	Church of England.	British.	Congrega-tionalist.	Wesley-ans.	Roman Catholics.
Before 1801	709	16	8	7	10
1801-11	350	28	9	4	10
1811-21	756	77	12	17	14
1821-31	897	45	21	17	28
1831-41	2,002	191	95	62	69
1841-51	3,448	449	269	239	166
Not stated	409	46	17	17	14
	8,571	852	431	363	311

Schools principally supported by endowments are not included in the above summary. The list of schools conducted on the principles of the British and Foreign School Society is admittedly incomplete. The Introduction to the Education Census contains a useful summary of the various parties met with at this time.

PROGRESS OF EDUCATION IN WALES.

A few words may be said about the progress of elementary education in Wales after the establishment

The Demand for Education.

of the Committee of Council. The social unrest that found expression in the Chartist riot at Newport in 1839 and the Rebecca Riots of 1843 had the effect of concentrating attention on the need for a better and more general system of elementary schooling. Thus the Commissioners who investigated the latter riots emphasised the importance of providing extensive facilities for instruction in the English language as the most likely means of leading to a more efficient working of the " laws and institutions,"[1] and of opening up avenues of advancement and increasing individual adaptability. The existing agencies fell far short of the demand. Indeed " the means of instruction of the children of the poor, and even those who may be styled the middle classes, are lamentably small . . . (with the result that) not only the children of the labourers, but of a large class of working farmers, are almost beyond the reach of mental improvement. It is needless to remark how greatly such a state of things is calculated to minister to those prejudices and misconceptions to which so much of the recent excitement of the country may be justly attributed."[2]

In order to understand the history of elementary education in the Principality during this period it

Some Difficulties.

is necessary to remember that Wales was at the time relatively poor. A great proportion of the people then as now were strong Nonconformists, but the wealthier part of the population belonged to the

---

[1] The obvious solution was of course to issue " laws and instructions " in both Welsh and English.

[2] See Report of the Commission on the Rebecca Riots.

Established Church. Accordingly without the operation of a State system there were great financial difficulties in the way of bringing an efficient day school education within the reach of all. The obstacles confronting the establishment of such a system in England have already been noted. These were even greater in Wales. It is only necessary to remember how large a part religion plays in the life of the Welsh people and how opposed the majority of Welsh Nonconformists have been to anything that savoured of " concurrent endowment " of the sects, to understand why the Principality became one of the strongest centres of "Voluntaryism" in the country. So strong was this feeling that for years districts too poor to establish day schools were led to decline all State aid and pinned their faith on the educative work of the Sunday schools. The policy proved to have been a mistaken one, and it did much to hinder the spread of a higher standard of elementary schooling.

Another point also calls for notice. At the present day when the spirit of Welsh nationalism is so strong, when every effort is made to develop Welsh education along its own lines, and when everything is being done to make the language and literature of the Principality a living force in the schools, it must not be forgotten that in the first half of last century it was not Welsh but English that was the favoured language in elementary schools. It was the ambition of the poorest Welshman that his child should learn English because of its market value,[1] and this sentiment was fostered, as we have seen, by those in authority, who honestly believed that in a widespread knowledge of the English tongue lay the salvation of Wales.[2] English

English v. Welsh Teaching.

[1] *Reports on Wales.* Minute of Committee of Council, 1847, p. 10.
[2] See *ibid.*, pp. 309-313, for the way in which many Welshmen regarded this.

was almost universally the language of the day schools, even though the teachers themselves had oftentimes a very imperfect knowledge of it.[1] In view of the low level of attainment of teachers at this time, what the educational value of the instruction was under these conditions may be left to the imagination.[2] So strong, however, was the determination of many of the teachers to do their best that penalties were inflicted, as in the schools of the Renaissance, on children found speaking their mother tongue during school hours.

What the existing state of education was in the mining districts of South Wales is described in the first reports of the Committee of Council. In the whole of the district investigated not a single National or British school existed. Some two thirds of the children never went to a school at all, the rest attended some 47 common schools or dame schools and paid from 3d. to 8d. per week. These differed in no important respects from poor schools in England. "The rooms were, for the most part, dirty and close. A rudely constructed desk for the master often occupied one corner; forms and desks for the children were ranged along the walls, and from side to side. The books being provided by the parents, mere fragments, consisting of a few soiled leaves, appeared to be generally deemed sufficient to answer the purpose for which the children were sent to school. A pile of detached covers, and leaves too black for further use, often occupied another corner, betokening the result of long struggles with unmeaning rows of spelling, with

Education in South Wales, 1839.

[1] *Ibid.,* p. 446.

[2] *Minutes of Committee of Council,* I., 1845, pp. xv-xix.

[3] Report of Mr. Tremenheere, *Minutes of the Committee of Council,* 1839-40. The district comprised the parishes of Bedwelty, Aberystruth, Mynnyddyslwynn, and Trevethin in Monmouth, and Merthyr Tydvil in Glamorganshire.

confinement and constrained positions, and the other adversities of elementary learning. In many silence was only maintained for a few moments at a time, by loud exclamations and threats." The main source of education was in the Sunday schools, of which some 80 existed.

Among the Welshmen who took a prominent part in advancing elementary education at this time **Beginnings of Educational Activity.** we find three well-known names, Sir Thomas Phillips of Newport,[1] Hugh (afterwards Sir Hugh) Owen, and the Rev. Henry Griffiths of Brecon.[2] Both Churchmen and Nonconformists shared in the movement. The Diocesan Board of Education for Monmouth came into existence in 1839, that for Llandaff in 1846. Between 1845 and 1847 the National Society conducted an investigation into the state of education in Wales. The great deficiencies existing led to the formation of a special fund for education in the Principality, to the granting of special facilities for Welsh teachers in training colleges, and to the formation of the Welsh Education Committee. One result of this activity was the opening of Carmarthen Training College in 1848.

Some years before this Hugh Owen had begun his valuable work on behalf of Welsh education. **Sir Hugh Owen.** Finding that people in Wales were generally unaware that the Government had undertaken to assist the work of education by means of grants, he endeavoured to arouse interest on the subject of State-aided undenominational education by issuing in 1843 a Letter to the Welsh People on day schools. "In order to provide the children with education you must have schools; in order to secure liberty of conscience you must have

[1] The author of *Wales*.

[2] Prominently associated with the establishment of the first normal school in Wales.

schools which shall not be identified with any particular religious denomination." Accordingly he favoured the British and Foreign system and recommended the establishment of a British school in every district[1]; the formation of a "British School Society" in each county for the purpose of collecting money, especially for the help of poor districts, and generally to advise and direct the spread of education; lastly he proposed the establishment of a local Committee for each school district. The necessary money was to be obtained from government grants, from donations by local landlords and from subscriptions.

A movement on these lines began in North Wales. An agent of the British and Foreign School Society was appointed and in three years some 40 schools with nearly 5,000 scholars were at work.[2] The great difficulty at this time was to secure efficient teachers and the fullest use was made of the Borough Road Training College.[3] In 1845 some 30 young Welshmen, many of them with very meagre educational qualifications, were passed through the College. The charge for board, lodging, washing, and instruction only amounted to 6s. a week. In South Wales the general feeling was against receiving State funds, and it was not until "Voluntaryism" had proved itself unable to accomplish the work of popular education that an agent of the British and Foreign School Society was appointed.

[1] In North Wales there were only two British Schools at the time.

[2] By 1871 the number of schools had increased to 271, with an average attendance of 32,455.

[3] The difficulty of getting efficient teachers was primarily due to the poor salaries that could be offered. As one of the Welsh Education Commissioners reported in 1848, "The meagre prospect of income which presents itself to a schoolmaster in Wales deters all but those whom poverty or want of activity compels to have recourse to so unenviable a status for their means of livelihood."

H. ED. 7

In 1846 the Cambrian Educational Society [1] was founded, with Hugh Owen as Honorary Secretary, to further the establishment of British Schools in Wales, to advise local committees and assist them in negotiating with the Committee of Council, to give pecuniary assistance in special cases; to assist young men to become teachers, and to appoint inspectors for the supervision of the schools. Owen also took upon himself the work of making the new pupil teacher regulations and the augmentation grants to teachers familiar to Welshmen, urging them to take advantage of the conditions offered, and not to leave the Established Church to capture the education of the country through adopting a mistaken "Voluntaryist" policy.[2]

That a good deal of attention needed to be given to education in Wales was evident from the Commissioners' Reports of 1848. As a result of a motion [3] in Parliament in 1846, for an Address to the Queen praying for "an inquiry to be made into the state of education in the Principality of Wales, especially into the means afforded to the labouring classes of acquiring a knowledge of the English language," three Commissioners, one of whom was Mr. Lingen, afterwards Secretary to the Education Department, were appointed by the Committee of Council "to ascertain . . . . the

The Welsh Education Commission, 1846.

---

[1] It was practically a Welsh branch of the British and Foreign Society.

[2] It was as an outcome of Owen's activities that the Bangor and Swansea Training Colleges came to be established. Owen showed a catholic interest in all branches of Welsh education, and is, in fact, the link between elementary and higher education. He was closely associated with the foundation of University College, Aberystwyth, 1872, and with the movement for extending the facilities of secondary schooling in the Principality. See *Life of Sir Hugh Owen.*

[3] This was moved by a Welshman, Mr. Williams, M.P. for Coventry.

existing number of schools of all descriptions, for the education of the children of the labouring classes, or of adults—the amount of attendance—the ages of the scholars—and the character of the instruction given in the schools." The Commissioners were assisted by a number of young men who possessed a knowledge of Welsh, but apparently had very little other qualification for the work. The investigation extended over the best part of a year.[1]

They reported in effect[2] that the school buildings were usually very inefficient, and often of a wretched character; that a large proportion of the entire number were un-provided with out-buildings essential to decency, and that a small proportion only of the existing buildings were secured for educational purposes; that suitable furniture and apparatus existed in a small number of schools only; that the supply of books was very scanty and exclusively English, without any suitable aids for enabling Welsh children to acquire what was to them a foreign language, and that the Holy Scriptures were commonly used as the spelling and reading book of the school. Moreover, very few of the teachers had had any previous training for their work, and those who had been at a training school had not continued there on an average more than six months. There was the usual complaint that many had undertaken school-keeping after having failed in mechanical trades; that but few of the schoolmasters taught efficiently what they professed to teach, and very few were skilful teachers or possessed of adequate mental cultivation. The incomes of teachers were very inadequate to secure the services of competent people, nearly half of the salaries being under £20 per annum, although two-thirds were unprovided

[1] *Reports of the Commissioners of Inquiry into the State of Education in Wales,* 1848, pp. ii, iii. [2] *Ibid.,* or Phillips' *Wales,* pp. 409-10.

with a residence by the school managers. There were no local resources adequate to the support of the schools. There was no effective supervision, and the discipline of the schools was generally poor. The attendance of the children was very irregular, being limited to "odd quarters" with long intervals between in the case of a large proportion of the scholars. Moreover, the school-leaving age was much too low. Too often it was found that on leaving school the children could not read with intelligence the most ordinary book of common information, while their own language had been ignored. In general the provision for girls was worse than that for boys.

The Commissioners in the course of their reports introduced many observations on the moral and religious conditions of the Welsh people, and succeeded in presenting to the outside world a most unfavourable picture of the general social conditions of the Principality. Both here and in the accounts of the stupidity that prevailed in the schools things are a little overdrawn. This, however, is a feature common to practically all the educational reports during this period. Investigators, apparently without any deliberate intention to be unfair, were led by their zeal for better things to emphasise the bad, and rarely gave equal importance to the good work that was being done. This defect is very marked down to 1870.

The Reports were repudiated by Welshmen of all parties. The comments were described as
Results. flippant, misleading, and untrue. They called forth the most indignant protests and a hail of abuse both in print and on the platform. The state of feeling is reflected in the name by which the Reports are known, *Brâd y Llyfrau Gleision*, The Treason of the Blue Books. It had been intended that the inquiry should pave the way for some comprehensive plan of

State education in Wales, but the agitation aroused by the Reports against the Committee of Council put a stop to any such scheme. Indeed the immediate effect was to confirm many Welshmen for the time being more than ever in their "Voluntaryist" position.[1] Nevertheless the inquiry gave a new impulse to Welsh education, and it is from this date that the forward movement may be dated. As the "Voluntaryist" position was abandoned the majority of Welshmen joined the secularist party.[2]

[1] The controversy has an interest of its own because of the part taken in it by the advocates of "Voluntaryism." Edward Baines succeeded in showing to his own satisfaction that all was well, and that State interference was quite unnecessary in the Principality. See *ante*, p. 86.

As illustrating the state of the feeling aroused we may take the cartoon published in Cardiff—" Pictures for the Million, No. 2," entitled "Gathercoal Scuttleworth's Final Charge to the Spies." It depicts Kay-Shuttleworth with horse's hoofs seated at a table with an inverted coal-scuttle on his head, addressing in these words the three Commissioners, who are very much out at the knee and are specially remarkable for their foxy ears :—

"The Whig Ministry are resolved to punish Wales for the dangerous example it gives to the rest of the Empire by its universal dissent from our Church. I now inform *you*, in confidence, that this is the real object of this espionage,—you are to help their lordships (of the Committee of Council) to make out a case against voluntary religion by collecting such evidence of its connection with immorality, disloyalty, and barbarism, as will disgust the public mind of England, thereby preparing it to sanction the (despotic) scheme in contemplation for driving the Welsh back to the *true Church*. The use of the Welsh LANGUAGE being known to be favourable to the propagation of earnest personal religion, both the LANGUAGE and the NATIONALITY of the Welsh, as well as their religion, are to be destroyed. Your *professional* with your personal art will enable you to select such witnesses, and call such evidence as may secure our object without exciting suspicion. My lords have authorised me to assure you that you will be made gentlemen(!) on your return."

[2] See *infra*, p. 121.

CHAPTER IV.

"We live in an age when the question is not *whether* but *how* the poor are to be educated."—DR. HOOK.

In 1846 something of a sensation was produced in the
Church by the publication of a pamphlet by
Dr. Hook's
Letter.
Dr. Hook, Vicar of Leeds, "On the means
of rendering more effective the Education of
the People," written in the form of a letter to the Bishop
of St. David's, a pamphlet that went through eight editions
in three months. Arguing that experience had demonstrated that the resources of Voluntaryism were inadequate
to secure a system of elementary education efficient either in
quality or quantity, he proceeded to advocate a "combined"
system of education whereby secular instruction should be
given by the State, supported out of public rates, and
definite doctrinal instruction should be given on two after-
noons a week and on Sundays by ministers of the different
denominations. Under these conditions, he argued that
both secular and religious instruction would benefit.
Teachers were to hold Government certificates; the school
was to provide a real mental and moral training; and the
curriculum was to be enlarged to include the elements of
mathematics, geography, music, drawing, and history.
Religious teaching would no longer be allowed to degenerate "into nothing more than a reading lesson, with no
peculiar interest, nor profit, nor object." Classes would
not be left in charge of ignorant and thoughtless monitors
"to read anywhere"; little children would not be set on the

Epistle to the Galatians; chapters would not be read without question or comment; and the Bible would cease to be a favourite spelling book.[1]

This pamphlet aroused a good deal of opposition, and marks the beginning to a new trend in the controversy on popular education. The question that now came to the fore between those who approved of State assistance centred round the principle of management. Men grouped themselves into two parties. Those who were disposed to regard the development of popular education mainly as a religious work held that the management of a school should rest in the hands of the Church or the congregation, and were altogether opposed to handing it over to the control of any popularly elected committee. They desired freedom of development on denominational lines, and favoured a scheme of concurrent endowment out of the rates. This party included the majority of the Church, the Roman Catholics, and many Nonconformists. On the other hand, those who saw in the spread of education the expression of a democratic principle, who believed that no complete system could be established without the uniform intervention of the State, were in favour of management by properly elected bodies *ad hoc*, arguing that local taxation without representation was intolerable. In the absence of any common basis of agreement between the various denominations with regard to religious teaching, this party favoured a system of secular instruction.

In 1847 a committee was formed in Manchester to promote a " plan for the establishment of a general system of secular education in the county of Lancaster." This developed into the Lancashire Public School Association, and after a repulse in Parliament it became the

The National Public School Association.

---

[1] *Letter*, p. 44.

National Public School Association in 1850, framed on a wider basis. Among its supporters were members of the defunct Central Society, eminent dissenters, and men like Cobden and Combe the phrenologist. The Secularist Bill of 1850 is interesting for the way in which it fore-shadowed the Act of 1870. It proposed that inspectors should be appointed to ascertain the educational deficiency of districts, and that compulsory powers should be given to the ratepayers to establish local school boards, and to levy rates for the purpose of establishing free secular schools for children between seven and thirteen years of age, and making up any deficiency in revenue. The importance of the personal factor was recognized by endeavouring to place the position of the teacher on a sound economic basis, and steps of a somewhat doubtful character [1] were to be taken to secure energy and initiative. No provision was made for existing denominational schools. The secularists were forced to make concessions through the strong opposition of the Church, Wesleyans, and Roman Catholics, without however saving the Bill.[2]

An active campaign was now begun to mould public opinion. Branches of the National Association were established in all the large towns, statistics and pamphlets were published and circulated, and free secular schools were opened in Manchester, Edinburgh, and elsewhere, to show the practicability of the secularist plan. A similar associa-tion came into existence at Leeds, but was somewhat overshadowed by the local " Voluntaryists." As the party attracted supporters from all classes it became less exclusive,

[1] For example, in order to stimulate or shame teachers, school reports were to be circulated, and salaries were to be dependent upon the number of children as well as upon the success of the teaching.

[2] *History of the Elementary School Contest*, Adams, p. 152; *Public Education*, Kay-Shuttleworth, p. 37 *et seq.*

and was prepared to extend to denominational schools not only the right to exist and to participate in Parliamentary grants, but even the benefit of local rates to supply the place of fees. The policy was inconsistent but opportunist, and had the merit of saving the proposals of the party from extinction.

To meet these proposals the advocates of the existing system had to devise some plan to accelerate progress. The result was the founding of the Manchester and Salford Committee on Education, its policy being to engraft a system of local rating upon the existing organisation.[1] It brought forward a private Bill only applicable to the boroughs of Manchester and Salford, proposing the levying of a rate of not more than 6d. in the pound in aid of existing schools, which were to be free but subject to a conscience clause and the management of which was to be undisturbed, the rate being administered by the Town Councils through the denominational managers. The Bill had the support of the Bishops, Wesleyans, and many dissenting ministers, but was opposed by Jews, Roman Catholics, Friends, etc., on various grounds, not the least of which was that it provided for the compulsory adoption of the Authorised version of the Bible in all new schools. It was strongly opposed by the " Voluntaryists," as was also a new Bill introduced by the secularist party. Both measures were referred to a Select Committee. A good deal of evidence was collected, and both Bills were set aside to make way for a Government proposal.[2]

The Manchester and Salford Education Committee.

[1] See *Public Education*, Kay-Shuttleworth, Chap. VI. and Appendix.
[2] A review of the evidence from the " Voluntaryist " standpoint is given in *The Case of the Manchester Educationists*, by J. H. Hinton, 1852, 1854.

On all hands it was felt that something must be done
to extend education by discovering some
Difficulties in the way of a State System. permanent source of local contribution to
supplement State grants. The difficulty lay
in providing that compulsory local contributions should be accompanied by local representation
in the management, without unduly interfering with
existing denominational schools.

During the next few years a number of Bills were proposed by the rival parties to meet the situation. In
1853 the Borough Bill was introduced by Lord John
Russell on behalf of the Government. Its object was to
give permissive powers of rating to Town Councils and
towns with a population of 5,000 to supplement the
revenue of existing schools by a sum equal to half of the
income derived from other sources; special grants might
also be made in aid of existing schools. No provision was,
however, made for local representation, and the Bill was
dropped. Even though this scheme was abandoned,
another, intended to supplement it, was put into operation
in rural districts by a Minute of the Committee of Council.
It provided for a system of capitation grants to be paid to
managers in order to encourage regularity of attendance.
The immediate result was to raise the Education Vote by
more than a half. These grants were a great boon to the
denominational system.

A new Manchester and Salford Bill was introduced, but
opposed on the ground that it neglected to provide local
representation. Another Bill was proposed by Sir John
Pakington in 1855, providing for the permissive establishment of local boards with power to aid existing schools,
subject to the adoption of a conscience clause, and to erect
and maintain new schools the creed of which was to be
decided in each case by the dominant religion of the

locality, provision being made to safeguard the rights of conscience. All the schools were to be free. This Bill, together with another introduced by the secularist party, was dropped. Various schemes of like nature were brought before Parliament during the next fourteen years, and prepared the way for the Act of 1870.

Two Acts of a different character call for notice at this point. Denison's Act of 1855, which gave permission to Boards of Guardians to pay the school pence of children in receipt of outdoor relief, is an indication of the importance attached to universal education. The following year, owing to the great expansion of the work of the Committee of Council, a Department of Education was created by an Order in Council, and a Bill was passed which provided for the appointment of a Minister.

Meantime dissatisfaction with the existing state of education was becoming more intense. A **Dissatisfaction with the State of Education.** series of drastic resolutions [1] to increase both the extent and the efficiency of existing means was rejected after a heated debate. The education vote was steadily increasing, and incidentally was establishing the existing system more and more firmly. A good deal had been accomplished, but amid the dust of conflict it was difficult to discern what effective progress had been made. For a quarter of a century the State had been making grants, and more than three and a half millions of public money had been spent on education. Opinion was divided as to the lines along which further operations should proceed. Had the Voluntary system shown itself capable of meeting the need? If so, was it capable of still further development? Or, on the other hand, were the various Voluntary agencies hiding fundamental defects under a show of activity?

[1] Introduced by Lord John Russell.

These were questions to which thoughtful men desired an answer. Accordingly, in response to a motion by Sir John Pakington, a Commission was appointed in 1858 under the Duke of Newcastle " to inquire into the present state of popular education in England, and to consider and report what measures, if any, are required for the extension of sound and cheap elementary instruction to all classes of the people." [1]

DUKE OF NEWCASTLE'S COMMISSION, 1858-1861.

The first duty of the Commission was to inquire into the complaints made against the existing
Subjects of Inquiry. system. The most prominent of these were that the cost of education was excessive and was still increasing, that it failed to penetrate the rural districts, that the instruction given even at the best schools was of an imperfect character, that the average school life was too short and attendance was very irregular. The system had confessedly accomplished great and beneficial results. Was it to be regarded simply as tentative and provisional, or did it contain elements of durability capable of a definite development into a national system?

---

[1] In 1857 a Conference on School Attendance, under the Prince Consort, reported that of 2,000,000 children at school

42 per cent. attended less than 1 year.					
22	,,	,,	1 or less than 2 years.		
15	,,	,,	2	,,	,,	3	,,
9	,,	,,	3	,,	,,	4	,,
5	,,	,,	4	,,	,,	5	,,
4	,,	,,	5	,,	,,	6	,,

The Committee recorded their opinion that the main defect in the existing state of popular education was not so much the lack of schools as the bad attendance of the children, many of whom left when they were from 9 to 10 years of age. See Final Report of the Cross Commission, p. 10.

No complete account of the state of education in any class of the population or of any district in the country being available, ten assistant commissioners were appointed to investigate the educational condition of ten specimen districts and to supplement existing information. Of the selected areas two were agricultural, one being in the east, the other in the west of the country; two were manufacturing, one comprising Lancashire and the West Riding, the other the Midlands. Similarly two mining, two maritime, and two metropolitan districts were chosen.

Method of Investigation.

The Report of the Commissioners was presented in 1861 after three years of assiduous labour. Briefly, it reported that the plan of leaving the spread of popular education to the initiative of religious communities had been justified by results. More than one in eight of the population was being brought under school influence, and the proportion was steadily increasing. The weakness lay rather in the value of much of the so-called educational provision, the early leaving age of the children—comparatively few remained after 11 years—and the poor standard of attendance. Even in inspected schools attendance only reached 74·35 per cent. of the number on the books. Of the two and a half million children at school, little more than one and a half million were in public schools, and only about half of these were in schools open to inspection. The value of inspection was recognised on all hands, and inspected schools as a class were much superior to others. There were of course some very good private schools, but the great majority gave an education that had little value.

The State of Education.

Under the superintendence of the Committee of Council a good type of education had been set up, but it was confined to too small a proportion of inspected schools, and a good deal of levelling up was necessary, for not more than one-fourth of the pupils in this class of schools were receiving a good education, and even in the best schools only about a fourth of the children reached the highest class and could be said to be " successfully educated." It is necessary to remark, however, that this last statement was challenged by Matthew Arnold and others as an assertion made without sufficient proof, and which in many cases would turn out to be untrue. Probably the criticism was more sweeping than it ought to have been owing to the lack of attention given at the time to providing suitable education for the younger children, and the tendency to concentrate all attention on the upper classes. The pupil teacher|system was regarded as " upon the whole excellent," while trained teachers had proved themselves " beyond all doubt greatly superior to the untrained." But the system as it had grown up under the Committee of Council was too complicated; its educational results were felt to be incommensurable with the expense entailed; the distribution of Government grants was too limited in its range, being confined to a comparatively small number of schools and, moreover, not reaching the districts most in need of assistance; and further, the instruction given in schools was too ambitious and superficial in character.

The problems confronting the Commissioners thus resolved themselves into how to raise the general level of school work, how to deal with the irregularity of attendance, and how to simplify the system and further the establishment of efficient schools throughout the country. The Commissioners were divided as to the steps to take. A minority who feared increasing central control, a gradual diminution of local interest in and liberality towards education, and the ultimate advent of public management favoured

Recommendations.

the gradual cessation of grants except for building purposes and trusted to awakened public interest and individual generosity to support schools. The majority, however, favoured increased aid, and the minority agreed to fall in with them. Denominational feeling being so strong it was decided to preserve the leading features of the existing system and to maintain the principles of non-interference in the religious training given by the different denominations and of central control over the direct management of schools. Teachers were no longer to be regarded as semi-civil servants receiving grants direct from the central authority, but all money was to be paid direct to the managers.[1]

At the same time a considerable extension of the existing system of grants was suggested. These were to be of two kinds : State grants from general taxation, and local grants from county and borough rates. They were to be directed toward increasing the efficiency, staffing, and average attendance of schools, and at the same time stimulating local interest. To be entitled to grants a school was to be registered, suitably housed, and provide at least 8 square feet of superficial area for each child in average attendance. The State grant was to be awarded on attendance, staffing, and the general tone of the school. The local grant—which was to be awarded by county or borough boards elected by quarter sessions or town councils—was to depend upon individual examination in reading, writing, and arithmetic. That is to say, the system of "payment by results" was recommended, with the object of making the actual teaching in schools more efficient and to distribute it more evenly among the scholars. "There is only one way of securing this result, which is to institute a searching examination by competent

[1] See *infra*, p. 347.

authority of every child in every school to which grants are paid, with a view to ascertaining whether these indispensable elements of knowledge are thoroughly acquired, and to make the prospects and position of the teacher dependent to a considerable extent on the results of this examination." [1]

It was not proposed to abolish school fees nor to introduce any system of compulsory attendance, such being regarded as neither attainable nor desirable in view of existing public opinion and the prevailing attitude towards child labour. As boys and girls could scarcely be expected to remain at school after 11 years of age it was important that they should commence schooling early, and it was in improving the education for infants and young children, and in establishing half-time and evening schools, that the hope of the future lay.

The Commissioners considered that by the adoption of some such plan existing requirements would be largely met. Poor districts would be supplied with the necessary means, local interest would be stimulated, and school work would increase in efficiency. At the same time by frankly recognising the value of the work done by the religious communities, by keeping existing relations unchanged, and by looking to them to supply the motive power for the further extension of popular education they would effectually check any reaction against a State system.

The Report was the result of compromise. Though outwardly unanimous it covered much deep-seated difference, and it inevitably aroused a good deal of criticism. Its statistics were challenged, its reports were regarded as untrustworthy, and it was soon evident that the division of opinion the Commissioners had sought to avoid was inevitable, so much so that the Government was not prepared

[1] *Report*, p. 157.

to face the danger of attempting to embody the recommendations in a Bill.

It now fell to Mr. Lowe, as Vice-President, to meet the criticism of the Commissioners and say what **Mr. Lowe's Criticism of the Report.** measures the Government proposed to adopt. He admitted that the system was expensive, that instruction was deficient, and that the machinery was complicated, and said that the Government would remedy as far as possible the evils complained of. The plan of a local rate could not be entertained, as it would inevitably entail locally elected representation and public management and introduce the difficulties they had sought to avoid. The organic principles of the present system would be retained, with its denominational character, its foundation on a broad religious basis, and its practice of giving State grants in aid of local contributions. Any change must come through a modification of existing Minutes, and the backbone of it must be to discontinue the practice of paying grants direct to teachers, throwing more responsibility on local managers, and making grants depend partly on the results of individual examination.

In order to present a clear view of the existing system and to facilitate its working Mr. Lowe had **The First Code.** the previous year collected the various Minutes in force, arranged them in chapters according to subjects, and published them. This was the original Code, the authoritative statement of the Education Department as to grants and the conditions determining their application.[1] This was now cancelled and a new series of Minutes—The Revised Code—presented to Parliament in 1861.

---

[1] An abstract of these regulations had been issued as a Parliamentary Paper in 1858, and a chronological list of Minutes in 1855.

This provided that grants should no longer be made to teachers holding certificates of competency,[1] but all payments to a school should be massed into a single Capitation Grant and paid direct to the managers, leaving them to bargain as they liked with the members of their staffs. In other words, the teacher ceased to be in any way an employé of the State. He must possess certain qualifications before his school was eligible for grant, but there the immediate interest of the State ended. At the same time, subject to the right of teachers already retired, the pension scheme was withdrawn. Grants could only be earned on pupils under 12 years of age, and were dependent on a certain number of attendances being made by the children, subject to the results of an individual examination by the Government Inspector of each child in reading, writing and arithmetic. The girls must also be taught sewing as part of the regular instruction of the school. Local co-operation was stimulated by regulating the amount of grant by reference to the income derived from school fees and subscriptions.[2]

The Revised Code.

Schools had to be adequately housed and staffed, but the scale of staffing was less in proportion to the number of scholars than before. At the same time a lower class of certificates was instituted with the object of opening up for grants schools taught by teachers of a lower order of attainment. Grants to Training Colleges were cut down, and no allowance was to be made in future for building and for improving the premises.[3]

[1] See infra, p. 347.   [2] See infra, pp. 143-4. A Reprint of the Revised Code is given in the Appendix to Matthew Arnold's *Reports on Elementary Schools 1852-1882*, edited by F. S. Marvin, 1908.

[3] The Training Colleges were supposedly voluntary institutions, although 90 per cent. of the cost was borne by the Government. Of the $4\frac{1}{3}$ million spent by Government on Education, $2\frac{1}{2}$ had gone to the training of teachers.

One reason for these drastic measures was the policy of economy to which the Government was **Opposition to the Revised Code.** pledged, and, as Mr. Lowe put it, "If the new system will not be cheap it will be efficient, and if it will not be efficient it will be cheap." The plan excited great hostility on all sides. The tendency of its provisions, it was contended, was to lower the qualifications of the teacher, to diminish the size of the staff, to reduce the importance of teaching any subjects beyond the mere rudiments, to restrict the total amount of the grant, and to take away the inducement to keep children at school after 11 years of age. On the other hand, it was maintained that under the new conditions every child would receive the educational attention to which it was entitled, that the managers and not the State would in future be responsible for the teacher, and that a door was opened for a humbler class of schools to come under the Government system. Teachers contended that the Government was under a moral obligation to continue the money payments conditionally due on their certificates. Managers protested that the system would injure religious instruction, and that " payment by results "was a delusive test of moral and intellectual advance. It showed a great want of trust in the educational oversight of the great societies, and was characterised as " an act of spoliation ever to be remembered with shame." Others, however, welcomed it as a check on the ambitious tendencies of primary education, and as absolutely essential if anything like efficiency was to be promoted.[1]

In introducing some modifications into the scheme in 1862 Mr. Lowe elaborated what he conceived to be the advantages of the plan. He pointed out that a religious

[1] For a discussion of the actual effects of the Revised Code on the school see *infra*, pp. 282-4.

element underlay the whole system of Privy Council education, that religious instruction in Church schools would
be inspected as before, and that the object of the Revised
Code was to deal with individuals rather than classes.   It
gave the managers almost entire freedom, made the interest
of the school identical with the interest of the public,
tested thoroughly the work done, and gave Parliament a
complete control over the educational grant.   " The object
of the Privy Council is to promote education among the
children of the labouring poor.   Those for whom this
system is designed are the children of persons who are not
able to pay for the teaching.   We do not profess to give
these children an education that will raise them above
their station and business in life—that is not our object
—but to give them an education that may fit them for that
business." [1]

The Revised Code came into operation in 1862.   The
grant was limited to 12s. a head, 4s. to be
The Working
of the Revised
Code.
paid on average attendance, and 8s. on the
results of examination, one-third of the
latter sum being withheld for failure in each
of the three R's.   Children under six years of age were
exempt from examination, but for the rest six standards
were laid down, and no child could be presented a second
time in the same grade.   Half-timers were eligible for the
same grants as those attending full time, and the development of evening schools was encouraged by making
similar grants, but on a smaller scale, for pupils over 12
years of age.[2]

The immediate effect of the application of the Revised
Code was a substantial and progressive reduction in the
total grant, together with a slow rise in average attendance

[1] See Final Report of the Cross Commission, 1888, p. 17.
[2] In 1862 there were only 317 evening schools.

due in some measure to an increase in the number of inspected schools.[1]

Supporters of the new system explained these figures as the result of greater efficiency in the administration of the grant, for whereas it had previously to be paid in full or not at all, it was now automatically regulated by the quality of the work done. Moreover, the decline in total grant merely exhibited pre-existing unsoundness in the children's knowledge, and was a necessary preliminary to better work. Some idea of the backward state of the schools may be gathered from the fact that in 1863-4 only 41 per cent. of the children in average attendance were presented for examination, and 86 per cent. of those over 10 years of age were examined in standards too low for their age.[2] With experience the number of passes slightly improved, but at best the schools showed up very badly.

On the other hand, various inspectors testified to the cruelty and the over-pressure of children that resulted. There was a falling off of all higher subjects; teachers were being sweated; managers were thrusting all responsibility on

Inspectors' Criticisms.

---

[1] The following list shows the average yearly attendance, together with the Parliamentary Grant :—

	Av. Attendance.	Parl. Grant.
1860	803,708	£724,403
1861	855,077	£813,441
1862	888,923	£774,743
1863	928,310	£721,386
1864	937,678	£655,036
1865	1,016,558	£636,806
1866	1,048,493	£649,307

The large drop in 1862 was partly due to the stoppage of grants for books and apparatus and to alterations in the system of building grants. See Final Report of the Cross Commission, p. 18.

[2] *Minutes of the Committee of Council.*

the staffs, inferior teachers were being employed; teaching was much less intelligent[1]; there was a serious reduction in the number of pupil teachers, and the scale of payments necessarily resulted in a lower grant per head than was earned under the previous system. Matthew Arnold, who was among those opposed to the plan, notes however one good result, viz. that it had wrought a great improvement in the quality of school reading books.

By 1867 sufficient experience had been gained to warrant the modification of the Revised Code in **Modifications** several important particulars. An additional **of the Revised** **Code.** grant was offered, designed to encourage more rapid promotion of the scholars, induce better staffing, and provide for the introduction of at least one specific subject so as to remove the reproach that all teaching was reduced to the " beggarly elements of the standard examination." At the same time, to prevent the supply of pupil teachers being checked at its source, special bonuses were to be granted to schools.

The introduction of the Revised Code had made Mr. Lowe one of the best hated men of the day. He was subjected to attacks on all hands, and in 1864 was (unfairly) driven from office. In the same year his successor was able to establish the right of the Department to refuse grants for building where a conscience clause was not accepted. Experience of the working of the Revised Code was proving conclusively that the existing system would never succeed in educating the country, and from the death of Palmerston in 1865 education was caught in the general reform movement.

[1] Cf. *infra*, pp. 282-4. See also Matthew Arnold's *Reports*, 1862, *et seq.*

Men were becoming weary of the incessant struggle that
centred round the education question. The
**Movements
leading up to
the Bill
of 1870.**
times of prejudice against popular education were past. Few people now believed
that it was dangerous for the poor to be
able to read and write : opinion was strongly
setting the other way. There were signs of a growing
spirit of reasonableness and of a determination to compromise. Evidence of this was seen in the joining of
secularists and denominationalists to form the Manchester
Education Aid Society, 1864, a society formed to investigate the educational condition of the city and to get the
children to school. The work of the society showed how
impossible it was for voluntary effort to meet the situation, and accordingly the Manchester Education Bill
Committee was formed, the first of three great organisations aiming at improving the machinery of education and
responsible for educating public opinion, the culmination of
whose labours was the Elementary Education Act of 1870.

The purpose of the Committee was to press Parliament
to establish a complete system of free com-
**The
Manchester
Education Bill
Committee.**
pulsory elementary education, supported by
local rates and under local management.
Existing schools were to be assisted subject
to a conscience clause, but not otherwise
interfered with. New schools were to be unsectarian in
character. All schools were to be open to local and
Government inspection. The Education of the Poor Bill,
drafted on these lines, was introduced by Mr. Bruce,
Vice-President of the Committee of Council, in 1867, and
was backed by Mr. Forster. It is interesting as being in
essential particulars the same as the original draft of the
1870 Bill. It was at this time that Mr. Baines finally
recanted his "Voluntaryist" views.

The same year (1867) saw the establishment of the Birmingham Education Aid Society,[1] the investigations of which showed that many parents were unable to pay school fees, and emphasised the lack of educational provision and the necessity of compulsion if proper attendance was to be secured. Two years later the Birmingham Education League came into existence, with Mr. Dixon as chairman, Mr. Joseph Chamberlain as vice-chairman, and Mr. Jesse Collings as secretary. Its object was to secure the establishment of a system of elementary education for every child in the country. It proposed making education free and compulsory, compelling local authorities to see that adequate school accommodation was provided in their districts, and founding and maintaining schools unsectarian in character by means of local rates, supplemented by Government grants. It also purposed to meet the conscientious objections of parents by giving only secular instruction to particular children, as well as by opening the schools at stated times to teachers of the various denominations, and on certain conditions it would not withhold rate aid from sectarian schools.

The Birmingham League.

To secure this the League instituted a great educational campaign, opening up over a hundred branch committees in Manchester, Sheffield, Leeds and all the important towns in the country, and starting with a guarantee fund of £60,000. Connected with it were many Churchmen as well as Nonconformists, and it is acknowledged by all parties to have stimulated an interest in popular education the like of which had not been known in the country before.

[1] *History of the Elementary School Contest*, by Francis Adams, Chapter V.

As was only to be expected, an association of this kind called into existence "Unions" of a

The National Education Union. distinctly denominational character at Birmingham and Manchester. The Manchester National Education Union, founded in 1869, is the third of the three great organisations already mentioned. It received the support of those who believed in developing education on already existing lines and feared the secularisation of the schools. Its policy was a very conservative one. Thus it proposed to make education compulsory by means of a vigorous application of the Factory and Workshop Acts. School fees of necessitous children only were to be paid, and all schools were to be denominational in character but subject to a conscience clause.

One other organisation must be mentioned, the Welsh Education Alliance, which had sprung up

The Welsh Education Alliance. through disagreement with the policy of the League in recognising denominational schools.

It demanded a system of secular schools, unsectarian in management, compulsory and free, leaving religious teaching to the parents and the churches. No recognition of any sort was to be given to existing denominational schools beyond allowing them to be transferred to the local authorities.[1]

The Coming of School Boards.

With the passing of the Reform Act of 1867 came the opportunity for dealing comprehensively with

The Bill of 1870. elementary education and introducing a national system. Politicians were fully alive to the importance of "educating their masters" as Mr.

[1] *Proposed National Arrangements for Primary Education*, H. W. Holland, Chap. III.

Lowe put it, and the matter was taken in hand by Mr. Forster in the second session of Mr. Gladstone's Government in 1870.[1] Mr. Forster's interest in education was well known. He had supported the Education Bills of 1867-8 ; he prided himself in his Puritan ancestry, and was looked upon as an advanced Liberal. He found firmly implanted on the country a great denominational system that in spite of its defects had done the great service of rearing a race of teachers, spreading schools, setting up a standard of education, and generally making the introduction of a national system possible. Accommodation for nearly two million children had been provided, three-fourths of which was in connection with the Church of England. In accomplishing this the Church alone had expended some £6,270,000 on buildings, and had raised £8,500,000 in voluntary subscriptions for the maintenance of the schools.[2]

Liberals were agreed that to ignore or wholly set aside these existing agencies was impossible, though extremists were prepared to go to such lengths. The question to be decided was whether a stop ought to be put to the further development of the existing system, or whether it should be encouraged to progress side by side, and even in competition, with a specifically State system. Liberals and Nonconformists as a body undoubtedly favoured the former alternative, but to the surprise and disappointment of many the Government took the other view.

Mr. Gladstone's statement was clear and unmistakable. " It was with us an absolute necessity—a necessity of honour and a necessity of policy—to respect and to favour

[1] See the volume of *Parliamentary Debates : Elementary Education Bill, 1870*, published by the National Education Union.

[2] The Church schools had also received some 6½ millions in Government grants.

the educational establishments and machinery we found existing in the country. It was impossible for us to join in the language or to adopt the tone which was conscientiously and consistently taken by some members of the House, who look upon these voluntary schools, having generally a denominational character, as admirable passing expedients, fit, indeed, to be tolerated for a time, deserving all credit on account of the motives which led to their foundation, but wholly unsatisfactory as to their main purpose, and therefore to be supplanted by something they think better. . . . That has never been the theory of the Government. . . . When we are approaching this great work, which we desire to make complete, we ought to have a sentiment of thankfulness that so much has been done for us." [1]

Similar sentiments were echoed by Mr. Forster, by Mr. Lowe, now Chancellor of the Exchequer, and by other prominent members of the Government, and adhered to unflinchingly throughout one of the greatest controversies of modern times, a controversy that continued for some years and for the time being effectually disintegrated the Liberal party.

In introducing the Elementary Education Bill 1870 Mr. Forster estimated that about 1,450,000 children were on the registers of State-aided schools, with an average attendance of 1,000,000, but in the schools there were only two-fifths of the working-class children between 6 and 10 years of age, and only one-third between the ages of 10 and 12. In other words, there were 1,000,000 children unprovided for between 6 and 10, and half a million between 10 and 12 years of age. An investigation [2] conducted the previous

The State of Education

---

[1] Speech, July 22nd, 1870.   [2] An inquiry conducted by Mr. (afterwards Sir) Joshua Fitch and Mr. D. R. Fearon into the educational provision existing in Manchester, Liverpool, Birmingham, and Leeds.

year had shown that a quarter of the children in Liverpool between the ages of 5 and 13 never entered a school, while another quarter attended schools where the education was worthless. A similar state of affairs existed in Manchester, Leeds, and Birmingham. It was to remedy this, " to complete the voluntary system and to fill up gaps,"[1] that the Bill was intended. It rested on two principles, viz. that there should be efficient schools within the reach of all, and that where such provision did not exist it should be compulsorily provided.

In drafting the measure, due regard was given to economy, to preserving existing schools from injury, and to offering no encouragement to parents to neglect the education of their children. Briefly, the Bill divided the country up into school districts—municipal boroughs and civil parishes, the metropolis being treated separately—and powers were given to ascertain the deficiency of school accommodation. To remedy any such deficiency, the denominations were granted a period of grace and aided by building grants. Should they fail School Boards were to be set up, with rating powers to establish and maintain public elementary schools, and able to compel the attendance of children between 5 and 12 years of age. Boards might be set up at once on the request of the ratepayers, and existing Voluntary schools might be transferred to these bodies. It was also proposed to abolish denominational inspection, to require a conscience clause, and no longer to insist on religious instruction being given a place in the curriculum as a condition of grant. An elementary school was defined as " a school, or department of a school, at which elementary education is the principal part of the education there given, and not including any school, or department of a

---

[1] *Debates*, p. 91.

school, at which the ordinary payments in respect of the instruction from each scholar exceed 9d. a week" (averaged over the whole school), a sufficiently general description, the interpretation of which became a fruitful source of controversy.[1]   On grounds of economy the Government could not see its way to make education free, but special powers were granted to School Boards to pay the fees of necessitous children attending any public elementary school.

The Bill shows a peculiar blending of the programmes of the National Education Union and of the Education League.   It followed the policy of the former in encouraging the development of Voluntary schools, which would generally be denominational in character, in continuing them under the same conditions of management as before, in requiring a conscience clause, and in proposing to make the school fees of necessitous children a charge on the rates.   It followed the League in proposing to set up Board schools, managed by local bodies elected ad hoc, and supported by local rates and government taxes.   It also agreed with the programme of the League in its proposal to assist existing denominational schools out of the rates, but it differed in not limiting the growth of these institutions, in allowing them to retain their distinctively denominational character, and in leaving the local Boards to decide the nature of the religious instruction to be adopted in their respective schools instead of making it definitely unsectarian.

The Bill a Compromise.

---

[1] The code of 1862 limited schools eligible for grants to such as provided for the children of those who supported themselves by manual labour. Children of a higher social grade might attend, but they could not be counted for grant (*Minutes*, 1862-3, p. 22).   Previous to this, however, schools attended by children of small farmers, small traders, and superior artisans were under no such restrictions, provided the fees charged were not such as to exclude the labouring class (*Minutes*, 1856-7, p. 42).   See *ante*, p. 116.

It is not proposed to enter into details with regard to
the controversies that centred round the Bill.
**Liberal
Opposition.** It contained sufficient common ground to
secure a welcome from all parties on its introduction, but opposition soon gathered. The main attack came from the League and was directed against the
policy of extending the existing denominational system,
both by giving a period of grace and by proposing to aid
such schools- out of the rates; against leaving religious
instruction in Board schools to be settled locally; against
the method of electing School Boards; against the nature
of the conscience clause in denominational schools, and
against the retention of school fees. The struggle centred
round the religious question.

The Church party were satisfied with the support given
to the denominational position and supported the Government, while the latter, in a desire to meet the wishes of a
considerable section of their own supporters, consented to
cut down by a half the period of grace granted to the
denominations to put their house in order. They also
adopted for these schools a time-table[1] conscience clause,
instead of requiring parents who objected to the religious
teaching to lodge a protest in writing. Beyond this, however, they would not go.

With regard to religious teaching in Board schools, the
Government admitted the incessant discord
**The Cowper-
Temple
Clause.** that might result from leaving the decision
to the local Boards. They proposed to get
over the difficulty by leaving the Boards to
decide in each case whether they would impose a purely

---

[1] The result of this was definitely to separate religious from secular instruction, a separation, it is true, in time only, but one that reformers held
to embody the great principle of freeing education from ecclesiastical control for which they had been fighting for nearly a century.

secular system or would include religious instruction. "The prevailing and very general desire and conviction of the people" being for including religious instruction in these schools, the Government adopted Mr. Cowper-Temple's amendment as likely to meet the case. This was to the effect that "no religious catechism or religious formulary distinctive of any particular denomination shall be taught in schools which receive rate aid." This, it will be noted, involved much more than "Bible reading without note or comment." It was hoped that by imposing such limitation upon the discretion of local Boards, it would on the one hand "bring together the conflicting opinions of various parties, and on the other, if not wholly get rid of what may be called denominational controversies, yet in a very large degree abate their acrimony and diminish their range besides, in a large number of cases, abrogating them altogether."

Mr. Disraeli's comment on this issue is, perhaps, worth recalling. "Nothing would be more unfair than that the children of this country, without any previous religious instruction, should be told by Parliament that they must find adequate religious instruction in merely reading passages from the Holy Scriptures ... but ... although no creed nor catechism of any denomination is to be introduced, yet the schoolmaster would have the power and opportunity of teaching, enforcing, and explaining the Holy Scripture when he reads. Now he cannot do that without drawing some inferences and some conclusions, and what will those inferences and conclusions be but dogmas? ... You will not intrust the priest or presbyter with the privilege of expounding the Holy Scriptures to the scholars, but for that purpose you are inventing and establishing a new sacerdotal class."[1]

[1] *Debates*, pp. 157-8.

The Government also went some way to meet the conscientious objections of its supporters to assisting denominational schools out of local rates by dropping the clause and providing instead higher Exchequer grants to these institutions. In the heat of the controversy, the clause (No. 25) which required School Boards to pay the fees of necessitous children at any public school—a clause that embodied identically the same principle—was overlooked, and became a fruitful source of irritation in the following years.[1] Various other modifications were introduced, but on the question of compulsion and free schooling the Government would not give way.

On these terms the Bill was passed by a coalition of Liberals and Conservatives, and became law on August 9th, 1870. Feeling, however, still ran high. Many Liberals thought they had been betrayed, the leaders of the Government were charged with bad statesmanship, with having missed a unique opportunity of settling once and for all the education question through weakness and over-consideration of vested interests, and the Act was characterised[2] as the worst passed by any Liberal Government since 1832. History, however, has agreed in pronouncing the Act, imperfect as it was in some respects, as the most important measure of the reform period, for none has entered so intimately into the life of the people, or had more far-reaching and beneficial results.[3]

[1] See *The Struggle for National Education*, J. Morley.

[2] By John Bright. For a discussion of the situation see *Life of Gladstone*, Morley, Book VI., Chap. III.

[3] See *Rise of Democracy*, Rose, Chap. XI,

CHAPTER V.

PARTITION AND ANNEXATION.

" You do not learn that you may live—you live that you may learn."—RUSKIN.

" We hold fast to the faith that the ' cultivation of the masses,' which has for the present superseded the development of the individual, will in its maturity produce some higher type of individual manhood than any which the old world has known."—T. H. GREEN.

With the Act of 1870 the experiment of partitioning the work of popular education between the State and the Voluntary associations began. A Voluntary system, aided and supervised by the State, was left to compete with a State system working through its local instruments, the School Boards. There was nothing inherently unfair in this, for at the time neither the magnitude nor the cost of the undertaking had been foreseen. The annual expense of educating a child had been steadily rising. During the past ten years it had increased by more than one-third. It was now 25s. 5d., but no one expected this to continue. The most reliable computations gave 30s. as the cost of an efficient secular schooling, and a 3d. rate was regarded as the utmost extent of the ratepayers' liabilities. On this basis the finance of the new measure was calculated. It was immediately evident, however, that the upward movement showed no signs of slackening, with the result that the Voluntary system was placed at a disadvantage that became more and more accentuated as time went on, for the subscription list had not the elasticity of a local rate. By 1897 it was costing £2 10s. 1¾d. to educate a child in a Board school, a sum 11s. 2½d. in excess of the sum available for a pupil in a Voluntary school. A Voluntary system in fact was rapidly becoming unworkable. To remove an impossible situation and at the same time to co-ordinate the various branches of public education was the object of the Act of 1902. The State annexed the whole of popular education, and made the Voluntary schools a charge on the rates, but left them their denominational character practically intact.

The history of elementary education since 1870 thus falls into two parts : (1) 1870-1902, a period of partition, (2) after 1902, a period of annexation. The first is an era of *ad hoc* bodies and of the gradual democratisation of education, and reveals a growing belief in the advantages of communism in educational affairs.[1] The second has seen the municipalisation of education, an immense forward movement in all branches of public instruction and a greatly enlarged sense of public duty in educational affairs. At the same time there has arisen a demand for reform in the finance of the system, to alleviate the rapidly increasing burden on the local ratepayer.[2]

I.—PERIOD OF PARTITION.

It has already been pointed out that equality of educational opportunity has been the demand of the working class movement since the thirties. A great step towards the attainment of this end was made by the Act of 1870. Huxley,

Education for Citizenship.

---

[1] Cf. Matthew Arnold's Report for 1882.

[2] In 1912 the annual cost per child in a primary school was £4 12s. 4d., and the education rate, including that for elementary education, varied according to the locality from 5d. to 2s. 10½d.

speaking as a member of the London School Board, only crystallised the views of many men up and down the country who were intimately connected with popular éducation when he said : " I conceive it to be our duty to make a ladder from the gutter to the university along which any child may climb." It was in response to sentiments like these that School Boards promoted the system of Higher Grade schools and scholarships that did so much to foster the demand for a secondary school education previous to the Act of 1902. In more recent times " the ladder " has given way to the demand for " a broad highway," though critics who have seen in the doctrine the manufacture of a great intellectual proletariat of only mediocre ability, unfitted for manual employments and discontented with all non-literary occupations, have called for a " sieve " instead. The truth is, the ladder, the highway, and the sieve are all similes arising from a somewhat one-sided view of the end of education in a democratic community. They imply, in short, a form of individualism that is foreign to the principle of the movement from which they spring. As J. S. Mill taught, the meaning and consummation of all self-realisation is not selfishness but service. During the period with which we are dealing, this message has been re-emphasised in different ways through the teaching of men like Ruskin, Herbert Spencer, and T. H. Green.

T. H. Green. T. H. Green's words spoken at the opening of the Oxford High School for Boys may be recalled in this connection. " Our high school, then, may fairly claim to be helping forward the time when every Oxford citizen will have open to him at least the precious companionship of the best books in his own language, and the knowledge to make him really independent ; when all who have a special taste for learning will

have open to them what has hitherto been unpleasantly
called the 'education of gentlemen.' I confess to hoping
for a time when that phrase will have lost its meaning,
because the sort of education which alone makes the
gentleman in any true sense will be within the reach of
all. As it was the aspiration of Moses that all the Lord's
people should be prophets, so with all seriousness and
reverence we may hope and pray for a condition of English
society in which all honest citizens will recognise themselves and be recognised by each other as gentlemen."[1]
Man· is by nature a citizen, and the end of all education, while allowing the utmost freedom for individual
development, is the production of the honest neighbour
and the good citizen. It was the "sons of artisans" to
whom he looked to become the social and educational
missionaries to the class from which they had sprung.[2]

No one attacked more vigorously or with greater influence the educational "gospel of getting
on" than Ruskin. "You do not learn that
you may live—you live that you may learn."[3]
The end of education is to make better men
and better citizens, imbued with a passion
for the public good. It is impossible to do more here than
to indicate the trend of Ruskin's educational message.
Education occupied a necessary part in his system of social
philosophy, the origin of which is to be found in his study
of art and in the teaching of Carlyle. "Let a nation be
healthy, happy, pure in its enjoyments, brave in its acts,
and broad in its affections, and its art will spring around
and within it as freely as the foam from a fountain."[4]

The
Educational
Teaching of
Ruskin.

---

[1] *Works*, Vol. III., pp. 475-6.
[2] See Essay on T. H. Green in *Six Radical Thinkers*, MacCunn.
[3] *Crown of Wild Olives*, Lecture IV., § 145.
[4] See *John Ruskin, Social Reformer*, J. A. Hobson, Chap. II.

Art is nothing but the manifestation of the perfectness and eternal beauty of the work of God. There was, however, little that was healthy or ennobling in the industrial system that Ruskin saw around him, so he was led to attempt to construct a truer social order, where "every man must do the work that he can do best and in the best way, for the common good and not for individual profit." But to organise such a society composed of the maximum number of noble and happy human beings two conditions seemed necessary: (1) that all citizens should be well born, (2) that all should be well educated. Though hereditary predispositions made individual equality impossible and accordingly favoured a gradation of society, yet within these limits there was to be equality of opportunity, and special educational, social and industrial machinery under strong paternalistic rule was devised. "I hold it indisputable that the first duty of a State is to see that every child born therein shall be well-housed, clothed, fed, and educated till it attain years of discretion."[1] There was to be a free, compulsory State system of education, workshops and manufactories were to be under Government control, there were to be State works for the unemployed and old age pensions.

At the same time Ruskin propounded a new view of wealth, which was nothing less than complete living. "There is no wealth but Life—Life including all its powers of love, of joy, of admiration." Education was a means of showing men how to live. It consisted not "in teaching men to know what they do not know, but to behave as they do not behave." It implied a development of the whole man, physical, moral and intellectual, a training in and through social service. Upon the growth of individual

[1] Note on Modern Education, *The Stones of Venice*, Vol. III., Appendix 7. The whole note is well worth reading.

and social character the very foundation of all social betterment rested, for reform from without apart from a change in the inner man was powerless to accomplish anything. In bringing about this change of heart, however, education had a great place, and in this connection Ruskin places a high value on the influence of character-forming ideas, on the study of mankind, and on an intimate communion with nature free from all undue interference on the part of the teacher. "The great leading error of modern times is the mistaking of erudition for education."[1]

His curriculum provided for (1) instruction in the laws of health, physical exercises—including riding, swimming, the art of offence and defence—and music; (2) training in reverence and compassion, in habits of gentleness, justice and truthfulness; (3) history and literature to be taught for enjoyment; (4) an accurate training in the use of the mother tongue, in natural science, and in mathematics, and (5) drawing and handicraft, which were to be compulsory, and, in the case of girls, training in domestic duties. At the same time the curriculum should be determined by local conditions and by the future occupations of the pupils. Thus in cities mathematics and the arts might well be emphasised; in the country, natural history and agriculture; while in maritime districts physical geography, astronomy, and natural history would seem appropriate, the object being to provide a generous meaningful elementary education upon which a technical education might be based.[2]

Ruskin and the School Curriculum.

"There are, indeed, certain elements of education which are

---

[1] Note on Modern Education, *The Stones of Venice*, Vol. III., Appendix 7.

[2] *Time and Tide*, Letter XVI.

alike necessary to the inhabitants of every spot of earth. Cleanliness, obedience, the first laws of music, mechanics, and geometry, the primary facts of geography and astronomy, and the outlines of history, should evidently be taught alike to poor and rich, to sailor and shepherd, to labourer and shop-boy. But for the rest, the efficiency of any school will be found to increase exactly in the ratio of its direct adaptation to the circumstances of the children it receives; and the quality of knowledge to be attained in a given time being equal, its value will depend on the possibilities of its instant application." [1]

No one was more alive to the suggestive influence of the school environment. The school building **Ruskin's** was to be the most important of all public **Ideal** **School.** institutions, noble and castellated in design, and provided within with a library of best books, an art gallery and a museum, while round its walls were to be hung historical paintings. A garden and workshops—especially a carpenter's and a potter's—were essential, for one of the great objects of the school was to train pupils to handiness and to a sense of the dignity of manual labour. The test of the work was the effort put forward and the spirit of joy that pervaded the whole. The school was to be no results grinding machine nor a place for doling out bits of knowledge. Showiness, superficiality, self-seeking, and punishment were to be unknown in an institution the motto of which was " Let nothing be done through strife or vain glory." [2]

Ruskin, in his reaction against the levelling tendencies of the day, finds no place for the modern **The Education** woman in his new social order, and he un- **of Girls.** doubtedly approves of the intellectual subjection of women. They are to feel and judge rather than know. They are to be primarily useful and secondarily beautiful home-makers. But within these limits he

[1] *Fors Clavigera.*   [2] See *Ruskin on Education,* Jolly.

provides for their physical education and for cultivating their imagination and sympathies by all that is best in nature, art and literature.[1]

The ordinary Englishman is frankly sceptical of theories, and it is undoubtedly true that the main

Industrial Influences in English Education. incentive to improving the means of education has been the fear that indifference in this matter would seriously affect the commercial prestige of the nation. This motive has been particularly prominent in the demand for science and technical knowledge, and in the reform of the school curriculum during this period. The demand in its modern form may be said to have arisen as a result of the International Exhibition of 1851, which gave an opportunity for the first time of comparing the products of English manufacture with those of other countries, and which served to emphasise the importance of science and art in relation to industry. One result was the founding of the Science and Art Department at South Kensington and the beginning of active propagandism by Dr. Lyon Playfair and others on behalf of technical education. The movement received a further impetus as a result of the Paris Exhibition of 1867. It found expression in the establishment of the City and Guilds of London Institute in 1880; it gave rise to the Royal Commission on Technical Education 1881-4, and to the rapid spread of technical instruction after 1890. In the primary schools the movement stimulated a feeling of intense dissatisfaction with the bookishness of the existing system, and a demand for the addition of new subjects, particularly drawing, science and manual work. Technical training was the watchword of the new movement. But under the influence of educational theory

[1] See *Sesame and Lilies.*

and as a clearer view of the end to be attained has developed, the reform spirit has found expression in such terms as vocational training and practical education, none of which, however, is very satisfactory.[1]

In the advance that has been made in popular education **Summary.** since 1870, three ideas then are clearly seen, viz. that each individual has a right to equality of educational opportunity, that education is a training for citizenship, and that on the right kind of school education the foundations of national prosperity rest. Since the school is so important in shaping the destiny of society and the life of the nation the doctrine of compulsory schooling follows as a corollary, while further deduction along these lines provides the justification for free education, school meals, medical attendance, school baths, educational oversight during adolescence, etc., as well as the attention that is being given in schools to arousing corporate life and evoking the qualities of leadership and service. Exactly how much the forward movement in popular education during the last 25 years owes to the enthronement of democracy by the Liberal Reform Bills of 1884-5 it is difficult to estimate, but their direct and indirect influences have undoubtedly been very great.

The Act of 1870 provided three chief topics of controversy to be thrashed out during the years **Three Topics of Controversy.** immediately following. Ought denominational schools to continue to receive public money; how far was the exercise of compulsion to secure school attendance desirable; was it

[1] It is important to note that dissatisfaction with the purely literary work of the schools had been expressed in the Reports of Inspectors in the fifties (see *Minutes*, 1856, p. 264), and for years an attempt had been made to encourage "Industrial or Manual work." It was only as the influence of the Revised Code began to wane that attention was again given to the Manual movement in the schools.

justifiable in districts where only denominational schools existed ?

Before the Act of 1870 had passed through its final stages, both parties, denominationalists and undenominationalists, were preparing for a new trial of strength—the former determined to use to the full the period of grace so as to put their house in order, the latter resolved on setting up School Boards at all costs. Educational zeal was never more successfully stimulated than by the sectarian differences at this time. The main activity came from those connected with the Church. The clergy and National Society exhibited amazing energy and succeeded, according to their own account, in doing in twelve months what in the normal course of events would have taken 20 years. By the end of the year they had lodged 2,885 claims for building grants out of a total of 3,342.[1] They also set to work, without any Government assistance, to enlarge their schools and so increased denominational accommodation enormously. The voluntary contributions in aid of this work have been estimated at over three million pounds. At the same time the annual subscriptions doubled.[2] In populous districts where the Church was either weak in numbers or where the growth of the working classes had outstripped any provision it could make, Churchmen took a prominent part in the founding and work of School Boards.

As if to counterbalance the enterprise of the denominationalists the Education League redoubled its activities and received the backing of the extreme section of Nonconformists. A great campaign was started to compel Parliament to revise the

Activity of the Denominational Party.

The Struggle round the Act of 1870.

[1] Of this total 376 were rejected and 1,333 were withdrawn.
[2] 1870, £329,000 : 1876, £750,000.

clauses of the Act that were held to favour the denominational system. In November a good deal of excitement was caused by the first School Board elections, when it was found that the system of cumulative voting, which was intended to safeguard the right of minorities, was able, when skilfully used, to carry a minority into power.[1]

These early years present a picture of turmoil, the battles that had been waged round the passing of the Act being fought again on the School Boards. Often enough one party on a local Board would desire to exercise its powers of compelling children to attend school, the other would resist compulsion to any save Board schools. Some Boards (*e.g.* Birmingham) steadfastly declined to pay the fees of poor children attending denominational schools. Others, like the Manchester School Board, had no such compunction ; indeed, the latter for several years availed itself of the permissive character of the Act,. and served as a relief agency for denominational schools. Passive resistance to the payment of the education rate was practised by a section of Dissenters, and quarrels between School Boards and Town Councils were not uncommon.

The extraordinary activity of the denominationalists induced the League in 1872 to adopt a definitely secularist platform and to urge the establishment of School Boards broadcast. For several years the League unsuccessfully attempted to pass a Bill embodying the main points of their programme—universal School Boards, secular schools, compulsory attendance, and the withdrawal of grants from denominational schools, leaving religious instruction to be provided by the various religious agencies at their own expense. The extreme agitation, however,

---

[1] As for example at Birmingham. See *History of the Elementary School Contest*, Francis Adams, Chap. VI.

gradually died away, for Dissenters as a body showed a want of conviction with regard to the relative merits of a secular and an unsectarian system. In 1876 the League disbanded. Its main good had been done in educating public opinion to the importance of compulsory attendance and of improving the quality as well as the quantity of instruction.[1]

It is interesting to compare the progress of the two systems. The returns of school accommo-
Progress of Board and Voluntary Schools. dation in the various parishes throughout the country, made in accordance with the Act of 1870, showed that in about 40 per cent. of the cases no deficiency existed in 1871, and in a large proportion of those where deficiency did exist it was being made up by voluntary effort. In 1872 over a thousand new Voluntary schools were built. By 1876 the number of school places in England and Wales was found practically to have doubled in seven years, and of the increased accommodation two-thirds had been provided by Voluntary schools.[2]

During the next five years accommodation was further increased by a half. By 1886 over 3,000,000 places had been added, one-half of which were due to voluntary

---

[1] See *History of the Elementary School Contest*, Chaps. VII.-IX.

[2] In 1869 there were in England and Wales 1,765,944 school places in inspected schools, equal to 8·34 per cent. of the population. In 1876 there were 3,426,318 school places, equal to 14·13 per cent. of the population. Of the additional 1,660,374 places, 1,104,224 (or 62·5 per cent.) had been supplied by voluntary agencies, 270,148 of these being in 1,077 new schools, erected at a cost of over £300,000 in grants and 1¼ millions in voluntary contributions. In the same period 1,596 Board schools, providing for 556,150 children, had been erected, and the loans granted to 1,107 School Boards for building purposes amounted to over 7½ millions. The average attendance in Voluntary schools had increased by 593,503 (or 55·83 per cent.), and 328,071 children were in average attendance at Board schools.—*Report of the Committee of Council on Education 1876-77.*

agencies, and Voluntary schools were providing rather more than two-thirds of the school places in the country. In 1897 the proportion had fallen to three-fifths, but even then accommodation in Church schools alone was considerably greater than in Board schools.[1]

But to augment school accommodation was itself not sufficient. The children had to be brought

The Problem of School Attendance.

into the schools, and to be induced to attend regularly when they got there. This was no easy matter. Indeed it was one of the most important problems of this period. School Boards might compel attendance within their own districts, but over a large part of the country no such powers were in existence. Besides, the mere exercise of compulsion on unwilling scholars is not very satisfactory in its results. Poor and irregular attendance was due to diverse causes. Many parents had no great faith in schooling; many others, who were not unwilling to send their children to school, had not realised the importance of regularity; others, again, merely followed custom in setting their children to work. The idea of sending children to school as a duty was necessarily a thing of slow growth, and it implied that the parents had experienced the benefits of education. Various steps had to be taken to remedy this state of affairs. It was felt that the school itself must be made more attractive, that parents should feel that something useful was being learnt there, means should be found to encourage teachers to take an active interest in improving the attendance at their own schools, and further steps should be taken to check the tendency to employ child labour, and to exert pressure on weak or indifferent

[1] 2,756,911 to 2,552,724 (*Report*, 1897-98). In the 25 years 1870 to 1895 the Church had spent nearly 7½ millions on buildings (*A Digest of the New Education Bill*, 1896, p. 9).

parents. In other words, reform was to be looked for through improvements in the curriculum, through improving the teaching power of the school, and through re-arrangement of grants, supplemented by compulsory powers of school attendance.

Indirect compulsion had existed previous to 1870, through the operation of the educational clauses of the Factory and Mines Acts. These had made education compulsory in two ways, either by making the employment of children between 8 and 13 years of age conditional upon part-time attendance at school—as was the case with the Factory Acts since 1833—or children might be exempted from further schooling if they could present a certificate of proficiency in reading, writing, and arithmetic—as was provided in the Mines Act of 1860 for children 10 to 11 years of age. This alternative method was incorporated into the Factory Acts in 1874. From 1870, however, alongside the Factory and Mines Acts, we have growing up a system of compulsion by means of Education Acts. The result is a highly complicated system that is a fruitful source of litigation, and which badly needs co-ordinating and simplifying. Besides bringing children into schools, the Education Acts have worked steadily towards establishing a higher minimum age for employment than is provided by the Factory Acts.[1]

The compulsory powers of the Act of 1870 were extended and made more effective by several other measures. In 1873 a short amending Act, among other provisions, made obligatory the attendance at school of children whose parents were in receipt of Poor Law relief, and required the guardians to pay the school fees.

The Growth of Compulsion.

[1] See *Child Labour in the United Kingdom*, Introduction and Part I., Frederic Keeling, 1914,

The Act of 1876, passed by a Conservative government, aimed directly at improving attendance. It Lord Sandon's Act: 1876. is memorable for its declaration that it was the duty of every parent to see that his child received efficient elementary instruction in reading, writing, and arithmetic, and for providing penalties for defaulters. No child was to be employed under 10 years of age under penalty to the employer, nor between the ages of 10 and 14 unless he had obtained a certificate from H. M. Inspector of having passed Standard IV. in reading, writing, and arithmetic, or having made 250 attendances for each of five years.[1] From the restriction thus put upon the employment of children special exemption was given to those who came under the Factory Acts which provided for half-time attendance at school. To administer the provisions of the Act local authorities were set up—the School Boards where these already existed, and elsewhere School Attendance Committees. In order to allay the fears of Nonconformists, the Committees were authorised to report any infringement of the conscience clause—a power that was either unnecessary or was overlooked, for it was not brought extensively into use. Provision was also made for the establishment of day industrial schools to which vagrant and refractory children might be sent, while, to encourage parents to keep their children at school, free instruction for three years was to be given to all who had attended regularly for five years.[2]

Finally a relaxation in the scale of grants was allowed, and special aid was given to poor schools in scattered districts. The cost of education was rising, and it was proposed to give a sum up to 17s. 6d. a head, that is to say, half the estimated cost of a child's schooling at this date,

[1] This was called the Dunce's pass. In 1900 350 attendances were required. [2] This provision was dropped shortly afterwards.

without requiring it to be met by a corresponding sum
from local sources as had been the condition of grant
hitherto. The Act was deliberately intended to assist the
Voluntary schools in what was already evidently to be an
unequal struggle.

A further step was taken by Mr. Mundella's Act of 1880.

The Act of 1880. School Boards and Attendance Committees
were now compelled to frame bye-laws, if
they had not already done so, to govern the
school attendance of children in their localities. No child
between 10 and 13 years of age was allowed to be absent
from school, even half time, without having obtained a
certificate stating that he had reached a certain standard of
education fixed by the local bye-laws.[1] At the same time
the Dunce's certificate became no longer available save for
children 13 years of age, though even then a child was
required to attend school half time for another year. The
Cross Commission of 1888 laid great stress on the indirect
incentives to regular attendance already mentioned, and
advocated the raising of the half time age to 11.[2]

In 1893 the lowest age at which children might be

The Rise in the School-leaving Age. wholly or partially excused from attendance
at school was 11, and in 1899 this was raised
to 12. Exception was, however, made for
children in agricultural districts who under
certain conditions might become half-timers at 11. In

[1] These standards still vary considerably between different districts, see
e.g. Report, 1881-2.

[2] The importance of these Acts on average attendance can be seen by
reference to the following statistics. In 1860 the percentage attendance in
grant-aided schools was 74·35, in 1870 68·07. The accession of feeble schools
and unwilling scholars brought the number in 1875 down to 66·95. In
1880 average attendance was 70·61, in 1886 76·31, and since then the
percentage has steadily risen. In England in 1905 it was 88·11, in Wales
85·4; in 1912 it was 88·86 and 87·22 respectively. This percentage was
lower than for the previous four years.

1900 local authorities were allowed to raise the age of compulsory attendance from 13 to 14. At the present day three-fifths of the population of England and Wales live in areas where no child under 14 years of age is wholly released from school unless he has passed the Seventh Standard. In 1909 the Interdepartmental Committee on Partial Exemption from School Attendance recommended the total abolition of the half-time system and the retention of all children at school beyond 13 years of age, save where necessity or the beneficial nature of the employ ment could be proved. Within recent years the number of half-timers has considerably declined. There are still over 70,000 in the country, but no one now undertakes to defend the practice. Even in Lancashire, the home of the system, it is, according to Mr. Shackleton, retained for no other reason than that "it is the custom of the district."

Steps taken to Increase the Efficiency of Primary Schools. Simultaneously with the expansion of educational accommodation, a steady effort was being made by the central authority to improve school buildings and staffing, to widen the curriculum, and to encourage a more generous view of what the primary school ought to accomplish. This "stringing up" process, as it was called, was effected by constant modifications in the conditions under which financial aid was dispensed to the schools. These conditions were set out year by year in successive Codes and in Instructions to Inspectors.

[1] The number of half-timers in 1886 was 168,543 out of a total of 4½ million. In 1876 it was 201,284 out of a total of under 3 million. In 1912 there were 70,119 half-timers out of a total of over 6 million. For further particulars see Report of the Interdepartmental Committee 1909, and the various annual Reports of the Board of Education.

Previous to 1870 the various Codes were nothing more than the codified minutes of the Education **The Code.** Department, setting forth the conditions, for the time being, on which Parliamentary grants would be distributed. After 1870 an important change was introduced. In accordance with provisions in the Elementary Education Act, the Code which contained a summary of regulations for the conduct of schools for the following year had to be laid on the table of the House of Commons for a period of 30 days, to allow members to exercise more definite control over the policy of the Department. Should the Code remain unopposed, it assumed all the force of a new Act of Parliament. It is by regulations set out in the Code that the provisions of the various Education Acts are carried into effect.

The first Code of the new series, The New Code 1871, introduced a number of important changes **The New Code of 1871.** in the manner of awarding grants. For the first time secular schools became eligible for grants, as the condition making the reading of the Scriptures compulsory was withdrawn. A further slight relaxation was introduced by extending the grants to efficient schools where the average school fees did not exceed 9d. a week, instead of limiting it as hitherto [1] to schools attended by children whose parents were engaged in manual labour. All school fees charged by School Boards had to be approved by the Department to check unfair competition with Voluntary schools.

At the same time the six standards of the Revised Code were modified, and a higher degree of attainment required. The old Standard I. disappeared, the remaining five were renumbered, the old Standard II. becoming the new

---

[1] See *ante*, pp. 116, 125.

Standard I., and a new Standard VI. was added. These standards underwent a further slight modification two years later, and in 1882 a Standard VII. was included. A more generous scale of grants was introduced, 6s. for attendance and 4s. for a pass in each of the three R's, while for infants a grant of from 8s. to 10s. was paid according to the accommodation provided.

In order to encourage a more liberal curriculum, 3s. was paid for a pass in not more than two "specific subjects"[1] by children in the three upper standards; 250 attendances was still a condition of grant, and the total grant could not exceed the total local income obtained from school fees, subscriptions or rates, etc. Evening schools were encouraged by a grant of 4s. for attendance and 2s. 6d. for a pass in each of the three R's. Accommodation had to be calculated on a basis of eight square feet per child (80 cubic feet),[2] and attention was to be given to ventilation and lighting. Two years later provision for warming schools was made essential. Surprise visits to schools might now be paid by inspectors. Time-tables had to conform to definite regulations, and from one-tenth to one-half of the grant might be deducted for various breaches of the regulations. Schools had to be in charge of certificated teachers, but certificates might be granted to efficient acting teachers of ten years standing over 35 years of age.[3] The Instructions to Inspectors at this time (1872) throw a lurid light on the policy of the Education Department that had reigned since Mr. Lowe's Revised Code. Inspectors are warned against over-interference, and told that "if satisfactory results be obtained no adverse criticism should be made on method."

[1] See *infra*, pp. 302-4.

[2] In Board schools 10 square feet were required for older children and 8 square feet for infants.   [3] See *infra*, pp. 318-319.

In 1874 the attendance grant was reduced to 5s., 1s.
being specially set aside to encourage the
Class Subjects. teaching of singing. The next year only 4s.
was paid for attendance, the shilling being paid on condition of receiving a satisfactory report on the discipline,
organisation, and moral training of the schools. At the
same time only 3s. was paid for a pass in each of the three
R's, but an extra 4s. per head might be earned if the
children throughout the school were able to pass creditably in any two " class subjects," [1] viz. grammar, geography,
history and plain needlework. This was a further effort to
liberalise the curriculum. Special grants of from £10 to
£15 were made in aid of schools in poor districts.[2]

In 1877 attention was given to improving the staffing
of schools. Not more than three pupil teachers were
allowed for each certificated teacher, and in schools where
the average attendance exceeded 220 an additional adult
assistant was required.[3] At the same time, further to
assist schools in poor districts, the grant was allowed to
rise to 17s. 6d. per child in average attendance before it
was liable to be reduced by excess over the local income.
In practice only the best schools were found to reach this
limit.

In 1882 some very important changes were introduced.
To prevent hardship and to check the
The Merit temptation to fraud, grants were paid on the
Grants.   average attendance over the whole school.
All children whose names had been on the books for
22 weeks were now examined, even though they had not
completed 250 attendances. The primary school syllabus

---

[1] See *infra*, pp. 302-4.
[2] *Special Reports*, Vol. I., p. 36.
[3] The regulation only came into force in March 1878. See *Minutes*,
1876-7, p. 309.

underwent further modification and a *merit grant* of 1s. 2d. or 3s. was introduced. Experience had shown that though two schools might obtain the same ratio of "passes," yet the quality of the work done might differ considerably. The object of this grant was to encourage better organisation and discipline, more intelligent instruction, and generally a higher quality of work, while at the same time lessening the harshness of the system of payment by results by allowing special local circumstances to count in determining the grant.

The effect of these various reforms was to increase considerably the burden of the Voluntary schools. **The Growing Burden on the Voluntary Schools.** In the twelve years that followed the passing of the Act of 1870, the Church, for example, had practically doubled the number of its schools and of its certificated teachers, the average attendance and the amount of annual subscriptions.[1]

During the same period the cost of maintenance had increased from 25s. 5d. to 34s. 6¾d. per child in average attendance. Of this sum 15s. 9d. was met by Government grants and 6s. 10¼d. by contributions. In Board schools the cost was 41s. 6½d., of which 16s. 2d. came from Government grants and 17s. from the ratepayer. The struggle to make ends meet, to conform to the increasing demands of the Education Department, and to compete with Board schools was daily becoming more severe. A powerful memorial from the National Society to Mr. Gladstone (1883), praying for further assistance, only elicited the

	1870.	1882.
[1] Number of schools	6,382	11,620
Accommodation	1,365,000	2,385,000
Average Attendance	8 14,000	1,538,000
Certificated Teachers	9,631	18,634
Annual Subscription	£329,000	£600,000

reply that the supporters of the denominational system had entered upon the terms of the Act of 1870 with their eyes open and with full knowledge of the amount of public assistance to be expected. Undeterred by the rebuff, however, an agitation was kept up in the country and in Parliament, and in 1886, with Lord Salisbury as Prime Minister, the denominationalists found a Ministry sympathetic to their cause.[1]

The time was ripe for an investigation of the progress during the past 15 years, and for this a Royal Commission was appointed, with Lord Cross as chairman, to inquire into the workings of the Elementary Education Acts in England and Wales. The points for investigation were, in brief, (1) how far existing provision was adequate and suitable, and how far the machinery provided by the Education Acts was able to meet further requirements; (2) the nature and efficiency of existing systems of school management, the composition and qualifications of the inspectorate, the professional preparation of teachers, and the working of compulsory attendance; (3) the system of moral and religious instruc-

The Cross Commission.

---

[1] In this denominational movement Roman Catholics occupied a foremost place. Their activity is shown by the following data :—

	No. of Schools.	Accommodation.	Present at Inspection.
1870	350	101,556	83,017
1874	567	....	119,582
1879	737	242,403	159,576
1884	828	284,514	200,158
1890	946	341,953	223,645

See *The Position of the Catholic Church in England and Wales during the last Two Centuries*, Edited for the XV. Club, p. 93. Cf. *The Catholic Encyclopaedia*.

One result of this denominational activity was the founding of the National Education Association, formed out of the fragments of the old Education League, and, as its Secretary, Mr. A. J. Mundella, pithily puts it, the Association has been fighting a " rearguard " action ever since.

tion, the suitability of the school curriculum, and the possibility of engrafting on to it some system of technical instruction; (4) the relation of elementary to higher education. The Commission sat for more than two years, collected a voluminous mass of evidence, and issued a majority and a minority report, the former signed by 15 and the latter by 8 Commissioners, the broad difference between the two being that the majority were predisposed to favour the extension of the denominational system, aided by local rates, alongside the Board schools; the minority were altogether opposed to rate aid divorced from popular management, and would make the denominational school the exception in a system of public education unsectarian in character.

On points of detail there was considerable agreement between the two reports. Both agreed that

Majority and Minority Reports: Buildings. school accommodation ought to be provided for one-sixth, and in certain industrial districts one-fifth, of the population, and that on the whole the demand had been fairly met. The time had come when the State might with justice be more exacting in its demands for higher hygienic conditions in schools, for playgrounds, for furniture and structural arrangements that primarily had in view the use of the building as a day school, for desks adapted to the size, age, and physical comfort of the children, while 10 square feet (100 cubic feet) should be the minimum accommodation per child in all upper schools, and 9 square feet in infant schools.

The small School Boards had in a number of cases not been very competently managed, and greater

The Smaller School Boards. efficiency would result if they formed voluntary associations; it would economise expense and bring to bear a greater variety of talent; a

similar arrangement was desirable among the managers
of denominational schools.

The inspectorate, it was considered, should be opened to
teachers. The staffing of schools should be
Training
College
Accommo-
dation.
increased: salaries should be fixed and should
not depend on the amount of grant earned;
steps should be taken to increase the educational efficiency of pupil teachers; additional
Training College accommodation was urgently needed, and
a third year of training was desirable, but while the
majority preferred the residential denominational college,
the minority were in favour of undenominational colleges,
and especially emphasised the importance of a system of
Day and University Day Training Colleges.

With regard to the working of compulsory attendance
Attendance.
there was no doubt that the magistrates had
not always supported the Attendance Committees. That no serious opposition had been encountered
was due to the cautious way in which it had been introduced. Now, however, the time was ripe for making
the minimum age for employment 11, and compulsion
ought to be more rigorous. Truant schools were especially
commended. The minority, even so, were strongly of
opinion that the real secret of good attendance lay in
improving the quality of the instruction and the general
interest and usefulness of the school. None of the Commissioners felt that they could recommend a system of
free education.

Both reports agreed that the sentiment of the country
Religious
Instruction.
was predominantly in favour of a religious
basis of instruction. The majority, however,
supported definite doctrinal teaching on the
ground that any plan of committing religious instruction
to Voluntary teachers was unworkable. Where con-

scientiously carried out the undenominational instruction in Board schools was highly valuable, and in all schools increasing attention should be given to moral training.

The quality of the instruction in secular subjects, as tested by examination, had on the whole shown continuous improvement. The system of payment by results had had a bad effect on promotion, for schoolmasters had not unnaturally aimed at presenting as many of their pupils as possible in the lowest standards where success could most easily be guaranteed. One of the great difficulties of the Education Department had been to see that a due proportion of children benefited from the work of the upper standards. In 1872 the children in Standards IV. to VI. numbered only 17·96 of the whole ; in 1886 the proportion had risen to 34 68. At the same time the index of backwardness had diminished. The proportion of scholars over 10 years of age presented in the three lowest standards had fallen from 63·71 per cent. in 1872 to 36·33 per cent. in 1886. The percentage of passes remained almost unchanged. It was 83·57 per cent. in 1864 and 85·87 per cent. in 1870, after which it fell off, but began to recover in 1878, and in 1886 it was 85·99 per cent. The standards after the New Code of 1871 were, of course, higher, and other subjects were gradually taking up part of the school day.

Improvement in Secular Subjects.

Both reports considered a more liberal curriculum than existed in many schools to be imperative, as well as a more elastic system of grading children than the rigid yearly standards allowed. Moreover, a uniform curriculum for the whole country was not desirable. There should be considerable diversity between schools, the determining factors being the special needs of the district and of the type of children in attendance. In all schools much more attention ought to be given to work of

Curriculum.

a more practical character, and steps should be taken to engraft on to the present system a curriculum of a vocational—"technical"—character for the older children. Special Government aid ought to be afforded for the erection of manual workshops, and there should be an active development of technical instruction under the care of the municipalities.

The system of " payment by results " had, in the opinion of the Commissioners, undoubtedly tended to stereotype instruction, to give a wrong emphasis, and to hinder healthy development. " We are unanimously of opinion that the present system of 'payment by results' is carried too far and is too rigidly applied, and that it ought to be modified and relaxed in the interests equally of the scholars, of the teachers, and of education itself." But while the majority were not prepared to recommend the total abolition of the system if it could be rendered less harsh in its operation, the minority would do away with it altogether. They considered the attitude of the Department was mistaken, and they proceeded to lay down the principles which have more and more guided the policy of the Board of Education, and may in fact be said to represent the position to-day, namely, to see that the educational conditions and the machinery are all right, and to expect everything else to follow as a matter of course. " We are of opinion that the best security for efficient teaching is the organisation of our school system under local representative authorities, over sufficiently extensive areas, with full power of management and responsibility for maintenance, with well-graduated curricula, a liberal staff of well-trained teachers, and buildings, sanitary, suitable, and well equipped with school requisites; that it should be the duty of the State to secure that all these conditions are fulfilled, and to aid

Payment by Results.

local effort to a considerable extent, but leaving a substantial proportion of the cost of school management to
be met from local resources other than the fees of the
scholars, ... and by its inspection to secure that the
local authority is doing its duty satisfactorily." [1]

Various alterations in the mode of assessing grants
Grants. were recommended, so as to abolish the
system of individual payments and concen-
trate on encouraging attendance and improving the general
efficiency and tone of the schools. Moreover, extra aid
ought to be given to rural schools, and for special expenditure on manual centres, science and domestic teaching, etc.
The majority went so far as to demand that the grants
should be fixed by Act of Parliament, so as to stop the
incessant changes at the whim of officials. In addition
they urged that once a school building had been passed
as efficient, if the Education Department required
further structural alterations they should make a grant
to assist in the carrying out of the work. They also
suggested the application of local rates to augment the
income of Voluntary schools so that they might compete
more effectively with Board schools, a procedure, as the
minority pointed out, that would upset the settlement of
1870.

All the Commissioners were strongly impressed with
the importance of evening continuation
**Evening
Continuation
Schools.** schools, and with the need for a thorough
revision of the existing system, which had
now outgrown its usefulness and was in a
state of decay. The average attendance had dropped
from 73,375 in 1870 to 26,009 in 1886. These schools,
which primarily aimed at teaching the three R's, were

---

[1] *Final Report, Cross Commission (Minority),* p. 249.

first aided by grants in 1851, and their usefulness
steadily increased up to 1870.[1]

The Act of 1870 still regarded them as elementary
schools held in the evening, and they were limited to
pupils between 12 and 18 years of age, or 12 and 21 by
the Code of 1876. But the number of students needing
this particular form of schooling was steadily declining.
In 1882 other subjects were admitted, but the rule that
every scholar must take an examination in the three R's
was still enforced. This was now felt to be a mistake.
What was wanted was a new type of curriculum more in
touch with the every-day needs of the pupils and determined by local conditions. Classes would still be necessary to revise the work of the day schools, but there was
need for preparatory classes for higher work in science,
art, and technology, for schools of a more recreative and
social type. In the words of the Report, " the evening
schools of the future should be regarded and organised
chiefly as schools for maintaining and continuing the
education already received in the day schools."[2] They
should be opened without upper age limit, and should
enjoy much more freedom to adapt themselves to particular conditions. Though compulsory attendance was urged,
the Commissioners were not prepared to recommend it.[3]

A good deal of evidence was also collected with regard
to the grading of schools and the relation of
elementary to higher education. The lack
of adequate secondary school provision, the
need for a great accession of lower grade
secondary school accommodation and the importance of

Relation of
Elementary
and Secondary
Education.

---

[1] Statistics are only available since 1862.

[2] *Final Report, Cross Commission*, p. 164.

[3] For other particulars see Cross Commission Reports, 1888, and Report
of Consultative Committee on Attendance at Continuation Schools, 1909.

democratising the whole system of secondary education had been emphasised by the Schools Inquiry (Taunton) Commission 1864-7. Among other things they recommended the establishment of local authorities with power to levy rates, to erect secondary schools and to enlarge existing establishments, but nothing had come of it. They divided secondary schools into three grades according as the leaving age of the majority of the pupils was 18-19, 16, and 14 respectively. A third-grade school they considered should exist in every parish, a second-grade school in every town with over 5,000 inhabitants, and a first-grade institution where the population exceeded 20,000. Even before 1870 the need for some higher education than that afforded in the ordinary primary school had led managers to establish here and there schools of a distinctly higher grade type, corresponding to the third-grade schools of the Taunton Commission.[1]

After 1870 this movement developed, but chiefly under **Higher Grade Schools.** School Boards. In the van were Sheffield, Birmingham, and Manchester. The definition of the Act of 1870 that an elementary school was one " in which elementary education is the principal part of the education given " was interpreted to mean that more advanced instruction could be given to a minority of the pupils at the expense of the ratepayers. The movement was further assisted by the liberal grants that could be earned by individual pupils from the Science and Art Department for a pass in a written examination in one or more of a long list of subjects. In 1872 another potential source of revenue was opened by the large grants offered by South Kensington for an organised

---

[1] The need for higher grade or secondary schools of a vocational character was recognised by the Committee of Council in 1856. (See *Minutes*, 1856-7, p. 42.)

three years' course in science, the object of which was to encourage systematic scientific training.[1] There was a great deal of diversity in the actual constitution of these higher grade schools. The one at Sheffield took children above Standard V. and the school was thrown open as a prize to the children of the town. The upper end of the school was arranged as an Organised Science School, teaching chemistry, machine drawing and construction, magnetism, electricity, light and heat, and drawing. The Central School, Manchester, one of the four higher grade schools in the city, was also an Organised Science School. Sometimes children of Standard III. were admitted. In other places these higher grade schools were practically elementary schools with supplementary classes. In some districts their effect was seriously to injure the endowed secondary schools by offering a modern education at a cheap rate.

Opinion about them differed considerably. Some, for example Matthew Arnold, thought they hindered the advent of a proper system of secondary education. Others were opposed to them on the ground of removing all the picked pupils from the elementary schools and so lowering the general standard of effort. Others considered them a middle-class provision. But many were enthusiastic in their support. Both reports of the Cross Commissioners viewed them with favour, but they pointed out the need for a sharp delineation of the respective spheres of different types of schools, primary, higher grade and secondary, the need for the establishment of a complete system of secondary schools, the importance of giving to all an

[1] This had the bad effect of diminishing the literary subjects of the curriculum to vanishing point. Only three schools of this type existed in 1886, but they developed rapidly later. In 1895 steps had to be taken to provide for the introduction of a larger proportion of literary subjects.

opportunity to benefit by means of exhibitions in either higher grade or secondary schools and of giving these institutions a bias determined by the locality. They also suggested that supplementary classes might, in certain cases, serve very much the same purpose as higher grade schools, and in large towns efficiency might be further secured by careful experiments in grading schools so as to get the maximum efficiency from staffing and from the congregation of pupils of approximately equal ability.[1]

Finally, the majority report considered that the time had come when, for the best interests of education, some more comprehensive system of administration should be found in order to remove, as far as possible, the grave and inequitable differences between the two systems of Voluntary and Board schools as at present existing, and to eliminate for the future the friction and collision that had often arisen between them.

The Report focussed public attention upon the problems of education, and during the next few years **Result of the Cross Commission.** steps were taken to give effect to many of its recommendations. The Code of 1890 introduced a number of important changes. Drawing was made a compulsory subject in elementary schools for boys, and science, physical exercises and manual work were encouraged. The method of awarding grants was modified to provide for a larger fixed grant, and an important extension of Training College accommodation was made by encouraging the establishment of University Day Training Colleges.

---

[1] The experiment of grading schools into junior, middle, and upper had already begun.

At the same time the evening school system was revised.

Revision of the Evening School System. It was no longer required as a condition of grant that schools should concern themselves mainly with elementary education, and students who could present a certificate showing that they had passed Standard V. were excused examination in the three R's. A much more important change was made in 1893 by the Evening Continuation School Code, which swept away the old conception of the evening school. Attendance of persons up to 21 years of age was recognised for the purpose of grants. Payment was made upon the instruction of the school as a whole instead of upon the attainments of individual scholars, and fixed grants were paid upon the number of hours of instruction received instead of upon average attendance. Examination was abolished and inspection without notice substituted. These changes gave the schools a new lease of popularity, and by 1900 the attendance was six times as great as in 1892.

A good deal of attention had been given for some time

Free Schooling. to the question of free schooling, for many felt that with a universal system of compulsory attendance in vogue the payment of school pence could not long continue if the system was to be efficient. It has already been pointed out that both Adam Smith and J. S. Mill[1] had been of opinion that the expense of elementary schooling might without injustice or without pauperising the recipients be made a State charge. To say, as many did, that because the State compelled parents to educate their children, therefore the State ought to pay for it, was of course neither a valid nor a convincing argument. The growth of public opinion in favour of free

---

[1] See *ante*, pp. 24, 67.

schooling is an outcome of the development of democratic sentiment which requires that each child shall have open to it the best available means of self-improvement without imposing any undue hardship on the parent.

In 1891 the " Free Schooling " Elementary Education Act was passed with few dissentients by a Conservative Government. This Act gave parents the right to demand free education for their children. A grant of 10s. on average attendance was made for each child between 3 and 15 years of age on condition that no fee was charged except where the average payment had exceeded 10s. a year, in which case the reduced fee and the aid grant together were not to exceed the amount formerly paid by the pupils. Moreover, if the Education Department was satisfied that there was inadequate free elementary school accommodation in any district, it might direct free schools to be established under the Act of 1870. The net result was to make the great majority of elementary schools free, to reduce greatly the fees in the remainder and to bring free education within the reach of all.[1]

Evidence of a quickened sense of State obligation in educational affairs begins to accumulate **Legislation** rapidly from this time. In 1893 the educa-**for Afflicted** tion of afflicted children was made a national **Children.** and local charge by the passing of the Elementary Education (Blind and Deaf Children) Act. This provided that children who were too blind to be able to read the ordinary school books or too deaf to be taught in class with normal children must be sent to special schools. Imbeciles and pauper children were excepted. The authorities concerned were the School Boards and the bodies

---

[1] In 1902 there were still over 600,000 elementary school children paying some fees, but the number has steadily fallen until to-day they do not total more than about a quarter of this number.

responsible for appointing School Attendance Committees. Attendance was compulsory between the ages of 7 and 16 years. The object was to lessen the handicap under which these children suffered, to train them to be self-respecting, and as far as possible self-supporting members of the community, and to check them from developing into habitual paupers. In 1899, as a result of a Departmental inquiry, a similar measure for defective and epileptic children—the Elementary Education (Defective and Epileptic Children) Act—was passed. It was, however, only permissive in character.

In 1888 the working of the democratic principle was seen in the passing of the Local Government **Development of Local Government.** Act, a measure of first rate importance that set up County and County Borough Councils on a popular basis all over the country. The following year authority to supply technical and manual instruction was given to these new bodies by the Technical Instruction Act (thus carrying out the recommendation of the Royal Commission on Technical Instruction). In 1890 the Local Taxation (Customs and Excise) Act allotted to the same bodies a large variable annual sum—the Whiskey Money—arising out of the customs and excise duties, which might be devoted to technical education.

These measures are important as exemplifying the trend of opinion in favour of committing education **Decline in Popularity of ad hoc bodies.** to some form of local authority other than the School Boards. The failure of the School Boards in rural districts has already been mentioned. Experience had shown that if local education was to be successfully administered, it must be in the hands of authorities of broad and enlightened outlook, working over comparatively large areas. As it was, a number of School Boards took rather a mean view of their responsibilities, others were accused of lack of sympathy with denominational ideals, of extravagance and the like. Besides, the system did not cover the country. For furthering the extension of local government in educational affairs men were losing faith in the value of *ad hoc* bodies and were concentrating their attention on municipal and county authorities. The next few years saw a struggle between these opposing views. In view of the urgent necessity of finding some body to take in hand not only primary but secondary and technical education, and to co-ordinate and develop the whole system of local education, it is perhaps not surprising that the School Boards were set aside by the Act of 1902. That the dissolution of the School Boards gave rise to a good deal of feeling was natural enough. The larger Boards had an unrivalled experience of local education, they had done a great work and had won for themselves a place in history.

The history of the Voluntary system between 1890 and 1902 is the story of an increasingly difficult

Financial Difficulties of the Voluntary Schools. struggle to make ends meet, for while Parliament augmented its grants, the result was more than negatived by the increasing demands of the Education Department as the standard of efficiency was steadily raised. During the whole of this period there is seen a growing determination on the part of a section of the community, and among conservative politicians in particular, to preserve the denominational system. Mr. Joseph Chamberlain eloquently vindicated the position and claims of Voluntary schools in 1890.[1] They represented, according to his estimate, a capital expenditure of anything from

---

[1] For nearly 20 years he had been their unfailing opponent.

28 to 40 millions, and were supported by voluntary subscriptions of over three-quarters of a million annually.
Lord Salisbury and Mr. Balfour, too, left no doubt as to
the goodwill with which they regarded denominational
schools.

In 1895, with the return of the Conservative party to
power, a conference was summoned by the
Demands of the Church Party. Archbishops on the subject of national
education. The result was a memorial to
the Prime Minister (Lord Salisbury), backed
by the whole weight of the Church, disclaiming any desire
on the part of Churchmen to free themselves of their
responsibilities, but setting out the principles that should
be kept in view in framing any new Education Act. These
were the maintenance of the religious character of education, the preservation to this end of the existing denominational system, the rights of parents to determine the
religious instruction provided for their children, the
safeguarding of the rights of conscience of the children of
Church parents in Board schools no less than of children
of Nonconformists in Church schools, the claim of
denominational schools and colleges to participate in
public grants for secular education, the educational value
of variety both in type and management of schools, and
the guarantee of efficiency afforded by public inspection,
examination, reports and audit. To carry out these
provisions the memorialists suggested the abolition of
the 17s. 6d. grant limit, the readjustment of grants so
that poor schools should not be penalised in comparison
with the rich, increased grants, preferably from the
Exchequer, further facilities for the federation of Voluntary
schools, the throwing open to all of educational facilities
provided by School Boards, facilities for denominational teaching in Board schools and for establishing

denominational schools where the parents demanded such provision.[1]

The Government replied by bringing in Sir John Gorst's Education Bill 1896, which for the first time aimed at co-ordinating the various branches of education under a single authority. It proposed making the County Council the chief local education authority with power to control and inspect elementary education and to supervise technical instruction and secondary schools, to abolish the 17s. 6d. limit and give a further grant of 4s. to Voluntary schools and to necessitous Board schools, to federate Voluntary schools, exempt them from rates and assist them with loans, to limit the rating power of School Boards to 20s. per child, and to provide separate religious instruction in all public schools where sufficient parents demanded it. Sir John Gorst sought to justify these drastic measures by pointing out that considerably more than a half of the children were in Voluntary schools, that since 1870 Churchmen had spent over seven millions on buildings and were subscribing another two-thirds of a million annually, that Board schools were able to spend nearly a quarter more per child than Voluntary schools, and that the Voluntary system represented a saving to the taxpayer of over $2\frac{1}{4}$ millions a year.[2]

The School Boards Attacked.

The Liberal party viewed the Bill with dismay, as a revolutionary measure designed for the purpose of killing the School Boards. They fiercely contested its propositions. There were many difficulties in the way of framing satisfactory local education authorities within the county

Relief of Voluntary Schools.

[1] *Elementary Education*, Gregory; also *The Church and Education since 1870*, published by the Church Committee for Church Defence and Church Instruction. [2] Cf. Mr. Chamberlain's estimate, *ante*, pp. 163-4.

area, and by skilful obstruction in Committee the Opposition caused it to be withdrawn through the exigencies of time. The following year a Voluntary School Bill was forced through Parliament abolishing the 17s. 6d. limit, freeing schools from rates and providing an "aid grant" of 5s. to be paid through the Association of Voluntary Schools formed for the purpose. A corresponding measure for the relief of necessitous School Boards was passed the same year. Both Acts were avowedly temporary and provisional in character—stop-gaps until a more comprehensive scheme could be brought forward. In the next few years various unsuccessful efforts were made by the Opposition to get Parliament to consent to the establishing of a universal system of School Boards.[1]

Meantime a good deal of attention was being given to secondary education, and to the passage of children from the elementary to the secondary school. Public interest had been focussed on the question by an important conference held at Oxford in 1893, and by the Report of Mr. (now Lord) Bryce's Commission of 1894-5, appointed to consider "the best methods of establishing a well-organised system of secondary education in England." A discussion of the best means of unifying elementary and secondary education under one local authority was debarred by the terms of reference. Nevertheless the Report has an important bearing on the development of elementary education.

The Education Ladder.

The Commission recommended the unification of the central authority by the creation of a general Board of Education under a responsible Minister with a permanent secretary and a consultative education council, of which one-third

The Bryce Commission.

---

[1] See *The Education Crisis*, published by the National Education Association.

should be appointed by the Crown, one-third by the Universities, and one-third co-opted. The new Board of Education was to absorb the Education Department and the Science and Art Department, and to undertake much of the work of the Charity Commission. The Report also recommended the establishment of County and County Borough Authorities for secondary education responsible for providing adequate secondary school accommodation in their respective areas and empowered to aid out of the rates secondary schools whether directly under their management or not. It also advocated a great extension of the scholarship system already begun by County and County Borough Councils as a result of the Technical Instruction and Local Taxation Acts of 1889 and 1890 for the further education of children from public elementary schools.

"We have to consider the means whereby the children of the less well-to-do classes of our population may be enabled to obtain such secondary education as may be suitable and needful for them. As we have not recommended that secondary education shall be provided free of cost to the whole community, we deem it all the more needful that ample provision should be made by every local authority for enabling selected children of poorer parents to climb the educational ladder. . . . The assistance we have contemplated should be given by means of a carefully graduated system of scholarships, varying in value in the age at which they are awarded and the class of school or institution at which they are tenable."[1]

Other important recommendations dealt with the inspection of secondary schools, with the establishment of a system of school examination by the central authority, and with the registration and professional training of teachers in secondary schools.

[1] *Royal Commission on Secondary Education*, Vol. I., pp. 299-300.

In 1895 the total number of County and County Borough scholarships offered to boys and girls from primary schools in England was under 2,500. Of these the majority were available at endowed schools, but a number of higher grade schools and technical institutes were included.[1] The difficulty in the way of any considerable extension of the system was the lack of adequate secondary school accommodation. By 1900 the number of scholarships had doubled, being now 5,500, a number, however, quite inadequate to the need. It is only since the establishment of new local authorities in 1902 that the passage from the primary to the secondary school has become in any way effective.[2]

Beginnings of the Scholarship System.

In 1899 the reorganisation of the central authority was taken in hand by the Board of Education Act, which co-ordinated the various activities at Whitehall and South Kensington by replacing the Committee of Council and the Science and Art Department by a central Board of Education with greatly extended powers, under a President and Parliamentary Secretary, and by providing for the establishment of a Consultative Committee.[3]

[1] There were, of course, scholarships offered by endowed schools themselves. These are not included in the above figures.

[2] In Wales facilities for a widespread system of secondary education were opened up by the Intermediate Schools Act of 1889. In 1896-7 some 1,364 scholarships were awarded from county funds. At the same time school fees were very low—the highest being £9 and the lowest £2 2s. per annum. The average was £4 14s. 10d. See *Special Reports of the Board of Education*, Vol. II., p. 40. For English schools see *Report of the Royal Commission on Secondary Education*, 1894, Vol. I., Appendix; also *Report of the Board of Education* 1911-12, Chap. I.

[3] For some years the policy of the Education Department had been approximating to that suggested by the Cross Commission Report, viz. to dispense with examining results and instead to scrutinise the conditions under which the work was conducted. In 1895 inspectors were allowed to

Further progress was held over for the next two years, through attention being absorbed by the South African War. During this period, however, important events were happening. In 1900 Mr. Cockerton, district auditor under the Local Government Board, disallowed the London School Board the money it had spent out of the rates on the education of pupils over 15 years of age, whether in higher grade or in evening continuation schools, as being of a type not provided for in the Code for public elementary schools, a decision upheld in the Court of Appeal in 1901. A special Act in 1901 authorised County and County Borough Councils and other local authorities to empower School Boards to carry on for one year any school that had been conducted in violation of the law—an arrangement renewed in 1902.

II.—PERIOD OF ANNEXATION.

Mr. Balfour's Education Act (1902) marks the close of a chapter in the history of English education **The Education Act of 1902.** and the beginning of a new era. It is the culminating point in the movement towards unification that found expression in Sir John Gorst's Bill of 1896 and in the Board of Education Act of 1899. It is a great venture in municipalising education. For the first time education of all grades, primary, secondary, and higher, was brought under the control of a single local authority. But it is no less interesting as affording an illustration of the vitality, at any rate for the time being, of the denominational ideal in this country.

substitute surprise visits of inspection for examination. Two years later the system of "payment by results" disappeared. In 1896 the Department of Special Reports was established under the charge of Mr. Michael Sadler, and the same year the Board of Education Library was opened.

For some years past there had been a growing determination on the part of a section of the
**Demands of
the Church
Party.** community to insist on the rights of parents
to denominational instruction in every type
of school, and this feeling grew as the
financial position of Voluntary schools became more and
more untenable.[1]

Opinion among Churchmen was divided, as it always
had been, as to the wisdom of accepting rate aid for
Church schools. The majority, however, had no such
scruples. Their position was well represented by the
resolutions passed at the joint conference of the House of
Convocation in London in 1901. These were (1) that the
cost of maintaining secular instruction in all schools
should be borne out of public funds, whether local or
Imperial; (2) that the capital expenditure on buildings,
structural repairs, and alterations should be thrown on the
body to which the school belonged; (3) that Voluntary
school managers should appoint and dismiss teachers, but
that one-third of their number should be appointed by
the local authority; (4) that wherever a reasonable number of parents of any denomination demanded it dogmatic

---

[1] In 1902 the cost of maintenance per child in a Board school was
£3 0s. 9¼d., as compared with £2 6s. 3½d. in Church schools.

	Board Schools.		Church Schools.		Total Voluntary Schools.
Number of schools	5,878	...	11,711	...	14,275
Accommodation	2,957,966	...	2,813,978	...	3,723,329
On registers	2,778,127	...	2,328,455	...	3,074,149
Average attendance	2,344,020	...	1,927,663	...	2,546,217
Grants earned	£1 1s. 7¼d.	...		...	£1 1s. 6½d.
Voluntary subscriptions ...		...	£670,324	...	

Report of the Board of Education, 1902-3, also *The Church and
Education since 1870.*

instruction might be provided in any school by that denomination at its own cost.[1]

The principles were embodied in the Education Bill of the following year. Owing to its importance **The Passing of the School Boards.** it was taken in charge by the Prime Minister. Its two main features were the creation of one local authority for public education with extensive powers over the whole field of education, and the making of Voluntary schools a charge on the rates equally with the Board schools. It aroused the bitterest hostility of Nonconformists and Radicals, who regarded it as a betrayal of all that had been fought for in 1870. The new local authorities were denounced as ineffective: the "clerical yoke" was being riveted into the educational system of the country: Voluntary managers were left undue independence. This and much other criticism, both intelligent and blind, continued through two sessions of Parliament; every species of obstruction was resorted to, but the Bill was forced through by the guillotine application of the closure, and became law at the end of 1902.[2]

The Act abolished School Boards and School Attendance Committees, and constituted the Councils of the counties and county boroughs the local authority for elementary and higher education, with the proviso that the Councils of non-county boroughs with a population of over 10,000 and the Councils of urban districts with a population of over 20,000 should be the local authority in their own area for elementary education only. Each Council was empowered to elect an Education Committee under a scheme approved by the Board of Education. The

---

[1] *Elementary Education*, Gregory, pp. 211-214.
[2] Cf. *The Education Crisis*, also *Diary of the Education Bill*, 1902.

majority of the members of the Education Committee
had to be appointed by the Council (a county might
adopt other arrangements) from their own number. The
rest were to consist of representatives of local interests,
persons of expert educational knowledge, and the like.
Each Committee had to include women as well as men.
All powers given to the Council under the Act, except the
raising and borrowing of money, might be delegated to
this Committee.

The duties of the local authority included those of the
School Boards and School Attendance Committees, with
the responsibility for controlling all secular instruction in
all public elementary schools in the district. They had also
" to consider the educational needs of their area, and take
such steps as may seem to them desirable, after consulta-
tion with the Board of Education, to supply or aid the
supply of education other than elementary and to promote the general co-ordination of all forms of education."
In this connection they had regard to secondary, technical,
and higher education generally, including the power to
establish a Training College for teachers. The rating
powers of the Council were unlimited, save that the higher
education rate in counties was not allowed to exceed 2d.
in the pound.

The Local Education Authority thus acquired control
over two classes of elementary schools, (1) provided or
Council schools, corresponding to the old Board schools,
and (2) non-provided or Voluntary schools. The former
were built, supported, and managed entirely by the
Local Education Authority. In county areas each school
had four managers appointed by the Education Committee. Non-provided schools differed in that they were
managed by a Board of six, four of whom—the foundation managers—were appointed under the provisions

of the trust deed, and two by the Education Committee. These managers had to keep the school fabric in repair, with the exception that the cost of ordinary wear and tear was a charge on the public purse. They had to carry out the instructions of the local authority with regard to secular education, and to allow this authority the use of the building for educational purposes, free of charge, on not more than three days in the week. The managers had also the right to appoint their own teachers subject to the consent of the Local Education Authority.

Religious instruction in provided schools and in any secondary school, college, or hostel under the Council was to be subject to the Cowper-Temple Clause of the Act of 1870. In non-provided schools the religious teaching had to conform to the trust deed, and was under the control of the managers. This is known as the Kenyon-Slaney Clause, and was introduced to check undue clerical interference.

A new system of grants was devised, applicable to all schools. The term elementary school was limited to a school held during the day-time, and might not include for grant, save under special conditions, children over 16 years of age. Powers were also granted to the Local Education Authority to pay the reasonable travelling expenses of teachers and children attending school or college.[1]

The Education (London) Act of 1903 extended and adapted these provisions to London.

However controversial some of the clauses of the Act may be, there can be no doubt that it represents an immense forward step in the history of English Educa-

[1] For a full summary of the Act see *The Educational Systems of Great Britain and Ireland*, Graham Balfour, pp. 33-37.

tion, parallel to that taken by the Act of 1870. The State abandoned its policy of supervising and assisting the work of Voluntary associations, and assumed full responsibility for the whole of the secular instruction of the people. In other words, it marks the close of a period of partition, and the beginning of an era of annexation.

The result has been that all grades of education have been brought into much closer relations than was possible at any previous period. The interdependence of all classes of schools has been more clearly realised, and the passage of children from the elementary school to higher institutions has been enormously facilitated.[1] Greater attention has been given to the organisation of continuation and trade schools, to the questions of child labour, blind alley employment, and the like. The position of teachers as a body, and especially of those in non-provided schools, has steadily improved. There has been a great development of interest in educational experiments, and a considerable expansion of training college accommodation and of means provided for enabling teachers to keep in touch with the latest developments in educational method. In short, the existence of strong and alert local authorities responsible for the educational policy of their particular areas has done a good deal towards raising the general level of national education. But at the same time the question of the right attitude of the State towards denominational schools has acquired a new importance.

Result of Act of 1902.

---

[1] In 1906 some 23,500 scholarships were offered by local authorities for this purpose. In 1911-12 the number had risen to over 38,000. At this date nearly 50,000 boys and girls whose previous education had been received in elementary schools, representing 32·5 per cent. of the total number of secondary school pupils, were in receipt of free tuition.

It was hardly to be expected that Nonconformists and
Radicals as a body would be prepared to
leave the denominational schools in the
favoured position in which they were left by
Mr. Balfour's Act. With the return of the
Liberal party to power, Mr. Birrell brought
in an important Bill in 1906 for remedying the grievances
of Nonconformists. The dual system of Council and
Voluntary schools was to be abolished. After January 1st,
1908, all public rate-aided Voluntary schools were to be
transferred to the local authority and become
" provided " schools. The terms of transfer
of these " non-provided " schools was to be
settled by the local authority and the school trustees, or,
failing them, by three special Commissioners, against whose
decision there was to be no appeal. The Cowper-Temple
clause was to be enforced in all schools and no teacher was to
be bound to give religious instruction. In the transferred
schools, however, teaching of a definitely denominational
character might be given on not more than two mornings
in the week at the expense of the particular denomination.
At the same time, to meet any special demand in urban districts for schools of a denominational character, "extended
facilities " for special religious instruction would be granted
on every school day providing four-fifths of the parents
demanded it. Under such conditions the ordinary teachers
might, if they so desired, and with the consent of the Local
Education Authority, give their services for the work.

The Bill was amended in the Lords so as to provide
every opportunity for denominational teaching in every
type of school, and at the same time to allow the setting
up of a class of State-aided schools entirely free from local
control. The latter provision was introduced to meet the
views of a considerable section in the Church who had

Attempt to remove the Grievances of Noncon-formists.

Mr. Birrell's Bill.

always opposed the policy of assisting denominational schools out of rates. Provision was also made for the erection of denominational schools in areas where the school provision was deficient.

As neither House was disposed to compromise, the Bill was dropped. This forms the most important attempt so far made to amend the Act of 1902. Three other Bills call for notice in this connection. In 1908 Mr. McKenna, **Mr. McKenna's Bill.** then Minister of Education, sought to limit rate aid to schools that conformed to the Cowper-Temple clause. Local authorities were to be responsible for seeing that adequate " provided " school accommodation was within the reach of every child who needed it. Accordingly the trustees of " non-provided " schools were to be invited to " transfer " their schools to the Local Education Authority. Facilities were to be granted for the use of the school premises on Saturdays and Sundays, and in " single school parishes " daily before or after school hours for denominational teaching. Where managers did not wish to transfer their schools they might " contract out." That is to say, they would cease to receive rate aid, they would be given an Exchequer grant not exceeding 47s. per child per annum, providing they satisfied the requirements of the Board of Education with regard to efficiency, staffing, etc., and they would be allowed to charge fees up to 9d. a week. This option was not open to managers where the school was the only one in the parish.

In the same Session the Bishop of St. Asaph's proposed **Bishop of St. Asaph's Bill.** a Bill on similar lines. He proposed to lease non-provided schools to the local authority, but he required undenominational instruction in all schools and facilities for denominational teaching on at least three days in the week in every school, whether

Council or transferred, during school hours, but not at the expense of the local authority.

Mr. Runciman's Bill (1908) proposed to limit rate aid to Council schools; to require undenominational religious instruction at the morning session; and to allow denominational teaching at the request of the parent on two mornings in the week providing there was sufficient accommodation for the purpose within the school building. He also proposed to recognise a special class of State-aided schools not under the control of the Local Education Authority provided they were organised into associations.

Mr. Runciman's Bill.

These various proposals to find a basis of compromise have had the effect of exciting a good deal of opposition on both sides. In the following year an Educational Settlement Committee, composed of people of all shades of political opinion desirous of maintaining and promoting religious education as an integral part of a national educational system on non-party lines, issued a series of proposals intended to pave the way to a settlement. As yet this has not been realised. Briefly, they proposed that wherever only one school existed in a particular area, that school should be provided by the Local Education Authority, and existing non-provided schools should accordingly be transferred, though provision should be made for denominational religious teaching not at the expense of the local authority. Proposals were also made for increasing the efficiency of religious teaching in Council schools, for continuing rate aid to denominational schools, and for encouraging a diversity of type of school in districts where more than one school was possible. There the matter rests for the present The real difficulty is the single school area. A settlement is beset with difficulties because of the diversity of con-

Educational Settlement Committee.

H. ED.   12

flicting ideals and interests involved, which are not limited to the members of the recognised religious communities.[1]

One of the most characteristic features of the twentieth century is the attention that has been given **Increasing Attention to Personal Hygiene.** to questions concerning the improvement of the physical condition of the individual. After realising that the environment of home and street is amenable to remedial treatment, it is a short step to the individual himself. Much thought has been given to the question of how to improve the physique of the nation and to determining whether or not the race has deteriorated. The Physical Training Commission (Scotland) of 1903 and the Physical Deterioration Committee of the following year are signs of the time. It has been shown that there is a great deal of physical unfitness existing among the people, and the determination has arisen to ameliorate and as far as possible prevent it by improving the health conditions both personal and material of the children. Attention has been focussed on the children because the State has for years been caring for their mental development. They are easily seen and easily examined, and it is with the children that the most valuable preventive and remedial work can be done. Two important Acts which are the result of this movement call for attention.

The Education (Provision of Meals) Act of 1906 is an outcome of the feeling that it is little use **Feeding of School Children.** attempting to teach children who are improperly nourished. It empowered local authorities to form committees (" School Canteen Committees "), whose business it was to provide

---

[1] See *Towards Educational Peace*, Longmans, 1910; also the recent publications of The National Education Association, etc.

suitable meals at a cheap rate for children within their area who were unable by reason of lack of food to take full advantage of the education provided for them. The Education Committee was required to provide land, buildings, apparatus and the like for the Canteen Committee, and to levy a charge on the parent for the food provided. In cases where it was evident that the parent could not defray the cost of the meals, the authority might, with the permission of the Board of Education, levy a rate for the purpose not exceeding $\frac{1}{2}$d. in the £.

The Education (Administrative Provisions) Act of 1907 took the further step of requiring each **Vacation** child in school to be medically examined, **Schools and** and allowed special provision to be made **Medical** **Inspection.** for children during the school vacations It empowered authorities to establish vacation schools, vacation classes, play-centres or other means of recreation during the holidays or at other times, either in the school itself or elsewhere, for example in the country. At the same time it imposed on all local authorities the duty of providing for the medical inspection of children immediately before, or at the time of, or as soon as possible after, admission and on such other occasions as the Board of Education direct.

This marks the beginning of the State system of school medical inspection in this country. Hitherto few authorities had undertaken anything in the nature of the systematic individual medical inspection, although it was a well-established practice abroad. Useful pioneer work had been done in London and elsewhere, and of course in a number of secondary schools. Each Local Education Authority had to set up its school medical department, and a corresponding department was established by the Board of Education. Special grants are made in aid of the expenditure incurred by local authorities on the medical treatment of children attending public elementary schools and on work ancillary to medical treatment, as well as for children attending special schools and suffering from tuberculosis or from ailments for which open-air treatment is specially suitable. Apart from the more strictly medical aspect of the work, the result is already seen in the emphasis on open-air teaching, the provision of school baths, increased attention to clothing and personal hygiene, to physical education, to the lighting, cleaning and ventilating of school buildings, to school furniture, reading books and the like. A good deal is also being done to educate careless and indifferent parents to a sense of their duties.[1]

Since 1902 the cost of education per child has increased by more than a half. The result has been a **Financial Problems.** steadily increasing burden on the local authorities, which has not been met by any proportionate increase of Imperial grants. At the same time other local expenditure has grown, and the rates are not indefinitely elastic.[2] The seriousness of the situation was recognised by Mr. Birrell's Bill (1906), which proposed to allot £1,000,000 for the relief of local rates, and Mr. McKenna's Bill (1908) had in view an extra contribution from the Government of nearly 1½ millions. To-day educational finance is one of the pressing problems of the moment. One way out of the difficulty would be to make the entire cost of education a charge on Imperial funds. Such a policy would be most unsatisfactory, as it would

---

[1] Compare also the attention that has been given during this period to the employment and school attendance of children. Cf. inter alia, *Child Labour in the United Kingdom*, Keeling.

[2] The cost of education per child per annum in 1912 was 92s. 4d. Local authorities are expending upwards of 25 millions on education, an increase of 5 millions in 7 years. During the same period Government grants have increased by one million.

lead to a highly centralised system of education and management that is contrary to prevailing sentiment in this country. English opinion undoubtedly favours local management as a check on bureaucracy. It is more democratic in character and allows of greater initiative, variety and elasticity.[1]

The problem on which attention is beginning to be focussed is how to increase the contribution from the central funds, by transferring some of the burden from the ratepayer and imposing it on the taxpayer, while at the same time guaranteeing an efficient local administration. Mere doles, it is recognised, will not do. At the same time other suggestions are being made, viz. to reform the present system of local rating by distributing the burden more equitably than at present and securing greater economy in administration by grouping education authorities and establishing a uniform system over large areas.[2] These are questions, however, that extend far beyond the limits of educational administration and finance.

For the moment the tendency seems to be to increase the contribution from the Government in such a way as to favour poor districts where the ratable value is lowest and where the burden of education is often highest. How far such a policy is capable of extension without overstepping the limit of sound finance is another question.[3]

---

[1] Thus a section of opinion to-day looks for a much greater freedom than is at present allowed. It seems to favour experiments on co-operative lines that recall the proposals of William Lovett in the thirties.

[2] Provision for this was included in the Act of 1902.

[3] Local education rates vary from 2s. $10\frac{1}{10}$d. (Wales) and 2s. $3\frac{7}{10}$d. (England) to $5\frac{8}{10}$d. The ratable value per scholar ranges from £13 to £106, and local expenditure from 52s. to 150s. The formula proposed by the Kempe Committee on Local Taxation was that the Government should give a grant of 36s. per child, plus two-fifths the local expenditure on education less the produce of a 7d. rate, but no authority should receive under

the formula more than two-thirds of its expenditure so long as the amount falling on the rates is equivalent to a rate of less than 1s. in the £. The Kempe Committee also recommended a grant for small schools of 5s. for each unit by which the average attendance in a school falls short of 200. It is very unlikely, however, that the recommendation will be strictly adhered to. (See *Board of Education Statistics*, 1911-12.)

Progress since 1902 :—

	1902.		1906.		1912.	
	Schools.	Accommodation.	Schools.	Accommodation.	Schools.	Accommodation.
Church of England ...	11,711	2,813,978	11,377	2,743,876	10,877	2,227,431
Wesleyan ...	458	183,673	345	129,358	214	65,749
Roman Catholic... ...	1,056	403,064	1,064	411,360	1,082	377,859
British and other ...	1,043	322,887				
Jewish ...			12	11,358	12	9,883
Undenominational and other ...			689	196,480	452	98,828
Total Voluntary ...	14,268	3,722,427	13,487	3,492,432	12,637	2,779,750
Board (and Council) Schools ...	5,943	3,003,247	6,980	3,520,093	8,196	4,065,240

The steady increase of Roman Catholic schools should be noticed. The decline in the number of other Voluntary schools is due to schools being closed or transferred to local authorities. The smaller number of school places is a result of the larger amount of floor space per child required by the Board of Education.

PART II.

THE EVOLUTION OF THE CURRICULUM AND THE INTERNAL ORGANISATION OF THE PRIMARY SCHOOL.

CHAPTER VI.

THE ELEMENTARY SCHOOL AT THE CLOSE OF THE EIGHTEENTH CENTURY.

> "'Tis education forms the youthful mind,
> Just as the twig is bent the tree's inclin'd."
> How needful then, the tender plant to rear
> With constant diligence and watchful care.

It has already been pointed out that the conception of an elementary education more or less common to all classes was non-existent at the close of the eighteenth century. Equality of educational opportunity was undreamt of, and as Crabbe's lines [1] suggest, the nature and scope of even an elementary schooling depended upon the social grade to which the individual belonged. The charity school had one ideal, the common school quite a different one. Not that the schools which fall into one or other of these two classes were uniform in type; on the contrary they presented wide differences in organisation and curricula. Thus the "school of industry" had a

---

[1] *Ante*, p. 5.

motive very different from that of the ordinary parochial charity school. The Sunday school, again, had features peculiar to itself. Similarly the term "common school" conveniently denotes the great number of private adventure schools resorted to by the working and lower middle classes, lying between the dame schools on the one hand and the academies for young ladies and for young gentlemen on the other.

But, minor differences apart, the motive of the charity school was primarily to give a moral and
The Aim of Cha^rity School Education. religious training, while the common school was principally concerned with imparting the elements of intellectual instruction. Thus Griffith Jones was voicing well recognised philanthropic sentiment when he wrote: "It is but a cheap education that we would desire for them (the poor), only the moral and religious branches of it, which indeed is the most necessary and indispensable part. The sole design of this charity is to inculcate upon such . . . as can be prevailed on to learn, the knowledge and practice, the principles and duties of the Christian Religion; and to make them good people, useful members of society, faithful servants of God and men and heirs of eternal life." [1]

In short the foundation of all charity school education was a training in the principles of the Christian
The Religious Character of the Instruction. religion (e.g. as set out in the Church Catechism). Instruction in reading, writing, and arithmetic might be added to augment the economic efficiency of the pupil, or the education might be "improved" by coupling with it a training in industry according to the judgment of particular school governors; but this does not alter the essentially religious motive that dominated the whole. The peculiar nature of the instruc-

[1] *Welch Piety*, 1742, p. 28.

tion called for a special method of teaching. This was carefully laid down for the guidance of those concerned.[1]. Thus in charity schools connected with the S.P.C.K. the children had first to learn to say the Catechism by heart distinctly and plainly, after which it was expounded by the master from some good exposition. This had to be done twice a week, and as soon as the children knew the work they were catechised by the minister in church. Afterwards the children were instructed in their duty towards God and Man—the master taking as his guide for exposition *The Whole Duty of Man*. Much attention was given to religious observances, to moral training, to inculcating habits of good behaviour, etc., illustrations for teaching purposes being freely drawn from the Bible and the Catechism. In all this work, as in the direct religious instruction, the master taught under the superintendence of the minister.

At the same time the children were learning to read by an alphabetic-spelling method, or, in con-

Charity School Routine. temporary phraseology, they were taught " the true Spelling of Words and Distinction of Syllables, with the Points and Stops which is necessary to true and good Reading and serves to make Children more mindful of what they read." [2] Girls commonly got no further than this, but spent the rest of their time in domestic occupations, sewing, knitting, etc. Boys, however, as soon as they could read tolerably well " might be taught to write " a legible hand " and " the grounds of arithmetic." The schools provided for children between seven and twelve years of

[1] In Salmon's *Education of the Poor in the Eighteenth Century*, pp. 4-5, is given a verbatim copy of these instructions.

[2] *An Account of Charity Schools lately erected in those parts of Great Britain called England and Wales*. 1708. Seventh edition.

age. The school day was from 7 to 11 A.M. and from 1 to 5 P.M. in summer, and from 8 to 11 A.M. and 1 to 4 P.M. in winter. Registers had to be kept morning and afternoon, and in day schools parents were required to guarantee the regularity, punctuality, cleanliness, etc., of their children, and to conform to the discipline of the school. Schools varied considerably in size, from under 20 to over 100, the average being about 30.

In such a school everything depended upon the nature of the exposition, and the interest of the **Exposition.** minister as shown by frequently catechising the children—a fact repeatedly emphasised by observers. Griffith Jones, writing in 1758, was at some pains to make clear what catechising meant. It does not mean "the bare asking the Questions and hearing them (the children) repeat the answers, just as they lie in the Catechism, for this is not to instruct, and examine them as the Rubric requires: and if no more than this be done, we had even as good do nothing; for they will learn but little, or nothing from mere repetition. . . . You (the clergy) must condescend to be at the pains of giving them an easy explanation of every part of the Catechism, to ask them the same question in other words, to furnish them with plain texts of scripture to confirm them in the doctrines they learn, and then to close every instruction of the catechumens with some short exhortation for their delection and encouragement." [1]

---

[1] *Welch Piety*, 1758.

Isaac Watts was equally emphatic on the importance of exposition. "Be not content merely to have them read the Bible, and be taught the Catechism at proper seasons, but let the truths and duties of it be explained to them in a familiar and easy way by taking the answers to pieces, and instructing the children till they understood the sense of it." *An Essay towards the Encouragement of Charity Schools, particularly among Protestant Dissenters*, 1728. *Works*, Vol. IV., p. 524,

To ensure the efficiency of the teachers in the circulating

The Training of Teachers. schools it was Jones' practice to instruct the masters in catechetical methods for some weeks before they embarked on their work, giving them simple and familiar explanations of what they would have to teach, training them to catechise one another, and the like.[1] The scholars as well as the masters were provided with simple expositions of the Catechism, etc., and it was laid down as a principle that the pupils should not only repeat " out of Book " but also give the sense of what they read or learnt in their own words. It is interesting to note that the method of reading recommended was by " look and say," [2] the alphabetic-spelling method being condemned as irrational and responsible for much slow progress and dulness in schools.[3]

How far the schools were from living up to this standard

Mrs. Trimmer's Account of Charity Schools, 1792. is described by Mrs. Trimmer in 1792. She enlarges upon the relative ineffectiveness of charity school education, the ignorance of the teachers, the disuse of catechising resulting from a lack of interest shown by the clergy and others, and the smaller proportion of verbal instruction in vogue than formerly. " The children in most Charity Schools are at first taught to read in a spelling book, the lessons of which consist chiefly of sentences collected from the Scriptures, most of them in figurative language; as soon as they can read and spell a little, they are put into the New Testament, and when they have read this from beginning to end, they proceed to the Old Testament and go through that in the same manner, without regard to anything further than improve-

---

[1] *Welch Piety,* 1743.   [2] *Ibid.,* 1742.

[3] For the system of training teachers recommended by the S.P.C.K, see *infra,* pp. 329-330.

ment in the art of reading.   They learn, by stated regular
tasks, the columns of spelling in the Spelling Book; and in
some schools they are taught English Grammar, writing,
and arithmetic.   Once or twice a week the scholars are
catechised, that is, they stand up in classes, and answer
in rotation the questions in the Church Catechism and explanations of it.   They learn, perhaps, besides, chapters,
prayers, etc., by heart, and are sometimes taught psalmody.
They go to Church twice every Sunday, and where there is
a weekly duty performed, they attend also on Wednesdays,
Fridays, and Holidays.   When the scholars leave school
to go out into the world as servants or apprentices, a
Bible, Common Prayer Book, and *Whole Duty of Man*, are
given to them: and it is supposed, from the years they
have been at school, they must necessarily be furnished
with a competent share of Christian knowledge, to enable
them to read with advantage and improvement as long as
they live." [1]

To improve the level of the teaching Mrs. Trimmer set
to work to provide a new supply of school
Charity School Readers. books.   At the same time she suggested
that dullards ought to be sent to " schools of
industry," and that the charity schools should be reserved
for the brightest and most respectable children, pointing
out that the Sunday schools might do valuable work in
this sifting process.   Some of the charity schools might
usefully become industrial in character, while others would
serve as training schools for selected pupils who would be
" eminently qualified for the office of schoolmasters and mistresses in the various descriptions of Charity Schools which
very few of the present generation fill with propriety."

[1] " Reflections upon the Education of Children in Charity Schools,"
cf. *Education of the Poor in the Eighteenth Century*, David Salmon,
pp. 17-18,

By way of illustration it may not be out of place to give a few examples of charity school books in vogue at this date :—

Fox's Introduction to Spelling and Reading.—This book, a 12mo 108 pp. volume, commences with a pictorial alphabet—angel, bull, cradle—and represents each letter in Roman, italic, and Old English characters. The first six lessons are devoted to word-building, a, ab, ac, ack, e, eb, ec, eck; the next 17 to monosyllabic words, first of the type clout, flout, gout, pout; then classes of objects, e.g. " *creeping animals,*" ant, asp, bug, eff, flea, frog, leach, louse, newt, nit, etc. The Bible story, from the Creation to the death of Sampson, is next told in a series of short lessons, the majority of which are illustrated by a wood-cut. As an example of the style we may take part of Lesson XXXVIII., dealing with Joseph's imprisonment :—

· "This punishment would have been very grievous to Joseph but that God, who protects and rewards injured innocence, was with him in prison, and gave him favour in the sight of the keeper of it, so that Joseph had authority over all the other prisoners, and not anything was transacted which Joseph had not a hand in."

Next follows a series of catechetical lessons. *Q.* Who made you? *Q.* Why did God make you? . . . *Q.* How did God make you? etc., the order of topics being suggested apparently by those in *The Whole Duty of Man.* Then come selections from the Proverbs; two history lessons; rules for spelling and for dividing words into syllables; and finally, a number of prayers. In using the book reading and spelling were taught together, spelling being learnt by memorising a variety of rules. Thus the reading would be constantly interrupted by the teacher interposing such a question as—By what rule do you spell such a word? etc.

Mrs. Trimmer's Charity School Spelling Book.—Part I., Words of One Syllable, 12mo, pp. 36, 1d. (a separate

book for boys and for girls).   Part II., Polysyllables, 12mo,
pp. 162, 1½d.

Part I. follows the customary practice of beginning with
the alphabet and going through much useless word-building before reading is commenced.   This is arranged supposedly in order of difficulty, but shows an entire want of
understanding of the psychology of the subject.   Lessons
like—A good man; A good boy; A bad man; etc.—are
followed by others composed of longer sentences and dis-
jointed paragraphs, moral and religious in tone—" Some
boys make it their sport to tie a bone to a poor dog's tail,
or to cry out, A mad dog! A mad dog! that people may
kill them."   Finally the pupil is introduced to short stories.

Part II. begins with a long alphabetical list of dissyllabic
words.   This is followed by simple moral reading lessons
consisting of words not exceeding two syllables.   Next
come words of from three to seven syllables, then fables,
then long lists of Scriptural names, followed by the Bible
story up to the entrance into Canaan.   Here a special
feature is made of the use of proper names :—

" And they went from Mithcah, and pitched in Hashmonah.
And they departed from Hashmonah, and encamped at Moseroth.
And they departed from Moseroth, and pitched in Bene-jaakan," etc.

Next come all the difficult words in the four Gospels arranged chapter by chapter.   These are followed by definitions of Biblical terms.   Finally come the Catechism and
selected prayers.

The Poor Girls' Primer.—Sheffield Girls' Charity School,
1789.   The interest of this book lies entirely in the subject-matter.   Two examples will suffice :—

LESSON V.

Learn to spin Wool and Linen.
Learn to sew Shifts and Shirts and Caps.
Learn to knit Hose.

Learn to bake and brew and wash.
Learn to clean Rooms and Pots and Pans.

LESSON VI.

Do no wrong.
It is a sin to steal a Pin.
Swear not at all, nor make a Bawl.
Use no bad Words.
Live in Peace with all as much as you can.

Sufficient has been said to emphasise the moral and religious character of the instruction given in charity schools, the decline of oral teaching at the end of the eighteenth century, and the growth of verbalism. The slow progress in learning made by the children in many of the schools—a direct result of the defective methods of instruction—was an important factor, as has been seen for example in the case of Mrs. Trimmer, in directing the attention of the philanthropically minded to an industrial as opposed to a bookish training. Other influences that operated to the same end have been referred to elsewhere.[1]

The following is a description of a typical "school of industry" at Fincham in Norfolk in 1802, designed for the children of that and the neighbouring parishes:—

Two Typical Schools of Industry.

"They are instructed twice a day in reading, and eight of them in writing. The rest of their school time, being seven hours of the day, is employed in the plaiting of split straw; for which, in addition to the advantages of education, they receive pay, according to the amount of their respective earnings.

There are at present in the school sixty-four children. Four have left it to go into service, and seventeen have acquired a competent knowledge in the straw platt, and have returned home to their parents. The school is under the care and direction of three sisters; who have divided it into three classes, making the under-mentioned weekly payments on the average to each of the children, for the time they are employed in the platt.

---

[1] *Ante*, pp. 11-13, 40-42.

Nineteen children, from 7 to 9 years old (average each per week), 1s.

Twenty-seven, from 9 to 12 years, each 3s.

Eighteen, from 12 to 14 years, each 4s."

Threepence a week was deducted for each child who learnt to write. The long day was not injurious we are told, and the children were led to form early habits of order, cleanliness, and application. It is also pointed out that straw platting, being a new industry, does not injure anyone by taking away their livelihood.[1]

At the Kendal "schools of industry" opened in 1799, of 112 children in attendance 30 of the older girls were employed in spinning, knitting, sewing, and in housework. Thirty-six younger girls were employed in knitting only. Eight boys were taught shoe-making, and the remaining 38 card-setting, *i.e.* preparing the machinery for carding wool, a work suited to small children. In addition, the children were taught reading and writing, geography and religion. Breakfast was provided in the school daily for about 40 children at a charge of $4\frac{1}{2}$d. a week. The elder girls assisted in rotation in preparing the breakfast and in washing up. The girls were also taught to wash, bringing their own family linen, and a regular training in simple cookery was contemplated. The school with four teachers, two for spinning and knitting, one for shoe-making, and one schoolmaster, cost £55 a year. The schoolmaster was assisted by monitors, according to Bell's system.

Early Sunday Schools. The most popular and influential means of elementary education at the close of the eighteenth century were undoubtedly the Sunday schools. Their model was rather the day charity school than the ancient practice of gathering

---

[1] *Digest of Reports (Education) S.B.C.P.*, No. XII. Cf. other typical schools at Oakham, Lewisham, Birmingham, etc.

children together for catechetical instruction. They were in fact charity Sunday schools, and took pride in calling themselves educational charities. They offered to teach reading, the principles of religion—including the duty towards God and man—and in some cases writing as well " without cost and without hindering the work of the week." The school hours were generally from 9 to 12 and 1 to 6. The scholars were required to attend Church morning and afternoon, on the latter occasion to be catechised by the clergyman. To accommodate this influx of children " mats and forms" were provided by the churchwardens.

These early Sunday schools were held in hired rooms which were fitted with forms and desks. Accommodation was generally strictly limited. Hence we find a large number of small schools, and, as teachers were paid for their services, a correspondingly large bill for salaries. Gradually, however, the practice developed of concentrating the children in larger schools and curtailing the number of teachers.[1]

To each school was attached a number of " visitors " who attended in turn, acted as superintendents and assisted the master (or mistress) in catechising and in the general work of the institution. Upon their efficiency the success of the school largely depended, for the teacher, no matter how zealous he might be, was commonly of very humble

---

[1] An instructive example of this is seen in the Sunday schools at Stockport.

	No. of Scholars.	Schools.	Teachers.	Total Salaries.
1785-6	?	11	23	£87 9s. 0d.
1786-7	Near 700	9	19	£55 15s. 0d.
1793-4	751	7	?	£67 9s. 0d.[1]

[1] Reports of the Sunday Schools at Stockport.

attainments.[1] Even under the most favourable conditions
the difficulty of organising a school of children of different
ages, some of whom were learning to read, others to write,
some reading from the Bible and having it expounded to
them, can well be imagined, and it is not suprising to find
the Governors of Sunday schools welcoming with open arms
anything that approximated to a system.   Instruction was
provided by means of spelling-books, Testaments, Bibles,
and in Church schools psalters, prayer-books, and some
exposition of the Catechism.[2] Before the close of the
century week-day evening schools had arisen in connection
with a number of these institutions to supplement the
work that was being done on Sundays,[3] and many schools
were employing unpaid teachers.

It must not be imagined, however, that all elementary
education at the close of the eighteenth
century was arid and deadening in character.
Educational insight is no monopoly of the
present day. There were teachers who strove to make
school work meaningful and to quicken the understanding,
just as there were writers of school books who knew how to
bring instruction within the range of their readers.
Compare for example the following account of the
Barbauld's school at Palgrave :—

A Good Private School.

" On Wednesdays and Saturdays the boys were called in separate
classes to her (Mrs. Barbauld's) apartment (for English Composition) :
she read a fable, a short story, or a moral essay, to them aloud, and
then sent them back into the schoolroom to write it out on the slates
in their own words. Each exercise was separately looked over by
her ; the faults of grammar were obliterated, the vulgarisms were
chastised, the idle epithets were cancelled, and a distinct reason was
always assigned for every connection : so that the arts of enditing
and of criticizing were in some degree learnt together."

[1] Cf. *Robert Raikes, the Man and his Work*, p. 94.
[2] *Ibid.*, p. 136.   [3] *Ibid.*, p. 72.

In the geography lesson "she relieved the dryness of a study seldom rendered interesting to children, by so many lively strokes of description, and such luminous and attractive views of the connection of this branch of knowledge with the revolution of Empires, with national manners, and with the natural history of animals, that these impressive lectures were always remembered by her auditors less among their tasks than their pleasures." [1]

The same good sense is shown in her *Lessons for Children* —a child's first reading-book with its easy narrative full of action, printed on "good paper with clear and large type and large spaces." There is no introductory spelling, no meaningless sentences, no harping on words of one syllable in a mistaken idea of grading difficulties. Instead the children plunged straightway into such lessons as the following :—

Mrs. Barbauld's Lessons, 1780.

"Come and give mamma three kisses.
One, two, three.
Little boys must come when mamma calls them.
Blow your nose.
Here is a handkerchief.
Come and let me comb your hair.
Stand still.
Here is the combcase for you to hold " ; etc.

Very soon they reach continuous narrative :—

"Look at puss ! she pricks up her ears, and smells about. She smells the mice. They are making a noise behind the wainscot. Puss wants to get into the closet. Let her in. The mice have been in the closet, and nibbled the biscuits. Ah ! there is a mouse puts her tail through the hole in the wainscot. Take care, little mouse, puss will catch you. Look, look, there she runs." Etc.

During the latter half of the eighteenth century a marked change had been coming over books intended for children. Authors vied with one another in endeavouring to give information in as pleasant a form as possible, and nothing is more striking

Children's Books.

---

[1] *Mrs. Barbauld's Works, with a Memoir*, by Lucy Aikin, pp. xxv-xxvii.

than the way in which book after book bases its appeal to consideration on the ground that it is simpler and presents its subject-matter in a more interesting manner than its predecessors. There is commonly a great affection for a highly latinised style of writing, and book makers still aimed at producing infant prodigies by loading children with all manner of information on History, Astronomy, Science, Natural History, Geography, etc., but they did it in the form of conversation, sometimes interesting, sometimes very insipid, between the pupil and an omniscient parent or tutor. Barbauld's *Evenings at Home*, Edgeworth's *Harry and Lucy*, *Swiss Family Robinson*, and many of Newbery's Children's Books are excellent examples of this method of instruction. The best books of this kind were at some pains to sift out unessential information, but others merely redished the most arid facts in a form calculated as they thought to please or to assist the memory. To these rhyme offered many possibilities. Thus children might learn without weariness the geography of their own country from a " *Poetical Nautical Trip round the Island of Great Britain*," to which was appended copious " entertaining notes in prose " descriptive of the usual topographical features :—

> " In coasting off Norfolk * you'll find a vast number
> Of beautiful views—you will then reach the Humber ;
> And then if a visit you'd pay to John Bull,
> Pray steer up the river, and call in at Hull." Etc.[1]

* " *Norfolk* is bounded on the N. and E. by the German Ocean, on the S. by Suffolk, and on the W. by the washes and fens of Lincolnshire and the Isle of Ely. It is sixty miles in length, and thirty-four in breadth" ; etc.

---

[1] Compare the use of " toys " for imparting the rudiments of spelling, reading, grammar, arithmetic, etc. The " Art of Teaching in Sport," a method of instilling the rudiments of letters " under the idea of amusement,"

In the effort to bring religion within the comprehension of young children Isaac Watts stands out pre-eminently. He at any rate could present his lessons in a language well within the range of his readers. His *Divine Songs for the Use of Children*, if less well known to-day than a generation ago, are still remembered by such verses as

" Let dogs delight to bark and bite,"

and

" How doth the little busy bee," etc.

For more than a century his *First Catechism* beginning

" *Q.* Can you tell me, child, who made you?
A. The Great God who made heaven and earth.
Q. What doth God do for you?
A. He keeps me from harm by night and by day, and is always doing me good."

was hardly less highly valued. Along with these efforts at religious instruction must be mentioned Mrs. Barbauld's *Hymns in Prose*.

Towards these and other similar examples of educational method at the close of the eighteenth cen-
Eighteenth tury it is customary to adopt an attitude of
Century good-natured tolerance. Whether this is
Practice—
Good and Bad. altogether justified is perhaps open to ques-
tion. We tend to be so taken up with the " new methods " of to-day that we are apt to overlook the fact that the value of time charts in history, of dissected globes and maps in geography, in short, of illustrations of

is commonly met with after 1780, and seems to have attained considerable popularity. It doubtless was stimulated by Basedow's experiment at Dessau. The idea, however, is much older. Watts writing half a century earlier warmly advocated the method. See *Improvement of the Mind*, I. Watts, pp. 229-231 ; also *A Discourse on the Education of Children and Youth*, pp. 389-90 and *passim*.

all sorts, was amply recognised by intelligent teachers a
century ago.   True there was too much worship of "useful"
knowledge, there were too many attempts to point a moral,
and too little appreciation of the meaning of childhood ;
but, allowing all this, there was a body of educational
thought and practice that was far from contemptible, and
which found worthy exponents in R. L. Edgeworth and
his daughter Maria.

Richard Lovell Edgeworth (1744-1817) was a prominent
figure in the literary and scientific world of
his day. He was an Irishman of independent means, possessing considerable literary
and social interests, and a well-marked
scientific temper. He was a born inventor
and educator, a man of shrewd insight into child nature,
who divided his attention between scientific and literary
pursuits and the education of his numerous family. He
is a representative of that considerable body of middle-
class opinion that favoured a domestic, in preference to a
school, education for its boys and girls, and in common
with many other cultivated parents of the time was not
only alive to contemporary educational thought, but was also
acquainted with the teaching of earlier writers, such as
Locke.

The Educational Teaching of the Edgeworths.

At the time Edgeworth's eldest son was born Rousseau
was the oracle of the day.   The *Emile* had
been published four years before, and its
novelty, eloquence, and plausibility, had made
a profound impression on thinking men and
women who were not unconscious of the deficiencies and
absurdities that characterised the treatment of children at
the time, by helping them to see things from a new angle.
Among many extravagancies and inconsistencies Rousseau
pleaded for the sanctity of individual personality, for the

Rousseau's Educational Ideas.

abolition of tyranny in all its subtle forms, whether in the family, the school, or society. He taught that man is born good, and unless interfered with develops according to law. Hence it is the business of education not to make men to this or that arbitrary pattern, but to allow man freedom to attain the fullest self-realisation. Since education is no longer a matter of imposing ideas and restraints, the attention of the teacher is withdrawn from the subject-matter of instruction and concentrated on removing obstacles. In other words, there is a shifting of emphasis from the curriculum to the child.

The great weakness of Rousseau's handling of the subject is that moral education is at a discount. Nevertheless, though his foundations were wrong, he succeeded in emphasising some valuable truths that were in danger of being neglected. Under the plea of a return to Nature he made a powerful appeal on behalf of physical education, while on the intellectual side he reminded his contemporaries that all education is essentially self-education, depending not on imposing ideas and learning by rote but on inciting the self-activity of the pupil, stimulating his curiosity, inventiveness, and practical capacity.

It was in strict accordance with Rousseau's plan, as set out in the *Emile*, that Edgeworth began to educate his son. At the end of nine years he regretfully admitted his mistake. The basis was wrong. "Whatever regarded the health, strength, and agility of my son," he says, "had amply justified the system of my master; but I found myself entangled in difficulties with regard to my child's mind and temper. He was generous, brave, good-natured, and what is commonly called good tempered; but he was scarcely to be controlled. It was difficult to urge him to anything

Edgeworth's Son.

that did not suit his fancy, and more difficult to restrain him from what he wished to follow. In short, he was self-willed, from a spirit of independence, which had been inculcated by his early education, and which he cherished the more from the inexperience of his own powers." [1]

In all this Edgeworth's attitude was strictly scientific. Rousseau was put aside, and he set out to discover a better method for himself. From 1768 he and his wife had kept a careful register of observations and facts relative to their children. These constitute some of the earliest child-study records we possess. In 1791 his daughter Maria began to note down anecdotes of the children and their father's conversations with them. Every effort was made to get a clear understanding of the personality of each individual, and to adapt his education accordingly. In doing this no preconceived system was followed. The fullest use was made of ideas culled from earlier writers, and practice was constantly revised in the light of experience. The object was to reduce education as far as possible to an experimental science, and to evolve a series of principles of universal validity. The results were embodied in *Practical Education*, 1798, in a series of children's books, and in the *Memoirs*, the joint production of R. L. Edgeworth and his daughter Maria.

Early Child Study.

In these various writings we get a picture of a man who was first and last an optimist in matters of education. No one believed more fervently in the potency of education in forming taste or directing talent. " Virtues, as well as abilities, or what is popularly called genius, we believe to

Edgeworth an Educational Optimist.

---

[1] *Memoirs*, Vol. I., pp. 273-4.

be the result of education, more than the gift of nature." [1]
What really distinguished one person from another was
his power of attention. Hence one of the chief objects of
the educator was to strengthen this faculty. By education
Edgeworth understood much more than instruction. It
consisted, among other things, in cultivating the understanding, developing initiative and inventiveness, evoking
a deep sense of religion, giving " moral habits, generous
sentiments, kind tempers and easy manners." [2]

The method proposed for compassing this was frankly
utilitarian, " to associate pleasure with what-

Pleasure and Pain. ever we wish that our pupils should pursue,
and pain with whatever we wish that they
should avoid." [3] This principle was founded on a deep-
rooted conviction in the inherent reasonableness of man.
It did not occur to Edgeworth that he was, to say the
least, putting humanity on a very low plane. " Would
you teach a dog or a horse to obey you ? Do you not
associate pleasure or pain with the things you wish that
they should practise or avoid ? " [4] As his daughter Maria
points out, this doctrine led him to a fundamental mistake
in his view of the moral principle of action, an error that
he came to recognise in his later years. " He had believed
that if rational creatures could be made clearly to see and
understand that virtue will render them happy and vice
will render them miserable, either in this world or in the
next, they would afterwards, in consequence of this conviction, follow virtue and avoid vice. . . . Hence, both as to

---

[1] *Practical Education*, Vol. III., p. 291, 2nd Edition.
In his later years he allowed that there was more difference than he had
been accustomed to admit between the natural endowment of individuals,
but he maintained that it was much smaller than was commonly supposed.—
Memoirs, Vol. II., p. 388.   [2] *Memoirs*, Vol. II., pp. 386-7.
[3] *Practical Education*, Vol. III., p. 291.   [4] *Ibid.*, Vol. I., p. 357.

national and domestic education, he formerly dwelt principally upon the cultivation of the understanding, meaning
chiefly the reasoning faculty as applied to conduct.   But
to see the best and to follow it are not, alas! necessary
consequences of each other." [1]   The fact is, of course, that
pleasure is not the mainspring of action.   There are many
ends that we desire and towards which we strive, and
happiness may or may not accompany or reward our
efforts.   The teacher's business is not to demonstrate to
his pupils that certain actions pay, but to evoke worthy
purposes and to assist in their accomplishment.

On the question of education Edgeworth neither allied
himself with those who believed that children
could not be set too young to read and
write, nor with those who, like Rousseau,
advocated leaving children entirely at liberty on the
ground that they would learn for themselves much better
than they could be taught.   His experience of the bad
moral effects that resulted from trusting too much to
nature, liberty, and the pupil's "experiments in morality,"
inclined him to extreme caution.   Government he held
was essential before children were able to regulate their
own conduct, but it should be uniform, determined on the
principle of pleasure and pain, and directed to form
settled habits.   Laws should be few, but once laid down
they should be strictly adhered to.   In order to avoid any
suspicion of personal caprice, the whole treatment of the
child should lead him to associate certain experiences as
the necessary consequences of his action.   Punishment he
held should always be remedial and not vindictive, it
should be intelligible and should inflict the minimum of
pain necessary to achieve its purpose.   At the same time

Rewards and Punishments.

---

[1] *Memoirs*, Vol. II., pp. 401-2.

it should be regulated according to the temperament of the individual—thus to some a sense of continued disapprobation is a much greater punishment than temporary physical pain. Reward should be administered on similar principles, remembering that the greatest reward that can come to any individual is the feeling of uplift that attends successful achievement, and that the natural consequence of virtue is esteem. "But plum pudding is not the appropriate reward of truth, nor is the loss of it the natural or necessary consequence of falsehood."[1] "Children are not fools, and are not to be governed like fools."

With regard to intellectual education Edgeworth's great aim was to develop capacity, evoke **The Aim and Method of Intellectual Education.** initiative, and ripen judgment. The great need of the time, he felt, was to break down the idea that existed in children's minds that "learning" was disagreeable, by infusing more of the spirit of play into the school. To accomplish this all meaningless tasks were to be abolished, the schoolroom was to be brought into relation with the outside world, so that the significance of the lessons was immediately obvious to the children. At the same time methods of teaching must be reformed. All needless discouragements were to be got rid of, and in order not to weary the children short lessons were to be introduced. There was to be no forcing, but the teacher must so govern his procedure as to compel attention. "If the pupil be paid for the labour of listening by the pleasure of understanding he will attend."[2] "No matter how little be learned in a given time, provided the pupil be not disgusted : provided the wish to improve be excited and the habits of attention acquired."

[1] *Practical Education*, Vol. I., p. 363.   [2] *Ibid.*, Vol. I., p. 112.

To train the power of attention was of primary impór-
tance and this demanded clearness, distinct-
**Training the
Attention.** ness, and opportuneness in the presentation
of the subject-matter of instruction. In other
words, teachers must be careful not to overwhelm their
pupils with too many ideas at once. They must relate their
teaching to the pupils' experience and it must be well
timed, great care being taken to introduce into the school
work a variety of occupations, so that one subject might
counteract the fatiguing effects of another. Various forms
of practical occupations, and the practice of agreeable arts
suggested many useful experiments in this connection.
" If we could exactly discover how to arrange mental employments so as to induce actions in the antagonist faculties of the mind, we might relieve it from fatigue in the
same manner as the eye is relieved by colour. By pursuing
this idea might we not hope to cultivate the general power
of attention to a degree of perfection hitherto unknown ? " [1]
In following up the subject, attention was to be given to
the difference of temperament that existed between individuals, Edgeworth realising that no one procedure could
be applied with equal success to everybody.

Notwithstanding the erroneous psychology underlying
this account of attention, it led Edgeworth to
**Education
through Play.** institute a number of useful reforms. Thus
he recognised in children's play a great
educational means ready to hand that only needed judicious
guidance. The child was essentially an active individual.
Doing was the keynote of his life. He was constantly
building up and pulling apart, ever seeking to objectify
his inner experiences, ever being led on under the stimulus
of curiosity to investigate and to invent. Increased scope

[1] *Practical Education*, Vol. I., pp. 172-3.

was to be given to this native tendency by providing more rational toys, and at the same time more use should be made of these practical activities in the actual school work. Elaborate toys were dispensed with and playthings were substituted that could be manipulated in different ways— round ivory or wooden sticks, square and circular bits of wood, balls, cubes, and triangles with holes of different sizes to admit the sticks. From these children would gradually familiarise themselves with the sensory properties of objects, and imagination and inventiveness would be stimulated. Baby houses were provided unfurnished so as to give employment to " little carpenters and sempstresses " to fit them up. Pictures were used as a valuable means of education at this stage. Children were encouraged to cut out animals in paper, to model in clay and wax; basket-making was practised, and so on. As skill increased and more call was made on the inventive powers, card, pasteboard, wire, gum, etc., were introduced. Similarly full use was made of the possibilities held out by gardening, woodwork, and experimental science. In all this work the teacher needed to be specially on his guard against unduly interfering. "As the merchants in France answered Colbert when he desired to know how he could best assist them, children might perhaps reply to those who are most officious to amuse them, ' Leave us to ourselves.' "[1]

Among Edgeworth's attempts to reform school work may be mentioned his invention of a phonic script

.The Reform of School Practice.

for teaching reading, which he elaborated in *The Rational Primer*. The need for more interesting reading-books of the standard of Mrs. Barbauld's *Lessons*, and for popularising scientific knowledge, led him to begin writing *Harry and Lucy*, a

[1] *Ibid.*, Vol. I., p. 56.

book that was expanded later in co-operation with Maria into the series of *Early Lessons*. The original object was two-fold: to diffuse by means of an "interesting" story the first principles of morality, together with the elements of science and literature, and to show parents how the various subjects of instruction might be taught without wearying children.[1]

In other directions Edgeworth's practice shows the impress of the born teacher. Spellings were taught by grouping them and in conjunction with writing. Arithmetic was introduced practically by manipulating small cubes. Geography was taught with the help of a large globe six feet in diameter. The dominant motive in the literature lesson was enjoyment, and much stress was laid on the stimulating effect of good reading by the teacher. Edgeworth, fully realising the value of some acquaintance with elementary science, sought to demonstrate that much might be done by way of conversations centred round every-day incidents to stimulate children to observe and investigate for themselves. At the same time he suggested lines along which children might be allowed to experiment for themselves, his plan approximating very closely to the modified heuristic methods of to-day. He reminds us that "Independently of all ambitiou there is considerable pleasure in the pursuit of experimental knowledge. . . . They love to see experiments tried and to try them. They show this disposition not only whenever they are encouraged, but whenever they are permitted to show it; and if we compare their method of reasoning with the reasonings of the learned, we shall be surprised."[2]

---

[1] *Sandford and Merton* (Thos. Day) was originally intended as a part of this work.

[2] *Practical Education*, Vol. III., p. 117.

In his anxiety to keep school work free from drudgery
he was apt to underrate the importance of
**Defects in
his Practice.** seeing that foundations were securely laid.
Any child of intelligence, it seemed to him,
had no need to trouble with reading, spelling, or writing a
legible hand. Similarly he undervalued the necessity of
some memorising, but in all these directions he considerably changed his position in later years without any loss
to the liberality of his practice.[1] Indeed the education of
his youngest child was accounted the most successful of
all.

We will close this account by recalling Edgeworth's
conception of a true education.

**A True
Education.** "We do not mean to promise that a boy judiciously educated shall appear at ten years old a
prodigy of learning; far from it: we should not
even estimate his capacity or his chance of future progress, by the
quantity of knowledge stored in his memory, by the number of
Latin lines he has got by rote, by his expertness in repeating the
rules of his grammar, by his pointing out a number of places readily
on a map, or even by his knowing the latitude and longitude of all
the capital cities of Europe ; these are all useful articles of knowledge, but they are not the tests of a good education   We should
rather, if we were to examine a boy of ten years old, for the credit
of his parents, pronounce proofs of his being able to reason ac-
curately, of his quickness in invention, of his habits of industry
and application, of his having learned to generalise his ideas, and
apply his observations and his principles : if we found he had learned
any or all of these things we should be in little pains about grammar,
or geography, or even Latin ; we should be tolerably certain that he
would not long remain deficient in any of these ; we should know
that he would overtake and surpass a competitor who had only been
technically taught, as certainly as the giant would overtake the
panting dwarf, who might have many miles start of him in the race.
We do not mean to say that a boy should not be taught the principles
of grammar, and some knowledge of geography, at the same time

---

[1] *Memoirs*, Vol. II., pp. 390-1.

that his understanding is cultivated in the most enlightened manner : these objects are not incompatible." [1]

Such is the message of *Practical Education*, a book written for parents and widely read in cultivated homes during the early nineteenth century. But its spirit reached a much wider circle through the medium of Maria Edgeworth's children's tales. To avoid any misunderstanding as to the relative share of father and daughter in elaborating the underlying principle, we need go no farther than Maria Edgeworth's statement in the *Memoirs* (1819).

"It was my father's delight to say, that, in literature his thoughts and mine were in common ; he never would permit me to attribute to him even what was peculiarly his own. In the work (*Practical Education*) of which I am now speaking, the principles of education were peculiarly his, such as I felt he had applied in the cultivation of my own mind, and such as I saw in the daily instruction of my younger brothers and sisters during a period of nearly seventeen years ; all the general ideas originated with him, the illustrating and manufacturing them, if I may use the expression, was mine."

"So commenced that literary partnership which, for so many years was the pride and joy of my life." [2]

Maria Edgeworth was a past master in the art of didactic fiction, and in her various children's books

Maria Edgeworth. she embodied the principles she held in common with her father. The books are still well known, so that a brief summary of their import will suffice. *Harry and Lucy* emphasises in popular form the importance of inciting children to be in measure their own instructors, by stimulating curiosity, suggesting questions for investigation and encouraging inventiveness. Its main theme is to bring out some of the chief principles of science and their application in every-day life. Sir Walter Scott's comment on it illustrates very well one aspect of

[1] *Memoirs*, Vol. II., pp. 369-70.   [2] *Ibid.*, Vol. II., p. 190.

public opinion toward introducing modern subjects in school education. "She should have limited the title to *Education in Natural Philosophy*, . . . for there is no great use in teaching children in general to roof houses, or build bridges, which, after all, a carpenter or a mason does a good deal better at 2s. 6d. a day. Your ordinary Harry should be kept to his Grammar, and your Lucy of most common occurrence would be kept on her sampler, instead of wasting wood and cutting their fingers, which I am convinced they did, though their historian says nothing of it."

The Parent's Assistant was intended to point a series of moral lessons, the importance of industry, the dangers arising from contact with bad acquaintances, from weakness of mind, and in general to shock children with representation of what they ought to avoid. *Frank and Rosamond* and the *Moral Tales* were drawn up on a similar plan.

The eighteenth century closes with a picture of an elementary education differing widely for different ranks. Much of the prevailing practice was arid and worthless to a degree, but here and there we see work of exceptional merit.

In the following chapters we shall trace a growing liberality of outlook in the instruction designed for the poor, and a rise in the average efficiency of school work.

CHAPTER VII.

TEACHING BY MACHINERY.

" As the sequence among the letters or simple elements of speech may be made to assume all the difference between nonsense and the most sublime philosophy, so the sequences in the feelings which constitute human thought, may assume all the differences between the extreme of madness and of wickedness, and the greatest attainable heights of wisdom and virtue : And almost the whole of this is the effect of education."—James Mill, Article on Education, *Encyclopaedia Brit. Supplement*, 1824.

These words of James Mill afford us the key alike to the educational optimism that characterised the early stages of the primary school movement and to the ideals of teaching in vogue. Broadly speaking, two rival conceptions of the educative process held the field. The one, objective, regarded education as primarily external, determined and imposed upon the individual from without; the other, subjective, considered education as conditioned by the spontaneous development of the individual. The one set up a standard man, and sought to manufacture him ; the other aimed at securing the fullest self-development of each in accordance with the law of his own nature —the aim, for example, of Rousseau and Pestalozzi.

It was the former of these two conceptions that implicitly or explicitly dominated educational thought in England during the first part of the nineteenth century.

The Mechanical View of the Educative Process.

210

Such a view represents the child as clay in the hands of the potter. What he is depends upon his knowledge, upon the " trains of ideas " he has acquired, and these—making allowance for certain physical differences in individuals— are, according to Mill, under the control of the educator. The child learns what seems good for him as judged by adult standards, and the business of the teacher is to methodise instruction that knowledge may be acquired as surely and as economically as possible. No time is to be lost. That childhood has its own ways of looking at things, its own standards of value, is forgotten. Instead, there is an inevitable tendency to place all emphasis on a study of the printed page. In the schools education tends to become purely a matter of machinery, the grading of instruction, the length of lessons, and the invention of ingenious devices for assisting the memory.

It is the purpose of this chapter to trace the working out of this idea and to examine its influence on the organisation and method of the primary school.

Our knowledge of the inner working of the common schools at the close of the eighteenth and the beginning of the nineteenth centuries is somewhat incomplete, but apart from some notable exceptions all the evidence points to a state of affairs chaotic in the extreme. Crabbe's description of a day school of the poorer sort agrees with what we know of similar schools at a latter date.

The Common School at the beginning of the Nineteenth Century.

" Poor Reuben Dixon has the noisiest school
Of ragged lads, who ever how'd to rule ;
Low in his price—the men who heave our coals,
And clean our causeways, send him boys in shoals.
To see poor Reuben, with his fry beside—
Their half-check'd rudeness and his half-scorn'd pride—
Their room, the sty in which th' assembly meet,

> In the close lane behind the Northgate-street ;
> T' observe his vain attempts to keep the peace,
> Till tolls the bell, and strife and troubles cease,
> Calls for our praise ; his labours praise deserves,
> But not our pity ; Reuben has no nerves.
> 'Mid noise and dirt, and stench, and play, and prate,
> He calmly cuts the pen or views the slate."[1]

Everything was calculated to foster mean educational ideals, harsh discipline, and wooden methods. Schools in the main were small, composed of pupils of all ages, and numbering anything from a dozen upwards, in charge of a single teacher, confined to one room, often enough ill-lighted, ill-ventilated, overcrowded, and with a minimum of furniture and apparatus, a few benches, books, pens and paper being all that was required. In successful schools an assistant or usher was employed, but large establishments employing a number of teachers were unusual. Schooling seems to have been entirely a matter of imitation, memorising, and the getting off of tasks with no attempt at exposition, though doubtless many a schoolmaster here and there with the instinct of a born teacher did his best as far as circumstances would allow to touch the understanding of his pupils.

What one type of common school was like can be seen from the accompanying illustration of John Pounds' School.[2]

---

[1] *The Borough*, Letter xxiv.

[2] Pounds (1766-1839) was the large-hearted cobbler of Portsmouth who, when fifteen years of age, had met with an accident that disabled him for life. His time was divided between cobbling and rescue work among the poorest and most degraded children in the neighbourhood, over whom he seems to have exerted an extraordinary influence. These children, boys and girls, he induced to attend his workshop, where he taught them, free of charge, to read, write, and sum, to cook their own victuals, and to mend their own shoes. He combined the functions of schoolmaster, doctor, nurse, and playfellow. So well did his work succeed that he is often spoken

The modes of teaching in vogue can be grouped under one or other of three heads, (1) simultaneous or collective, (2) individual, and (3) mutual.[1]

Mode of Instruction.

It was the second of these that was characteristic of elementary schools at the end of the eighteenth century. The simultaneous or collective method so familiar to-day could only be used effectively in schools sufficiently well staffed to enable the children to be divided into groups according to individual attainment, each group being in charge of an efficient teacher. As used in Sunday schools and for catechetical purposes it was generally ineffective, for, as often as not, the whole school was taught as one group irrespective of age, and fully deserved all the hard things that were said about it during the early years of last century. The individual system was equally ineffective and uneconomical. The better schoolmasters, as Professor Pillans[2] tells us, did make some attempt to group their children into several grades for reading, as many more for writing, as many again for arithmetic, and so on, but amid such a distracting diversity of occupations it was well-nigh impossible to do effective work, the time given to any section was too short and the pupils spent the bulk of their time in idleness. The scene of confusion in the majority of these schools, conducted as they were without any method at all, by teachers with no special capacity for the work, and where every child was occupied with a different task, can well be imagined. That progress was slow

---

of as the founder of Ragged Schools. His workshop, which served as a schoolroom, was about 6 ft. by 18 ft., and accommodated some 40 children. It is a good example of one kind of unorganised elementary school that is met with down to 1870.

[1] Cf. Gréard: *Education et Instruction—Enseignement Primaire*, p. 39. (1904.)

[2] Pillans: *Contributions to the Cause of Education* (1856). See *ante*, p. 4.

is hardly surprising. The defects of both a simultaneous and an individual system as commonly practised must have been obvious to all, and it is reasonable to suppose that some form of mutual instruction was common in at any rate the better schools.[1]

Robert Raikes describes how he made use of the plan in his early experiments on Sunday schools :—

"I endeavour to assemble the children as early as is consistent with their perfect cleanliness—an indispensable rule. The hour prescribed in our rules is eight o'clock, ... Twenty is the number allotted to each teacher, the sexes kept separate. The twenty are divided into four classes ; the children who show any superiority in attainments are placed as leaders of the several classes, and are employed in teaching the others their letters, or in hearing them read in a low whisper, which may be done without interrupting the master or mistress in their business, and will keep the attention of the children engaged, that they do not play or make a noise."[2]

This apparently innocent device, re-discovered independently by Bell and Lancaster and worked up by each into an independent system, was destined to exert a determining influence on educational practice in this country for half a century. So much so that mutual instruction came to be regarded abroad as the distinctively English method of elementary schooling. The rival systems, though differing considerably in detail, are the same in principle and will accordingly be discussed together.

THE MONITORIAL SYSTEMS OF BELL AND LANCASTER.

Neither Bell nor Lancaster were in any sense educational theorists. Their ideals of education were little if at all in advance of those of the better primary schoolmaster of the day, being confined to imparting the ele-

[1] Cf. *ante*, p. 43.
[2] *Letter of Robert Raikes*, November 8th, 1787, reprinted in *Robert Raikes: the Man and his Work*, p. 324, Harris.

ments of reading, writing, and arithmetic, with the addition
of sewing in the case of girls ; but they aimed at doing this
more efficiently and more cheaply than hithertofore. To
this end both pupils and subject-matter were to be carefully graded. Short lessons and working to a time-table[1]
were to be insisted upon. Each class was to be put in charge
of a picked boy (or girl) teacher in order to insure systematic
drill and oversight, thereby greatly increasing the number
of children that could be looked after by one schoolmaster ;
and, most important, emulation was to be substituted for
the harsh discipline of the day. In Lancaster's own
words : " Every pupil in school shall, at all times, have
something to do, and a motive for doing it." Bell was
equally explicit : " To attain any good end in education,
the desideratum is, to fix attention, to call forth exertion,
to prevent the waste of time in school." [2] " The entire
machinery of the New School is fitted to prevent idleness
and offences, to call forth diligence and exertion, and
thereby to supersede the flagellation which he (Quintilian)
so justly reprobated." In short, the Monitorial Systems
introduced (1) a new plan of school organisation, and
(2) improvements in the method of instruction.

In carrying out these reforms both men showed not
only considerable resource, but a shrewd knowledge of
, children. It was upon his own observation of boys that
Lancaster's monitorial principles were largely based.
Boys are naturally active and full of spirits, he tells us.
Instead of attempting to repress it, use it for the good
of the school ; keep all busy and give the mischievous

[1] It is worth noting that the *term* Time-table is not met with until the
forties, when it appears in the Reports of Government Inspectors. Cf.
Minutes of Committee of Council, Vol. II., 1846, p. 354. See *infra*,
p. 220.   [2] *The Madras School*, p. 10,

positions of responsibility.[1] Boys are imitative and sug-
gestible; use this fact as a means of exciting emulation,
promoting a healthy public opinion and *esprit de corps*.
Motive and self-exertion lie at the root of all education;
study the dispositions and cultivate the affections of the
children. Such is a brief outline of the main points of
monitorial theory.

ORGANISATION.

As already indicated the root principle of monitorial
instruction was the setting of children to teach children.
The ideal school was conducted in a large square or oblong
room, lofty and well lighted, a barn, it was said, furnish-
ing no bad model as to shape and proportions. Six square
feet of floor space was recommended for each child.

In Bell's schools the centre of the floor was kept free of
furniture, so as to accommodate the various
classes standing. Round the walls was fixed
a row of desks at which the children sat for
writing with their backs to the centre of the room.
Parallel to the desks were placed not more than three rows
of forms. The only other furniture in the room consisted
of a few cupboards and the headmaster's desk. The
centre of the floor was marked out into squares for the
different classes. The pupils of each class formed three
sides of a hollow square, while the class "teacher" with
his "assistant" stood on two dots marked T and A respectively on the fourth side. They stood for all lessons
save writing. The accompanying illustration shows the
central school of the National Society at Baldwin's Gardens
at work. The room was 60 feet wide and 100 feet long,
and was divided by a partition into two unequal parts,

The Madras Plan.

----

[1] *Improvements in Education*, 1806, p. 31 and *passim.*

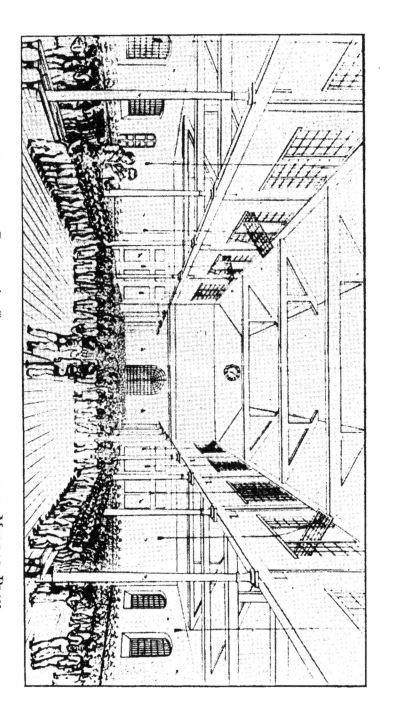

To face p. 216.

THE SCHOOL AT BALDWIN'S GARDENS, ORGANISED ON THE MADRAS PLAN.

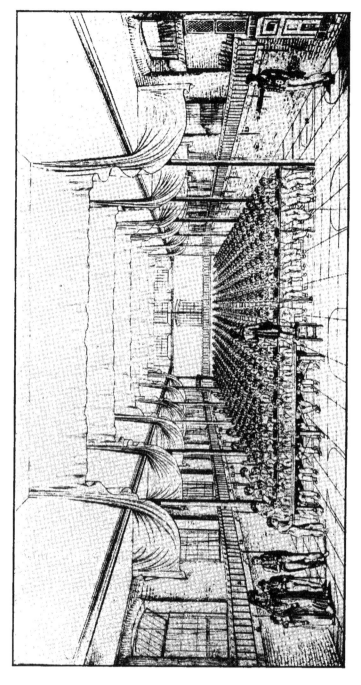

THE SCHOOL AT THE BOROUGH ROAD, ARRANGED ACCORDING TO THE LANCASTERIAN PLAN.

To face p. 217.

the one for 600 boys and the other for 400 girls. The girls' school shows the benches distributed over the floor for a sewing lesson ; the boys' school illustrates the every-day working conditions.

The size and number of classes depended very much upon the number of children attending the school ; but, in general, the fewer the classes the better. In a large school where many children would have made the same progress each class consisted of from twenty-four to thirty-six scholars. In small schools the classes were smaller, but never more than six or eight classes would be found. Allotted to each class was a *teacher* and an *assistant teacher*. The former was chosen from the top class (or classes) of the school, the latter was the best scholar of the particular division. In addition every boy in a class was paired, the best helping the poorest, and so on.[1]

Size of Classes.

In Lancasterian schools the centre of the floor was occupied by long unbroken rows of desks, leaving a wide passage all round the walls. This free space was marked out into semi-circles much smaller than Bell's squares, each intended for eight or ten boys. The general method of organisation is shown in the accompanying illustration of the Borough Road School.[2] The room was 90 feet long by nearly 40 feet wide, and sloped gently towards the back. There were twenty desks each 25 feet long, and thirty-one semicircles. The boys of each row were divided into two " drafts " of from eight to ten, each in charge of a *monitor* as the boy teacher was called. As in the Bell school, the scholars stood for all lessons except writing. The use of

The Lancas-terian Plan.

---

[1] At Madras the *teacher* ranged from fourteen to eleven and the *assistant teacher* from eleven to seven years of age.

[2] The common method of heating was by means of a stove.

small "drafts" instead of comparatively large classes brings us to an important difference in the monitorial plan as elaborated by Bell and by Lancaster. The determining factor was cheapness. In the ordinary school of the day, and in schools following the Madras model, reading-books were used by the children; but these books, varying in price from 1d. upwards, very quickly wore out. Lancaster "improved" this by using *reading* (and arithmetical) *sheets* 17 inches by 10 inches, printed in larger type and mounted on cardboard, which, though involving a greater initial outlay, were practically everlasting. It was round these sheets, hung on the walls, that the "drafts" gathered. The smaller classes made more individual drill possible, but it was at the expense of more monitors and more noise, a school of 200 having now instead of six some twenty monitors shouting out lessons simultaneously. Not only so, but the existence of a stock of imperishable sheets inevitably tended to prevent schools adapting themselves readily to new ideas.

There was no part of school organisation that Lancaster did not "improve." "A place for everything and everything in its place" was one of his mottoes. Accordingly, he devised elaborate rules for slinging hats across the shoulders, for marching to and from desks; every seat was numbered and had its corresponding slate hanging from it[1]; reading-sheet No. 1 went on nail No. 1[2]; every boy in the same class was supposed to write the same number of letters in the same time, and so on. To keep this machinery going a small army of monitors was employed. Besides teaching

Lancaster's Improvements.

---

[1] Considerations of economy led Lancaster to use slates to an extent hitherto unprecedented. He popularised the slate at the expense of paper and ink.

[2] Cf. the illustration above.

monitors there were order monitors, monitors for ruling books, mending pens, for enquiring after absentees, for inspecting, monitors-general for writing, for reading, etc., until the whole organisation was practically at the mercy of a very fallible body of lieutenants. In short, Lancaster's improvements went too far and resulted in a loss of flexibility. Hence it was the less precisely organised Bell system, with fewer monitors and larger classes, that showed itself more adaptable to newer conditions, and so formed the link between the practice of the eighteenth century and the school organisation as we find it in the fifties after the coming of the pupil teacher system.

Two other points of organisation call for remark: the grading of lessons and promotion. Lancaster had eight grades (or classes) in reading, and ten in arithmetic. The arithmetic was only begun when the fifth reading class (or grade) was reached; that is to say, the upper part of the school was re-classed for arithmetic. In schools following Bell's plan six (or eight) grades was the ideal, and instruction in the three R's went on contemporaneously.

A Village School on the Madras Plan.

The exact number of classes depended, of course, upon local circumstances. Thus a small village school would only have three classes, each with its own " teacher." The method of conducting such a school is shown in the accompanying table. Attention should be directed to the occupations of the different classes, the length of lessons, and the way in which the master distributed his time.[1] The " teachers " referred to are of course the monitors.

[1] For the breakdown of the system in larger schools see *infra*, pp. 267-8.

DISTRIBUTION OF TIME IN A SMALL VILLAGE SCHOOL ON THE MADRAS SYSTEM.

MORNING.			
	1ST CLASS.	2ND CLASS.	3RD CLASS.
¼ past 9	Catechism.	Collects.	Lord's Prayer.
½ past 9	Reads and spells to the master.	Reads and spells from lesson to teacher.	Reads spelling cards to teacher.
10 o'clock	Repeats tables —cyphers and spells from cards.	Spells from cards —writes from copper-plate cards to teacher.	Reads and spells to the master— goes out.
½ past 10	Reads and spells from lesson to the teacher.	Reads and spells from the lesson to master—goes out.	Writes copper-plate cards— sitting.
11 o'clock	Spells on the cards to the master — goes out.	Writes a lesson from the spelling cards.	Writes tables and figures—go out again.
½ past 11	Writes in copy-book, or if girls, sew.	Go out five minutes — writes tables—repeats them from cards.	Reads and spells to master.
¼ to 12	Repeat religious instruction— fill up registers, etc.		

From *A Small Manual for the Use of Village Schools, to assist Masters and Mistresses to understand and to adopt the Rev. Dr. Bell's System*, W. Burkwell, Leek, c. 1818.

Promotion in these institutions appears to have taken
Promotion. place at no fixed date nor after any particular period. Perfect familiarity with the particular set of lessons was the deciding factor whether for the
individual or for a group of boys. Emulation with attendant place-taking was an essential feature of all monitorial
schools, and the progress of each boy was carefully recorded each day by his position in class. To the marks
register kept for this purpose Bell gave the name of the
"paidometer." If a boy succeeded in keeping his place
at the head of his section he was moved to the middle of
the class higher. Should he succeed in retaining or in improving his position well and good; if he dropped to the
bottom he was degraded. No degradation of this sort was
practised in Lancasterian schools.

Of teaching properly so called there was comparatively
Method. little in the majority of these schools. It
was too much a matter of learning or help-
ing children to learn lessons in the most mechanical way,
regardless of whether what was learnt was assimilated or
not. Reading was taught as a mechanical art, arithmetic
was the manipulation of figures, writing was concerned
with penmanship and spelling. There was no such thing
as composition. Class lessons in which the teacher nar-
rated, described, expounded, were unheard of. Any questioning there was generally came cut and dried from a
book, followed by the answer which had to be memorised.

To teach reading was the chief end of the monitorial
Reading, school, yet as a rule little or no attention was
Spelling, and given to content. Reading simply meant the
Writing. power to recognise words and to string them
together orally. The customary method was to begin with
the alphabet and to proceed to read by means of spelling.
Both reformers adopted this method, but proceeded to

improve it in detail. First they carefully graduated the lessons. Not until all ordinary monosyllables and words had been spelled were children allowed to approach dis-syllables. Again, all syllables and words of two letters had to be known before those of three letters were dealt with, and so on. Secondly, in order to fix the forms of the syllables clearly in mind they had to be written—that is to say spelling, reading, and writing went hand in hand. Only after the children had gone through a long drill in spelling and writing monosyllables and monosyllabic words were they introduced to the reading of sentences, and even then care was taken that these did not make too good sense, for fear the children would memorise them rather than concentrate their attention on the individual words. Lancaster's scheme of spelling, reading and writing, which was typical of monitorial practice, was as follows:—

Class I.   learns to read the alphabet and to trace the letters on sand.

Class II.   spells words and syllables of two letters and writes them on slates.

Class III.   spells and writes words and syllables of three letters.

Class IV.   spells and writes words and syllables of four letters.

Class V.   spells and writes words and syllables of five and six letters and begins to read words of one syllable.

Class VI.   spells and writes words of two syllables and reads short passages containing dissyllabic words.

Class VII.   spells and writes words of several syllables and reads longer passages.

Class VIII. reads from the Bible.

The last one, two, or three classes wrote on paper with pen and ink.

Though each reformer introduced "improvements" the basis of their work was *Mrs. Trimmer's*

Method in Reading. *Charity School Spelling Book,* and the New and Old Testaments furnished the reading material. As a means of ensuring alertness, the pupils in Madras schools would be asked to build up syllables on the model ab, eb, ib, etc. A sharp distinction was drawn between *spelling on book* and *spelling off book.* It was "spelling on book" to look at a word and say i-b ib, c-a-t cat, whereas it was "spelling off book" to first say the word, *e.g.* cat, and then spell it from memory.[1] The reading of monosyllables proceeded thus. Suppose the sentence to be "The way of God is a good way." This was first copied on slates, then from dictation, every word being spelled alphabetically. When the class stood up to read the passage was attacked in the same way : T-h-e the, w-a-y way, o-f of, G-o-d God, etc. It was next read in *pauses*: The way-of God-is-a good way; then it was read again without a stop. Next it was "spelled off book" thus, The t-h-e, way w-a-y, etc.; afterwards it was written from dictation, the monitor only pronouncing the words. As a further means of maintaining attention each boy would be required to spell only one letter of a word, and if any missed his turn he lost his place in the class.

Polysyllables were split up into single syllables, but now without any spelling, each syllable being pronounced separately : "Thus-he-pro-ceeds-through-the-child's-book-part-first-and-se-cond-Mis-tress-Trim-mer's-spel-ling-book," etc., afterwards counting one for a comma, two for a semi-colon, and three for a full stop. In order to ensure "ceaseless activity," while one boy was reading the

[1] *The Madras School,* p. 60.

lips of all the rest were to be moving, and individual lessons were to be short—10 to 20 minutes. Nevertheless the same sort of grind went on for the whole of each school session.[1]

To make sure that the children grasped the sense of a passage two forms of explanation were gradually introduced, one directed to getting the general sense of the passage, the other directed to particular words, both questions and answers being set out in a book in the hands of the monitor.

Arithmetic was taught with the same want of under-standing as reading. Of ways in which number concepts develop there was no thought whatever. It was all a matter of "cyphering." The figures were learnt by copying them, and all the rest was a matter of drill and rules. According to the extract[2] from the Master's Report of a Sunderland School, 1822, Lancasterian Schools were graded for arithmetic as follows :—

Arithmetic.

Class I.	learnt to cypher and to combine figures.[3]
Classes II. to V.	learnt to add, subtract, multiply, and divide simple numbers respectively.
Classes VI. to IX.	learnt the same rules for compound numbers.
Class X.	learnt reduction, practice, and the rule of three.

---

[1] The old method of meeting a new word like "misrepresentation" was to attack the separate syllables as though they had never been seen before, *e.g.* m-i-s mis, r-e re, misre, etc. Bell would not allow this, the word must be spelled m-i-s—r-e—p-r-e, etc.

[2] "Monitorial Schools and their Successors," *Educational Record,* Vol. XVIII., p. 21. The chapters under this heading contain a full and valuable account of the inner working of the monitorial systems.

[3] Bell carried this to septillions.

The tables had to be thoroughly learnt, and in Madras schools these were built up as follows :—

Addition.[1]

```
0 0 0 0 0 - - -  to 12.
1 1 1 1 1 - - -
1 1 1 1 1 - - -
  1 1 1 1 - - -
  2 2 2 2 - - -
    1 1 1 - - -
    3 3 3 - - -
```

Combined addition and subtraction of twos :—

```
2 3 4 5 6 7  to 12.
2 2 2 2 2 2
4 5 6 7 8 9
2 2 2 2 2 2
2 3 4 5 6 7
```

Combined multiplication and division of nines :—

```
   9 10 11  12
   9  9  9   9
9) 81 90 99 108
   9 10 11  12
```

The children were well drilled in combinations such as—

$$9 + 6 \text{ and } 6 + 9 = 15.$$
$$15 - 6 = 9 \text{ and } 15 - 9 = 6.$$

In teaching addition the monitor in both Bell and Lancasterian schools read out from a book :—

```
     lb.
2 7 9 3 5
  3 9 6 3
  8 6 7 9
1 4 3 2 7
```

---

[1] Lancaster's method was for the monitor to take a long table and read thus, the boys writing the numbers as dictated :—9 and 1 are 10 ; 9 and 2 are 11 ; . . . 25 and 2 are 27 ; 25 and 3 are 28.

Each line was inspected as written. Then taking the key the monitor begau : *First Column :* 7 and 9 are 16, and 3 are 19, and 5 are 24. Set down 4 under the 7 and carry 2 to the next, etc., and so on through the various "rules."

Such was the monitorial method of rendering "simple, easy, pleasant, and economical the acquisition of letters," which, together with morality and religion, "are the leading objects of Elementary Education."[1] That the actual value of letters acquired on such terms was small need hardly be pointed out. At the same time the judgment of contemporaries leaves no doubt that the schooling, such as it was, was enormously more efficient than that afforded, almost without exception, in the primary schools of the day.

But what of the moral training given in the monitorial schools? For, according to Bell, the "ultimate object" (of the Madras system) was "to make good scholars, good men, good subjects and good Christians; in other words, to promote the temporal and spiritual welfare of our pupils."[2] To Lancaster it was "to train children in the practice of such moral habits as are conducive to the welfare of society."[3]

Moral Training.

Both men firmly believed this end was an inevitable accompaniment of the machine-like regularity of the school, its strenuousness, the constant sense of personal responsibility felt by pupil and monitor alike, supplemented as it was by definite moral and religious teaching. "Look at a regiment or a ship," says Bell, "you will see a beautiful example of the system which I have

[1] *The Madras School,* p. 6.   [2] *The Madras School,* 1808, p. 7.
[3] *Improvements in Education,* 1806, p. 25.

recommended for a single school." [1] In it "every boy has his place and every hour its proper business "; . . . and "there grows up imperceptibly a sense of duty, subordination, and obedience." . . . "The hope of reward . . . the fear, not of corporal pain, but of disgrace, are the effective springs by which the *mighty machine is to be moved.*" "The smart of bodily pain soon subsides and is forgotten, but the sense of shame strikes close and will not suffer the offender to be at peace, till the fault that occasioned it be obliterated by subsequent meritorious action. . . . These things daily and hourly preached . . . are wrought into the sentiments," and they become "the fixed and settled habits both of body and mind." [2]

By realising that children like to be kept busy, by substituting order for chaos and emulation for the harsh corporal punishment of the day, a great advance was made. To place boys in positions of trust and so endeavour to awaken a feeling of personal responsibility was excellent. The practice of trying boys whose names appeared in the black book by a jury elected by the school had at least the merit of endeavouring to eliminate any suspicion of caprice in inflicting punishment, and in so far as it was an attempt to cultivate a healthy public opinion, and to accustom boys to self-government, it emphasised an aspect of social training that is sometimes forgotten. But too often, owing to the incompetence of the master, these elements were entirely in abeyance.

It is unnecessary to detail the elaborate scheme of rewards and punishments. Emulation was the watchword of the systems, and supposedly the key to all individual enterprise. But at a time when schooling consisted in "driving in knowledge at the end of a stick" it did a good

---

[1] *The Madras School*, p. 312. [2] *Ibid.*, pp. 270-72.

deal towards popularising a more humane view in the school.

In estimating the value of the monitorial systems we must not confuse the machinery with the **Merits and Defects.** spirit that directed it. Both Bell and Lancaster were men who could, and did, infuse new life into whatever school they entered, but neither distinguished between the relative importance of machinery and personality. Mechanism was in the air and both men believed firmly that it was possible to mechanise education, just as Pestalozzi had done.[1] "*Any boy who can read can teach . . . although he knows nothing about it,*"[2] said Lancaster. "An automaton might be a schoolmaster." Both believed that they had discovered a short cut to knowledge, and they succeeded in convincing others that this was so. That the monitorial systems of school organisation marked a great forward step in the direction of bringing instruction within the reach of all is indisputable.[3] The wave of enthusiasm that attended the introduction of the systems into both day and Sunday schools is shown in numerous contemporary records. Old furniture was discarded, and local generosity was stimulated to effect the fitting up of the schools on the new plan. The number of scholars increased rapidly, listlessness disappeared in the school-room, and a new spirit reigned. Evidence of boys "spelling in their sleep" was received with satisfaction.[4]

---

[1] *Life and Work of Pestalozzi*, J. A. Green, p. 127.

[2] *Improvements in Education*, 1806, p. 84.

[3] Cf. *The Training System*, Stow, First Edition, Chap. I.

[4] An interesting example of this enthusiasm is found in the records of the Church Sunday schools at Stockport, where Bell's system was introduced in 1812. In 1810-11 the total income was £91 9s. 8d., the expenses £70 8s. In 1812-13 the total income was £233 9s. 7d. (this includes no grant from the National Society). The expenses due to a heavy joiner's bill for desks and other fittings, a large bill for books and stationery, in-

But the weakness of the monitorial plan was apparent even while Bell was boasting " If you or I live a thousand years we shall see this system spread over the world." There could be little education where the ideal of the school-master was to do nothing beyond acting as an organiser and an inspector, and where the real work of the school was committed to children.

Accordingly it is hardly surprising to find that the average day school conducted on monitorial **The** lines was far from reaching the standard **Ordinary** set by the inventors of the system. Among **Monitorial** **School.** the complaints lodged against these institutions were included bad discipline, the tyranny of the monitors, the late and irregular attendance of schoolmasters, and the poor results of the instruction. It has already been pointed out that the monitorial system was too much concerned with " stuffing the memory," and it was to improve the intellectual value of school work that reformers first directed their attention.

One of the leaders of this movement was John Wood of the Edinburgh Sessional School. A careful **John Wood's** study of children with whom he was brought **Intellectual** into contact (1820) soon led him to the **System.** [1] discovery that pupils are not machines or irrational animals to be driven, but intellectual beings who may be led; that success depends upon studying the individual and adapting circumstances accordingly; and that it is the spirit—not the external arrangements and

creased salaries, etc., amounted to £476 9s. 11d. The improvement in the efficiency of the schools is seen by the increase in attendance. Within a year 600 new scholars entered and two new schools had to be opened. Two years later 2,500 children were in regular attendance. The income was then £439 6s. 7d., and the expenditure £552 12s. 7d.—*Reports of the Church Sunday Schools.*

[1] *Account of the Edinburgh Sessional School,* John Wood, 1828.

mechanism—that counts in education. Teaching that did
not strike a responsive note in the pupil, that did not
quicken his understanding, was dead. School work to be
of any value must be meaningful and must start from the
pupils' experiences. Unintelligible rote work must be
abolished, exposition was to come in, and it was the
teacher's business to see that nothing was learnt that was
not understood. Knowledge was accordingly looked for in
the schoolmaster, but at the same time he must be "apt
to teach." This was Wood's contribution to educational
practice. His principles were set out in his *Account of the
Edinburgh Sessional School*, and further elaborated by
Professor Pillans in his *Letters on Elementary Education*.
He invented no new system of school organisation, but took
the monitorial system as elaborated by Bell and sought
to infuse it with a new spirit. Higher qualities were
demanded of master and monitor alike; the latter must
not merely know the lesson by heart, he must understand
it and be prepared to get the pupils to understand
it likewise. Great store was set upon questioning, though
the use of books of set questions was not forbidden so long
as they were not used mechanically. A real effort was
made to brighten the school, and to stimulate a vigorous
intellectual life. Emulation and place-taking were retained,
and might be supplemented by corporal punishment under
exceptional circumstances, but sarcasm and ridicule were
abolished. "There is no stronger mark of incapacity in a
teacher," says Wood, "than his being under the necessity
of resorting to punishments more frequently than others
placed in like situation : nor any higher recommendation
in one than his maintaining equal authority with less
severity than his neighbours."[1]

[1] *Account of the Edinburgh Sessional School*, John Wood, 3rd Edition,
p. 144.

In reading great stress was laid on making the work
interesting and instructive. The children
Improvement in Practice. were set to read simple passages as soon as
they knew the alphabet. Much attention
was given to seeing that they understood what they were
reading about, and in a mistaken endeavour to achieve this
there was an absurd waste of time on learning the mean-
ings of individual words and lists of prefixes and roots,
while at the same time the lesson was allowed to degenerate
into a vehicle for conveying miscellaneous information.
Grammar was also emphasised as an aid to understanding the reading-book. In arithmetic a good deal of
emphasis was laid upon principles and mental work, and
the children were encouraged to evolve solutions and
methods for themselves. In geography an effort was made
to see that every place learnt was located on the map and
stood for something; and so on.

These improvements required the name of the *Intellectual
System,* and were adopted in principle by the monitorial
schools. Not that they were evolved by any one individual.
All these ideas were in the air, and can be studied to-day
in the pages of the large contemporary literature intended
for the consumption of middle-class children. Rather they
represent an inevitable stage in the evolution of the
common school, reforms that thinking teachers have
fallen upon again and again. They are associated with
the name of Wood because his school embodied them
more perfectly than the majority of similar schools. It
stood out like an oasis in a desert, but to imagine that
the ideas were peculiar to him would be to misread
history.

Other improvements came with the development of infant
schools. It has already been pointed out that the primary
function of the initiatory and dame schools of the working

classes during the early nineteenth century was to mind children while their parents were at work.

> " Yet one there is, that small regard to rule
> Or study pays, and still is deem'd a school:
> That, where a deaf, poor, patient widow sits
> And awes some thirty infants as she knits;
> Infants of humble, busy wives, who pay
> Some trifling price for freedom through the day.
> At this good matron's hut the children meet,
> Who thus becomes the mother of the street.
> Her room is small, they cannot widely stray—
> Her threshold high, they cannot run away;
> Though deaf, she sees the rebel-heroes shout;—
> Though lame, her white rod nimbly walks about;
> With band of yarn she keeps offenders in,
> And to her gown the sturdiest rogue can pin.
> Aided by these, and spells, and tell-tale birds,
> Her power they dread and reverence her words."[1]
>
> —CRABBE.

Sometimes the elements of reading were imparted, but any attempt at instruction was most perfunctory. It was the improvements in common school education, brought about by the introduction of the monitorial method, that directed attention to the need of reform in infant education. To leave unprovided for children who were too young to begin to use slates and to learn to read, and for whom the drill of the monitorial school was unsuited, was to risk the stability of the whole edifice. Without efficient initiatory schools there was no provision for checking the formation of bad habits and stemming the growth of juvenile depravity. Some organisation was, in fact, wanted to supplement the monitorial school and to help in disciplining the children, a matter of especial importance in view of the early age at

---

[1] *The Borough*, Letter xxiv.

which children were accustomed to enter upon some form of daily occupation.

It was Robert Owen's Infant School at New Lanark that set a new standard.[2] The school was attended by children from one and a half to six years of age: these were divided into three classes, each with its own class-room, and placed in charge of an old weaver, James Buchanan, and a young mill worker, Molly Young, assisted by several others. Owen's object was to banish all harshness in word and action from the school, and to adopt every means to inculcate a spirit of loving-kindness, brotherliness, and social service. Great emphasis was laid on physical training and an education in contact with realities. Instead of teaching the three R's, he proposed to direct the interest of the children to nature and the objects around by means of conversation. Spontaneity was to be the keynote of the school. All formalism was to be abolished. There were to be no set tasks. Much time was to be spent in the playground, and games and story-telling were to occupy a prominent part in the work of the school. In practice, however, the importunity of the parents made it impossible to follow out this scheme in its entirety, and a good deal of formal instruction was included. Children of from two to four years of age were occupied with games, singing, object lessons, conversation and story lessons, and were also taught the alphabet. Those from four to six had lessons in reading, geography, natural history, singing, and drawing.

Robert Owen's School.[1]

[1] The school was housed in the New Institution, a large building erected in the centre of the village. The ground-floor was divided into three rooms, and was occupied by the infants. The first floor, consisting of a large room 90 ft. by 40 ft. by 20 ft. and a smaller one, accommodated the upper school. See illustrations in Podmore's *Robert Owen, a Biography*, Vol. I,

[2] Cf. *ante*, pp. 33 *et seq.*

An equally liberal outlook governed the work of the children from six to ten or twelve years of **Upper School.** age. Kindliness and a spirit of mutual service pervaded the whole. All artificial rewards and punishments were excluded as having a pernicious influence on character. Every liberty consistent with the maintenance of good order was allowed, and every effort was made to lead children to understand wherein their true self-interest lay. Instruction was conveyed in as pleasing a manner as could be devised, the object being to evoke and maintain interest and quicken the understanding. Failure led the teacher to self-examination and to devise means of improving his procedure. The importance of illustration and exposition was fully realised, but too little attention seems to have been given to encouraging inventiveness and spontaneity in the intellectual part of the work.

The curriculum was very liberal including, in addition to the three R's, geography, history (ancient and modern), natural history, religious instruction, sewing, singing, dancing, and drill. The school was first organised on the Lancasterian plan; but experience having shown the inconvenience of this, the children were divided into classes of 40 or 50 under adult teachers.[1] After 1818 Pestalozzian methods were gradually introduced. But what impressed visitors most was the note of freshness and spontaneity that pervaded the establishment. To find children reading Miss Edgeworth's tales, illustrated accounts of voyages and travels, using time charts in history, singing " The Birks of Aberfeldy " and other lively Scotch songs from note, entering with enthusiasm into the various Scotch reels and country dances, and to see

. [1] *An Outline of the System of Education at New Lanark*, R. D. Owen 1824.

girls cutting out their own garments in the sewing lessons, the boys organised into a cadet corps, suffice even to-day to explain why the school should attract visitors interested in the social aspect of education from all over Europe.[1]

Thanks to this emphasis on the physical and moral aspects of education the infant schools in this country took on a direction very different from that of the monitorial schools. Owen shows a truer conception of children than was customary at the time. To the majority they were merely adults in miniature, childhood was a time to be hurried through as quickly as possible, education meant storing the memory, and young children learnt the same lessons as their elders only in a briefer and more concentrated form. This intellectual view had its outcome in the prodigy system. John Stuart Mill began to learn Greek at the age of three. Basedow's daughter Emilie spoke and read French and German, could compose a simple letter, was familiar with the elements of arithmetic, and was a capable housekeeper at four years of age; and Bentham's scheme of the proposed Chrestomathic school which children were to enter at seven years of age made no provision for instruction in reading, writing, and arithmetic.

Owen's Influence.

But in other quarters a still more vicious idea prevailed. Acting on the assumption that the poor must be trained to poverty many were in favour of capturing the children young and inuring them to " habits of industry " by setting them to various industrial occupations utterly reckless of any physical consequences, at the same time pro-

---

[1] Cf. " The Daily Routine of the New Lanark Institution " as given by the Headmaster in *The New Views of Mr. Owen of Lanark Impartially Examined*, by Henry Grey Macnab, 1819. A good account is also given in *Adventures in Socialism*, Alex. Cullen.

viding merely the dry bones of intellectual instruction.[1]
What the times needed was imagination, and this was
what the seer of New Lanark provided.

    If the infant school movement owed its origin and
direction to Owen, it was to the energy and

Wilderspin.   ingenuity of Wilderspin that the ideas were
reduced to a system and spread up and down
the country.[2] Wilderspin had a genuine interest in and
sympathy with the poor, and in the infant school as organised at New Lanark he saw a means of checking the growth
of juvenile depravity in large towns. With the development of his scheme and the controversy that centres round
the source of his ideas we are not concerned. Many of
them were cognate with Pestalozzi's doctrine, nor is this
surprising when for the past twenty years visitors had been
attracted to Switzerland to study at first hand the ideas
and work of the great reformer. All the ideas vital to the
plan were in the air at the time and only awaited application. So much may be granted without in any way milita-
ting against his reputation as one of the great educational
influences of the day, or as a man who deservedly won the
affectionate esteem of enlightened working class opinion
throughout the country.[3]

---

[1] See *ante*, pp. 40-41.

[2] Cf. *ante*, p. 56.

[3] G. W. Goyder tells us (*Autobiography of a Phrenologist*, pp. 108-9)
that Wilderspin got his first knowledge of the working of infant schools
from James Buchanan, and that Wilderspin's school in 1820 differed in no
way from Buchanan's. Indicative of the importance of Pestalozzi at this
time we have Goyder's statement that Buchanan urged him to make himself acquainted with Pestalozzi's system in order that he might be eligible for
the headship of a new Infants' School to be opened at Bristol. *Infra*, p. 243.

    Of the Pestalozzian literature in England at the time we find *The
Mother's Book*, "exemplifying Pestalozzi's plan of awakening the under-
standing of children in Language, Drawing, Geometry, Geography and
Nature," *Pestalozzi's Intellectual or Intuitive Arithmetic*—both by P. H,

Wilderspin's success was due not so much to any profound educational insight as to his genuine **High Educational Ideals.** sympathy with children, his flashes of intuition, and his considerable organising ability. Above all he had faith in his work and was essentially an opportunist. He speaks of the importance of physical and moral education, of making school work meaningful, and of training children to think : .but in practice he was not averse to much meaningless rote work, to superficiality, and to show. Thus he lays it down as a first principle that infant schools must have regard to the physical development of children, "an inactive and healthy child under six years of age is never seen." Hence a playground is essential: games have to be devised: periods of intellectual work are to alternate with periods devoted to recreation: moreover, care has to be taken not to keep the children in one posture too long. Similarly he realises the importance of making the school bright and cheerful and so adapting instruction as to "amuse" the children. "The first thing (to be) attempted in an infant school is to set the children thinking": teaching is to proceed by means of objects and pictures: pupils are to be led to examine, compare, and express what they see, the inferences they draw, and so on. With regard to moral training he taught that to preach morality without giving children opportunities of practising it was of little use, and that it was better to rule by love than by fear.[1]

Pullen—and his six pamphlets entitled *Hints to Parents*, devoted to various aspects of Method. Pestalozzi's *Letters on Early Education*, written to J. P. Greaves, the Secretary of the London Infant School Society, were published in 1827.

[1] For an account of Wilderspin's teaching see his *Infant Education, The Infant System, Early Discipline, The Education of the Young*.

The spirit is excellent, and at any rate has the merit of **His Practice.** approaching the question of education from the standpoint of the child. But Wilderspin's school fell short of realising these ideals. After making all allowance for the difficulties of embodying ideals in practice, after making every allowance for opportunism to avoid the objections that at the time would have been raised by the parents themselves to a really enlightened system of education, it is difficult to avoid the conclusion that Wilderspin himself was far from understanding the real significance of much that he preached. Nevertheless, he did a great pioneer work and was worthy of the high praise bestowed upon him by his contemporaries. His efforts were greatly handicapped by the ignorance of his disciples, and though the spirit of his teaching was often missing, he succeeded in riveting upon the schools practices the effects of which are still found to-day.

He persistently confused education with instruction. He thought he was laying a basis of sense experience when as a matter of fact the children were mechanically memorising names. He seems to have imagined that if he manipulated a ball frame the children would inevitably build up number concepts, that spacial ideas came from learning the names of geometrical figures especially if they were illustrated from surrounding objects; his oral questioning too often laboured the obvious, or confined itself to facts which the children might or might not know: it was not sufficiently provocative of thought, nor calculated to lead the children to investigate things for themselves. In short, he had not grasped the significance of Pestalozzi's Anschauung. Concreteness he associated with something material, and he never seems to have understood how ideas actually develop.

To face p. 238.

THE PLAYGROUND OF A WILDERSPIN SCHOOL.

LITTLE CHILDREN LOVE ONE ANOTHER

WILDERSPIN'S INFANT SCHOOL.

To face p. 239.

Wilderspin's ideal infant school is shown in the accompanying illustration. It was an oblong

A Wilderspin Infant School.
building 80 ft. by 22 ft., with a classroom 20 ft. by 18 ft. at one end, and was intended to accommodate some 200 children. Seats were placed for the children against the wall. At one end was the master's desk, at the other a large gallery before which was a rostrum. On the floor were a number of lesson posts. Outside was always a playground bordered with flower beds, containing if possible fruit and other trees, and in the centre of the area were several rotatory swings. It was a place for games and physical exercises, a sort of open-air classroom where children might be seen playing together in groups with their bricks. It provided excellent opportunities for the teacher to observe the children in moments of freedom, and of training them to self-restraint and to respect for the property of others.

The school was in charge of a master and a female assistant, preferably his wife. Much attention was given to training children in good personal habits, cleanliness, tidiness, punctuality, etc., and to moral training. Great stress was laid upon information; the "prodigy" element loomed large. The curriculum included reading, writing, arithmetic, geometry, lessons on common objects, geography, singing, and religion, and an effort was made to make the work interesting and "concrete." To this end much importance was attached to object-lessons, to the use of illustration, to questioning and exposition, while the memory was aided by means of didactic verse. A new system of school organisation was devised. Monitors were still employed, but only for the more mechanical parts of the work. The real teaching devolved upon the master and mistress. This was of two kinds : class teaching to a section of the children of approximately equal attainments either on the floor or in the classroom, and collective teaching to the whole school, regardless of age, on the gallery. The gallery was also used for the simultaneous repetition of hymns, didactic verse, etc., in which case it might be conducted by the senior monitor while a number of picked children were being separately instructed in the classroom.

The following was the procedure in a typical lesson in the classroom. A picture would be placed **Specimen Lessons.** in front of the class. The master repeats the passage of Scripture beginning " And Joseph dreamed a dream, and told it to his brethren." Pointing to the picture the following questions might be asked:—*Q.* What is this ? *A.* Joseph's first dream. *Q.* What is a dream ? . . . *Q.* Did you ever dream any-thing ? . . . *Q.* What did you see in your dream ? . . . *Q.* How did you know it was a dream ? . . . *Q.* What did Joseph dream about first ? [1] etc., etc.

A typical geometry lesson by the master to the whole school on the gallery would proceed somewhat as follows :— A large board with geometrical figures is placed before the gallery. The master points to a straight line. " *Q.* What is this ? *A.* A straight line. *Q.* Why did you not call it a crooked line ? . . . *Q.* What are these ? . . . *Q.* What does parallel mean ? . . . *Q.* If any of you children were reading a book that gave an account of some town which had twelve streets, and it said that the streets were parallel, what would you understand ? " etc., etc. Instead of dia-grams a jointed strip of metal—the gonograph—was some-times used. In these lessons the children often answered simultaneously, and though to begin with only the older ones might be able to enter into the work, yet as the same lesson recurred it was argued that the younger children would gradually pick up the necessary ideas.

[1] *Infant Education.*

Number was similarly taught by means of a ball frame. Afterwards the whole gallery would be set· to memorise what had been demonstrated. A monitor would ascend the rostrum and repeat aloud in sing-song fashion, the children repeating after him. Thus—"One and one are two; two and one are three; three and one are four, etc." At other times didactic verses would be learnt :—

> " Sixteen drams are just an ounce
>   When my mother goes to shop ;
> Sixteen ounces make a pound
>   When she buys a mutton chop," etc.

Or again—

> " Two pints will make one quart
>   Of any wine, I'm told :
> Four quarts one gallon are of port
>   Or claret, new or old.
>
> .   .   .   .   .   .
>
> A little wine within
>   Oft cheers the mind that's sad ;
> But too much brandy, rum, or gin,
>   No doubt is very bad," etc.[1]

The alphabet was taught in like manner to the whole school on the gallery, but with it was associated spelling and the maximum of general information. At the same time the children were practised in oral expression. Thus the teacher holds a large card inscribed with letter A, and the lesson proceeds :—

A Gallery Lesson.

" *Q.* Where am I ? *A.* Opposite to us. *Q.* What is on the right side of me ? *A.* A lady. *Q.* What is on the left side of me ? *A.* A chair. . . . *Q.* What do I hold in my hand ? *A.* Letter A for apple. *Q.* Which hand do I hold it with ? . . . *Q.* Spell apple.[2] . . .

---

[1] *The Infant System.*

[2] That only a few can do this does not matter. The rest will learn !

Q. How is an apple produced? . . . *Q.* What part of the tree is in the ground? . . . " and so on, the teacher going over the parts of the trees, discussing blossom, sap, etc.[1]

Geography was similarly taught by reference to a map or globe, after which the information was summarised, as for example by singing the capitals :—

> London is the Capital, the Capital, the Capital,
> London is the Capital, the Capital of England.

To break the monotony of too much of this sort of thing, action songs were sung. These were supposedly good for the physical development of children; they also " let off steam " and were an aid to discipline. Thus, " The Winds " begins with the teacher calling for " a dead calm ": perfect silence ensues. " A breeze," and the children gently rub their hands, " a gale " and slight hissing is added; " a storm " and the feet are used gently; " a hurricane " and all the movements are performed vehemently. In addition, there was a whole series of finger, hand, and arm stretching exercises, animal cries, and animal motions; the prepositions were illustrated by postures, and so on.[2]

When not on the gallery, the children were divided into small classes, each in charge of a little moni-
Lesson in Drafts.
tor who was re-appointed daily. Each child had his own particular seat on the bench round the walls, and each draft was grouped for drill in, say, reading and in object-lessons, round one of the lesson posts. Special boards fitted these. One board might contain the alphabet, another syllables, another an appropriately illustrated reading-sheet, another pictures of animals, or trades, another a series of articles. (Wilderspin had some 34

---

[1] *Infant Education.*

[2] A good account of the inner working of these early infant schools will be found in Chambers, *Infant Education from Two to Six Years of Age.*

pictures of Scriptural history, 60 of natural history, and so on.) Thus the board might contain a piece of hemp, a piece of rope, string, bagging, sacking, canvas, hessian, sheeting, unbleached linen, etc., or it might confine itself to cotton in various forms, different kinds of wood, etc. The monitor in charge of a board or sheet knew it by heart, and drilled his draft until they had memorised it too.[1]

This will suffice to show the working of one of these early infant schools. Their influence on the elementary schools is seen in the gradual introduction of the mixed system of simultaneous and monitorial instruction, with corresponding changes in the planning of the schoolroom ; in the use of object-lessons and pictures ; and in the wider range of reading material.

But the credit for this does not wholly belong to Wilderspin. With the reform movement is inextricably associated the name of David

David Stow.

Stow, than whom no one exerted a more far-reaching influence on the development of primary education during this period. Of the man himself it is sufficient to say that he came from a comfortable middle-class home, was deeply religious and imbued to the full with ideas of social service. His thoughts were turned to a study of education as a result of experience gained in social work in a poor

---

[1] Goyder's school at Meadow Street, Bristol, differed in important respects from Wilderspin's, and is interesting as showing clearly the influence of Robert Owen and Pestalozzi. The organisation was not nearly so highly perfected as in Wilderspin's school. There was no gallery and no classroom. The floor was marked out in lines to facilitate the assembly of the children ; a single row of forms was arranged round the walls ; there were no reading posts, but instead the children were grouped, as in Lancasterian schools, round the sides of the room. " Hardly a letter" was taught to pupils under four years of age, but otherwise there is the same anxiety to impart a great deal of mere information. Picture lessons, marching, action songs, open-air games, and singing occupied an important part of the school day. Arithmetic was taught according to Pestalozzi's method. Reading and spelling

district in Glasgow. His aim was nothing less than the moral elevation of the masses, particularly in large towns. He first devoted himself to Sunday school teaching, then to conducting an evening school; but as the conviction forced itself upon him that it would be easier to prevent error than to eliminate bad habits once they were established, he concentrated his attention in 1827 on infant education. It is with the principles he elaborated rather than with his experiments that we are concerned.

Briefly his position was that schools had exerted less influence than had been expected because they **His Educational Position.** were founded on an erroneous assumption, viz. that morality would result from the mere acquisition of the elements of reading, writing, and arithmetic. The general attitude towards education was fundamentally wrong. It was too commonly imagined to consist in imposing precepts and knowledge on the individual from without; education was confused with instruction; the appeal was to the intellect. But man is not thus made. He is a moral and physical being, a creature of emotion and sentiment, a being in a constant state of development. It was absurd to compare the mind to wet clay ready to be fashioned when all education was essentially a self-education, the beginning and end of which was morality, and the key to which was *doing*. The business of the teacher was to evoke this activity

were taken together. Didactic verse had a recognised place in the curriculum, and every effort was made to make the school work attractive.

> " The hour is come; I will not stay,
> But haste to school without delay ;
> Nor loiter here, for 'tis a crime
> To trifle thus with precious time."

—*Manual of the System of Instruction*, D. G. Goyder, 4th edition, 1825. Goyder organised a number of schools in various parts of the country, and claimed that Stow had adopted his plan without acknowledgment, and to direct it, to arouse worthy motives and to implant ideals.[1] To express the idea Stow invented the term Training, a word peculiarly unfortunate. " Education in the sense in which it is generally understood never has and never can morally elevate a community."[2] What he desired to see established was a " Moral Training System," as he called it, a system that among other things should approximate the school to a true home life, and that should train children to the true principle of giving, for " knowing is not equivalent to doing."[3] " The child that can be induced to part with a penny or half of his bun, or to call on a poor neighbour, will very shortly feel a pleasure in the act, and the *doing* will eventually form a habit, which, coupled with principle, he will carry with him through life."[4]

"Training " implied two things :· understanding and action. " I am only under training when I am caused both to understand and to do the thing specified." The true educational system, he felt, must be based on universal principles applicable throughout life, for education is progressive and never completed. Accordingly he had no sympathy with those who would invent one system for infants, another for children, and another for adults.

Training.

Stow readily acknowledged that his system was eclectic in character.[5] Like Pestalozzi he taught that " it is life that educates," and he condemned the schools of the day on the ground that they were not constructed so as to enable the child to be superintended in real life, viz. in

Importance of Trained Adult Teachers.

[1] *The Training System*, 10th Ed., p. 13.   [2] *Ibid.*, p. 12.
[3] *Ibid.*, pp. 137, 145.   [4] *Ibid.*, p. 145.
[5] See *The Training System*, 1st Ed., 1836, Chap. I. He took as his starting-point the improvement in school organisation effected by Bell, the reform in instruction due to Wood and Pestalozzi, and the advance in

play.[1] "A dirty, dingy, airless schoolroom" might suffice for instructing the head, but some of the best education could only be got out of doors. Accordingly a playground—"the uncovered schoolroom" as he called it—was a necessity. Monitors, too, were all very well for carrying out the mechanical details of the school—giving out pens, arranging desks, hearing spellings—but they were useless as teachers, for the very essence of education, according to Stow, consisted in the interaction of a cultivated on an uncultivated mind, in "awakening thought, stimulating and directing inquiry, and evolving the energies of intellect." Accordingly, great stress was laid upon oral class teaching on the ground that it was provocative of thought, and the teaching could be adapted to the needs of the particular circumstances. For this to be effected the number of children that could be committed to the care of a single teacher was strictly limited, and it was desirable that they should be of approximately equal ability.

Stow also laid much emphasis on what he called the "sympathy of numbers," that is to say, upon those subtle influences of suggestion and imitation that play such a large part in corporate life, in raising the standard of individual endeavour, and in evoking a healthy public opinion.

Sympathy of Numbers.

This demanded a new method of school organisation, and a system of "graded schools" grew up at Glasgow and elsewhere. Each of these "schools" was in fact one large class pursuing the same studies and receiving the same lessons under an adult teacher, the whole being controlled by an organising head master. The infant (or initiatory) school, for children

Organisation.

infant training effected by Wilderspin, especially on its physical side. What he claimed as original was his attention to moral training as the chief end of all school instruction.

[1] *Ibid.*, 10th Ed., p. 6.

of from two to six years of age, was to contain not more than 140 children in charge of a master and mistress. In the junior school, for children between the ages of six and twelve, one master might take charge of eighty pupils; should the school contain more than this number an assistant was required, another was needed if the number exceeded 120, and so on. Monitors were still used for the routine work. The objection to this method of organisation was the expense it entailed and the difficulties it presented in sparsely populated districts, for it was obviously impossible to educate simultaneously a group of children varying from six to thirteen years of age. This, however, was commonly attempted, and led to the grossest absurdities. On a large gallery the whole junior school would be gathered to be instructed at the same time and in the same subject.

In emphasising the oral lesson Stow sought to abolish all meaningless repetition. Nothing was to **Picturing Out.** be memorised unless it was first understood. Moreover, in treating a subject the correct order was to begin with what was significant and immediately connected with the experience of the pupils—to sketch out the broad outlines first and leave the detail to be filled in gradually. This was often misunderstood to mean teaching summaries first and then expanding them. In these oral lessons much emphasis was laid on questioning—individual and simultaneous—and in " picturing out in words." By this he meant making clear an idea to the pupil by description, aided by analogy, familiar illustration, gesture and questioning, much use being made of ellipses and any device that suggested itself at the moment. The following is a typical example :—

" As the hart panteth after the water brooks, so panteth my soul after thee, O God."—Psalm xlii. 1.

(In this stage of training, the children are supposed to have acquired a considerable amount of Scriptural knowledge.)

POINTS TO BE PICTURED OUT.

TRAINER : The Bible is full of imagery and emblems drawn from nature and the arts of life. The verse you have now read is of that description, and is full of . . . *natural imagery.*

I must tell you, children, before we commence our lesson, that it is supposed this Psalm was written by David, who was obliged to flee from his enemies, to the land of Jordan, and that, when there, he probably took up his abode in the mountains, away from the public worship of God's . . . *house*, and seeing the harts running . . . *about the mountains*, and panting for thirst, most likely induced him to use the . . . . What metaphor or emblem did he use? Look at your books, if you please. David says, " As the hart panteth after the . . . *water brooks* " (read on) " *so panteth my soul after thee, O God.*"

The first thing we must speak about in this picture is . . . *the hart.* What is a hart? Can you tell me any other names given to the hart? *Stag—deer—gazelle.* Very right ; these are the names given to . . . *this animal*, or . . . *species.*[1]

Between Stow's practice and that of Wilderspin there were many points in common, and also much of difference that it is unnecessary to elaborate further. But while Wilderspin is best known in connection with infant education, Stow's influence was probably greatest on primary schools. By his statement and elaboration of the thesis that education presupposes the interaction of mind upon mind, the cultivated upon the relatively uncultivated, he made a contribution of permanent value to the educational thought and practice of his time. Too little value had been attached to the living voice in elementary education, and too much to the printed page. Stow aimed at setting this right, but the result, as will be seen in the sequel, was that teachers went to the other extreme, and schooling became talking. Even in Stow's own practice the pupil was

[1] *The Training System*, 10th Ed., p. 382.

too much within a strait-jacket; the teacher's thought was dominant, and the pupil was not left sufficiently alone. The *doing* that was talked of was very one-sided. It was confined to oral work. The teacher never created the circumstances, and left the boy to "muddle through." There was nothing to evoke the need of the various manual activities, and nothing that called for observation and experiment. But this does not detract from the fact that Stow was a light to his generation by his emphasis on studying the pupils, by his call for concrete teaching, for training children in oral expression, by getting his pupils to practise morality, by his use of phonic methods in reading, and above all by his demand for trained adult teachers, and for a new system of school organisation as the only way of making the school an effective instrument of moral education.

The effect of these reforms on the average school was, however, small until 1840. The monitorial school, where it had not degenerated, remained much as it had been thirty years before.

CHAPTER VIII.

TRANSITION AND REACTION.

"Education will cause every latent seed of the mind to germinate and spring up into useful life which otherwise might have been buried in ignorance and died in the corruption of its own nature. . . . The ignorant man can never be truly happy."
—LOVETT AND COLLINS : *Chartism*, pp. 75-6.

The present chapter is concerned with the history of school practice between the date of the first

General Summary.

Parliamentary grant and the coming of the School Boards. The limits are arbitrary, but convenient. The period falls into two parts, before 1862 and after. Between 1833 and 1862 the reforms in organisation, staffing, curriculum, and method that had appeared during the two previous decades slowly made their way into general practice. These years present a picture of extraordinary diversity between schools. Some were good, others were poor, but it is doubtful whether such a thing as an "average school" can properly be said to have existed. With improvements in staffing came a widening of the curriculum of individual schools, and the signs are not wanting of a movement in favour of introducing manual activities as a necessary part of school education. This liberal development was checked, however, by the system of payment by results, avowedly designed to secure a higher average efficiency. Hitherto the Committee of Council had aimed at stimulating and encouraging teachers to work out their own salvation. This policy was now replaced by one that exalted machinery, that took no thought of anything but results, and left methods and general conditions to take care of themselves. The outcome of this was the reaction that is seen after 1862. There was a checking of growth due to the loss of freedom, an establishing of wrong standards, and a discouragement of initiative. If a higher standard of accuracy was set up in the schools, it was at the cost of an enormous waste of time and of educational opportunity through a mistaken concentration on the 3 R's.

During the past fifty years the facilities for obtaining education—deficient as they were—had increased enormously, and with them the number of those who had been instructed in reading and writing. Education had at last identified itself with public opinion; it was felt to be needful for the advancement of every physical, intellectual, and moral good, but this had been accomplished at the price of disillusionment, and with it came a storm of criticism against the very agencies that had contributed most to the change. Some charged them with manufacturing economic misfits, with stuffing the mind and confusing instruction with education. Others denounced them as illiberal and anti-social, as middle-class schemes designed for maintaining the social *status quo*. Many of the day and Sunday schools did not hesitate to call themselves educational charities, and to a section of public opinion a charity school was anathema.

Dissatisfaction with existing Education.

" Knowledge she gives, enough to make them know
How abject is their state, how deep their woe ;
The worth of freedom strongly she explains,
While she bows down, and loads their necks with chains.

Faith, too, she plants, for her own ends imprest,
To make them bear the worst, and hope the best;
And, while she teaches on vile int'rest's plan,
As laws of God, the wild decrees of man,
Like Pharisees, of whom the scriptures tell,
She makes them ten times more the sons of hell." [1]

All this is very healthy and marks the beginning of a
new epoch in popular education. Men were beginning to
realise that the monitorial plan of which so much had
been hoped had merely tinkered with the subject. It
had accepted the ideal of popular education as it existed
in the eighteenth century, and had confined its attention
to improving its technique. The inculcation of religious
truth according to the capacities of the children was still
the main function of the elementary schools. Committees
still believed in the children treasuring up the materials
of religion in their memories, for " though at present they
may perhaps enter very little into the sense of them, yet,
as their understanding ripens with time, and their appetite
for knowledge increases, it will be no small advantage that
they have the words and sentences of heavenly wisdom
ready stored up for use; and that during the active and
busy scenes of life they may be able to put these good
resolutions and maxims into practice." [2]

Not until 1839 did the British and Foreign School
Society see the necessity of abrogating the
Examples of Monitorial Practice. rule which bound its schools to use no other
reading lesson book than the Bible, a rule
that provided an excuse for excluding any
book of general literary or scientific information. The
National Schools were in no better position, and what
changes were made were principally confined to " im-

[1] See *Quarterly Journal of Education*, Vol. 10, p. 324.
[2] *Report on the National Sunday School at Stockport*, 1816-17.

proving" the Scriptural instruction. Arithmetic took a Scriptural cast, and the result was such curiosities as the following :—

"Mesha, King of Moab, was a sheep-master and rendered unto the King of Israel 100,000 lambs. 2 Kings 3rd and 4th Chap. Write down the number.

"There were seven days between the birth of Jesus and his circumcision, and five days from that event to the Epiphany, the time when the star led the Gentiles to worship the holy child. How long was it from the Nativity to the Epiphany?

"There are twenty-four chapters in the Gospel of St. Luke and twenty-eight chapters in the book of the Acts of the Apostles. What difference is there in the two?

"At the marriage in Cana in Galilee there were six waterpots of stone, holding two or three firkins a-piece. If they held two firkins how much water would it take to fill them? and how much if they held three each?

"Our Lord showed himself to the Apostles forty days after his passion. For how many weeks was he seen?"[1]

In 1825 sets of geography and grammar lessons were first issued for British schools. A similar Biblical tone characterised much of the geographical instruction, as witness the following model treatment that was adhered to for over a quarter of a century. The lesson is on the Holy Land and Tyre is the subject of discussion.

"*M.* (reading from a book) : What occasioned its (Tyre's) erection on an island? *P.* Its being attacked by Nebuchadnezzar. *M.* In what tribe was it included? *P.* Asshur. . . . . *M.* Was the second Tyre ever taken? . . . . *M.* Cite a passage of Scripture relating to the event ; etc., etc."[2]

---

[1] *Elementary Arithmetic*, by Rev. J. C. Wigram ; see *Central Society of Education*, Second Publication, p. 358.

[2] *British and Foreign School Society Manual.*

For further examples of the Scriptural method of teaching geography the reader is referred to Mrs. Sherwood's *Geography*, where each topic is accompanied by an appropriate Biblical text.

Equally absurd was the practice of combining Scriptural references with the letters of the alphabet, that held in many infant schools :—

A—is an angel, who praises the Lord ;
B—is for Bible, God's most holy word ;
C—is for Church, where the righteous resort ;
D—is for devil,—D is for devil,—D is for devil who wishes our hurt.

Or again, introducing sacred geography :—

G—is for Goshen, a rich and good land ;
H—is for Horeb, where Moses did stand.

There were, of course, good schools conducted on more liberal lines, as may be gathered from the list of reading-books used in the British School at Lancaster, 1827 :—1st class, Blair's Class Book ; 2nd, History of Greece ; 3rd, History of Rome ; 4th, History of England ; 5th, Dublin Reading Book ; 6th, Esop's Fables ; 7th, Selden's History of the Bible ; 8th, The Bible ; 9th, Testament. In 1837 the Report of the British school at Harp Alley, City of London, records that "about 130 boys have visited the Zoological Gardens ; 30 the British Museum ; and about 20 attended Mr. Adam's Lent lecture on Astronomy . . . 30 to 40 subscribe one penny per month to the school library."[1] The school fees were 2d. a week. Contemporary observers are unanimous as to the useful work that was being done at the central school of the Society under Mr. Crossley in face of great difficulties. Drawing on paper and round the walls was introduced in 1836, the children practised vocal music, and much attention was given to mental arithmetic, questions like the following being answered immediately :—

" Square of 96 ? 17 oz. of tea at 15s. per pound ? Cube of 65 ? Interest of £47 at 5 per cent. for 9 days ? Square root of 9658 ?

---

[1] See *The Educational Record*, Vol. XVIII., p. 204.

Scraps of history, geography, geometry, natural history, and natural philosophy were taught by tacking them on to spelling lessons and by making the Scriptures the vehicle of all sorts of extraneous information. But the instruction was largely words. No apparatus was provided, pictorial illustrations were at a discount, and no attempt was made to base instruction on things. Physical education was completely ignored, and drawing was entirely from copies. It is noteworthy that in a number of schools small libraries existed, and it was to these that intelligent masters looked to supplement the trite Scriptural reading.[1]

Writers at this period are unanimous in their condemnation of the attitude of the average **Unsatisfactory** school committee towards education. "We **Condition of** have been brought into contact with many **Monitorial** **Schools.** British School Committees," writes a well-informed contributor to the *Education Magazine,* "and although we never yet found one where there were not some of its members desirous of extending education without limitation, we never found one in which the great majority were not either opposed to it, or so indifferent as to make no exertions to introduce more comprehensive methods. The masters of the schools, however ardent they may be when they commence their work, are soon chilled by this opposition and indifference. . . . It is thought if a man attends much to secular instruction he must neglect that of a higher kind, and he is looked upon with extreme suspicion; and should anything go wrong with the school it is attributed to this cause. This remark applies not to all schools in the system : there are some, although the number is extremely limited, where no shackles, either directly or indirectly, are placed upon the spread of intelligence, and where every facility is given to

[1] *Central Society,* First Publication, p. 172.

the master to carry out his views ; but this number bears no proportion to that in which knowledge is painfully restricted."[1]

Girls' schools were in a much worse condition than boys' schools, and a greater degree of fear and jealousy was manifested in them. " In many schools writing on paper is confined to half a dozen or so of the principal monitors, in others it is not permitted at all; and in arithmetic, they are nearly all most lamentably and miserably deficient. We find in a few schools the dry rigid rules of grammar attempted, and the barren definitions of geography; but the children rarely enter into the spirit of what they are about for want of the required books, maps, etc."[2] Sewing was continued practically unchanged, and some of the girls were trained in domestic duties.

Unsatisfactory as the average British school was, the National schools were in no better condition, and many were a good deal worse. In the late thirties some of these institutions were too poor to afford anything beyond a few reading-books. In the majority reading, writing, arithmetic, with sewing for girls were taught. Half the day was given to religious teaching.[3] In a few schools a little geography was permitted, but even at the central school at Westminster this represented the whole course of instruction. In forming a just estimate of them it is necessary, however, to remember the enormous financial difficulties under which these schools worked. Many of them were set up in an outburst of enthusiasm that quickly died away, and the whole burden of conducting the school over many years fell upon a devoted few, and oftentimes upon a single

The State of National Schools.

---

[1] *Educational Magazine*, 1838, pp. 166-7.   [2] *Ibid.*

[3] Cf. *Central Society*, Second Publication, 1838, pp. 356-8; also Rev. J. C. Wigram's Evidence before the Select Committee, 1834,

individual—the clergyman of the parish. Many of them began with good intentions. £100 a year might be paid to the headmaster and his wife, the latter undertaking to act as schoolmistress. In addition an assistant master would sometimes be appointed. Often enough, however, the Committee soon found itself in difficulties. A cheese-paring policy would be forced upon them, the assistant would be dropped, the supply of apparatus would be cut down, and significant entries like the following appear in the School Minutes : " To consider the subject of school fees paid by the day scholars with a view of increasing them for such as learn writing and accounts." The struggle would continue for years. As the supply of books and pencils was curtailed, and the general efficiency of the school was impaired, numbers dropped, until finally the policy might be resorted to of attempting to throw some of the financial burden on the headmaster. The Minutes record sugges-tions for withdrawing the salary of the master and mistress and giving them instead " the pennies " paid by the scholars.[1]

This is not meant to imply that the majority of British schools were free from financial worries.

British Schools. On the contrary, they too led an existence of constant struggle, so hampered that even with a low fee they could not retain the children long enough to carry them beyond the merest elements. Nevertheless some British schools undoubtedly adopted the policy of catering for a higher class of children, and it is futile to compare the achievements of schools that charged from 4s. to 16s. a quarter with those paying 1d. a week, as was often done perhaps unconsciously in an effort to prove that liberality of outlook was exclusively confined to one class of

[1] Minutes of the National School, Stockport, Feb. 1844.

the community.[1] British schools were fewer in numbers and generally planted with a care that was not always observed in the case of National schools; but that the British and Foreign School Society had in Dunn a secretary more alert than its rival to the educational thought of the time seems to admit of little doubt.[2]

The failure of Place's project of a middle-class secondary school conducted on monitorial lines has already been mentioned. That he anticipated a real need is borne out by the success with which certain British schools in favoured districts gradually approximated their curriculum to a higher elementary type and catered for a superior class of pupils. Some twenty years after Bentham's Chrestomathic scheme was dropped, the question of middle schools was occupying the attention of the National Society on the ground that the lower classes were in many instances receiving a more comprehensive education than the class immediately above them. Defective as the National schools might be, the common day schools were considerably below them in point of discipline, information, and religious instruction.[3] The problem was how to offer to the middle (as distinct from the poorer) classes, on moderate terms, a useful general education based on the religious principles of the Church. The matter was investigated by the Committee of Inquiry and Correspondence, which reported (1838) that they had "reason to believe that a promise of

Middle Schools of the National Society.

---

[1] Cf. *The Educational Record*, Vol. XVIII., p. 203.

[2] For further information the reader is referred to the evidence in the *Journal of Education*, Central Society's Reports, Pillans' writings, Articles in the *Educational Magazine*, the Select Committee's Reports 1834, 1838, and the Reports of the British and Foreign and National Societies. These may be usefully supplemented by a study of the Reports and Minutes of a typical National school.

[3] Cf. *Four Periods of Public Education*, Kay-Shuttleworth, p. 195.

prompt and steady exertion in this department will be welcomed by a large portion of the middle classes, who will find in a connection between the teachers of these schools and the clergy of the Church a better guarantee than they can at present obtain, both for the religious principles and the intellectual attainments of those to whom they entrust their children." The plan suggested, especially for rural districts, was to engraft superior schools on already existing Normal schools, providing there were a master and assistant who were competent to undertake the work. In other cases, and generally in towns, the best course seemed to be to establish commercial schools in connection with the local Diocesan Boards. They were to be conducted by masters duly qualified and under clerical superintendence. The fees of the scholars, it was anticipated, would be adequate to maintain the institutions. Projects for founding schools on these lines were set on foot, and schools were gradually established in London, Canterbury, York, Manchester, Lincoln, and elsewhere. The school at York, for example, was connected with the Training College. It provided accommodation for day boys and boarders and was (1848) arranged in six classes, the lowest class containing some children only 5 to 6 years old. In addition to the three R's mensuration, grammar, Latin, and history were taught. Some of the senior boys attended lectures along with the students in the Training College, while some of the weaker students attended the Middle School. At Manchester the first of four commercial schools contemplated by the "Manchester Church Education Society" was opened in 1846. Its curriculum was much more modern in character, and its object was to supplement the provision offered by the Grammar School. The staff consisted of a headmaster (a clergyman), two assistants, and masters for French, German, and drawing.

In the volume of criticism directed against primary
education at this period, and in the stirring
Schools to Equip for Life. of dry bones, we find the working more or
less consciously of a common sentiment, viz.
that the school must equip for life. No such unanimity
however attended the means of its accomplishment. On
the one hand were those who, impressed with the value of
useful knowledge, sought to widen the curriculum, and
exalted the intellect and the understanding. On the other
hand were men who, with greater or less clearness, looked
to education to develop capacity. The educational creed
of the former was simplicity itself. It dated from the
" bran new days " of politico-economic zeal, when men had
become all at once wise, and when man was regarded as a
curious machine capable of being directed at will. It had
animated the reform party since the beginning of the
century, and its very simplicity gave it a glamour that was
almost irresistible when men seriously turned their attention to the question of popular education. Moreover it is
a view of education that, in spite of every effort to uproot
it, is still very popular in some quarters to-day.

On the Continent a systematic attack on this position
had been made by Pestalozzi. To him is
Pestalozzi's Teaching. due the merit of having firmly gripped the
organic as opposed to the mechanical view
of human development, and having striven consistently to
embody it in the practice of the school. His root principle
was that the impulse to development lies within. In
other words, spontaneity is a principle of mental as much
as of organic growth, and the business of education is to
see that this striving towards self-realisation is aided
rather than checked. But for this the educator must
work in accordance with natural laws, which laws are
discoverable by observation, and furnish the only basis of

an educational method. Moreover, as mental life is one, morality and practical capacity must not be sacrificed in an attempt to exalt intellectual training, but all three must proceed harmoniously together. At the same time it is necessary to remember that the mind does not develop in a vacuum; it must be supplied with the materials for growth, but these to be of any value must be assimilated. In other words, only what is concrete or meaningful has any value in terms of mental development. No one realised more clearly the importance of the social factor in education, or the necessity of bridging the gulf that separates school life from the life of the home. The true school recapitulated the activities of the outside world. It was not a place for merely learning and memorising set lessons, nor was it a means of inuring children to habits of industry through the medium of treadmill occupations. Rather it was the place for doing meaningful work, having due regard to intellectual occupations on the one hand and practical activities on the other, its object being to train the children to lead moral, useful, and complete lives in the sphere in which they might happen to be.[1]

Such a conception of education is much more elusive and far more difficult to realise in practice than the mechanical view already mentioned. Hence it is not surprising that many who were infected with Pestalozzi's zeal for educational reform never caught the spirit of the master, and were content to transplant a practice that very imperfectly embodied the pregnant ideas in which it originated. Consequently Pestalozzian method came to be associated with such reforms as beginning the teaching of

Examples of Pestalozzian Influence.

---

[1] Cf. *The Life and Work of Pestalozzi*, J. A. Green.

arithmetic in contact with objects, laying great stress on
object-lessons to provide children with a basis of sense
impression, emphasising the importance of language training in connection with such lessons, grading all instruction from its logically simplest elements, and in general
with a procedure that had the merits of thoroughness
and simplicity, and was calculated to "train the mind,"
though it appeared at times meaningless and insipid.
Pestalozzi, in fact, commonly stood for a reformed method
of instruction rather than for a new educational ideal, a
method, it is interesting to note, that in 1818 was regarded
as very suitable to the middle classes, though too elaborate
and costly for the ordinary elementary school,[1] but which
twenty years later was looked to as a means of reforming
the whole structure of popular education.

Nor is it altogether surprising that men accustomed to
look beyond the surface of things should
have failed to grasp Pestalozzi's message.

Fellenberg's Influence.

Men like Mr. Wyse, of the Central Society
of Education, who ardently desired to see education
established on a more scientific basis, considered the system
doctrinaire, too much given to the abstract development of
the intellectual and moral man, and as paying far too little
regard to fitting children for the workaday world.[2]   Consequently it is not Pestalozzi so much as Fellenberg that
dominated the educational thought of this country in
the fourth and fifth decades of the nineteenth century.
Pestalozzi was the idealist, the dreamer, whereas Fellenberg was the practical man, the man who embodied what
was best in the social teaching of the former, and showed
how to present it in practical form.   His was an eclectic
system, that believed in the importance of cultivating the

[1] Cf. *A Century of Education*, Binns, p. 86.
[2] *Intellectual Education.*

whole being, moral, physical, and intellectual, that was acutely conscious of the supreme value of manual activities in education and the stimulus that comes from productive work, that regarded the child not as the mere recipient of the ideas of others, but as an agent capable of collecting, originating, and producing ideas from contact with experiences of all kinds. Nevertheless it was a system that had no undue predilection for cultivating the mind to the neglect of positive knowledge and practical application, and that neither regarded the pupil as a machine, moved at the will of the teacher, nor yet left him to wander aimlessly about without guidance; but it sought to establish a series of schools calculated to fit pupils to be intelligent, industrious, and useful members in the particular sphere of life in which they happened to be. Thus one type of curriculum was evolved for well-to-do boys, another for those in moderate circumstances, and another for the poor, but the same principles animated the work of each. On the educative effects of a training on the land Fellenberg set a high value, not only for its physical results, but its disciplinary powers, intellectually and morally. It was throughout a training in contact with things, evoking forethought, handiness, and resourcefulness.[1]

It was in thus reacting against the tyranny of the school-room by pointing out the educative value of all kinds of productive work, by showing how such activities might be connected with ordinary instruction, by indicating a means of adapting the curriculum to the needs of particular classes, that Fellenberg exerted a great influence on his generation. Under his teaching benevolent individuals like William

Industrial Training.

---

[1] *Letters on the Educational Institutions of De Fellenberg, with an Appendix containing Woodbridge's Sketches of Hofwyl*, 1842.

Allen and Lady Byrom at Ealing were stimulated to set up a better type of industrial school; the Irish Commissioners of National Education developed industrial education, "not to teach trades, but to facilitate a perfect learning of them, by explaining the principles upon which they depend, and habituating young persons to expertness in the use of their hands,"[1] and under the guidance of Kay-Shuttleworth and others education in workhouse schools underwent a complete reformation. At the same time the reformed school of industry opened up new possibilities for educating neglected and vagrant children in large cities who were excluded from the ordinary elementary schools, and many ragged schools became definitely vocational in character. The success of such institutions led somewhat later to the establishment of reformatory schools for juvenile criminals.

A further example of the way in which the combined system of school and vocational training had captured the popular imagination is seen in the Chartist programme of education published by Lovett and Collins in 1840, which specially provides for the establishment of industrial and agricultural schools for orphan children up to 12 or 14 years of age. It is laid down that part of the time spent in the agricultural school should be devoted to cultivating the land, while the industrial school should provide for instruction and practice in "such manufactures and occupations as may be combined with it."[2]

It is interesting to note that in the ordinary Chartist day school Lovett will have nothing to do with vocational training. His ideal is a cultivated working class with disciplined, alert and receptive minds, and with every latent faculty developed to the full. Absence of wealth or social

---

[1] *Report of the National Commissioners*, 1837.   [2] *Chartism*, p. 118.

position is to be no bar to educational opportunity. It is the fully developed individual, not the individual trained for this or that sphere, that he has prominently in mind. Accordingly vocational work is put aside, and in its place he provides a laboratory where the pupils may obtain a training in experimental methods, and a workshop in which they may cultivate handiness in the use of tools. In short, Lovett rejects the class system of Fellenberg in favour of the more democratic ideal of Pestalozzi.

With the spread of Pestalozzian practice in this country

The Mayos. two names are especially associated, the Mayos and Kay-Shuttleworth, the one as practical teachers and writers of text-books, the other as an administrator. Dr. Mayo had been at Yverdun in 1819, and on his return to England had conducted, together with his sister, a school on Pestalozzian lines, first at Epsom and later at Cheam. The practice of this school was set out in a series of text-books, the best known and most successful of which was Miss Mayo's *Lessons on Objects*, 1830. Half a century before the author of *Evenings at Home* had remarked that " we daily call a great many things by their names without inquiring into their nature and properties, so that in reality it is only their names and not the things themselves with which we are acquainted." Miss Mayo's book, the first of its kind published in this country, was intended to remedy this defect. It consists of a series of lesson summaries, enumerating such qualities, parts, uses, etc., of the several objects under consideration as may be mainly obtained from a first-hand examination, and setting out such supplementary information as seems likely to interest children. The lesson on Glass proceeds as follows :—

" Glass has been selected as the first substance to be presented to the children, because the qualities which characterise it are quite obvious to the senses. The pupils should be arranged before a blackboard or slate, upon which the result of their observations should be written. The utility of having the lesson presented to the eyes of each child, with the power of thus recalling attention to what has occurred, will very soon be appreciated by the instructor.

The glass should be passed round the party, to be examined by each individual.

Teacher. What is this which I hold in my hand?

Children. A piece of glass.

Teacher. Can you spell the word *glass*? (The teacher then writes the word "glass" upon the slate, which is thus presented to the whole class as the subject of the lesson.) You have all examined this glass; what do you observe? What can you say that it is?

Children. It is bright.

Teacher. (The teacher having written the word "qualities," writes under it—It is bright.) Take it in your hand and *feel* it.

Children. It is cold. (Written on the board under the former quality.)

Teacher. Feel it again and compare it with the piece of sponge that is tied to your slate, and then tell me what you perceive in the glass.

Children. It is smooth—it is hard." Etc.

The influence of the book was very great. Not only did it serve to popularise object teaching in schools, but it set up a recognised procedure in lessons of this type that was adhered to for nearly three-quarters of a century.

The Mayos also exerted a great influence through their connection with the Home and Colonial Infant School Society. From this institution went forth a series of text-books—the best known of which is probably Dr. and Miss Mayo's *Practical Remarks on Infant Education*—and many generations of teachers scattered Pestalozzian practice broadcast. In the model school of the Society the children between 2 and 10 years of age

The Home and Colonial Infant School Society.

were divided into four divisions. Great attention was given to inculcating religious and moral ideas, to exercises involving sensory discrimination—colour, form, size, weight, sound, etc., to object teaching, to careful training in expression, to singing and so on. Instruction in arithmetic was based on the manipulation of objects, geography began with a study of the school neighbourhood, attention was given to physical education, some provision was made for the constructive activities of children by means of blocks, etc., and drawing was introduced. But in all this there was none of the spontaneity, the freedom, the games, the practical occupations so characteristic of schools of to-day. Orderliness was a fetish, everything was in steps, the near and remote were ideas carried out to the bitter end. So concerned was the school to see that ideas were properly built up, that the whole procedure was artificial and mechanical. Story-telling, it is true, was introduced in connection with the Scripture lesson, and simple poetry was not excluded, but the treatment was too didactic; there was a failure to recognise the educative value of well-told stories. Nevertheless the general influence was good in emphasising the need for system and for objective teaching at a time when school organisation and instruction were often chaotic, entirely divorced from principles of any sort, and when the teaching consisted mainly of words.

Kay-Shuttleworth's influence was of a different kind. As first secretary to the Committee of **The Need for a New Method of School Organisation.** Council he had opportunities and difficulties of no usual order. The popularity of the method of mutual instruction was a thing of the past. What it resolved itself into in the ordinary National school is well described by an inspector at the time.

"I have often witnessed with pain the attempts of a master
. . . to leave some impression of his knowledge upon the minds of
the children ; to exercise, in short, some of those functions of an.
instructor for which he has been carefully prepared. Standing
surrounded by his school, perhaps of 150 children, divided into ten
classes, with as many teachers, and as many different subjects of
instruction all going on at once, and each at such a pitch of the
voice as to be audible above the surrounding tumult—a tumult
which has a perpetual tendency to rise to a hubbub, because every
boy, speaking only just loud enough to make himself heard, any
accident which raises the voice of one must be followed by the
elevation of the voices of all the rest,—I have seen an excellent,
accomplished and painstaking teacher make the attempt under such
circumstances to give a lesson to the first class in his school—say a
lesson in geography. With the map before him, and the class
grouped around, he collects his thoughts and endeavours so to
arrange them as to give to the knowledge he desires to impart
the easiest access to the minds of the children—to enlist their
interest and command their attention. But with this effort he is
making another—he is labouring to subdue the excitement which
has been awakened in his mind by noise and disorder, which he
perceives to have been gradually increasing from the moment that.
his attention has been diverted from a general supervision of the
school, and his eye taken off it. It is obvious that the schoolroom
has become to him one vast sensorium—that his feelers are thrown
out over the whole surface of it, and his sensibilities awakened
everywhere to the quick.

Sometimes he pauses in his discourse and listens ; the perspiration
begins to appear on his forehead, and a blow with his cane upon the
map indicates the state of his feelings, and for a few seconds allays
the tumult. At last, when it is too much to be borne, he darts
perhaps from behind the map, recovers with his actual presence
and the formidable suggestions of his cane his ascendency in the
school, and gives up his task." [1]

A whole new system of school organisation and method
was urgently needed, a new race of teachers needed to be
called into being, a better type of teaching apparatus was

[1] Mr. Moseley's Report on the Midland District, *Minutes of the Committee of Council*, Vol. I., 1845, pp. 246-7.

necessary, and a new standard of elementary education set up, and all this with the strictest regard to economy.

Kay-Shuttleworth was no mere official. He was a man with profound faith in education, who for **Kay-Shuttleworth's Influence.** a number of years had made a special study of the social aspects of the subject. He had gained much first-hand experience of the problems involved during his apprenticeship as an Assistant Poor Law Commissioner, and to this knowledge he added a first-hand acquaintance with the teaching of Pestalozzi and Fellenberg and the educational systems of Western Europe. For ten years, until compelled through ill-health to retire from public life, he applied himself unstintingly to the reform of elementary education along the lines laid down by the two Swiss educators. Though compelled by circumstances to be an opportunist he inaugurated a number of far-reaching reforms. Elementary teaching became a profession, the method of mutual instruction was replaced by the modern class system, and a type of Pestalozzian practice was imposed upon schools and retained almost undisputed possession for half a century.

Among the services rendered by Kay-Shuttleworth was the drawing up of instructions on method **His View of the Educative Process.** in the form of Minutes. Unfortunately he started from the false psychological position of imagining that the earliest mental activity of a child is synthetic, and that analysis only comes later. Or, to use his own words: "In observing the process which nature pursues in developing the intelligence, we use the senses of the infant first in activity : they are employed in collecting facts; the mind then gradually puts forth its power, it compares, combines, and at length analyses the facts presented to it. Thus the child raises his attention above material objects. But whatever may be the differences which mark these successive periods of intellectual progress, the method of education which suits them is always the same. From the most elementary knowledge to the highest speculations one method is universally applicable. This consists, first, in carefully examining the constituent parts of any object before us, *i.e.* in *analysing it*; secondly, in classifying and separately considering these component parts. All this is the work of the teacher in elementary schools; thirdly, in reconstructing the object which has thus been decomposed by the analysis of the educator, *i.e.* in operating by synthesis. This is the work of the pupil, by which he is prepared for the more difficult work of analysis. When his mental powers are exercised in this way the attention is actively engaged." [1]

In other words, the correct method of instruction is for the teacher first to take the knowledge which is to be imparted to the scholar, decompose it into its mechanically simplest elements, classify these, and then present them in order of apparent simplicity. In writing this consists of beginning with straight strokes, then pothooks, then simple combinations, and so on. To carry out these ideas a series of manuals were produced and published under the sanction of the Committee of Council,—reading-books on a phonic method, a manual of writing on Mulhaüser's method, and another on singing adapted from Wilhem's Method by Hullah. Moreover, on the principle that in order that the scholar may be taught it is necessary first to teach the teacher, special classes were arranged on the new methods at Exeter Hall.

Committee of Council Manuals for Teachers.

[1] *Minutes of the Committee of Council,* 1840-1, p. 42.

One of the first acts of the Committee of Council was to assert control over the planning of new schools by requiring as a condition of grant that plans, specifications, etc , should be submitted for approval. At the same time Kay-Shuttleworth availed himself of the opportunity to advocate a new scheme of school organisation, that was calculated to replace the system of mutual instruction by the modern class method. No one was more conscious of the defects of the monitorial system, or more alive to the truth of Stow's teaching, that education depends for its success upon the stimulus and personality of the cultivated teacher.

School organisation was, in fact, passing through a critical period. The shackles of the old monitorial systems remained to hamper the **A New Plan of School Organisation.** development of a new spirit. Bell and Lancaster had made no provision for an enlightened instructor in the school. The master was essentially a disciplinarian, a man of order and authority. The system was not based on contact of the mind of the master with the minds of the children;[1] but with the rise of other conceptions of education alert masters had tended more and more to enter into the actual work of teaching. In other words, a new system of school organisation was needed to meet the changing view of the educative process. There is little doubt that Kay-Shuttleworth's ideal would have been a trained adult teacher for every forty children;[2] but at a time when elementary teaching as a profession had not yet come into being, and when the strictest economy was imperative, any such plan was altogether outside practical politics. His actual proposals can only be regarded as tentative and as making the best of circumstances.

[1] See *ante*, p. 226.   [2] *Public Education*, p. 132.

Every school he considered should have its children divided into at least four grades, according to their individual attainment, and it is the business of the teacher to see that he comes into personal contact with every group of children for some part of every day. In a small school this is a relatively simple matter. The school is provided with a gallery on which are placed desks to accommodate the whole of the children. These are divided into four groups. One or two of these come down on to the floor for oral instruction, while the others are engaged in some kind of silent work, and for certain lessons the whole school is taken together.

But when the numbers increase above a certain amount assistance is required, and the so-called *mixed method* of management becomes necessary. This consists in employing pupil-teachers, or in the case of large schools one or two assistant teachers as well. Kay-Shuttleworth frankly describes it as a device entirely determined by considerations of economy. The pupil teacher is generally an old scholar from fourteen to seventeen years of age. At the close of his apprenticeship he should further qualify in a training college, and then serve for some years as an assistant before becoming a master. Such a plan would have the merit, however, of recruiting a body of expert professional teachers. Monitors were to be altogether superseded as teaching agents.[1]

In adopting this method of simultaneous instruction classrooms provided with galleries were strongly recommended to give the necessary isolation and quiet. It was

---

[1] *Minutes of the Committee of Council*, 1839-40, p. 52. *Note.*—The essence of the pupil-teacher system was devised by Kay-Shuttleworth as an Assistant Poor Law Commissioner before his visit to Holland. What he saw there only "confirmed" his "conviction of their value." See *Four Periods of Public Education*, pp. 287-9.

proposed that each classroom should be shared by two classes, separated from one another by a partition, and that the teaching should be divided between an adult and a pupil teacher. In order to promote such a method of organisation, and at the same time to assist managers, plans for schools of different sizes were issued (1840), showing the arrangement necessary in order to carry out each of the three systems, Madras, Lancasterian, and mixed. It must be remembered that all this was proposed six years before the establishment of the pupil-teacher system, and the drawback to it was of course the large demands it made upon staffing.

A few years later an alternative method of organisation was put forward with the approval of the Committee of Council.[1] It divided the children into three grades, and provided for each being personally instructed by the master once each session. The subjects of instruction were divided into (1) subjects of oral instruction, (2) reading, (3) silent occupations. For the first, silence was regarded as essential, and accordingly they should be taken in a classroom provided with a gallery. For silent work parallel desks were arranged on the floor, and an open area was reserved for reading, which might be taken in drafts. The master was to be assisted by two pupil teachers, and monitors might also be used to supplement these. This system, it is to be noted, was specially favoured by British schools.

The Tripartite Scheme of School Organisation.

The accompanying plan illustrates the conditions at the Borough Road in 1856. The room accommodated nine classes of 45 each, and was divided into three parts by curtains, which are represented by dotted lines, and which were dropped while lessons were in progress. Lessons lasted

[1] By Mr. Moseley. See *Minutes*, Vol. I., 1845, pp. 250-2.

for three-quarters of an hour, and the pupils might be arranged at a given moment as follows: gallery—English history; desks—written arithmetic; drafts on the floor—Scripture reading. At the change of lesson each set of three classes, e.g. 1, 2, 3, would interchange places.

There is no need to enter into a discussion of the merits and defects of these plans. They are interesting as attempts to give something like system to the increasing tendency to introduce more and more collective teaching into the work of the schools. As the reports of inspectors show, school organisation at this period varied widely in character, and examples of a purely monitorial or a purely simultaneous type were practically non-existent.

Developments in School Organisation. With the coming of pupil teachers the influence of the two methods of organisation already described became very marked. But, again, they are not reproduced true to type. There is a peculiar blending of old and new. National schools are found retaining some of the forms and three-sided squares of the original Madras model alongside rows of parallel desks and a gallery. The spirit and the details of Kay-Shuttleworth's original proposals were alike violated. Large schools were often conducted solely with the assistance of pupil teachers, and curtains stretched across a large schoolroom took the place of the partitions and classrooms he considered so essential. Along these lines school organisation evolved, but without any considerable modification until the coming of School Boards after 1870.

Improvements in Apparatus. At the same time that these developments were in progress attention was being given to improving the teaching apparatus, which was sadly deficient in many schools. First came a grant for school furniture, including desks, blackboards,

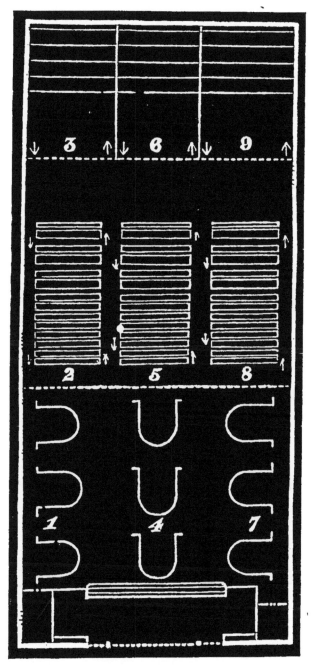

THE BOROUGH ROAD SCHOOL, ARRANGED ON THE
TRIPARTITE SYSTEM.

To face p. 274.

and easels, and in 1847 a further grant was made for the purchase of maps, books, etc., for not only was reading material generally very scanty, but, such as it was, it was oftentimes confined to Scriptural reading. Of the desks it is unnecessary to say more than that they differed little from those in the original Lancasterian schools, and the seats were never provided with backs. These grants ceased in 1862, on the introduction of the system of payment by results.

Until the issue of the "Revised Code" (1862) the central authority exerted no direct control **The School Curriculum.** over the school curriculum. Any changes that were made depended entirely upon the initiative of the master or the school managers, or were due to the stimulus of a Government inspector, who, like Matthew Arnold, looked to the schools to inspire some elements of culture into their pupils, to open their minds and to touch their imagination. What the curriculum of the "average" school was during this period is difficult to determine. According to the Census Returns (1851) the great majority of elementary schools, both public and private, taught nothing beyond the three R's. A considerable number included grammar and geography, and a diminishing number taught singing, drawing, mathematics, and industrial occupations; a condition of things that accords very well with the reports of inspectors.[1] History, etymology, lessons on common things, and physical exercises also found a place in some schools, the latter in particular becoming increasingly popular. In 1847 grants were made towards the cost of hiring field-gardens, erecting workshops for the teaching of handi-

[1] It is very noticeable how a gradual extension of these "higher subjects" followed the improvements in school organisation after 1846. See *Minutes*, 1850-1, Vol. I., p. ciii; 1851-2, Vol. I., p. 143.

crafts, and providing school wash-houses and kitchens.
Between 1850 and 1860 gardening and domestic subjects
received considerable attention.[1] Thus an inspector reports
in 1856 : "It is very doubtful whether the usual practice
of keeping boys at their lessons in school from five
to six hours a day is the best. My impression is that
four hours' schooling, with two hours' industrial work,
and home lessons at night, would be a much better
arrangement."[2]

The fact is that during this period schools showed wide
differences of quality. Many of the better-
class schools undoubtedly had a liberal
curriculum, and, as Matthew Arnold tells
us, were attended by a type of children
whose parents had every right to expect a generous
education. In 1854 another inspector reported that a
boy of fair average attainments in a good school has
learned—

Education in
State-aided
schools

"To read fluently and with intelligence any work of general
information likely to come in his way ;

To write very neatly and correctly from dictation and from
memory, and to express himself in tolerably correct language ;

To work elementary rules of arithmetic, including decimal and
vulgar fractions, duodecimals, and interest, with accuracy and
rapidity ;

To parse sentences and to explain their construction ;

To know the elements of English history ;

To have a satisfactory knowledge of geography, physical and
political, and to draw maps well."[3]

---

[1] In 1854 Froebel's system was first introduced into infant schools. See
Mitchell's Reports—*Minutes*, 1854-5, pp. 473-4, and 1856-7, p. 340.

As a further indication of the level of educational thought during this
period see Tate's *Philosophy of Education*. Cf. also the volumes of
Pleasant Pages, following Pestalozzian method.

[2] *Minutes*, 1856-7, p. 264.

[3] *Minutes*, 1854-5, pp. 393-4; cf. *ibid.*, 1857, p. 253.

Besides this a good school would include lessons on physical science, natural history, and political economy. Natural philosophy, it is worth noting, was a subject especially recommended by Matthew Arnold for general adoption in schools.

Classing schools as excellent, good, fair, bad, the attainment of a fair school, representing 80 per cent. of those under inspection, was thus described in 1854 :—

"In the first class the children will be able to read a page of natural history—about an elephant, a cotton tree or a crocodile—with tolerable fluency and with scarcely a mistake. They would answer collateral questions on this, not well, but not preposterously ill ; they would have a general knowledge of the distribution and conventional divisions of land and water on the surface of the globe ; most of them would name the counties on an unlettered map of England, and the kingdoms on one of Europe. They would work a sum in compound addition—two-thirds of them without a mistake ; they would write out a short account of any object named to them which they had seen or read about—an animal, a tree, a flower—intelligently, and not without thought and observation, but with trifling errors of grammar and of spelling. In such a school the remaining four or five classes would show attainments proportionably graduated from that which I have represented as usually belonging to the first. With respect to acquirement, boys are ordinarily a little in advance of girls, because they have more time for it. The girls compensate by a somewhat livelier intelligence, by prettier reading, by better discipline and by needlework, on which two-fifths of their time are spent." [1]

while a "bad" school, said to be typical of many country schools in 1854, was described as follows :—

"Their only books are a few torn Testaments which they learnt to read with precisely the same amount of intelligence as if they were attempting to read the Greek language in English character. They have no more idea whether Jerusalem was in Palestine or

---

[1] *Minutes*, 1854-5, p. 500,

Palestine in Jerusalem than they have of the outside of the moon ; or whether the event from which all Christian time is reckoned occurred before or after the Battle of Waterloo. Very few indeed of them can work the humblest multiplication sum correctly. Their writing, if legible, is rendered unintelligible by the spelling. While their minds are thus left utterly uncultivated, their morals can be deriving no advantage from their communion with each other about their street experience. They are perpetually engaged in eluding and cheating the master." [1]

Inspectors' Reports leave no room for doubt that throughout this period one of the gravest defects of the schools was the systematic neglect of the younger children to enable the master to give all his attention to the upper division, with disastrous results on the attendance. Moreover opinion gained ground that much of the work being done in elementary schools was superficial and would not stand close scrutiny. Evidence of this was afforded in plenty by the Newcastle Commission, and the system of awarding grants on individual examination in the three R's was recommended as the only way of guaranteeing thoroughness in the school work, a recommendation that was carried out by the Revised Code.

A new era now began for the elementary school. Reading, writing, and arithmetic were divided in
Progress
under the
Revised Code.
six stages or standards, and immediately attained an exaggerated importance, for these rudimentary subjects, along with plain needlework for girls, were compulsory, and the bulk of the grant that could be earned depended upon the success with which each child could pass an annual examination in them. As will be seen from the following syllabus the standards were not high.

[1] *Minutes*, 1854-5, p. 502.

SYLLABUS.

	READING.	WRITING.	ARITHMETIC.
Standard I.	Narrative in monosyllables.	Form on blackboard or slate, from dictation, letters, capital and small, manuscript.	Form on blackboard or slate, from dictation, figures up to 20. Name at sight figures up to 20. Add and subtract figures up to 10, orally, from examples on blackboard.
Standard II.	One of the narratives next in order after monosyllables in an elementary reading-book used in the school.	Copy in manuscript character a line of print.	A sum in simple addition or subtraction and the multiplication table.
Standard III.	A short paragraph from an elementary reading - book used in the school.	A sentence from the same paragraph slowly read once and then dictated in single words.	A sum in any simple rule as far as short division (inclusive).
Standard IV.	A short paragraph from a more advanced reading - book used in the school.	A sentence slowly dictated once by a few words at a time, from the same book but not from the paragraph read.	A sum in compound rules (money).

	READING.	WRITING.	ARITHMETIC.
Standard V.	A few lines of poetry from a reading-book used in the first class of the school.	A sentence slowly dictated once by a few words at a time, from a reading - book used in the first class of the school.	A sum in compound rules (common weights and measures).
Standard VI.	A short ordinary paragraph in a newspaper or other modern narrative.	Another short ordinary paragraph in a newspaper or other modern narrative, slowly dictated once by a few words at a time.	A sum in Practice or bills of parcels.

Reaction. That some decided steps needed to be taken to raise the average standard of efficiency in elementary schools cannot be disputed, but that it should have taken the form laid down by the Revised Code must always remain as a blot on the administrative policy of the Education Department. It marks the beginning of a process of reaction. The natural evolution of curriculum, organisation, and method that had been going on under the fostering care of Sir J. Kay-Shuttleworth and his successor, Mr. (Lord) Lingen, came to a stop. Enthusiasm for results got anyhow was to replace enthusiasm for education, for improving methods, for alertness to make the school work meaningful. The child became a money-earning unit to be driven; the teacher a sort of foreman whose business it was to keep his gang hard at work. No wonder Sir J. Kay-Shuttleworth was dismayed.[1] A more short-sighted policy could hardly have been devised. It betokened an entire want of imagination and understanding of what was and what was not fundamental. It denied that there was such a thing as a science of education. Initiative on the part of the teacher was not wanted; he was a cog in a machine, and it totally disregarded what in these days is regarded as essential, viz. varying local conditions with their different types of children and varying potentialities. The school in a poor neighbourhood was to reach exactly the same standard as the comfortable school attended by a good class of children. If it did not it was to be penalised. Six cast-iron annual standards were applied to the whole country. The whole arrangement was ridiculously simple, and educational administration was reduced to a mere question of arithmetic. The school became a money-earning institution, and a place for doling out bits of knowledge.

The harshness with which the Code was bound to operate was certainly not intended by those responsible for drafting it. Thus Mr. Lingen, in his Instructions to Inspectors upon the administration of the Revised Code, expressly states that "the grant to be made to each school depends, as it has ever done, upon the school's whole character and work. . . . You will judge every school by the same standard that you have hitherto used, as regards its religious, moral, and intellectual merits. The examination under Art. 48 (*i.e.* in the three R's) does not supersede this judgment, but presupposes it. That article does not prescribe that *if thus much is done, a grant shall be paid,* but, *unless*

---

[1] *Four Periods of Public Education:* Fourth Period,

thus much is done, no grant shall be paid. It does not exclude the inspection of each school by a highly educated public officer, but it fortifies this general test by individual examination. If you keep these distinctions steadily in view you will see how little the scope of your duties is changed."

At the same time, however, the school managers generally threw the responsibility of the new system on the shoulders of the teacher by making his salary depend upon the amount of grant earned. It is little wonder that the real education in the school was reduced to a minimum. Children were kept grinding at the three R's in an endeavour to ensure success in the examination, but to make the grant still more certain they were put into as low standards as possible. In this respect it certainly had the result of strengthening the attention given to the lower part of the school. In a very short time the percentage of apparently backward children was enormous, and successive Codes had to struggle with the difficulty of speeding up the rate of promotion.[1] At the same time it had the effect of narrowing the curriculum to the three "rudimentary" subjects. The Annual Report of 1865 admits that while "the system has secured greater attention to the lower classes and to the less proficient children, and has led to more uniform progress in Reading, Writing, and Arithmetic . . . it has tended, at least temporarily, to discourage attention to the higher branches of elementary instruction—Geography, Grammar, and History."

Results of the Revised Code.

---

[1] In 1863-4 41 per cent. of the number of scholars in average attendance were individually examined ; and 86 per cent. of those over 10 were examined in too low standards. From this time, however, there was a steady improvement. In 1881, with 69·69 per cent. examined, 47·84 per cent. were in standards too low for their age.

According to Matthew Arnold the system of payment by results had one good effect. It stimu-
Matthew Arnold's Account of the System. lated the production of a better and more intelligent type of reading-book, but otherwise school examinations under the system were a fraud, "a game of mechanical contrivance in which the teacher will and must more and more learn how to beat us." Already it was "found possible, by ingenious preparation, to get children through the Revised Code Examination in reading, writing, and ciphering, without their really knowing how to read, write, and cipher." "To take the commonest instance: a book is selected at the beginning of the year for the children of a certain standard; all the year the children read this book over and over again, and no other. When the Inspector comes they are presented to read in this book; they can read their sentence or two fluently enough, but they cannot read any other book fluently. Yet the letter of the law is satisfied. . . . Suppose the Inspector were to produce another book out of his pocket, and to refuse grants for all children who could not read fluently from it. The managers and teacher would appeal to the Code, which says that the scholar shall be required to read 'a paragraph from a reading book used in the school,' and would the Department sustain an Inspector in enforcing such an additional test as that which has been mentioned?

"The circle of the children's reading has thus been narrowed and impoverished all the year for the sake of a *result* at the end of it, and the *result* is an illusion.

"The reading test affords the greatest facilities for baffling those who imposed it, and therefore in reading we find fewest failures, but the writing test is managed almost as easily. . . .

"In arithmetic, the rate of failure is much more considerable. To teach children to bring right two sums out of three without really knowing arithmetic seems hard . . . (a child) is taught the mechanical rule by which sums of this sort are worked, and sedulously practised all the year round in working them; arithmetical principles he is not taught, or introduced into the science of arithmetic."[1]

[1] Report, 1869.

The effect of the Revised Code is well illustrated by the following Time Table analysis, the one taken from the British and Foreign School Society *Handbook*, 1856, the other from *The Elementary School Manager*, Rice-Wiggin and Graves, 1879.

1856.

Time spent on each study per week.	Times.	Hours.
1. Scripture Reading and Scripture Lesson ...	5	3¾
2. Secular Reading — Prose and Poetry	5	3¾
3. Writing	5	3¾
4. Written Arithmetic ...	5	3¾
5. Mental Arithmetic ...	2	1½
6. Map Geography and Map Drawing	4	3
7. Physical Geography ...	1	¾
8. Grammar	2	1½
9. Composition — Oral and Written	2	1½
10. Etymology	1	¾
11. Dictation, Spelling, Drawing, Singing, etc. .	5	3¾
12. English History	1	¾
13. Object Lesson and Manufactures	1	¾
14. Natural History	1	¾
Total school time		30

1879.

Secular Instruction only.

Boys' Schools.		
Reading	6½	hours
Writing (including Transcription, Dictation and Composition)	3½	,,
Arithmetic	7	,,
History (Stds. IV.-VI.)	3	,,
Geography *or* History	3	,,
Singing and Recreation	2	,,
	25	

Girls' Schools.		
Reading	6	hours
Writing, etc.	3	,,
Arithmetic	7	,,
Needlework	4	,,
Grammar *or* Geography *or* History	3	,,
Singing and Recreation	2	,,
	25	

CHAPTER IX.

THE NEW SPIRIT IN EDUCATION.

" New times demand new measures and new men ;
The world advances, and in time outgrows
The laws that in our fathers' day were best;
And, doubtless, after us some purer scheme
Will be shaped out by wiser men than we,
, Made wiser by the steady growth of truth."

—LOWELL.

"The modification going on in the method and curriculum of education is as much a product of the changed social situation, and as much an effort to meet, the needs of the new society that is forming, as are changes in modes of industry and commerce."

—DEWEY : *School and Society.*

It remains to deal with the changes that have taken place in the elementary school, in its ideals, its organisation and staffing since 1870, and to trace the forces that have been instrumental in shaping its method and curriculum in its passage from the warping system of payment by results to the comparative freedom of to-day.

In the preceding chapters it has been seen how the curriculum has constantly adjusted itself to meet new social and economic conditions or to give expression to particular social philosophies. The measure of success attained in any given instance has been proportionate to the intensity of the new faith, to the degree in which the curriculum has met prevailing needs, and to the efficiency of the teachers. Under a system of State education similar influences are at work, but how readily they find expres-

285

sion depends upon the sensitiveness and elasticity of the educational machinery. The increase of foreign competition, the growing specialisation of modern industry, the steady rise in importance of democracy, and the advance in scientific method and hygiene have been responsible for giving to elementary education during the last 40 years, and especially during the last two decades, a character of its own. There has been an increasing tendency to emphasise the social responsibilities of the school, to break down the barriers that have been erected between the life in the school and the life in the home and the outside world, to make school work more practical and less bookish, to develop, in short, handiness and practical capacity. At the same time increasing stress is being laid on putting children in the way of acquiring knowledge for themselves, greater attention is being bestowed on the encouragement of individuality both in children and teachers. Much importance is attached to developing the physical nature of the child, and to training for citizenship and service. The school has developed a new social importance that seems likely to increase rather than diminish. The demands that are being made on the teacher are also steadily increasing. Personality has become a matter of first-rate importance. But it remains to be seen whether, as the teacher abandons the character of policeman, he will attain his rightful position as an educator.

In the development of educational thought and practice during this period the influence of Froebel, Herbart, and Pestalozzi has been very marked. Of contemporary writers Herbert Spencer, John Ruskin, and, of more recent date, Professor John Dewey occupy a foremost place, each having contributed in his own way to interpret in terms of the school the social movements and thought of the time.

Herbert Spencer (1820-1903) is a representative of that

Educational Teaching of Herbert Spencer. scientific and utilitarian movement that in the forties found expression in the secularist schools at Manchester and elsewhere, and in the teaching of George Combe.[1] At an earlier date we meet with it in the writers of the revolutionary period, in the teaching of the Benthamites and in the work of the Society for Diffusing Useful Knowledge.

Biologist, sociologist, psychologist and philosopher, Spencer ranks among English writers on education next to Locke in foreign esteem. In this country his value is felt to lie in the powerful plea he made for a training in scientific method and for the introduction of science into the school curriculum; in arousing men from dogmatic slumber by challenging the accepted values of school studies; in pointing out the haphazard character of existing education—a patchwork based on tradition, and in calling for a system of instruction based on scientific principles. Further, he pleaded for realism in education; he denounced the bookishness of the prevailing system, and urged that the useful is not necessarily non-educative. Rather it is the most educative. "It would be utterly contrary to the beautiful economy of nature," he declares, "if one kind of culture were needed for the gaining of information and another kind were needed as a mental culture." It is to his special credit that he demanded, and got people to believe, that the fullest attention should be paid to matters of hygiene, to the feeding and the physical education of children, of girls no less than of boys.

Lastly, he urged the more rational grading of instruction so that it might harmonise with the mental development of the individual, and pointed out that in the history

---

[1] See *Discussions on Education*, George Combe, p. 154, and Chap. VIII.

of the race might be found many useful suggestions for the teacher's guidance. "Alike in its order and its methods, education must conform to the actual process of mental evolution . . . there is a certain sequence in which the faculties spontaneously develop, and a certain kind of knowledge which each requires during its development . . . it is for us to ascertain the sequence and supply the knowledge." [1] In short, Spencer restated amidst much specious reasoning much of what was best in the educational thought of the last 200 years, and focussed attention once again on the teaching of Bacon and of Pestalozzi.

Spencer's interest in school reform must be attributed to the importance he assigned to education in his philosophical system, for though the laws of evolution are inexorable, yet he leaves a place for human effort and human obligation in helping on the progressive improvement of humanity. Education, he considered, is capable of exerting a determining influence not only on the rising generation, but on mankind in the future. Hence its first-rate importance. It is a matter that concerns the whole of humanity and especially parents and teachers. "The subject which involves all other subjects, and therefore the subject in which education should culminate, is the theory and practice of education."

But a rational system is impossible save on a scientific basis, and the materials for this are as yet **Spencer's Essays.** inadequate. The four short essays, *Education : Intellectual, Moral and Physical* (1861), which in bulk form a very insignificant part of Spencer's writings, are intended as a contribution towards such a system. The treatment is very incomplete and one-sided. In the anxiety to provide a utilitarian education the development of personality tends to be overlooked, and

[1] *Essays*, Chap. II., p. 59, Small Edition.

the use of "science" as an undefined middle term leads
to conclusions that will not always bear analysis. The
influence of the book it is hardly possible to exaggerate.
Among other things it inspired the work of the Code
Reform Association (1881), and the demand for a reform
of the standards and curriculum imposed by the Education Department.[1]

According to Spencer, the end of man is complete living.
Spencer's Five Categories. This being so, knowledge has value in
proportion as it favours more or less the
exercise of those essential activities that
conduce to individual and social happiness. The first need
of man, it seemed to him, is knowledge calculated to assist
the individual to his own self-preservation; the second,
knowledge such as will enable him to gain a livelihood;
third, knowledge of how to bring up a family; fourth, of
how to live the life of the good citizen; and last, the means
for occupying the leisure moments of life. In preparation
for all these, "science," understood in a broad sense, seemed
to be the subject of primary importance, and he proceeded
to arrange the sciences according to their utility in serving
these universal ends. Physiology, hygiene, sociology, all
have their place. "For discipline as well as for guidance
science is of chiefest value." But as the categories are
arranged, the inner life of the average man tends to be
neglected. All that touches the affections, that serves to
implant worthy motives and high ideals, is regarded as of
least importance. The school is to become a dull place
once more, devoted to the inculcation of science and reason.

[1] The essays were originally published separately—" What Knowledge is of Most Worth " (Chap. 1), in the *Westminster Review*, 1859 ;
" Intellectual Education " (Chap. 2), *British Review*, 1854 ; "Moral
Education" (Chap. 3), *British Quarterly*, 1858 ; " Physical Education " (Chap. 4), *British Quarterly*, 1859.

As would be expected, however, Spencer firmly grasps the biological view of the educative pro-

Spencer and Pestalozzi. cess. Education is not something that can be given to children ready made. It is essentially an individual process, and the business of the teacher is to put children in the way of educating themselves. Accordingly, telling must give way to providing pupils with opportunities for discovering—" making "— knowledge for themselves. " Children should be led to make their own investigations. They should be *told* as little as possible and induced to *discover* as much as possible. Humanity has progressed solely by self-instruction. .... Those who have been brought up under the ordinary school drill, and have carried away with them the idea that education is practicable only in that style, will think it hopeless to make children their own teachers." [1] Sense impression, observation, heurism, experiment, inventiveness, inference, realism—these are the watchwords of the new method. Instruction was to proceed according to the carefully graded steps so dear to Pestalozzi, though the teacher was to beware of falling into many of the latter's mistakes. Everything was to start with the concrete, the simple, and the definite, and by a process of mental elaboration was to be arranged into nicely compacted systems of knowledge. But unfortunately " concrete," " simple," " abstract," etc., are purely relative terms that are either misleading or so trite as to be of little value. A similar want of analysis characterises the use of the term " interest," the evoking of which is supposed to be an infallible test of the value of any subject or method of instruction.

Spencer was no believer in the innate goodness of children. Punishments he considered necessary, but he would free

[1] *Essays*, Chap. II., p. 69.

them, as he thought, from harshness and caprice by making them "natural" and removing the personal factor as far as possible. He confessed himself sceptical of moral instruction, and looked rather to the innate "moral sense" of children and the operation of experiences of pleasure and pain. Finally, in urging the importance of physical education, he was led, through his belief that interest and pleasure are trustworthy guides to what is educationally sound, to emphasise the superiority of plays and games to formal gymnastic exercises.

The demand for instruction in science and for a more practical education resulted in increased **Elementary Science and Nature Work.** attention being paid to object lessons and lessons on common things in the lower part of the school. At the same time various scientific subjects—domestic economy, physiology, physical geography, mechanics and botany—were encouraged by the Education Department, and began to be provided in the more ambitious schools for the older children. But the instruction was commonly nothing but words. The presence of an object or picture was supposed to raise a hackneyed and rambling discourse to the level of a " new method," and the performance of a few "class demonstrations" to transform the memorising of a highly systematised and arid array of facts into a course of scientific training. The value of the teaching may be gathered from the first two questions of a typical examination paper set to Standard V. boys, about 11 years of age, for the purpose of grant.

(1) Impenetrability and elasticity do not apply to atoms. Explain this and give illustrations.
(2) In what bodies may you say that molecular attraction is balanced by the repulsive force of heat?[1]

---

[1] *Final Report, Cross Commission,* p. 151.

That something very different was contemplated is seen from the instructions laid down in the Code. "It is intended that the instruction in the Science subjects shall be given mainly by experiment and illustration, and in the case of Physical Geography by observation of the phenomena presented in their own neighbourhood. If these subjects are taught to children by definition and verbal description, instead of making them exercise their own powers of observation, they will be worthless as means of education. It cannot, therefore, be too strongly impressed upon teachers that nothing like learning by rote will be accepted as sufficient for a grant, and that the examinations by the Inspectors will be directed to elicit from the scholars, as far as possible in their own language, the ideas they have formed of what they have seen."

Huxley, Lubbock, and others were outspoken in their condemnation of prevailing methods of science instruction. The poor quality of the work and the incompetence of teachers induced the Cross Commission to recommend, presumably as a temporary expedient, the unsatisfactory system of peripatetic science instructors. Teachers in the bulk had not yet realised what science really was, nor what it aimed at.

Some further guidance was afforded by Mr. Mundella's Code of 1882, which for the first time sought to encourage the teaching of elementary science throughout the whole school. Teachers were to provide a progressive course of simple lessons on common objects such as familiar animals, plants and substances employed in ordinary life, " adapted to cultivate habits of exact observation, statement, and reasoning." In the upper part of the school a more advanced knowledge of special groups of objects was required. For example, children were to be led to study the animals or plants that have special reference to agriculture, the simpler kinds of physical and mechanical appliances, the thermometer, lever, etc., the principles they involve, substances and processes employed in arts and manufactures, and the like. The great difficulty, however, in the way of handling such a course successfully was that the teachers had themselves been trained on bookish lines, and the implication of terms like "observation" was not properly understood.[1]

A further step in advance was made at the International Conference on Education at London in 1884, *Investigational Methods.* when Professors Meiklejohn and Armstrong independently urged in effect that science to be of any educational value must not be presented as a ready-made system, but as a subject that the student saw being gradually built up, and in the building up of which he had a hand. It is from this date that heurism as an educational method has been brought prominently before teachers by an enthusiastic band of disciples, helped by reports and syllabuses of British Association Committees, etc. Although it presents a partial and one-sided view of the problem of scientific training, it has done inestimable service in vitalising the subject by substituting thought, observation and invention for the passive getting up of facts taken on trust. The first attempt to put the new method into practice was in 1891 in some of the schools under the London School Board.

Since 1890, owing to the removal of certain restrictions in the Code, elementary science has shown *The Coming of Nature Study.* a remarkable growth in popularity. The movement having fairly started, it rapidly took on a new character. Knowledge of common things and elementary science, no matter how useful it might

---

[1] Elementary Science at this time was a permissive and not a compulsory subject. See *infra*, p. 305.

be or how valuable the training it might afford, did not altogether meet the need of the time. The poets had been eloquent in their praise of nature. In the cities men were looking more and more for some means of escape from the grimy monotony of bricks and mortar. In the country much thought was being given to some method of checking the rush to the towns, and to making rural life more attractive. Ruskin was emphatic as to the duty of schools to cultivate in children a love of nature. The followers of Froebel had always emphasised the educative influence that may result from contact with living things. Foreign experience, especially in Switzerland and Germany, was seen to be strongly in favour of school excursions. These and other influences had a powerful effect on science teaching in elementary schools in this country. Isolated schools were giving more and more attention to nature work, to school gardening and to school excursions to the great benefit of the work done. In 1900 the Board of Education sought to give direction to these tendencies by emphasising the importance of making the science scheme fit local conditions. Mechanics and chemistry were recommended as suitable for town schools ; bee-keeping, poultry management, and lessons centred round agricultural processes as useful in rural districts, and so on. These experiments were given a wide publicity by the Nature Study Exhibition of 1902, and from this date the Nature movement may be said to have begun with the whole-hearted support of local authorities and others.

The present tendency in nature work and elementary science is to make the teaching more real, **Present Tendencies.** more practical, and less bookish. As a result of experience rather than through any widespread understanding of its theoretical justification, there has been a steady growth of opinion that nature

work provides an essential foundation for elementary
science, that the latter should be postponed to the last
years of the school course, and that even then the tendency
to present anything in the nature of a system of science
should be steadily repulsed ; that, in short, it should concern itself with practical situations and the development,
at a later stage, of the point of view that the purpose of
science is economic description and not dogmatism. These
tendencies have found expression in the demand for
experimental work by the pupils, in elaborating courses
and methods specially suited to children, in centring the
work round the school gardens, local industries, every-day
appliances, in connecting it with geography, and the like.
In the case of girls, similar influences are seen in the desire
for a more scientific treatment of domestic subjects.

The result has been a growing demand for greater freedom in school organisation and for considerable changes in
the planning of schools, so as to provide rooms and
benches where practical work may be done.

The various terms, "object lessons," "observation
lessons," "elementary science," "nature study," and
"experimental science," are the record of so many attempts
to emphasise important aspects of the training in scientific
method. It is because each represents only a partial view
of the goal to be reached that they are such a fruitful
source of misunderstanding.

Another outcome of the scientific movement is seen in
the spread of Hygiene and Physical Training.
Hygiene and Physical Exercises. One or both of these subjects had found a
place in individual schools throughout the
nineteenth century—for example in Robert
Owen's school at New Lanark, in the schools of Stow and
Wilderspin, and in the secularist schools in London,
Manchester and elsewhere. Open-air lessons were advo-

cated in the thirties.[1] Sanitary reform was one of Kingsley's special themes. Martial exercises were warmly commended by Adam Smith. But it was Herbert Spencer who more than anyone else was responsible for educating public opinion to a sense of the supreme importance of hygiene and physical training in the school. Other influences had, of course, been at work. Physical education in particular owes a great deal to foreign influence. Every great war since 1870 has given a further stimulus to the subject. Thus in 1871 military drill was first recognised in elementary schools as a result of a conference with the War Office, and ex-army sergeants were recommended as instructors.[2] Physiology and domestic economy were also encouraged at the same time. Swedish drill appeared in girls' schools about 1879 and somewhat later in boys' schools. Each of these subjects came in for special commendation by the Cross Commission. But neither military drill nor Swedish exercises nor physiology quite met the needs of the time. For some years teachers had been quietly developing school games. In 1885 the first Inter-school Athletic League came into existence. A few years later organised physical exercises were introduced by the London School Board, and shortly afterwards they appeared in the Code.[3]

Meantime increasing attention was being given to the hygienic condition of buildings and furniture, and playground accommodation was receiving attention. As a result of the consideration that was being given to the question of physical unfitness, no school could earn the maximum grant after 1895 that failed to make provision for some form of physical exercises. Since then a rapid

[1] *Central Society of Education*, First Publication, pp. 38, 39.
[2] Cf. the influence of the Boer War in this respect.
[3] Cf. *Special Reports of the Board of Education*, Vol. I.

advance has been made. Syllabuses of physical exercises were issued by the Board of Education in 1902, and of recent years hygiene and physical training have received more and more attention. The tendency in physical education has been to attach increasing importance to freedom and enjoyment rather than to formal exercises, and to provide opportunities for the growth of corporate spirit and for training in leadership. Accordingly we find a good deal of attention being given to dancing. There has been a great revival of old-time games that were in danger of extinction. The Boy Scout movement is encouraged, and so on. Open-air lessons, too, where these can be conveniently held, have increased in popularity. In this movement much is due to the introduction of medical inspection in 1907.[1]

The venerable character of industrial and agricultural training and housecraft in elementary schools **Handwork and Handicraft.** has been pointed out in preceding chapters.

We have seen the steps that were taken to encourage this branch of instruction by the Minutes of 1846, and how all this disappeared with the Revised Code, leaving needlework as the sole indication of the former existence of a specifically vocational ideal in elementary education. Some attempt was also made to show how the demand for vocational training has arisen from time to time as a protest against the bookishness of the schools and their tendency, in the opinion of many, to manufacture economic misfits or to give children " pretensions." This feeling was again very marked in Western Europe after 1860, largely as a result of the rapid changes that were taking place in industry and commerce. The result was seen in a demand for " technical " training and for manual

---

[1] See also *ante*, pp. 178-180,

work with a view to making school education more useful and more practical, and checking the tendency to look down on manual employment. Ruskin gave the weight of his support to the new movement, and would make the workshop a prominent part of every school building.

At the same time there was a revival of interest in educational theory. The teaching of Pestalozzi and Fellenberg had lost its compelling power. The forms were there, but the spirit was lacking. Herbert Spencer had done good service by directing attention anew to Pestalozzi's teaching. Men were realising that education must be meaningful and built on sense impression. But it was from Froebel that the new note of inspiration came. Education must work through bodily activities. In the kindergarten activities of all sorts were to be found. The children were doing things, and, what seemed very attractive, a foundation of sense impression was being laid through "Hand and Eye Training." In the elementary schools children were still learning the three R's and little besides. The "technical training," the "practical" education that men were groping after appeared in a new light. Instead of turning the schools into workshops, what was needed was to use manual activities as a new educational means.

Influence of Froebel.

It was with somewhat similar ideas in mind that Cygnaeus and Salomon sought to turn slöjd to educational ends. Schools were not to aim at training young carpenters, but to exercise the bodily activities in contact with materials, to give suppleness and dexterity to the hand by means of a graded series of exercises "from the simple to the complex," to implant ideas of form, to evoke ideals of carefulness and accuracy, to promote self-reliance, and generally to make good the training that was neglected by the ordinary school subjects,

Slöjd.

The result was the setting up of a highly artificial view of manual work and the implanting of a boundless faith in training the hand and the eye. Professedly following Froebel and Pestalozzi, it overlooked practical capacity and worshipped technique, and forgot that work that did not spring from a felt need, that failed to arouse and cherish the desire to achieve a particular goal, had no educative value. The popularity of the system was due to the simplicity of its underlying principles and to the fact that it offered a tangible means of combating the unpractical character of the schools. Where it was not accepted in its entirety it became a model for other systems, and so a standard of manual instruction has been implanted on the country which to-day seriously hampers progress.[1]

The movement may be said to have begun with the publication of the First Report of the Royal **Manual Instruction.** Commission on Technical Education in 1882. Experiments with manual work were made in Manchester and Sheffield. In 1884 the Commissioners urged the payment of grants for "proficiency in the use of tools for working in wood and iron." The Cross Commission considered such instruction ought to have a place in the elementary school curriculum. Voluntary managers were pleading for Government help to erect workshops. Grants were paid by South Kensington for manual instruction after 1890, and since that time the work has spread rapidly.[2]

A quasi-technical character was given, perhaps unintentionally, to the work by limiting it to boys over 11 years of age who had passed Standard IV. This was further

---

[1] *Enquête historique sur l'enseignement manuel*, A. Panthier; also *The Teacher's Handbook of Slöjd*, Otto Salomon.

[2] In 1891 145 schools were giving instruction in manual work, in 1899 there were 1,587, and in 1910 4,261 with 187,111 boys.

accentuated by the accidents of organisation. The subject was generally in charge of craftsmen, and was carried on at some distance from the school, with the result that it became almost completely divorced from the rest of the school instruction. There were other objections to the system. Backward boys, who of all others might have been expected to profit by work of this character, were excluded because of their position in the school, and no handwork of any kind existed in the lower classes.

In recent years various causes have contributed to remedy these defects. Among them may **The Handwork Movement.** be mentioned the initiative of individual teachers who have availed themselves of the freedom that has resulted since the abolition of payment by results in 1897, coupled with the demand for a practical education and a growing belief in the educative value of " doing." In this connection the writings of William James and Professor Dewey have directly and indirectly had considerable influence. The early experiments were dominated too largely by a belief in the value of hand and eye training. Work in clay and plasticene, paper and cardboard modelling, much of it of a very formal and uneducative character, was introduced into the lower classes.

But teachers have gradually withdrawn from this extreme position, and the present tendency, while not despising workmanship and technique, is to utilise handwork more and more as a method, as a new educational organon, to encourage handiness and resourcefulness when face to face with situations of a kind such as are met with outside the school. It is much more than a means of illustrating, oftentimes quite unnecessarily, the various subjects of the curriculum, though this is important. It has received additional attention because of the opportunities it affords of training children to co-operation, but the possibilities of the subject are hardly as yet realised.

Similar changes had begun to make their appearance in the work of the older boys, but it is not yet clear what direction the movement will ultimately take. Signs are not wanting that we are moving to a position that is strikingly reminiscent of that taken up by Fellenberg. Advanced opinion already favours, at any rate for boys destined for industrial occupations, a much more generous and varied system of work than is met with outside a few special schools. It emphasises making things as they are rather than the models of things, and would entrust the work to trained teachers who are craftsmen as well as students.[1]

It was pointed out in the last chapter that the effect of the Revised Code was to limit instruction in elementary schools receiving Government grants to the three R's and needlework (for girls). To counteract this tendency the Committee of Council in 1867 offered grants on the result of individual examination to schools that introduced a three years' course of instruction extending over Standards IV., V., and VI. in one or two "specific" subjects, for example, geography, grammar, or history, in addition to the compulsory subjects fixed by the Code of 1862. It is on these lines that the elementary school curriculum has been built up. Broadly speaking, the factors that have determined it at any period have been (1) the minimum needs of the community, and (2) the subjects necessary to discipline

Building up the Curriculum.

---

[1] Compare the attitude of educational writers in the thirties in *The Quarterly Journal of Education*, the publications of the Central Society, etc.

the mind or give it a little culture.[1] The point of view is entirely adult, and of the needs of children as children there is no consideration whatever. It is here that we have the root of the difficulties that confront teachers as the number of subjects increases. This will be dealt with later.

In 1871 the standards of examination for the compulsory subjects were raised and the list of "specific" subjects was greatly extended to include algebra, geometry, natural philosophy, physical geography, the natural sciences, political economy, languages (*i.e.* English literature or the elements of Latin, French, or German), together with any other definite subject of instruction approved by the Inspector. About the same time drill and singing were encouraged.

A further step was taken in 1875 by the introduction of "class subjects"—grammar, geography, history, and plain needlework—designed to liberalise the curriculum of the lower part of the school. Not more than two subjects could be taken, and if taught at all, had to be taught throughout the whole school above Standard I. The teaching was assessed by the general proficiency of the class as a whole, not by individual examination. The curriculum was thus divided into three main parts :—

Attempts to Liberalise the Curriculum.

(1) The elementary or obligatory subjects, reading, writing, arithmetic, with needlework for girls.

(2) The class subjects, optional for the whole school.

(3) The specific subjects which might be taught to individual scholars in Standards IV. to VI. These now included mathematics (algebra, Euclid, and mensuration),

---

[1] At the same time it is necessary to point out the complete absence of any definite principle that has characterised the constant changes by the Education Department of subjects and their categories. See *infra*.

Latin, French, German, mechanics, animal physiology, physical geography, botany, and domestic economy (for girls).[1] English literature reappeared as a specific subject in the following year. In addition a special grant was made to encourage singing, and instruction in cookery was permitted, though no grant was paid for it.

Some idea of the character of the instruction in class

Specimen Schemes. subjects may be gained from the syllabus laid down in the Code at this time :—

ENGLISH.

Standard II.: To point out nouns in the passages read or written.

Standard III.: To point out the nouns, verbs, and adjectives.

Standard IV.: Parsing of a simple sentence.

Standard V.: Parsing, with analysis of a simple sentence.

Standard VI.: Parsing and analysis of a complex sentence.

GEOGRAPHY.

Standard II.: Definitions, points of compass, form and motion of the earth, the meaning of a map.

Standard III.: Outlines of geography of England, with special knowledge of the county in which the school is situated.

Standard IV.: Outlines of geography of Great Britain, Ireland, and the Colonies.

Standard V.: Outlines of geography of Europe—physical and political.

Standard VI.: Outlines of geography of the World.

[1] After 1876 girls taking specific subjects were required to offer domestic economy as one.

HISTORY (not taken below Standard IV.).

Standard IV.: Outlines of history of England to Norman Conquest.

Standard V.: Outlines of history of England from
Norman Conquest to accession of
Henry VII.

Standard VI.: Outlines of history of England from
Henry VII. to death of George III.

It is interesting to compare with this the syllabus of
English literature taken as a specific subject:—

1st Year: One hundred lines of poetry, got by heart,
with knowledge of meaning and allusions.
Writing a letter on a simple subject.

2nd Year: Two hundred lines of poetry, not before
brought up, repeated; with knowledge of
meaning and allusions. Writing a para-
phrase of a passage of easy prose.

3rd Year: Three hundred lines of poetry, not before
brought up, repeated; with knowledge of
meaning and allusions. Writing a letter
or statement, the heads of the topics to be
given by the Inspector.

In 1880 the list of class subjects was extended, as a
result of representation to the Education Department, to
include any others " which can be reasonably accepted as
special branches of elementary instruction and properly
treated in reading-books." Natural history, chemistry, and
agriculture now appeared in a few schools as class subjects.

The Code of 1882 introduced other important changes.
In view of the fact that children were stay-
**Standard
Seven.** ing longer at school and the level of attain-
ment was rising, a Seventh Standard was
introduced for examination purposes, the syllabus of

which was "To read a passage from Shakespeare or Milton, or some other standard author, or from a History of England. To write a theme or letter; composition, spelling, and handwriting to be considered. In arithmetic to work sums in averages, percentages, discount, and stocks."

Steps were also taken to encourage more attention to English and elementary science, and to the practical training of girls. The class subjects were re-arranged to include English (literature and grammar), physical geography, and a new subject called elementary science. Wherever class subjects were taken English had to be one. The list of specific subjects was further extended to include agriculture, chemistry, sound, light and heat, magnetism, and electricity. A grant was also paid for instruction in cookery.[1]

Further developments were considerably influenced by the Report of the Cross Commission. Briefly, the Commissioners reported in favour of a much more liberal curriculum than existed in many schools. All children ought as far as possible to be grounded in all four of the "class" subjects, and where this was impossible the choice should be left to the school authorities. They pointed out the mistake of confining history teaching to the upper part of the school; and emphasised the importance of simple instruction in elementary physiology for girls. Drawing they considered should be taught to all boys, and special recommendations were made with regard to instruction in manual work for boys over 11 years of age, and in physical training. Special syllabuses were advocated for small schools and for schools in rural

---

[1] Of the class subjects geography was by far the most popular. In 1890 English was taught in 20,304 departments, geography in 12,367, history in 414, elementary science in 32.

districts, and special facilities for teaching the Welsh language in Wales.[1]

The following represents in their view the *essential* sub-

A Minimum Curriculum.

jects of the elementary school curriculum: Reading, writing, arithmetic; needlework for girls; linear drawing for boys; singing; English, so as to give the children an adequate knowledge of their mother tongue; English history, taught by means of reading-books; geography, especially of the British Empire; lessons on common objects in the lower standards, leading up to a knowledge of elementary science in the higher standards.[2]

In accordance with the spirit of these recommendations

---

[1] As a result of this Welsh was admitted as a "specific subject" in Welsh schools. It became a "class subject" in 1893.

[2] *Final Report*, p. 146. It is important, however, to note that very few schools had such a curriculum before 1900. It was only the exceptional school that took subjects unless grants were paid for them. Any further encouragement of this attitude was done away with by the introduction of the "block grant" (1900). In place of the elaborate system of grants payable for different parts of the curriculum (viz. a principal grant of 12s. 6d. or 14s.; discipline and organisation grant, 1s. or 1s. 6d.; drawing grant, 1s. 9d.; needlework grant, 1s.; singing grant, 6d. or 1s.; grant for one or two "class" subjects, 1s. or 2s.; grant for "specific" subjects, 6d. or 1s.) a principal grant of 21s. or 22s. was instituted. Previous to this the following examples are typical of the curriculum and grants in a good and a poor school:—

Good Mixed School.	*Poor Girls' School.*
Main grant, 14s.	12s. 6d.
Discipline, 1s. 6d.	1s.

Boys :
Stds. I -III., Object Lessons } 2s.
  ,, IV.-VII., Geography }
    English, 2s.
Girls :
Stds. I.-III. Object Lessons } 2s.
  ,, IV.-VII. English }
    Needlework, 2s.
    Singing, 1s.

Stds. I.-III., Object Lessons } 1s.
  ,, IV.-VI., English }
    Needlework, 2s.
    Singing, 1s.

See for example *Report of the Committee of Council*, 1897-8, p. 116.

the next few years saw an increase in the amount of time given to science, mathematics, domestic subjects for girls and manual instruction for boys. At the same time commercial subjects received attention, while there was a decline in the importance of the literary side of the curriculum. History was no longer confined to the upper part of the school and alternative courses were laid down in the various class subjects. Drawing was made compulsory for boys; manual instruction was recognised but not awarded any special grant. Physical exercises, including swimming, gymnastics, and Swedish drill as distinct from military drill, appeared. Shorthand, navigation, horticulture, and hygiene were made specific subjects. After 1893 one class subject became obligatory in all schools. Grants were made for laundry work, dairy work, and housewifery, and domestic economy was made a class subject for girls.

With the abandonment of the system of individual examination and payment by results, which began in 1895, a considerable extension of the curriculum took place, and we have gradually approximated to the position as we find it to-day.

Indicative of the new spirit is the Board's Circular to Inspectors in 1893 on the "Instruction of Infants." Hitherto " varied occupations " had been recommended, "such as will relieve the younger children, especially during the afternoon, from the strain of ordinary lessons, and train them to observe and imitate." Now something of true Froebelian spirit was to be seen. It was strongly urged that sufficient attention had not been paid in the past to the following principles : " (1) The recognition of the child's spontaneous activity, and the stimulation of this activity in certain well-defined directions by the teachers. (2) The harmonious and complete development of the whole of the child's faculties. The teacher should pay especial regard to the love of movement, which can alone secure healthy physical conditions ; to the observant use of the organs of sense, especially those of sight and touch ; and to that eager desire of questioning which intelligent children exhibit. . . . It is often found that the kindergarten occupations are treated as mere toys, or amusing pastimes, because they are attractive for children, and the intellectual character of the ' Gifts of Froebel ' is disregarded, whereas the main object of these lessons is to stimulate intelligent individual effort." At the same time emphasis was laid on training children to express their ideas.

. In the Code of 1902 the Board of Education set out for the first time what it considered to be a properly co-ordinated curriculum suited to the needs of the children, together with " an indication of the relation the various subjects of instruction should bear to each other in place of the relatively haphazard list of possible branches of knowledge which were formerly presented to the choice of individual schools or authorities." The principal aim of the infant school was stated to be to provide opportunities for the free development, physical and mental, and for the formation of habits of obedience and attention. Stress was laid on free play, games, singing, and breathing exercises, providing children with opportunities of doing things, on the importance of story work, etc. The curriculum of the primary school, allowing for local variations, had to provide a training in the English language (including speaking, reading, composition, literature) ; handwriting taught to secure speed as well as legibility ; arithmetic, including practical measurements ; drawing, including drawing from objects, memory and brush drawing, the use of ruler and compasses, with special provision for handicrafts; observation lessons and nature study, including the teaching of gardening to both boys and girls; geography, history, music, hygiene and physical training (together with cookery, laundry work, housewifery), and moral instruction given both directly and indirectly, besides providing for the teaching of special subjects suited to the particular locality.

As the curriculum has steadily widened, teachers have been faced with an overloaded time-table. **The Child and the Curriculum.** The artificiality of a long list of disconnected subjects, the result of dividing instruction into a great number of watertight compartments, has been more and more apparent. The economy of time and effect that would result from a proper grouping has led to many attempts to evolve schemes based on the principles of correlation and concentration.[1]

These principles have a theoretical justification in the teaching of Herbart and his disciples. **Herbart.** According to Herbart the end of education is the production of character. Character, however, depends upon willing, willing upon desire, desire upon interests, interests upon ideas, upon "the circle of thought." Ideas are the result of instruction; it is by instruction that the mind is built up. Hence the business of the teacher is to establish in the pupils a wide, coherent circle of thought, for on the content and unity of the latter the whole moral life depends. In Herbart's own words, "the circle of thought contains the store of that which by degrees can mount by the steps of interest to desire and then by means of action to volition." "If the circle of thought has been so perfectly cultivated that a pure taste entirely rules *action in the imagination*, then anxiety for the formation

---

[1] The ideas are in themselves very old. Cf. their working in the monitorial schools.

of character in the midst of life is almost at an end, for the individual left to himself will so choose opportunities for external action, or so *use* those that force themselves upon him, that the right will only become strengthened within his heart." "Those only wield the full power of education who know how to cultivate in the youthful soul a large circle of thought closely connected in all its parts."[1]

The material of instruction was the whole field of human knowledge and activity. The aim of the **Concentration and Correlation.** educator was to see that his pupil acquired an all-round, well-balanced culture, the materials of which should be closely interwoven. To accomplish this, instruction would follow two main lines, one aiming at cultivating the understanding, the other having regard to the feelings and the imagination. For the first the subject-matter of mathematics and science was available; for the second, history and humanistic material. The school curriculum, therefore, would exhibit two great concentration centres, two great cores of instruction, round which the various auxiliary studies would be grouped or correlated. In this way the unity of the circle of thought would be insured. The curriculum would, for example, be dependent on a strong core of humanistic material of high ethical value that traced the history of mankind from the earliest times. With it would be correlated the literature, moral lessons, the bulk of the drawing, geography, etc. Other schemes have made geography the concentration centre, and so on. The objection to plans of this sort is their obvious artificiality and the way in which they lend themselves to all kinds of absurdity. Thus a lesson on the miraculous draught of fishes is followed by a nature lesson on the stickleback.

---

[1] *Science of Education*, Felkin's translation, pp. 92, 213, 220.

But a more fundamental objection is raised to such theories. They give an over-emphasis to instruction, to imposing education from without, whereas modern theory under the influence of biological thought inclines to lay stress on the spontaneity of the individual and on self-education. The one appraises things by adult standards, the other sees a new meaning in childish impulses and activities. Human knowledge in all its majesty, carefully systematised and pigeon-holed, is arrayed against the immature attainment of the child. It is a heritage to be entered upon as soon as possible, and in order to effect this the various sciences are to be arranged in steps and made "interesting." That this logical, impersonal, highly systematised view of experience has no place in the narrow, personal and practical world of the child does not appear to have been fully appreciated. There is an antagonism between the two that no amount of correlating will remove. The school material is too formal in conception. Instead of seeking to arouse a feeling of demand, attention tends to be turned to the modification of the subject-matter. So many facts have to be learnt, and the teacher has to resort to various devices to interest the children and sugar the pill. A new way of approaching the problem of school instruction is in fact needed. To have helped to impress this on the thought of the present generation has been the work of Professor Dewey.[1]

The Child v. the Curriculum.

He teaches that the problems that centre round the curriculum will never be solved by concentrating attention either on the subject-matter as something to be learned, or on the activities of the child as ends in themselves. We must take full

Teaching of Professor Dewey.

[1] *The School and the Child*, John Dewey. Edited by J. J. Findley, Essay I.

advantage of childish impulses and activities, but they must be interpreted and given direction, remembering that they have meaning only in the light of their promise of higher things. Similarly we must not attempt to impose our own experience or our own highly specialised view of the world on children; rather we must recognise that we have ourselves attained to our present condition as the result of long development. Accordingly the subjects of the curriculum must be taken as representing the goal towards which children will be directed as the narrow world of childish experience progressively widens. To children knowing and doing are not separated. Their school is the world as they know it. Consequently the problem of the school is how to make the work in it meaningful by bringing it into closer relationship with the home and the life of the neighbourhood, how to make it a place dominated by purposeful activities, rather than where certain lessons have to be learnt. How can history, science and art be given a positive value and real significance in the child's own life as something worthy of attainment? How can reading, writing and arithmetic be carried on in such a way that children shall feel their necessity through their connection with things that mean something to them?

Dewey himself sought for a solution by gradually working up to the definite subjects of the curriculum, by centring the early instruction round the life of the home and the neighbourhood, round various social and industrial occupations, by reviewing the problem of primitive man in connection with the experience of camping out and the like. Much opportunity was given in this way for manual occupations of very varied character and the subject-matter of instruction was no longer confined to water-tight compartments.

It is in emphasising the every-day experiences of the children as the starting-point of instruction **Present Tendencies.** and grouping subjects under larger headings that reform is proceeding. Geometry is no longer something apart from arithmetic, nor is geography treated as something divorced from nature work, mathematics and history. But the difficulty of advance is two-fold. There is the weight of tradition to overcome, and when this has been surmounted it is necessary to convince teachers that the advance towards the reasoned and logical treatment of experience has not therefore been abandoned, but only postponed. Unless this is understood the reform movement is in danger of leading to results at least as pernicious as the older system, by altogether under-estimating the capabilities of children and leaving them indefinitely at the Kindergarten stage.

The Gradual Abandonment of "Results."

It has been seen how the first effect of the system of assessing grants by individual examination was to minimise the educational value of school instruction and to set a premium on results "got anyhow." Such a state of things could not last indefinitely. From 1875 a new note is evident in the attitude of the Education Department. In that year a small part of the grant was made to depend upon discipline and organisation, and in the following year the moral aspects of this part of the school work were specially emphasised. " The managers and teachers will be expected to satisfy the Inspector that all reasonable care is taken, in the ordinary management of the school, to bring up the children in habits of punctuality, of good manners and language, of cleanliness and neatness, and also to impress upon the children the importance of cheerful obedience to duty, of consideration and respect for others, and of honour and truthfulness in word and act."[1] This summary in one form or another remained for many years a guide in determining grants.

Two years later we find it asserted in the Instructions to Inspectors that the intention of " my lords " had always been to promote the development of general intelligence rather than to seek to burden the children's memories, and " to encourage such training in school on matters affecting their daily life as may help to improve and raise the character of their homes."

The intention of the " Merit Grant " of 1882 to encourage a higher standard of school organisation and discipline, more intelligent teaching and greater thoroughness in the work done has already been referred to. Schools were to be classed as " fair," " good," or " excellent " for the purpose of participating in this grant. The description of an " excellent " school—one of distinguished merit—is worth quoting as embodying in practical form the ideals of the time.

An "Excellent" School in 1882.

" A thoroughly good school in favourable conditions is character-ised by cheerful and yet exact discipline, maintained without harshness and without noisy demonstration of authority. Its premises are cleanly and well ordered ; its time table provides a proper variety of mental employment and of physical exercise ; its organisation is such as to distribute the teaching power judiciously, and to secure for every scholar—whether he is likely to bring credit to the school by examination or not, a fair share of instruction and of attention. The teaching is animated and interesting, and yet thorough and accurate. The reading is fluent, careful, and expres-sive, and the children are helped by questioning and explanation to follow the meaning of what they read. Arithmetic is so taught as

---

[1] For important changes made in the curriculum at this time see *ante*, p. 302.

to enable the scholars not only to obtain correct answers to sums, but also to understand the reason of the processes employed. If higher subjects are attempted, the lessons are not confined to memory work and to the learning of technical terms, but are designed to give a clear knowledge of facts and to train the learner in the practice of thinking and observing. Besides fulfilling these conditions, which are all expressed or implied in the Code, such a school seeks by other means to be of service to the children who attend it. It provides for the upper classes a regular system of home exercises, and arrangements for correcting them expeditiously and thoroughly. Where circumstances permit, it has also its lending library, its savings' bank, and an orderly collection of simple objects and apparatus adapted to illustrate the school lessons, and formed in part by the co-operation of the scholars themselves. Above all, its teaching and discipline are such as to exert a right influence on the manners, the conduct, and the character of the children, to awaken in them a love of reading and such an interest in their own mental improvement as may reasonably be expected to last beyond the period of school life." [1]

A fair picture of the actual work being done in the schools is given in the Report of the Cross **Primary School Education in 1886.** Commission, which specially calls attention to the fact " that witnesses of all classes testify to the imperfect hold of knowledge gained in elementary schools." With regard to instruction in the three R's, it recorded the conviction of the Commissioners that the practice of providing only three reading-books for each standard for the year was a mistake. More reading material was desirable, and a stop ought to be put to the practice of converting the reading lesson into a spelling lesson and the reading-book into a spelling-book. Far too much importance was attached to spelling as a separate subject. Again, reading had to do with the sense of the printed page, not with the

[1] Instructions to Inspectors.—*Report of the Committee of Council,* 1882.3, p. 158.

individual words and letters. " A child who has thoroughly acquired the art of reading with ease has within its reach the key of all knowledge, and it will rest with itself alone to determine the limit of its progress. Good reading is, however, at the present time often sacrificed to instruction in spelling."

Very little was said about the teaching of writing. With regard to arithmetic there was great need for a more practical type of work, such as would deal with the situations that are met with in every-day life and in local industries. There was too much juggling with figures, too much teaching of rules, and too little attention to establishing principles and training the children to think mathematically.

The teaching of the four class subjects, English, geography, history, and elementary science, came in for a good deal of criticism. English was too much a matter of formal grammar, of learning prefixes and of word-building, altogether beyond the capabilities of children. Much more attention needed to be given to English literature, and especially to getting the children to learn by heart suitable passages of poetry. It had been suggested that the intelligent reading of standard authors might be allowed to take the place of grammar, but this was not recommended ; rather the Commissioners favoured the retention of parsing and analysis.

In geography the need of alternative syllabuses suited to different teachers was emphasised. Too much of the geography teaching was nothing more than lists of names, brute facts and definitions without any content. The aridity of much of the work would be removed if teachers confined themselves to fewer countries and to the striking distinctions between the different areas of the earth, and dealt with them in a more descriptive manner. At the same time the intimate connection of geography and elementary science was pointed out. In Standard VII. some specialisation was highly desirable, for example a study of the causes that contribute to the distribution of animal and plant life, the influence of the physical features of a few countries on the density of population, habits, pursuits, character and history of the people.

In history teaching the importance of studying special epochs, typical personages, the growth of national institutions was emphasised.

Finally the Commissioners recorded their conviction that great elasticity was needed in grading children, and that progress would be furthered by giving less attention to results and more to the conditions that made the attainment of any lasting results possible. It is on these lines that advance has been made.

In 1902 the Board of Education ventured for the first time to state for the guidance of teachers **The Aim of** and parents the proper aim of the public **the Primary** **School.** elementary school.

"The purpose of the public elementary school is to form and strengthen the character and to develop the intelligence of the children entrusted to it, and to make the best use of the school years available, in assisting both boys and girls, according to their different needs, to fit themselves, practically as well as intellectually, for the work of life.

"With this purpose in view it will be the aim of the school to train the children carefully in habits of observation and clear reasoning, so that they may gain an intelligent acquaintance with some of the facts and laws of nature; to arouse in them a living interest in the ideals and achievements of mankind, and to bring them to some familiarity with the literature and history of their own country; to give them some power over language as an instrument of thought and expression, and, while making them conscious of the limitations of their knowledge, to develop in them such a taste for good reading and thoughtful study as will enable them to increase that knowledge in after years by their own efforts.

"The school must at the same time encourage to the utmost the children's natural activities of hand and eye by suitable forms of practical work and manual instruction ; and afford them every opportunity for the healthy development of their bodies, not only by training them in appropriate physical exercises and encouraging them in organised games, but also by instructing them in the working of some of the simple laws of health."

The Code goes on to point out that the school should enable promising children to pass on to the secondary school, and that moral training should never be lost sight of by the teacher. The elementary school should inculcate habits of industry, self-control and perseverance, implant ideals of purity, truth and honour, and through its corporate life instil notions of fair-play and loyalty. Further, the school and parents should work together so that the pupils may become "upright and useful members of the community in which they live, and worthy sons and daughters of the country to which they belong." [1]

It remains to consider briefly the improvements in school staffing since 1870. It has been pointed out [2] that the originators of the pupil teacher system contemplated only two types of instructors, the pupil teacher and the trained certificated teacher. From the outset, however, a class of uncertificated ex-pupil teachers—"assistant" teachers they were called—had gradually won a place in the schools, though every inducement was given them to become certificated. In 1870 the number of certificated teachers was insufficient to

Staffing.

---

[1] In 1905 the first edition of the "Suggestions to Teachers" was published.

[2] *Ante*, p. 272.

provide one for each school department under inspection. The New Code (1871), however, made the employment of such a teacher a condition of grant, and by 1877 we find that the total number of certificated teachers was slightly in excess of the number of departments. Immediately this happened it became possible to attempt to improve the standard of staffing. The value of an adult over a pupil teacher was already beginning to be recognised. In 1878 an additional adult teacher was required in departments exceeding 220, and in 1882 a further step was taken by limiting the number of pupil teachers to three for the head teacher and one for each certificated assistant. At the same time the class of " supplementary " or " additional woman " teacher over eighteen years of age [1] was called into existence and allowed to count for staffing purposes at the same rate as the pupil teacher. To encourage further the appointment of certificated teachers the following scale of staffing was drawn up:—

Principal certificated teacher	. 60 children in average attendance.	
Other ,, ,,	. 80 ,, ,, ,,
Uncertificated assistant teacher	60 ,,
Pupil teacher 40   ,,
Candidate 20   ,,
Additional woman teacher over 18	40 ,, ,, ,,

From this time staffing received a good deal of attention, and complaints of the excessive size of classes were reiterated again and again. The Cross Commission reviewed the whole question in detail. Already advanced opinion was in favour of limiting the number of children to twenty-five in the lowest infants' class

Cross Commission Recommendations.

_____

[1] The present Supplementary Teacher Schedule I.D,

and at the top end of the elementary school. In other classes forty was the ideal number.[1] It was shown that the general level of staffing over the country was considerably in excess of the Code minimum, which the Commissioners were of opinion ought to be raised. All the evidence emphasised the great gain in teaching power that came from staffing with adult teachers. With regard to the question whether or not a head teacher should be responsible for a class, opinion was divided. It was a point to be settled on the merits of each case. The outcome of the Report was that in 1890 a new scale of staffing was issued. The staff value of certificated assistants was cut down from eighty to seventy, that of uncertificated assistants to fifty, of pupil teachers and supplementary teachers to thirty, and a special scale was devised for small country schools.

Four years later the first attempt was made to restrict the size of classes by limiting the number of children on the register under the control of one teacher to a number not exceeding 15 per cent. of the staff value of the grade to which the teacher belonged. This condition was relaxed the following year by substituting the " number habitually present." In 1897 the values of head, certificated, and uncertificated teachers were reduced to fifty, sixty, and forty-five respectively. These changes are a necessary consequence of the new attitude towards education that was creeping over the schools. The result was that Voluntary schools could not keep pace. What the staffing was like at this time can be seen from the table given on the opposite page.

Limiting the Size of Classes.

---

[1] Matthew Arnold thought forty-five in average attendance, or fifty on the register, would be satisfactory.

| | 1897. | | 1902. | |
	Voluntary Schools.	Board Schools.	Voluntary Schools.	Board Schools.
Number of departments .	20,656	10,191	20,385	10,987
Number of scholars in average attendance .	2,471,996	2,016,547	2,546,217	2,344,020
Average number of scholars to a department	120	198	125	213
Head teachers :—				
Certificated . .	20,557	10,152	20,107	10,919
Others . . .	55	26	251	49
Assistant teachers :—				
Certificated . .	7,886	20,219	9,226	27,476
Uncertificated . .	14,182	11,024	20,116	15,796
Additional women .	11,412	2,743	14,073	3,515
Pupil teachers . .	17,002	15,596		
P.T.'s and " Provisional Assistants" . .			13,501	15,815
Probationers . . .			1,781	827
All teachers . . .	71,094	59,760	79,095	74,397
Number of scholars per teacher :—				
All teachers . .	35	34	32	32
All adult teachers .	46	46	40	41
All certificated teachers . .	87	66	87	61

It must be remembered that the Departments in Voluntary Schools were smaller than in Board Schools. (See *Report of the Board of Education*, 1909-10.)

In 1903 to the numerical test of good staffing was added that of its suitability and efficiency for each particular school, and in later Codes [1] stress was laid on the

[1] 1908 and 1909.

arrangement of the premises, the nature of the curriculum, and the special qualification of the teachers for their several duties. At the same time (1909) the size of classes was limited to *sixty on the register*. This means rather more than fifty in average attendance. (Steps have also been taken to supersede supplementary teachers by refusing to recognise them for any but the lowest classes of the primary school, and for infant schools.) Many localities, however, staff on a much higher scale, and uncertificated teachers are being replaced, more and more, by those with higher qualifications Of the various influences working in favour of smaller classes none is more important than the tendency to substitute more practical methods of study and instruction, but we are still a very long way from the ideal staffing advocated before the Cross Commission.

Alongside the improvements in staffing have gone developments in building. As the pupil teacher gave way to the adult assistant, class-rooms became more common. The type of school building with a room for each class opening out of a central hall, adopted by the London School Board in 1873, was obviously of limited application in the absence of an adequate supply of adult teachers. Accordingly the majority of the early Board schools were built with a large room, from which opened off two or three class-rooms. In some of these rooms the old gallery arrangement was commonly retained. Gradually, however, these rooms have been partitioned, and new schools, built on the class-room plan, have conformed to one or other of two types, one with central hall, the other without it. Of these types there is endless variety. There is no such thing as a standard school building, for the arrangements must vary according to the changing demands of the day and the particular neighbourhood in

School Buildings.

which the school is placed. The practical movement in education has led to the demand for workrooms, and the conversion of one or more class-rooms for this purpose. Hygienic considerations have wrought many changes in furniture and planning. There is a demand for school baths, for open-air class-rooms, and for beds in infant schools. Much greater stress is laid on adequate playground accommodation. With a growing sense of the responsibility of the school, there has been a demand for bright and tastefully decorated class-rooms, for good pictures and the like. More attention is being given to grading and to keeping schools within manageable size. There is not and cannot be any finality in these matters so long as educational thought is alive and active.

In Wales a new era began with the founding of the Welsh Department of the Board of Educa-
Recent Developments in Wales. tion in 1907. The Welsh language had been gradually winning its way into the schools. For some years it had formed a subject, and, in a greater degree, a medium of instruction in some at least of the elementary schools in almost every county of Wales and Monmouthshire. The first Welsh Code crystallised the aspirations of many in the Principality by requiring that the Welsh language should, as a rule, be included in the curriculum. Any subject might now be taught in Welsh, and stress was laid on provision being made in every school for teaching the literature, history, and geography of Wales. The full results of this departure have yet to be seen, but it has undoubtedly had the result of infusing a new spirit into the educational life of the Principality.

PART III.

CHAPTER X.

THE TEACHER.

" Any boy who can read, can teach. "
—LANCASTER : *Improvements in Education.*

" I think you would be more amused if you saw those who were kings and satraps upon earth reduced in the nether world to beggary and forced to sell kippers or to teach the elements of reading and writing."—LUCIAN : *Nekuomanteia.*

"In all cases the success of a school depends mainly upon the character of the teacher. . . . I concede the institution of schools for masters to be at the very foundation of all improvement in national education."
—Professor PILLANS : *Report of Select Committee, 1834.*

Demosthenes in abusing his rival Aischines taunts him with having been a schoolmaster—" You taught letters, I went to school "—and he proceeds to remind him how he used to be employed " grinding the ink and sponging the forms and sweeping out the schoolroom, the work of a servant, not of a free boy." [1] To find a parallel in our own country to this menial view of the office of the primary teacher we need go back little more than half a century. It was then no uncommon thing to find the headmaster

The Menial View of the Schoolmaster.

---

[1] Cf. *Schools of Hellas*, Freeman, pp. 81-3.

even of a National school combining in his person the duties of teacher, caretaker, messenger, and general handyman.[1]

The question of the professional and economic status of the teacher is inextricably associated with the history of elementary education in this country during the nineteenth century. Indeed it is no exaggeration to say that no other factor has had so determining an influence on the progress of the schools. The educational literature of the century is one long record of the fact that the primary school has been unable to offer social and monetary inducements adequate to retain the services of its best men. The problem was already so acute in 1800 that one of the claims of the monitorial systems to the gratitude of philanthropists was that it afforded a steady supply of cheap and relatively efficient labour. Thus Sir Thomas Bernard wrote in 1799 in describing the Kendal Schools[2] :—

The Status of Teachers in 1800.

" It has been observed that whenever ushers of *mature years* are *completely* fitted for teachers, they are capable of earning a greater salary than the school can afford; so

[1] Thus, according to the Minutes of the Committee of the Stockport National School (October 2nd, 1846), we find that the duties of headmaster of the boys' department included superintending the (school) building, lighting the fires, keeping an account of the gas, cleaning the school, and undertaking the general charge of the building—all for a salary of £65 a year with house, coals, and gas—a condition of things that lasted for another eleven years until the school came under Government inspection.

Such a combination of duties is in no way derogatory to the Committee. The post of caretaker was eagerly sought after. The practice had been to award it to one of the conductors of the Sunday schools for meritorious service, but with the advent of a day school the post had been claimed by the headmaster as a perquisite. The Minute referred to was merely continuing with a new master a well-established custom.

[2] *Digest of Reports (Education) S.B.C.P.*, 1809, pp. 135-6.

that all who are *really fit* for the situation are looking out for something better. A similar circumstance may attend those selected from the pupils themselves, but what is an evil in one case operates as a benefit in the other. The spirit of the establishment, which has raised one boy above the situation, has fitted and prepared others to succeed him."

Few institutions have received such universal condemnation as the dame schools and common schools of the first half of the nineteenth century. Macaulay's rhetorical description of the common schoolmaster is well known— "the refuse of all other callings, discarded footmen, ruined pedlars, men who cannot work a sum in the rule of three, men who do not know whether the earth is a sphere or a cube, men who do not know whether Jerusalem is in Asia or America. And to such men, men to whom none of us would entrust the key of his cellar, we have entrusted the mind of the rising generation, and with the mind of the rising generation, the freedom, the happiness, the glory of our country."[1] There were of course many schoolmasters of a very different calibre, but in the main the indictment was only too true. But Lancaster, a private schoolmaster himself, leaves us in no doubt as to the reason.[2] Of all occupations school-keeping was one of the most precarious, attendance was very irregular, fees were very uncertain, and mean parents have been a bye-word since the days of Theophrastus. In an age when an educational reformer like Pestalozzi believed that anyone who could read could teach ; when teaching was an un-skilled occupation ; when Rousseau, along with the men of the enlightenment, taught that the poor have no need of

---

[1] Speech in House of Commons, 1847.
[2] Cf. *Improvements in Education*, passim.

education; it is useless to expect a highly organised or expert body of common school teachers.

In the haste to bring the elements of letters within the reach of all, the supreme importance of the **Personality v. Mechanism in Education.** personal factor in education tended to be overlooked. Almost without exception the attention of reformers was directed to the machinery of instruction. Pestalozzi hoped that his A B C books would be infallible educative instruments in the hands of the most ignorant parent. The ingenuity of Bell and Lancaster was turned to devising a great teaching machine. Similarly a State mechanism, designed among other things to manufacture teachers in normal schools, was the ideal of the advanced reformers. It is doubtful, for example, whether Brougham, with all his knowledge and enthusiasm for popular education, ever realised the relative importance of personality and machinery. Speaking in 1820 he said that "he looked upon the schoolmaster to be employed in an honourable and useful capacity—so honourable that none was more highly esteemed, if the individual were faithful in the discharge of his duty—so useful that no man, he believed, effected more good in his generation than a good parish schoolmaster. That class would not, however, be offended when he observed that they moved in an inferior situation of life."[1] Accordingly, he considered a salary of from £20 to £30 per annum adequate remuneration for their services, and would leave any augmentation of it to private initiative. To improve the quality of the education given in schools all that was needed was to train the teachers.[2]

---

[1] Speech in House of Commons, 1820.
[2] Cf. Evidence before Select Committee, 1834.

The evidence of the period leaves no doubt as to the mischief exerted by this ban of social inferiority. Dunn emphasises it in his evidence before the Select Committee (1834), and the feelings of all self-respecting teachers are portrayed in such indignant protests as the following : "Point to an individual as a physician, a clergyman, or a lawyer, and though his cranium be as devoid of eminences as the surface of a plate of glass, yet you give him a passport to the name of gentleman and the best society; but let any one be named a schoolmaster and a feeling of insignificance and disrepute, and the idea that he is a fit companion for the vulgar, will be the consequence." [1]

The Social Inferiority of Teachers.

In this connection it is interesting to note the efforts towards self-help that were being made by the teachers at this time. Before the project of a State Normal School was launched in 1839, teachers up and down the country were banding themselves together into societies for mutual improvement,[2] and giving expression to ideas that have still to be realised in this country. One of these schemes for professional advancement, drafted by a teacher, appears in the *Belfast Christian Patriot* (1839). It proposes the establishment in every district of a Teachers' Library, "consisting exclusively of works on education and school books. In this way for a few shillings annually the treasures of Edgeworth, Hamilton, Pestalozzi, Wood, Wilderspin, Wyse, *The Journal of Education, The Educational Magazine, The American Annals of Education,*

Early Teachers' Improvement Societies.

[1] See *Educational Magazine*, 1839, p. 84.

[2] *E.g.* The London British Teachers' Society; cf. the Berne Society of Teachers, with Fellenberg as President, founded 1832; see *Letters on the Educational Institutions of Fellenberg*, p. 360.

etc., etc., would be laid open to all. Ere a new work would be completely dry, it would be in the hands of thousands of teachers"—a plan common enough in America at the present time. "Poverty would not then stamp its victims with the seal of eternal ignorance, good schools would no longer stand like oases in the desert," school-keeping would no longer be the refuge of the economic mis-fit, and the teacher would secure that recognition that his pastoral work entitles him to.[1]

The need for training teachers in Charity schools was recognised at the beginning of the eighteenth century, and a plan for establishing a training school for masters and mistresses—probably inspired by Francke's Training Institute at Halle—was discussed by the Committee of the S.P.C.K. in 1712.[2] Although nothing came of it, it points to a feeling of dissatisfaction with the method of initiating novices into the art of school-keeping that had been hitherto recommended :—

The Training of Charity School Teachers.

"And here it may be noted, That it will be adviseable for any new-elected Schoolmaster to consult with some of the present School-masters of these Schools, for the more ready Performance of his Duty. And it is recommended to them to communicate to such new elected Master their Art, and the divers Methods of Teaching and Governing Scholars used according to the different Capacities, Tem-

---

[1] As long ago as 1581 Mulcaster had urged the dignity of the teacher's profession, its specialised character, and the need for training schools. "Is the framing of young mindes and the training of their bodies so meane a point of cunning? . . . He that will not allow of this carefull provision for such a seminarie of maisters, is most unworthy either to have had a good maister him selfe, or hereafter to have a good one for his (children). Why should not teachers be well provided for, to continue their whole life in the schoole, as Divines, Lawyers, Physicians do in their severall professions?"— *Positions*, Quick's Edition, p. 248. [2] *Ante*, pp. 14-16.

pers, and Inclination of the Children. And, moreover, it will be convenient that such new-elected Master have Liberty, on certain days, to see and here the present Master Teach the Scholars, and upon Occasion to be assisting to them in Teaching ; that such new Master may thereby become yet more expert, and better qualified for the discharge of his office. The due and faithful Execution whereof, as it is a Matter of very great importance, so it does deserve much Commendation and may hope to meet with a proportionable encouragement."[1]

It is significant of the educational thought of the time that Robert Nelson included in his list of fit objects of charity (1715)[2] the founding of superior schools of secondary type for the training of Charity school teachers. A similar proposal was made by Mrs. Trimmer some 70 years later,[3] and seems to suggest the Bursar system that has arisen since 1902.

With the advent of the monitorial systems the first movement in the direction of special preparation for the teacher's office in this country began. A complicated piece of mechanism had been invented, the successful working of which demanded considerable skill. To obtain this the inventors sought to improve the method of " training " already familiar in Charity schools. Lancaster accordingly opened a " training " institution in connection with his school at the Borough Road. There he lodged, boarded, and clothed a number of picked monitors who were trained to organise and conduct similar schools as required. He also established a training school for country teachers at Maiden Bradley in Somersetshire. To his lavish expenditure on this branch of his activities was due, in no small

The Monitorial Training Schools.

---

[1] *An Account of Charity Schools lately erected in those parts of Great Britain called England and Wales*, 1708.

[2] Kirkman Grey : *History of Philanthropy*, p. 84.

[3] *Œconomy of Charity*, 1787.

measure, his bankruptcy in 1808. Various schools, for example Mr. Davis' school at Whitechapel and the Barrington school, Durham, similarly initiated teachers into the working of Bell's system. These masters left fully trained at the age of 15 to 17.

But " schoolmasters and others of good character " were also admitted to these institutions at their own expense to be instructed in the new method. The practice of the Barrington school affords a typical example of training in 1810.[1] First the manual explanatory of the method used in the school was studied. This being in some degree mastered, practice began. Each individual was put in charge successively of every class in the school, beginning with the lowest. This occupied some 6 or 8 weeks. They were also subjected to occasional examinations to test their knowledge of how to adapt the system to different conditions, the mode of teaching particular lessons, of examining and classing scholars, etc. They were next examined successively in the initiatory processes and books of the school, and required to say their lessons just as if they were in the actual classes, beginning with the monosyllabic spelling-book. Mistakes were inevitable, and promotion and degradation followed exactly as in one of the ordinary children's classes, the idea being thoroughly to familiarise them with the lessons and to initiate them into the difficulties the children were likely to meet with. In short, school management, wooden and inelastic in character, and wholly divorced from principles, was the end and aim of the course. Along these lines all attempts at training teachers proceeded for nearly a quarter of a century.

Training in 1810.

[1] Sir Thomas Bernard: *The Barrington School*, Third Edition, pp. 131-3.

With the founding of the National Society and the British and Foreign School Society a great impetus was given to training. More teachers were needed, and one of the principal objects of these societies was to supply school masters and mistresses from their central training schools at Baldwin's Gardens and the Borough Road. Other schools of similar character under district societies were gradually established up and down the country, each contributing its quota of teachers.[1]

The Development of Central Training Schools.

Meantime the practice of lodging and boarding a number of picked monitors until they were old enough to go out as schoolmasters seems gradually to have disappeared. The system was very costly, and with the advent of new ideas the young master of 15 to 18 years of age was no longer popular. At the time of the first Parliamentary grant, no teacher under 21 years of age was admitted to the central school of the National Society. A few entered the Borough Road under 19, but the usual age was between 19 and 24. Dunn entirely disapproved on the grounds of immaturity of any attempt to begin training anyone under 18 years of age, and even then he held that the period of training should last for three years instead of three months. Under these conditions he would devote the first and last period of three months to practice in school, and would devote the whole of the third year to a study of the " science of teaching."[2]

---

[1] By 1834 2,039 teachers had been sent out from the central training school of the National Society, and 35 district schools, *e.g.* at Durham, York, Norwich, Bath, Bangor, etc., were in existence. (*Select Committee on Education*, 1834, also Reports of National Society, 1828-1833.) Four years later they had increased to 47, but as a rule they only trained two or three teachers a year. (*Select Committee*, 1838, Evidence.)

[2] *Select Committee*, 1834, Evidence.

The method of training prospective schoolmasters at the Borough Road at this time is thus de-

Training at Borough Road in 1834. scribed.[1] "They are required to rise every morning at five o'clock, and spend an hour before seven in private study. They have access to a good library. At seven they are assembled together in a Bible class and questioned as to their knowledge of the Scriptures; from nine to twelve they are employed as monitors in the school, learning to communicate that which they already know or are supposed to know; from two to five they are employed in a similar way: and from five to seven they are engaged under a master who instructs them in arithmetic and the elements of geometry, geography, and the globes, or in other branches in which they may be deficient. The remainder of the evening is generally occupied in preparing exercises for the subsequent day. One object is to keep them incessantly employed from five in the morning until nine or ten at night. We have rather exceeded in the time devoted to study the limit we would choose, on account of the very short period we are able to keep them, and we have found in some instances that their health has suffered on account of their having been previously quite unaccustomed to mental occupations."[2]

---

[1] *Select Committee on Education*, 1834: Minutes of Evidence, p. 232.

[2] These conditions remained practically unchanged in 1846. See Fletcher's Report, *Minutes of Committee of Council*, 1846, Vol. II.

It is noteworthy that comparatively few of those who trained at the central schools had been brought up under the monitorial systems. A few had kept private schools, but the great majority had been engaged in some other occupation. Some had been teachers in Sunday schools and had acquired a genuine liking for the work. (*Select Committee on Education*, 1834: Minutes of Evidence, p. 232.) The cost of training was borne by the candidates themselves or by some local committee. In the competition for headships of monitorial schools the candidate who promised to train at a

The condition of entry to a training school was a certificate of character, and ability to read, write, and cypher. The first fortnight was a probationary period to weed out those who were unsuited to the work. A certificate was awarded on successfully completing the course. The mode of training in schools connected with the National Society was similar to that in vogue at the Borough Road, though it seems to have been less arduous, and attention was confined to practice in the three R's and religion. Moreover, there does not seem to have been, at this date, any general feeling of dissatisfaction with the system such as Dunn expressed. It was during the next few years that criticism grew apace.[1]

We are, in fact, at the beginning of a new era. The influence of Pestalozzi and Fellenberg abroad and of Woods and Stow at home was leading to a new view of education. It was something more than mere ability to read and write badly. It demanded of the teacher knowledge, maturity, and personal qualities to a degree hardly realised twenty years before.[2] The result was a feeling of intense dissatisfaction and a quickening of the educational conscience of the nation that was reflected in every branch of education. At the same time increased attention was given to educational methods abroad. Men's eyes were turned to the Ecole Primaire Normale of France, and to the Normal schools of Switzerland and Prussia. The word "training" had acquired a new meaning, so much so that the Secretary of the National Society was fain to admit (1838) that in "the high sense

The Ferment in Training.

central school at his own expense not infrequently triumphed over his more needy rivals.

[1] *Select Committee on Education*, 1834: Minutes of Evidence, *passim.*

[2] Cf. *Select Committee on Education*, 1838: Minutes of Evidence, *passim.*

which is now attached to the words, 'model or normal schools,'" the district central schools of the Society could not be said to train at all.[1]

Indeed, at this date there was, according to Dr. Kay,[2] only one genuine training institution in the country—the Glasgow Normal Seminary, the home of Stow's training system. Here two objects were kept in view: (1) to convey general knowledge to the candidates; and (2) to make them acquainted with the principles upon which the methods of instruction were based, at the same time giving them practice in putting these principles into execution, first in a small school, and then from time to time in a larger school conducted on the same plan. The qualifications of students entering and the time spent in the seminary varied considerably.[3] Thus of forty-one men admitted in 1840[4] one was a preacher, twenty-one had been teachers in small adventure schools, one had been a carpenter, one a teacher of dancing, one a portrait painter, one a baker, three shopmen, and five students at colleges. The previous occupation of the remaining seven was not ascertained, nor was that of the fourteen women students. The average duration of the course was eight to nine months. A minimum period of eighteen months was felt to be necessary for those who came with poor academic qualifications. The course was divided as follows: out of forty hours a week, sixteen were devoted to academic studies—physics, natural history, geography, arithmetic

The Glasgow Normal Seminary.

---

[1] *Select Committee,* 1838: Minutes of Evidence, 889. An expression of this unrest is found in the vote of £10,000 in 1835 for the erection of model schools. The money was not allocated, however, until four years later. [2] Kay-Shuttleworth.

[3] *Select Committee,* 1838: Minutes of Evidence (265-6).

[4] Committee of Council, 1840, *Minutes.*

and algebra, English grammar, sacred history—together with elocution, music, drawing and gymnastics. The professional work included: I. Observation in the model schools (8 hours), II. Practice lessons in gallery and class (11½ hours), III. Bible lesson to fellow-students (1 hour), IV. Public criticism lessons (3½ hours).[1]

All sorts of schemes were in the air and awaited being put to the proof.[2] Stow had not preached in

Need for Improving the Conditions of Teachers. vain the great truth that all real education depends upon the interaction of the cultivated with the less cultivated mind, and that to teach meant to incite to learn. Admitting this, a new method of school organisation was necessary; school staffs must be increased by the addition of assistant teachers who should exhibit a greater degree of culture and increased professional skill. Reformers looked eagerly to an improved training college course, beginning at 18 years of age and lasting for two or three years, and to ensure a steady supply of good material men were seeking for some means of retaining the services of picked monitors. The economic aspect of the teacher question was recognised

---

[1] A critical account of the system of training is given in the *Minutes of the Committee of Council*, 1840, pp. 412-424. Some ten years later, under the system of Treasury grants to training colleges, Stow bewailed the fact that the entry of younger pupils less well prepared had resulted in the gradual encroachment of academic studies to the detriment of the purely professional work. Less interest was shown in this part of the course, and he was forced to the conclusion that the only solution was a two-year academic course followed by one year devoted to purely professional work.

[2] The erection of Normal schools with model schools attached held a prominent place in the Chartist plan of educational reform as propounded by William Lovett. They were to be adequately staffed, supplied with the best works on physical, mental, moral, and political training, and with proper apparatus. Certificates should be awarded, and no one should hold a post in a Chartist school without one. The length of training was not stipulated. (Lovett and Collins: *Chartism*, p. 41.)

as serious, and palliatives had to be discovered. The following proposals emanating from the National Society will serve to illustrate the trend of opinion at the time : " Probationers should enter at the age of 18 into a normal school in London; that they should remain two years; that after two years they should undergo an examination as to character and acquirements, and if they went through it creditably, receive a certificate, and be appointed as assistant schoolmasters in the first instance; that having passed that, they should receive a second certificate, which should entitle them to promotion under the (National) society ; that if they acquitted themselves well in their situations as schoolmasters, at the end of a certain number of years, say every ten years, they should be entitled to a small increase of salary, or to promotion to some higher school; and that when they were in a state which required them to be superannuated, they should be entitled to a retiring pension from the Consolidated Fund." [1]

Activity in
the National
Society.

Under the influence of the new religious spirit in the Church, and with the growth of opinion in favour of a State system of education, the National Society had, in fact, awoke to a new sense of its responsibilities. In 1838 a Committee of Inquiry and Correspondence was appointed for the purpose of stimulating local interest on the subject of education, and of bringing various orders and classes throughout the country to act together in a combined plan for extending the operations of the society. One of its main objects was to devise means " to provide a better class of teachers, by improving the education, condition, and prospects of schoolmasters." To carry out this object it was proposed at once to connect training schools with

[1] *Select Committee on Education*, 1838, Minutes of Evidence.

the cathedrals in several dioceses, and, if sufficient funds could be raised, to found "an Institution of a superior order in London, for still further improving the education and training of masters." Other plans were under consideration as indicated in the preceding paragraph for improving the status and prospects of teachers and providing for their old age.[1]

The real difficulty was concisely put by the Secretary of the Committee of Council a few years later.[2]

Poor Salaries the Obstacle to Educational Progress. "There is little or nothing in the profession of an elementary schoolmaster, in this country to tempt a man having a respectable acquaintance with the elements of even humble learning to exchange the certainty of a respectable livelihood in a subordinate condition in trade or commerce for the mean drudgery of instructing the rude children of the poor in an elementary school.

"For what is the condition of the master of such a school? He has often an income very little greater than that of an agricultural labourer, and very rarely equal to that of a moderately skilled mechanic. Moreover it is beset with uncertainties. He tries all manner of means to eke it out, and even if he be successful, these additions barely keep him out of debt, and in old age he has no prospect but helpless indigence and dependence." He added: "The first business of the State is to improve the lot of the teacher. To build spacious and well-ventilated schools, without attempting to provide a position of honour and emolument for the masters, is to cheat the poor with a cruel illusion. . . . Whilst their condition remains without improvement, a religious motive alone can induce

---

[1] See National Society Report; also abstract *Educational Magazine*, November 1838. See also *ante*, p. 258.

[2] Kay-Shuttleworth: *Four Periods of Public Education*, pp. 474-5.

the young men who are now (1847) trained in Normal Schools to sacrifice all prospects of personal advancement for the self-denying and arduous duties of a teacher of the children of the poor." [1]

This candid recognition of the fact that the supply of efficient teachers is first and foremost an economic question marks a great advance in the educational thought of the day and the beginning of a new movement. Hitherto all the attention had been given to improving such teaching material as was available by seeing that it was properly " trained." Thus the first proposal of the Committee of Council in 1839 was to set up a State Training College. This tendency to magnify the importance of mere training, rather than the quality of the individual who was to be trained, was perhaps inevitable at a time when the need for bringing about a change in existing methods was acutely realised, and before the nature of the problem had been very clearly understood.

It was at this time that attention was given to the improvement of teaching in infant schools. **The Training of Infant-School Teachers.** Previous to 1836 no provision existed in England for the systematic training of this class of teacher. Although the training of teachers was the chief object in view in founding the Infant School Society in 1824, no central training institution had been established, though use had been made temporarily of the schools at Spitalfields and Walthamstow. Lectures were also given on infant education by the secretary of the society, J. P. Greaves, but it was to the " missionary " journeys of Wilderspin that the spread of the system was mainly due. Wilderspin acted

[1] The yearly stipends of the 234 head teachers in Lancashire schools whose salaries were ascertained in 1846 amounted to £9,676 10s.—Report on the Northern Division, 1846.

as a sort of organising master, and travelled up and down the country in response to invitations from local committees who were interested in the movement. He would expound his system and then, if the committee were agreeable, he would undertake to open and organise a school on their behalf, and conduct it until he had initiated the teachers who were to take charge of it into the method. These, for the time being, acted as his assistants. His stay in one place varied considerably, but six weeks was an average time for planting a school and training the teachers. The defects of such a system were soon obvious.[1]

The Home and Colonial Society, founded in 1836, put infant education and the training of infant teachers on a somewhat more satisfactory basis. A central model school was established, to which students of both sexes and married couples were admitted for a period of not less than 12 weeks.[2]

Meantime an experiment that was to have far-reaching results was about to begin. With the pass-**Early Experiments with Pupil Teachers.** ing of the Poor Law Amendment Act, 1834, considerable difficulty was experienced in getting suitable teachers who were able at once to give both the intellectual and industrial training

---

[1] In spite of all Wilderspin's exertions the system was scarcely known by name in many parts of the country, while in London infant education was under an eclipse. "Without means, without methods, without common sense to guide those who took upon themselves the office of instructors, the veriest drivelling and nauseating gibberish . . . the most stupid masses of imbecile twaddle (called intellectual training) was attempted to be crammed into the minds of children by the most absurd methods." The wonder is that the infant system had not utterly disappeared.—*Educational Magazine*, 1838, p. 429.

[2] So ill supported was the society at the outset, that by January 1838 the total donations and subscriptions received were only £383.—*Educational Magazine*, 1838, p. 7.

that was demanded in workhouse schools. It was the practice to send teachers to certain picked schools of industry to study organisation and to acquire the necessary industrial proficiency. The need for a special type of teacher for schools of this nature influenced Dr. Kay, at that time one of the Assistant Poor Law Commissioners, to suggest the apprenticing of a number of picked monitors as pupil teachers for a period of five years. In this way it was hoped to ensure a supply of teachers inured from their earliest years to industrial occupations, and yet possessed of the necessary intellectual attainments. The plan was successfully introduced into the Norwood School of Industry and elsewhere.[1]

In 1840, with the abandoning of the plan of a State Normal School, Dr. Kay—now secretary of An Experiment in the Training of Teachers. the Committee of Council on Education—in conjunction with Mr. Tufnell, began a further experiment in the training of teachers. He was profoundly convinced that the first business of a training college was to turn out teachers of character. At the same time it had to develop the intelligence of the students, and provide appropriate training in industry, and in the methods and principles of teaching. He was also anxious to show that, "without violating the rights of conscience, masters trained in a spirit of Christian charity, and instructed in the discipline and doctrine of the Church, might be employed in the mixed schools necessarily connected with public establishments, and in which children of persons of all shades of religious opinion are assembled."[2] What was wanted was an entirely new system of training. To conceive that a few months' attendance at a Model School should make a man of the humblest

[1] *Select Committee of Education*, Minutes of Evidence, 1834.
[2] *Four Periods of Public Education*, p. 426.

academic attainments acquainted with the theory of its organisation, convert him into an adept in its methods, or even to rivet on his memory any but the least significant factors, "is a mistake too shameful to be permitted to survive its universal failure." [1]

The training college was to be imbued with the spirit of Pestalozzi. It was to train a race of teachers who, with the expectation of little pecuniary recompense, were to devote their lives to the education of poor children in workhouses and elsewhere. Hence they must be trained to habits of frugality and inured to manual occupations. The model was found in the work of the Christian Brothers in France and in Vehrli's Training School in Switzerland. A manor house with five acres of land was purchased at Battersea, and two types of students were admitted : boys over 13 years of age—pupil teachers— from the Norwood School of Industry, and young men 20 to 30 years of age. The former were to stay some five years, first as pupil teachers and then as assistant teachers. The men entered only for one year. . The academic attainments of the candidates were not high. They were formed into two groups and instructed in English, mathematics, heat, natural history, geography, history, religion, drawing, music, and gymnastics, according to the most approved methods, and always with an eye to the practical utility of the course for their future work. Thus arithmetic was taught on Pestalozzian lines, mechanics by discussion of every-day contrivances; heuristic methods were the order of the day; excursions in connection with the natural history, geography, and history lessons were a recognised part of the work, and so on. In addition the students were given a practical training in such industrial occupations as were suited to rural districts—gardening,

[1] Four Periods of Public Education, p. 410.

trenching, management of animals, putting up simple buildings, etc. They were also required to perform all the domestic duties of the establishment. Food was plain and the appointments were of the simplest. Practical training in teaching was provided in the village school. At the outset of the experiment the working day lasted from 5.30 a.m. to 9 p.m., variety of occupation and a good deal of outdoor work taking the place of any interval for recreation.[1]

The foreign note about the whole scheme is very striking. Experience soon proved that without considerable modification it would not serve its purpose in this country. The founder still believed in the soundness of the underlying principles, but the scheme as arranged turned out teachers unsuited to schools save in quiet rural areas. In large towns the young teachers found themselves lacking in the worldly wisdom that was needed to adapt their training to the complicated conditions with which they were confronted. The result was to strengthen in the mind of the founder a belief in the pupil teacher system as opposed to the practice of secluding students from an early age in a college. What was lost in this way was more than made up for, he felt, by the familiarity gained of the peculiar circumstances the young people would later have to deal with. Moreover the experiment had convinced him that a training college course begun before 18 years of age was of very little value owing to the immaturity of the student. In 1843 the College was transferred to the National Society.[2]

---

[1] See Kay-Shuttleworth : *Four Periods of Public Education*, pp. 293-431.

[2] *Ibid.* Compare the interesting experiment in training masters for Workhouse schools at Kneller Hall. See *Minutes of the Committee of Council*, Vol. 1., 1851-2.

Meantime great activity was going on in other quarters.
Development of the Training College Movement after 1839. The two great societies had been definitely entrusted by the Committee of Council with the work of training teachers, and the Government grant of £10,000 had been divided between them. Both societies set to work to improve their central training schools at the Borough Road and at Westminster. At the same time the National Society put into operation its scheme for extending the facilities for training. Many of the provincial Model Schools were improved and Diocesan Training Institutes were immediately established in the Dioceses of Chester, Exeter, Oxford, Salisbury, etc. St. Mark's College, Chelsea, was opened in 1841, Whitelands early in the following year, and from this time the founding of training colleges was steadily pushed forward, assisted by a capitation building grant from the Committee of Council of £50 per place in 1844. Model schools were also assisted on the same terms as ordinary schools. A further grant of £10 per head was contributed by the National Society. Homerton was opened by the Congregational Board of Education (1845), and other Nonconformist training colleges at Rotherhithe, and for Welsh teachers at Brecon—the latter being afterwards removed to Swansea. St. Mary's, Hammersmith, was established by the Roman Catholic Poor School Committee in 1847, and two colleges for women came into existence eight years later.

It was, however, one thing to open training colleges and another to fill them. It was the experience of the next few years that taught men that the first step towards raising the general level of efficiency in schools was to make teaching more attractive. It was useless to attempt to fill the colleges with students who were physically and mentally unfitted for the work, who had "too often no further education than what can be obtained in an elementary school of average character during the usual period of attendance till 13 years of age." But ill-adapted as this class of student was, their number was barely sufficient to keep the schools alive. There was no opportunity for selection, the supply was imperfect and precarious, and the opening up of other sources was a matter of urgency. Many more teachers were needed. Schools still existed with upwards of 200 children in charge of a single master or mistress, while the average number of pupils per teacher in inspected schools in the North of England was 80. It was necessary to reinforce the school staffs as cheaply as possible and to replace the monitor, now fallen into disrepute, by something better.[1] In order to appreciate the difficulties of the situation we must remember that whatever dignity the primary school has to-day was altogether lacking at the middle of last century. People had not yet realised that elementary education is necessarily costly, and even if they had realised it, there was nothing like adequate secondary school accommodation to provide a race of well-educated teachers. Indeed the movement for the higher education of girls even of the middle classes had not yet begun.

It was at this stage that the Committee of Council definitely took in hand the work of creating an efficient teaching profession. The most promising way seemed to be to capture picked boys and girls and apprentice them to the head master or mistress as had been done at Norwood,

A Semi-State Service of Teachers.

---

[1] With the general school-leaving age being very low, especially in agricultural and manufacturing districts, the monitorial system had broken down in spite of valiant efforts to secure efficient monitors. The youth of these individuals had shaken the confidence of parents and had reacted very seriously upon the attendance of even the young children.

and at the same time to improve the prospects of the teachers. This step was taken in 1846.

In every school under Government inspection one or more of the brightest scholars might be apprenticed

The Beginning of the Pupil Teacher System. to the head master or mistress for five years from 13 to 18, providing that the teacher was competent to conduct the apprentice through the stipulated course of instruction and that the school conformed to certain requirements as to organisation, apparatus, etc. The pupil teachers had to present themselves for examination yearly, and if they acquitted themselves creditably the Government paid the master or mistress by whom they had been trained the sum of £5 for one, of £9 for two, of £12 for three pupil teachers and £3 per annum more for each additional apprentice.[1] In special cases, where a head teacher was unable to conform to the whole of the necessary conditions, " stipendiary monitors " serving for a period of four years might be appointed. These were required to pass easier examinations, and the master drew a smaller bonus than in the case of pupil teachers. The stipends of pupil teachers and monitors alike were paid by the Government. These ranged from £10 to £20 and from £5 to £12 10s. respectively according to the length of service. In many cases some small additional rewards of clothes and books were given by the school managers.

At the close of the apprenticeship pupil teachers might submit themselves to a competitive examina-

Queen's Scholarships. tion for Queen's Scholarships which would admit them to a training college for three years. Unsuccessful candidates who had acquitted them-

---

[1] An additional grant was given for training the pupil teacher in gardening, workshop practice, or in the case of girls domestic economy, including cookery and laundry work. Head teachers were required to instruct pupil teachers 1½ hours per day out of school hours.

selves creditably might be offered posts in the Civil Service. At the close of each year of training a Certificate Examination offering three degrees of merit was to be held, on the result of which large grants were to be paid to the training college. The object of this was to produce greater efficiency and at the same time to give much needed financial assistance to training colleges.[1]

A similar Acting Teachers' examination for granting certificates to those who had not been through a Normal school was provided for.

In connection with these certificates liberal grants were paid by the Government. These grants were **Attempts to make Teaching Attractive.** intended to provide a basis for a scale of salaries that was calculated to make elementary teaching more attractive. According as a teacher had spent one, two, or three years in a training college he received grants of £15-18, £20-23, and £25-30, the actual sum depending upon whether he held a first, second, or third class certificate. These payments were, however, subject to the condition that the school managers provided a house and a further salary of at least twice the amount of the Government grant, and that the teacher continued to receive a satisfactory report from the inspector. The scale of payments to schoolmistresses was two-thirds of that to men. At the same time a pension scheme was proposed for teachers having a minimum of

---

[1] The average expense per student per annum in a Normal school was estimated at £50. Under the new conditions the training college would obtain for every student grants of £20 at the end of the first year, £25 at the end of the second, and £30 at the close of the third year, providing he obtained in each year the Government certificate of merit. In other words, the Government proposed to spend in educating a male teacher £190 ; £75 during apprenticeship, £20 to £25 as a scholarship, £75 paid to the training college, besides an additional £15 to £20 paid to the master of the school where he served as a pupil teacher. The value of a scholarship in women's colleges was in 1850 made equal to two-thirds that awarded a man.

15 years' service. This did not come into operation until five years later.[1] Within two years over 2,000 pupil teachers had been apprenticed.

At this time a great deal of variety existed among the different training colleges. In the absence

General Education v. Professional Training.

of tradition to guide them, they showed wide differences in the nature and length of the training they offered, in the character of the curriculum and in the age at which students were admitted. Some provided a course stretching over a period of from one to three years. In others students might leave at the end of three months. Borough Road concentrated attention on professional training, St. Mark's, Chelsea, and the majority of the other colleges devoted their energies to advancing the general education of the students. Thus we are told that in 1846 there was little to distinguish St. Mark's "from the schools of the upper and middle class or as a place for the education of teachers rather than any other class of persons," and the question that troubled the onlooker was how far all this was fitting the students for their work as teachers. The problem of the relative emphasis to lay upon academic and upon professional work had in fact already arisen, and within the next few years it was decided in favour of furthering the general education of the students and putting the study of " school management " on a level with any other subjects.

---

[1] The amount to be distributed in pensions was limited to £6,500 per annum and the maximum pension to £30. These various benefits were extended as a result of a petition from the British Schoolmasters' Association to untrained certificated teachers. See Minutes of Committee of Council, 1846, pp. 16-17. Lord Lingen, in evidence before the Cross Commission, maintained that the purpose of this pension scheme was to aid in the removal of inefficient teachers, just as the augmentation grants were to aid in attracting better teachers. (*Report*, p. 83.) It is certain, however, that the teachers themselves did not read it in this way.

The students were picked up, as it were, by accident. Many had no previous experience of teaching **The Low Attainments of Students.** and few had more than they might have obtained by teaching in a Sunday school. Their age might vary anywhere between 16 and 33. They had generally everything to learn and the qualifications for admission were uniformly low. At St. Mark's, for example, one of the best colleges of the day, they were required "to read English prose with propriety, to spell correctly from dictation, to write a good hand, to be well acquainted with the outlines of Scripture history, and to show considerable readiness in working the fundamental rules of arithmetic." The reports of inspectors show that even these meagre attainments were imperfectly acquired. Thus we read of colleges where "few students could read with correct emphasis or just expression, who had not overcome the mechanical difficulties of reading, and whose compositions showed such a defective education as to make it questionable whether they ought to be allowed under any circumstances to teach."

In spite of this the training college curriculum was generally conspicuously ambitious. In 1844 **Defects of Training College Curricula.** we find colleges attempting to teach four or five subjects such as algebra, Euclid, trigonometry, mechanics, chemistry, and land-surveying, Greek and Roman history, Latin and Greek, etc. The work was necessarily characterised by superficiality ; it appealed entirely to the memory and ignored principles. The following is typical of the criticism directed against these establishments in 1847. "Why should we, in our Training Colleges, set at nought the principles on which instruction in our best schools and our Universities is founded, viz., that of teaching well a limited number of subjects. . . . . Let us see that the trained master possesses the knowledge which he will be called upon to communicate; and more, let us lay in his mind a sound scientific foundation for every part of this knowledge to rest steadily upon; so that the structure may have connection, unity, and completeness, as far as it extends. If we send forth the teacher to the discharge of his lowly but momentous duties with, in most cases, only a moderate range of attainment, let us provide that he have acquired such a readiness on all that concerns the art of teaching as will render his knowledge at once available. Nothing like this has yet been satisfactorily realised by any of our Training Colleges, and perhaps they might have approached more nearly to it had their aim been more strictly limited to a range defined by the practical objects for which they have been instituted." [1]

Whether the colleges were entirely to blame in this respect is doubtful, for at this time the Committee of Council itself had adopted an over-sanguine view of the situation. The examination questions set to individual training colleges were often highly absurd and calculated to perpetuate wrong standards. Thus we find candidates being required to outline the history of China in a question on a geography paper, " to trace briefly the changes of government which Athens, Sparta, and Rome underwent previous to the commencement of modern history " as the first of seven questions on general history, and the like. After six years' experience of this sort of " training," the Committee of Council made provision for the establishment of a three years' course for all students, an ideal that has still to be realised for the majority to-day, and at the same time it proposed a certificate examination which, in view

Responsibility of the Committee of Council.

---

[1] Committee of Council Minutes, 1847-8, II., p. 537.

of the defective state of education, seems to spread itself somewhat unnecessarily and did little or nothing to check the waste of energy that was the cardinal weakness of training college instruction. Thus candidates were to exhibit in writing a competent ability in religious knowledge (in Church schools), English grammar and paraphrasing, English history, general geography, especially the descriptive, physical and historical geography of the British Empire and Palestine, arithmetic, Euclid, Books I. and II., algebra as far as simple equations, the elements of mechanics, popular astronomy, and the composition of the notes of a lesson or some observations on the practical duties of a teacher. One or two of the following might, however, be substituted and indeed were necessary for a higher class certificate—vocal music, drawing from models, history and etymology of the English language, modern history, ancient history, physical science, higher mathematics, Latin and Greek.[1]

Much was hoped from the pupil teacher system which **The Training Colleges between 1846 and 1856.** was to bring the first batch of Queen's Scholars into the training colleges in 1852 with attainments much in advance of what it had hitherto been possible to look for. Besides skill in vocal music, drawing and teaching, these students would have passed through "an elementary course in religion, in English grammar and composition, in the history of their country, in arithmetic, algebra, mensuration, the rudiments of mechanics, in the art of land-surveying and levelling, in geography, and such ele-

---

[1] Women substituted natural history, bookkeeping and needlework for the more mathematical part of the men's syllabus. At St. Mark's, Chelsea, Latin and Greek were still included in the curriculum; at Chester, optics and the properties of bodies, land-surveying and agricultural chemistry at York, natural philosophy and natural history, logic, Latin and Greek.

ments of nautical astronomy as are comprised in the use of the globes." Additional accommodation was provided to meet the anticipated demand, but the results were disappointing. There was nothing like the readiness to enter the training colleges that had been expected. Moreover few students showed any willingness to stay more than 12 months. Accordingly the colleges were experiencing severe financial strain, and at the same time the value of the work that they were doing was being more and more called in question. First their syllabuses were restricted so as to emphasise the study of those subjects that are taught in primary schools.[1] A common examination was set to all colleges, and grants were made to encourage more efficient staffing. The Queen's Scholarship Examination was thrown open to all over 18 years of age regardless of whether they had been apprenticed or not. Every inducement was made to get ex-pupil teachers to enter the colleges and to stay there at least two years. To begin with, the number of Queen's Scholars in any college was restricted to 25 per cent. of the total number taking courses of one year and upwards. This restriction was now abolished. Efforts were made to induce training colleges to cease acting as secondary schools and to bestow more attention on professional training. Such was the position in 1856.

---

[1] Subjects of examination 1856.—Religious knowledge, arithmetic, grammar and English language, school management, reading, spelling, penmanship, class teaching, history, geography, drawing, music, geometry, mechanics, algebra or Latin (these four in first year only), physical science, higher mathematics, English literature or Latin (all in second year only). In the third year *one* of the following subjects might be taken in addition to religious knowledge, school management, vocal music and drawing, viz. mental science as applied to education, experimental science, higher mathematics, languages—Latin, Greek, German or French, history, English literature.

The Rev. F. Temple's [1] Report on Church Training Colleges for this year presents a masterly survey

Temple's Report, 1856. of the situation. The work in these institutions was characterised as generally good and steadily improving, and the limitation of the training college syllabus had been beneficial to both lecturer and students. The practice that had been instituted of testing the proficiency of the actual training by making second year students teach before an inspector had had the result of checking undue attention to academic subjects. Various changes were, however, still necessary. Far too much of the training consisted in acquiring facility in giving oral lessons, and no other type of lesson was ever presented at a training college inspection. This was a mistake, seeing that the business of the schoolmaster was "not so much to teach as to make the children learn." Equal attention ought to be given to the other activities that enter into school work, not only as far as different types of lessons were concerned but with regard to the general mangement and organisation of the school. Again, every training college needed to have associated with it two types of school, one a demonstration school in the highest sense of the term under specially skilled teachers, where students went not to teach but to study, where they went with definite questions in mind and sought for an answer to them. The other was a practising school, where they might endeavour to put into practice what they had learnt both in lectures, by reading and by observation.

Moreover, far more attention needed to be given to presenting students with good models of teaching by the training college staff. No member had a right on such a

[1] Afterwards Headmaster of Rugby, Bishop of Exeter, Bishop of London, and Archbishop of Canterbury.

staff who was not himself a good teacher, and each lecturer ought to be made responsible for the special method of his own subject; in all his lecturing he ought to have in view the special needs of training college students. So far as lectures on teaching were concerned, the great need of the day was simplicity, the abandonment of abstract verbiage that meant nothing to anybody, and a real determination to come down and study the problems that actually confronted the teacher. Lecturers required a far better preparation for their work. He would have them study the science and history of education and the systems and methods of teaching, but he was sceptical of the value of contemporary psychology. "Mental Science is in general too abstract, too removed from all practical applications to be of much real value to a normal master." Indeed he would altogether discourage the study of psychology by training college students. The position is incongruous, but few will deny that psychology is better left alone than taught badly.

Finally, he altogether dissociated himself from any attempt to relax the standard of the certificate examinations, on the ground that, in spite of apparent exceptions, an ill-informed, ill-educated person can never make a good teacher.

By 1860 the training college system was in full working order, and some 34 colleges were providing accommodation for 2,388 students, an increase of 18 colleges and 1,397 places in ten years.[1] On all hands the superiority of the trained over the untrained teacher was admitted. "As a class they are marked, men and women, by a quickness of ear and eye, a quiet energy, a facility of command, and

Superiority of Trained over Untrained Teachers.

---

[1] The number of pupil teachers in 1861 was 13,871.

a patient self-control, which, with rare exceptions, are not observed in the private instructors of the poor."[1] This commendation is borne out by results. Taking the 686 schools in one inspectorial district, 470 under trained and 215 under untrained teachers, and dividing them into good, fair and inferior, it was found that of the former 24 per cent. were good, 49 per cent. fair, 27 per cent. inferior; of the latter, 3 per cent. were good, 39 per cent. fair, 58 per cent. inferior.[2]

Much of the credit for this was given to the pupil teacher system. The reports of inspectors **The Pupil Teacher System at Work.** speak highly of the pupil teachers. Matthew Arnold refers to them as the "sinews of English primary instruction." In ordinary power of class management they were often superior to the older type of teacher, but the system was open to criticism. It was being used as a means of cheap staffing. To prevent this, in 1859 the number of apprentices allowed was one to every 40 children, and a maximum of four under any one master or mistress. There was also the objection that the pupil teachers had too heavy a day. Some $5\frac{1}{2}$ hours were given to teaching, half an hour to looking after books and apparatus, $1\frac{1}{2}$ hours to lessons, and whatever time remained was available for private study. The result was that not uncommonly a great accumulation of facts would be found, allied to a low degree of mental culture and general intelligence.[3] This had an inevitable effect on the value of their work as teachers. They are described as being often "too pedantic, too mechanical, and too much lost in routine." Their teaching was apt to be

---

[1] Newcastle Commission Report, p. 151.

[2] Newcastle Commission Report, p. 149.

[3] Matthew Arnold's Report, 1852, quoted in Newcastle Report, p. 106.

"meagre, dry, and empty," or it would go to the oppo-site extreme of "presumption and ostentation." How-ever well they might "manage" their classes, there was little of the elements present that make for real discipline and for inciting to learn.

Important changes affecting both teachers and training colleges were introduced by the Revised Code. Mr. Lowe had denied that there was such a thing as a science of education.

Influence of the Revised Code.

Building grants to training colleges ceased, and a new and narrower curriculum was imposed. It was in fact an elementary school syllabus magnified and made more difficult.[1] The same syllabus was retained for pupil teachers. Students were then kept grinding at the same subjects, each very limited in range, for seven or eight years. Anything more deadening it is difficult to imagine. A premium was immediately set on memoris-ing. The most trivial details were attended to and learnt, while anything calculated to broaden the outlook and to increase the cultivation of the individual was conspicuously absent.

For the old agreement between the master and appren-tice was substituted one between pupil teacher and managers. Instead of continu-ing to pay the salaries of pupil teachers, the Committee of Council made a grant to the managers, who were left to make what terms they liked with the pupil teachers. Under the old conditions salaries had averaged £15, now they averaged £13 9s. for boys and £12 15s. for girls. This, combined with the withdrawal of payments

Falling off of Pupil Teachers.

---

[1] It comprised for men religious knowledge, arithmetic, reading, spelling, penmanship, history, geography, geometry, political economy, music, and drawing. For women, sewing and cutting out and domestic science took the place of political economy, geometry, and algebra.

direct to certificated teachers, resulted in making elementary teaching less attractive. By 1866 the number of pupil teachers had fallen to 8,866, a drop of more than one-third,[1] and the standard of the Queen's Scholarship examination had to be lowered. At the same time there was a fall in the staffing of schools. The ideal had been one pupil teacher or an equivalent adult teacher for every 25 scholars. In 1861 the ratio was 1 to 36, by 1866 it had fallen to 1 in 54. The threatened shortage of teachers induced the Government to give an extra capitation grant to encourage better staffing, and extra grants were paid on the results of the scholarship and certificate examinations. By 1868 the number of pupil teachers was over eleven thousand, and by 1870 was 14,621.[2]

The history of the next 20 years may be conveniently summarised round the Report of the Cross Commission. The coming of the School Boards had done something to restore for the time being the attractiveness of the elementary teaching profession. Various attempts were made to improve the pupil teacher system. The system of examination grants was revised, the age of apprenticeship was raised from 13 to 14, and efforts were made to attract a somewhat different type of pupil teacher by relaxing the number of years of apprenticeship to those who had attained a higher standard of education. The signs were unmistakable that the pupil teacher system had begun to raise exactly the same kind of doubts in the minds of many observers as the old monitorial system that it had replaced. Much of this was undoubtedly

Doubts about the Pupil Teacher System.

[1] See *ante*, p. 354.

[2] Between 1860 and 1870 the number of training colleges remained stationary and the total accommodation only increased by about 100.

due to the steady rising of the educational standard of the day and the competition of the assistant teacher. The assistant teacher was an outcome of the pupil teacher system. He was generally an old ex-pupil teacher, who might or might not be certificated, and was obviously a more useful and efficient member of a school staff. In other words, a higher ideal of what the staff of an elementary school ought to be was coming over the country. One result of this was seen in the demand that first-year pupil teachers should not be counted on school staffs at all.

At the same time it was realised that the plan of making a head teacher responsible for the academic education of the apprentice was unwise, in that it presupposed qualifications that only the exceptional teacher could be expected to possess. The result of this feeling was seen in the movement for Pupil Teachers' Centres that arose about 1875. Owing to various causes they did not come into operation until 1881. Further advance was made in 1884, when pupil teachers were not required to teach more than half time, and might attend classes for general instruction at pupil teachers' centres during the day, instead of as hitherto during the evening. The system was one that was particularly suited to large centres of population, and it spread rapidly to all parts of the country. It was the object of much conflicting opinion. Many saw in it the germs of a reformed pupil teacher system. Others, among them some of the best elementary school teachers, conscious of the interest they had taken in their pupil teachers, were opposed to the change. Looking back, it is hardly possible to doubt that the establishment of Centres was a tacit admission of the breakdown of the old pupil teacher system.

Rise of Pupil Teachers' Centres.

The Report of the Cross Commission (1888) shows a marked divergence of opinion with regard to **Divergent Views of the Cross Commissioners.** pupil teachers, and affords additional evidence that the system was being rapidly outgrown. The Commissioners were unanimous as to the value of central classes, and the majority concurred with the senior inspectors of the Education Department that there was no " equally trustworthy source from which an adequate supply of teachers " was likely to be forthcoming, and with modifications for the improvement of their education the apprenticeship of pupil teachers ought to be upheld. On the other hand, the minority were of opinion that the pupil teacher system was the weakest part of the educational machinery, and that the best security for good teachers would be a prolonged period of preliminary education. " The complaint is general that the pupil teachers teach badly, and are badly taught, . . . and the remarkable thing is that the witnesses, while complaining generally of the backwardness and ignorance of pupil teachers, lay special stress on their inability to teach and on their ignorance of school management." They emphasised their argument by pointing out the crude and unprepared state in which students entered training colleges. The Centre system was a palliative so long as the hours during which pupil teachers were required to teach were diminished, but it could not be regarded as a final arrangement. The result of the Report was to set the pupil teacher system on its trial.

Meantime developments of importance were taking place with regard to the training colleges. The **Lack of Training College Accommodation.** importance of training was being more and more recognised. For some years previous to 1888 the number of persons admitted as pupil teachers varied from 8,000 to 9,000 per annum, and about 6,000 completed their apprenticeship each year. Theoretically all those who passed in the first or second class of the Queen's Scholarship examination were eligible to enter a training college, and the colleges who were free to do so usually chose those who were highest on the list. In 1888 there was training college accommodation for about 1,600 students per annum. In the same year over 2,800 were eligible by their place on the scholarship list for admission. There was thus a considerable shortage of accommodation, although there were nine more colleges in existence than in 1870.[1] The situation was further complicated owing to the fact that the majority of the colleges belonged to the Church of England, and only eight were undenominational. Of these six belonged to the British and Foreign Society.[2]

Growing Liberality of Training College Curriculum. With such a choice of material it would have been surprising if the training colleges at this time had not been doing good work. They had to a great extent outgrown the warping influence of the restricted curriculum that was imposed in 1862. Since 1870 it had been possible for students to enter for various science subjects under the Science and Art Department. Extra grants were earned in this way, and additional marks were

[1] Allowance must of course be made for those who had no intention of entering a training college.

[2] The data of the forty-three colleges were as follows :—

	Colleges.	Accommodation.			Students.
Church of England	30	2,232, i.e.	66·3	per cent.	2,210
Undenominational	2	151 ,,	4·5	,,	147
Undenominational Brit. & For. Soc.	6	517 ,,	15·3	,,	515
Wesleyan	2	240 ,,	7·1	,,	227
Roman Catholic	3	238 ,,	6·7	,,	173

awarded in the certificate examination. The effect had been to give a somewhat undue importance to certain science subjects in the colleges. Later languages and political economy also found a place, and these together with science were allowed as alternative subjects in the certificate examination. The latitude that had resulted had enabled the best colleges to prepare students for the degree examinations of the London University. At the same time the demand for a three-year course arose in various quarters, and attention was directed to the question of bringing picked students directly under University influence.

In spite of these results a good deal of criticism was directed against the colleges on various **Criticism of** grounds. The working hours were too **the Training** long,[1] too much was done for the students, **Colleges.** many of the colleges were very ill-equipped for science teaching, the staffs were too largely recruited from old students, with the result that there tended to be a certain narrowness about the work, and the outlook was too parochial. The minority report of the Cross Commission suggested that what the colleges as a whole needed was "not a more extensive curriculum, but a more thorough and intellectual study of the matters included in the curriculum; lecturers who shall combine a wide knowledge of their subject with the technical ability in handling classes." Moreover more variety both in type of student and of training college was required.

What the colleges at this period were like as viewed from within may be gathered from the following extracts. Speaking of women's colleges in 1886 Sir Joshua Fitch

---

[1] At Battersea, for example, in 1887 the seniors had 32½ hours' lectures and class work per week, and 22 hours' private study.

reported : " The teaching staff of the colleges consists very largely of certificated governesses selected on the ground of their success as college students or as mistresses of schools, but with necessarily limited reading and intellectual experience, and often with salaries inferior to those of the mistresses in Board Schools. The teaching, therefore, though for the most part extremely careful and conscientious, is often sadly lacking in breadth and vigour."

The following is a description by an old student of a London college for men in 1875. It must not, however, be regarded as applicable in detail to all :—

". . . during the seventies, the students, about 130 in number, had no place for recreation worthy of the name, no library and reading-room ; no pictures appeared on the walls of the dingy class-rooms, and there were no facilities for sitting out of doors or meeting in the open air.

The paved yard of irregular shape, surrounded by forbidding walls, was all too small even for the ordinary drill exercises taken once a week, in two sections ; whilst the small and badly-equipped gymnasium could only be used by a few men at a time—the enthusiasts in boxing and Indian club exercises. In short, it may be said that the College authorities made practically no provision for physical exercises and games.

Recreation took the form mainly of walking through the neighbouring streets for an hour before dinner and half-an-hour before tea.

. . . .

The ordinary class-rooms were used for recreative reading after class hours, and few men could find a comfortable place in which to sit, and in winter the fires could be approached by only a small section of those who needed warmth and brightness. Magazines and newspapers were purchased by the students from funds subscribed by them and handed to a committee of their fellow students, duly elected to perform the necessary duties.

Similarly, concerts and debates were organised by the men, and these (all of them interesting, some ennobling) took place at regular intervals after the classes were closed for the day. The resident superintendent took a personal interest in these meetings, and the men were encouraged by his presence and commendation. The principal class-room—'The Theatre'—was used on such occasions.

The men slept in cubicles, separated by wooden partitions some 6 feet high, arranged in long rows down the corridor 'landings.' The rooms were plainly furnished, but scrupulously clean. No real privacy was possible; and during the winter the bedrooms were subjected to draughts and were bitterly cold." [1]

Much criticism was directed against the denominational character of the majority of the training colleges, but the majority of the Commissioners did not see their way to recommend that these should be thrown open to all and made subject to a conscience clause. Instead they recommended that experiments should be undertaken in the establishment of Day Training Colleges in localities where the necessary demand existed. Such colleges in the opinion of the minority might be supported by local rates and popularly managed, or they might be attached to local Universities. It was also suggested that the ordinary residential training college should open its doors to day students. It is interesting to note that all the Commissioners were of the opinion that some system of residence was a very valuable adjunct of training college life.

With 1890 a new era in the history of training began. The Education Department adopted the **Rise of University Day Training Colleges** suggestion of the majority report, and provided for the establishment of University Day Training Colleges. At the same time day students were admitted to residential colleges and a third year of training was sanctioned. To begin with the total number of day students for the

[1] See Report of Board of Education, 1912-13.

whole country was limited to 200, but this restriction was removed in 1891, and since that time the University system has steadily developed. By 1903 there were seventeen Day Training Colleges with accommodation for 2,000 students. To begin with only a proportion of the students entered upon full degree courses. Several important results followed. The degree and sessional examinations in academic subjects held by the Universities and University Colleges were accepted instead of the certificate examination. The variety of curriculum and examination this allowed was in part extended to residential colleges, and students reading for degrees were admitted under similar conditions to the Day Training Colleges, and worked side by side with those reading for the ordinary certificate examination. The effect of this multiplication of syllabuses and examining bodies was the abolition in 1903 of the traditional three grade classification of outgoing teachers and the publication of a single class list. At the same time the competition of the Day Training Colleges had a beneficial effect in improving the staffing of the older colleges.

During this period the pupil teacher system was the object of much attention. Special steps **The Pupil Teacher System on Trial.** were taken to improve the general level of educational efficiency of the apprentice. Between 1896 and 1898 a Departmental Committee made a careful investigation of the whole system. They reported that the time was ripe for a considerable advance, and though the pupil teacher system was the main, it was not the only, nor indeed, ultimately, the cheapest source of supplying teachers for primary schools. " We wish to record as emphatically as possible . . . our conviction that the too frequent practice of committing the whole of the training and teaching of

classes to immature and uneducated young persons is
economically wasteful and educationally unsatisfactory,
and even dangerous to the teachers and the taught in
equal measure. We do not, however, wish to see at present
the entire abolition of a system which ensures an early
acquaintance with the process of teaching, and we have
felt ourselves bound to recognise the established place
which an existing institution has made for itself." Nevertheless they believed that the efficiency of the profession
would be raised by recruiting more and more from those
who had passed through a secondary school, and they
were of opinion that Pupil Teacher Centres should approximate more and more to the spirit of secondary
schools by abandoning the "class" ideal, and giving
more attention to cultivating a social and corporate life,
by strengthening their staffs and striving to give a liberal
education. Pressure of circumstances had compelled many
to be little more than "cramming" institutions. The
Committee looked forward to the ultimate conversion of
the best of these Centres into real secondary schools.
They made various suggestions for liberalising the pupil
teacher examinations, and urged that the age of apprenticeship should be raised to fifteen, and ultimately to sixteen
years of age.

Effect was given to a number of these recommendations
by allowing certain Local and Matriculation
Pupil Teachers examinations conducted by Universities to
and Secondary
Schools. be substituted for the Queen's Scholarship
examination (1899), by reducing the period
of apprenticeship to three years (1900), by examining
pupil teachers only at the beginning and end of their
course (1902), and at the same time a good deal of attention was given to improving the Pupil Teacher
Centres. In this work the School Boards and the

County and County Borough Councils co-operated. At Scarborough the joint efforts of the Borough Council and the School Board had led to the establishment of a secondary school for pupil teachers, where they were instructed as ordinary scholars until 16 years of age and afterwards continued to receive instruction in the school on five half-days a week. Similar though less complete attempts at rendering secondary schools available for the instruction of pupil teachers are met with. Any considerable extension of this movement was not possible until after 1902.

The Rise of Municipal Training Colleges. The Act of 1902 opens up another chapter in the history of the training of teachers. By it local authorities were empowered to establish training colleges at the expense of the rates. The need for some such step had been long recognised. The Act of 1870 had greatly increased the number of elementary schools without providing any corresponding increase in the facilities for supplying trained teachers. Some relief was afforded by the institution of University Day Training Colleges in 1890, but in spite of this the annual output of trained teachers was only 2,791, while the average attendance had risen to 5,030,219.[1]

In order to encourage local authorities to spend public money on the training of teachers, the Board of Education proposed to contribute three-fourths of the cost of buildings. At the same time a number of new denominational colleges came into existence. The result of this policy is

---

[1] In 1872 the average attendance in inspected schools in England and Wales was 1,336,158 and the training colleges could admit some 1,500 students.

seen by the fact that the output of trained teachers between 1900 and 1913 was doubled.[1]

In 1904 the training college regulations were issued for the first time apart from the Code, and the **Recent Changes in Training Colleges.** Board of Education adopted a new attitude towards the Colleges. In the first place it assumed control over appointments to the staffs, and in the second the general curriculum was remodelled on more generous lines. English,

[1] The progress is shown by the following table :—

Year.	Number of Colleges.	Number of students for whom places were provided.
1850	16	991
1860	34	2,388
1870	34	2,495
1880	41	3,275
1890	49	3,679
1900	61	6,011
1905	72	8,987
1910	85	12,625
1913	87	13,093

Cf. the increase of Government grants apart from sums contributed for building, etc., viz. £53 to each resident man student, £38 to each resident woman student, and £13 to non-residents, the form and rate of which grants have remained substantially unchanged.

Year.	Grants from Government.
	£
1860	68,272
1870	78,485
1880	109,299
1890-91	126,429
1900-01	178,220
1910-11	355,210

history and geography, elementary mathematics, and elementary science were compulsory, but alternative schemes now took the place of a uniform syllabus.[1] A comprehensive list of optional subjects was also included to provide opportunity for specialisation and more care was exercised in allowing students to enter for degrees. At the same time students in training colleges were no longer allowed to take the ordinary certificate examination, but another specially provided for them.

By the Act of 1902 "model schools" were removed from the control of the colleges and placed under the Local Education Authority. In 1904, in order to make the professional training more real and to give wider opportunities of practice, the Code required all elementary schools in receipt of grants to open their doors to students for the purpose of practical instruction. That something more is needed is seen by the movement to bring the demonstration schools which are assigned by the local authority to the colleges more immediately under their control. As was pointed out by the Report of 1856, both demonstration schools and practising schools are necessary, but the question has been thrown into relief by the growing interest in the study of education and the problems consequent on the decay of pupil teachership.

Two interesting developments have taken place of recent years in the direction of the complete severance of professional and academic studies.

The Four-year System.

Complaints of overpressure in the University Day Training Colleges have led to a movement in favour of prolonging the period spent by students in this type of institution for a fourth year, thus leaving the students free during their first three years to devote practically the whole

---

[1] Since 1913 geography has ranked as a subject apart from history.

of their attention to working for a degree. The post-graduate period is then spent exclusively in professional training. The system is only in its infancy and has for the moment to struggle with the poor financial prospects that await the student at the close of a long and expensive course. How it will fare under these circumstances in competition with a three-year system that makes the study of education an integral part of a degree course and is spread over the whole period remains to be seen. In spite of the hard things said about it, the three-year system under the conditions described does not differ in principle from the ordinary two-year system in that both academic and professional work are followed.

Another interesting experiment has been the partial abandonment in certain two-year colleges of the combined system and the devotion of more time to purely professional work. The objection to these, and in fact to all existing schemes at present in vogue is that they are all governed by a more or less academic outlook; there is nothing of the industrial element that Kay-Shuttleworth, for example, attempted to bring into the work at Battersea. That experiments on such lines will arise in the near future is hardly to be doubted, for it is the sequel to the present demand for a more practical and vocational education at the upper end of the primary school. To expect the school to take on a more practical character while every training college aims at manufacturing nothing but students is clearly absurd. The present regulations with regard to handwork merely tinker with the question. Why should it not be possible to enlist for training purposes a number of other than purely academic institutions?

Need for more Variety.

H. ED. 24

The unifying of all grades of education under one local authority by the Act of 1902 was the signal for the breakdown of the pupil teacher system. In 1903 the new movement began with the issue of special pupil teacher regulations, and by 1907 a new system was at work. Briefly, two principles underlay the various changes that characterised this period. The first was to facilitate and continue the preliminary education of future teachers by giving them a good secondary school education up to 16 or 17 years of age. The second was to limit strictly the employment of pupil teachers to half the number of school meetings and to provide for their education at other times. No one could become a pupil teacher under 16 years of age and the apprenticeship was limited to two years. During these years he had to continue to receive instruction in a recognised Pupil Teacher Centre. On the other hand, at the age of 16 any boy or girl who had been three years in a secondary school and signified his intention of becoming a bonâ fide teacher might, if his circumstances required it, claim a bursary for a year, at the close of which he might, providing he had passed the necessary qualifying examination, enter a training college straightway or serve for one year as a student teacher, teaching half time.

The Coming of the Bursar and Student Teacher.

The result of these changes has undoubtedly been to increase the general efficiency of students entering training colleges, but they have served to check the entry of many into the profession. Many parents are unable to afford to allow their children to remain non-wage earners until 16. The more stringent conditions of pupil teachership have practically closed the profession to boys and girls in country

The Shortage of Teachers.

districts.[1] A considerable number who under the old conditions would have become teachers are attracted by more profitable careers that open out to secondary school pupils at 16 or 17 years of age. At the same time the cost of training has steadily risen without any corresponding increase in the return to be looked forward to. Indeed, the prospects of headships and promotions have, if anything, grown steadily less.[2] These and kindred causes have resulted in a great deficiency of intending teachers, a decline of entrants unparalleled even under the Revised Code.[3]

[1] In 1904-5 2,141 pupil teachers in rural districts entered the profession. In 1911-12 the number had fallen to 29.

[2] In 1847 the salaries of 8,691 teachers in Church schools averaged only £29 12s. 0d. (masters £35 11s. 4d., mistresses £23 14s. 3d.), *independent* of the augmentation grant from the Government. In 1860 the average salary *including* augmentation was £95 and £65 respectively; in 1888 £119 and £72; in 1912-13 £129 3s. and £94 6s. for assistants and £178 and £125 2s. for head teachers. See Reports of the Cross Commission and Board of Education Report, 1912-13, etc.

[3]	Pupil Teachers Commencing.		Bursars.		Total Entrants (England).
	Boys.	Girls.	Boys.	Girls.	
1906-7	2,468	8,550	—	—	11,018
1907-8	2,092	6,205	637	1,406	10,340
1908-9	1,302	3,907	1,112	2,393	8,714
1909-10	894	2,956	1,090	2,251	7,191
1910-11	583	2,029	723	2,041	5,376
1911-12	393	1,562	723	2,135	4,813
1912-13	296	1,173	614	2,225	4,308
1913-14	251	1,203	598	2,434	4,486

In Wales the decline was from 883 in 1906-7 to 646 in 1913-14.—Board of Education Report, 1912-13.

To remedy the evils a modified pupil teacher system, accompanied by generous grants, was reverted to in 1913 in rural districts where neither secondary schools nor Pupil Teacher Centres are available. Grants have also been made in aid of maintenance allowance to children in secondary schools who are intending to become teachers, previous to their Bursar year. Various other schemes are also on foot.

The crux of the situation is how to devise inducements to make it worth the while of good people to enter and remain in the profession. It has been the problem that has embarrassed elementary education throughout the century. Originally, as we have seen, the solution was to dispense with adult teachers and make use of child labour. That is no longer possible. We are again at the parting of the ways. Unless the elaborate system of professional training that is being built up is to collapse, unless the nation is content to see the millions bestowed to elementary education wasted, it will have after more than a century of struggle to make up its mind that the teacher is worthy of his hire and be prepared to give him a return in some degree commensurate with his skill and responsibilities. There are, of course, misfits in every profession, but they flourish in direct proportion to the number of good men squeezed out. To expect universal enthusiasm among a class, many of whom are harassed by a perpetual struggle to make ends meet, without prospect and without hope, is to look for the impossible. If the history of elementary education during the last 200 years shows anything it is this, that the truest economy and the only way to progress lies in considering how to improve the efficiency[1] of the

---

[1] Whether the elementary school is attracting man for man the same class of material as formerly is a matter of opinion.

teacher. This is what distinguishes the régime of a Kay-Shuttleworth from that of a Robert Lowe.[1]

[1] The following statistics show the numbers of men and women teachers in 1856, 1876, and 1911-12 in inspected schools.

	Certificated.		Assistant Teachers.		Pupil Teachers.	
1856	Men.	Women.	Men.	Women.	M.	F.
England	1,948	1,400	140	38	4,189	3,824
Wales	141	35	10	3	296	145
1876						
England	9,834	12,128	1,022	1,777	10,487	18,727
Wales	829	471	40	78	615	709

	Trained.		Untrained.		Uncertificated.		Supplementary.	
1911-12	M.	W.	M.	W.	M.	W.	M.	W.
England	23,016	32,481	8,982	32,625	4,813	34,312	—	12,249
Wales	2,386	1,948	521	1,556	1,017	4,320	—	1,616

	Student Teachers.		Pupil Teachers.	
1911-12	M.	W.	M.	F.
England	509	1,198	916	3,472
Wales	63	71	198	560

The total Training College accommodation in 1911-12 :—

England   11,797 places in 80 Colleges.
Wales   1,070   ,,   ,,   7   ,,

For other details see *Report of the Board of Education*, 1912-13.

INDEX.

ABERYSTWYTH, University College, 98
Accommodation, school, 13, 15, 17, 19, 51, 60, 73, 92, 95, 97, 116, 123, 140, 149, 150, 170, 182
Account of Charity Schools, 1, 14, 15, 185, 330
—— *of the Edinburgh Sessional School*, 229, 230
Adams, Francis, 75, 104, 120, 139, 140
Address to Persons of Quality and Estate, 8
—— *to the Working Classes on the Subject of Education*, 65
Ad hoc bodies, 69, 83, 92, 103, 125, 130, 162 f.
Adventures in Socialism, 235
Afflicted children, legislation for, 161
Aikin, Lucy, 195
Aischines, 324
Allen, William, 43, 264
Allen and McClure, 14
Alphabet, method of teaching, 222, 241-2, 254
Andrew Bell, 47
Anglican revival, 32, 74, 77
Annexation of education by the State, 64, 90, 130, 169, 174
Anschauung, 228
Apparatus, deficient, 89, 99, 256, 257, 268, 277 ; Grants for, 90, 117, 274-5
Archbishops' conference on education, 164

Arithmetic, method of teaching, 206, 224-6, 241, 243, 253, 254, 262, 267, 283-4
Arithmetical sheets, 218
Armstrong, Prof. H. E., 293
Arnold, Matthew, 110, 114, 118, 130, 158, 275, 276, 277, 283, 320
"Art of Teaching in Sport," 196
Ashley, Lord (Earl Shaftesbury), 81
Assistant teacher, Bell's, 216, 217 ; Kay-Shuttleworth's, 272
Attendance, school, 52, 54, 89, 100, 106, 108, 109, 111, 116, 117, 120, 140, 143, 144, 147, 149, 152, 155, 160, 180 ; Prince Consort's Conference on, 108
Attention, training the, 201, 204
Autobiography (J. S. Mill), 32
—— *of a Phrenologist*, 236

BACON, 288
Bain, Alex., 32
Baines, Edward, 62, 85, 101, 119
Baldwin's Gardens, school in, 50, 51, 332 ; description of, 216-7
Balfour, Graham, 173
Balfour, Mr., 164
——, Education Act of, 169, 175
Baptist Voluntary Education Society, 85
Barbauld, Mrs., 5, 194, 195
——, school at Palgrave, 194-5

Barbauld's Works with a Memoir, Mrs., 195
Barnsley, 15
Barrington, Dr. (Bishop of Durham), 38, 49
Barrington school, 49, 331
Barrington School, The, 49, 331
Basedow, 197, 235
Baxter, Richard, 9
Belfast Christian Patriot, 328
Bell, Dr. Andrew, 28, 42, 43-4, 214, 221, 224, 228, 229, 230, 245, 271, 327
—— ——, educational aim of, 215, 226
—— ——, first schools organised by, 44, 49
—— ——, Madras plan of school organisation, 216 f.
—— ——, monitorial system invented, 44
—— ——, plan of a national system of education, 41, 47, 49
Bentham, 31, 33, 53, 235, 258
Benthamism, 31-32
Benthamites, 26, 31, 33, 65, 287
Bernard, Sir Thomas, 8, 15, 22, 38, 325, 331
Bevan, Madam, 9, 16, 17
Bible in school, use of, 16, 99, 103, 252, 277
Binns, H. B., 47, 262
Birmingham, 120, 121, 123, 139, 157, 192
—— Education Aid Society, 120
—— —— League, 120, 125, 126, 138, 139, 140, 150
——, state of education in, 124
Birrell, Mr., 175
——, Education Bill of, 175-6, 180
Bishop of St. Asaph's Bill, 176
—— of St. David's, Letter to, 102
"Block grant," 306
Board of Commissioners for Education, 71, 72, 74

Board of Education, 72, 73, 74, 154, 166, 167, 168, 171, 172, 179, 297, 308, 317
—— —— Act, 168, 169
—— —— Consultative Committee, 166-7, 168
—— —— Library opened, 169
—— —— *Reports*, 145, 168, 321, 363, 371
—— ——, *Special Reports*, 148, 168, 296
—— —— *Statistics*, 182
Board Schools, 147, 151, 153, 155, 159, 164
—— ——, cost of education in, 130, 149, 170
—— ——, progress of, 140
Bookishness of schooling, reaction against, 136, 191, 293, 294, 297, 300, 312
Borough, The, 5, 212, 232
Borough Bill, 106
Borough Road, school at, 45, 52; described, 217; under Mr. Crossley, 254-5; in 1856, 273-4
—— —— Training College, 97, 330, 344
Brâd y Llyfrau Gleision, 100
Brailsford, H. N., 25
Brecon, 96
Bright, John, 128
Bristol, 12, 53, 72, 243
British and Foreign School Society, 33, 52, 60, 70, 73, 74, 76, 90, 91, 92, 97, 98, 115, 252, 258
—— ——, District and Foreign associations of, 53
—— ——, Rules of, 52, 252
British and Foreign School Society Handbook, 284
—— —— *Manual*, 253
British Association committees, 273
British Quarterly, 289
—— *Review*, 289
British School at Harp Alley, 254

British School at Lancaster, 254
—— —— committees—attitude towards education, 255
British Schools, 95, 182, 257-8, 279
—— —— in North Wales, 97
—— ——, Management Clauses for, 91
Brougham, Lord (Mr. Henry), 31, 33, 55, 57, 80-1, 327
—— and religious teaching, 72, 75, 89
——, Commission and Select Committees, 39, 57-8
——, Education Bills of, 59-60, 72, 89-90
——, educational returns, 61
——, *Popular Education*, 61
——, tribute to work of clergy and voluntary agencies, 49, 68
Bruce, Mr., 119
Bryce, Mr. (Lord), Commission, 166 f.
Buchanan, James, 55, 232, 236
Building grants, school, 58, 66, 69, 70, 82, 89, 111
—— ——, training college, 114, 366
Burke, Edmund, 24
Burkwell, W., 220
Bursars and student teachers, 370
Byrom, Lady, 264

CAMBRIAN Educational Society, 98
Cardiff, 101
Carlyle, 32, 63, 66, 132
Case of the Manchester Educationists, 105
Catechetical schools, 9, 13, 16
Catechising, 6-7, 10, 16, 193
——, meaning of, 186, 187
Catholic Emancipation, 63, 71, 77
Catholic Encyclopaedia, 150
Census Returns — Education (1851), 92, 275

Central Authority, reorganisation of, 168
—— control, fear of increased, 110-111.
—— Society of Education, 63, 65, 72, 74, 104, 262
Central Society of Education (Publications), 73, 253, 255, 256, 258, 296, 301
Century of Education, A, 47, 262
Chamberlain, Mr. Joseph, 120, 163, 165
Charge to the Clergy of the Archdeaconry of Middlesex, 90
Charity education, 1, 3, 5-6, 13 f.
Charity school movement, 9 f.
Charity schools, 3, 5, 6, 8, 38, 39, 183, 185, 193
—— ——, aim of education in, 10, 13, 14, 184
—— ——, cost of conducting, 14-15, 45
—— ——, curriculum and routine, 14, 185-6, 187-8
—— ——, Dissenting and Roman Catholic, 14
—— —— in Wales, inefficiency of, 16
—— ——, industrial occupations in, 11, 14, 191, 192
—— ——, investigations into, 39, 58
—— ——, masters' qualifications, 15
—— ——, popular dislike of, 251-2
—— —— prayer, 8
—— —— reading books, 188 f.
—— ——, training of teachers for, 14, 188, 329-330
—— ——, variety of type, 5, 183
Charity Sermon quoted, 11
Charles, Rev. Thomas, of Bala, 17
Chartism (Carlyle), 66
——, *a New Organisation of the People* (Lovett and Collins), 39, 66, 250, 336

Cheam, 265

Cheap Repository Tracts, 22

Child and curriculum, 211, 309, 311

Child labour, 11, 30, 82, 112, 140, 143, 152, 174, 180

—— ——, minimum age for, 142, 143, 152

Child Labour in the United Kingdom, 142, 180

Child-study records, 200

"Children are not fools," 203

Children at school, 60, 61, 73, 117, 123, 140, 145, 149, 150, 366

Children's books, 195 f.

Children's Employment Commission, 82

Chrestomathia, 33

Chrestomathic secondary school, 33, 53, 54, 235, 258

Church alone has power to educate, 48, 78 f.

——, compulsory attendance at, 51, 53, 56, 83, 118, 193

—— distrust of Lord John Russell, 92

—— expenditure on education, 122, 138, 164, 165, 170

—— monopoly of education challenged, 31, 60, 63, 65, 69, 72, 74-5, 77

—— party, activity of, 50 f., 70, 75-6, 89, 92, 96, 138, 164 f., 337

—— ——, demands of, 77 f., 164 f., 170

—— schools, management clauses for, 91

Church and Education prior to 1870, The, 75

—— —— *since 1870, The*, 165, 170

Churton, Ed., 50

Circulating schools, 5, 10, 16 f.

—— ——, training teachers for, 187

Citizenship, education for, 67, 130-3, 137

City and Guilds of London Institute, founding of, 136

Civic ideal in education, 20 f., 33, 68, 72 f., 103, 150, 154, 175 f. (*see also* Birmingham Education League, Brougham, *and* Russell)

Class view of society, 6, 7, 29

"Clerical yoke," the, 171

Cobbett, William, 3, 61

Cobden, Richard, 104

Cockerton Judgment, 169

Code, Mr. Mundella's, 1882, 292, 304

——, the, 113, 145, 146, 156, 160, 169, 296

——, The New, 1871, 146-7, 153

——, The Revised, 1862, 113, 114 f., 137, 147, 278, 297, 301, 356

—— ——, effect on curriculum, 282, 284

—— ——, effect on promotion, 117, 153, 282

—— ——, Matthew Arnold on, 283-4

—— ——, reaction caused by, 280 f.

—— of 1890, 159, 293

—— of 1902, 208, 318

Code Reform Association, 289

Colbert, 205

Coleridge, 32

Colfe, Rev. Abraham, 6

Collective method of instruction, 213

Collings, Mr. Jesse, 120

Combe, George, the phrenologist, 104, 287

"Combined" system of education, 80, 83, 87, 102

Committee of Council on Education, 64, 74, 81, 83, 90, 92, 106, 107, 109, 110, 301, 339, 344, 345, 350, 356

—— ——, concordat between the Church and, 90)

Committee of Council on Education, controversy around, 75 f.
—— ——, educational policy of, 75, 88 f., 147, 154, 251, 270 f., 280 f., 302
—— —— manuals and lectures for teachers, 270
—— —— Minutes, 75, 106, 113, 297
—— ——, suspicion against, 89, 101
Committee of Council on Education, Minutes of the, 88, 92, 94, 95, 99, 117, 125, 148, 157, 216, 268, 270, 272, 275, 276, 278, 333, 335, 336, 343, 348, 350
—— ——, *Reports of the,* 140, 141, 306, 315
Committee of Public Instruction, 65
Common schools, 26, 95, 183, 184
—— —— —— described, 95-6, 211-12
Communism in educational affairs, 130
Compayré, 20
" Comprehensive " system of education, 80, 87
Compulsory schooling, 22-24, 40, 65, 66, 68, 82, 84, 119, 120, 121, 124, 128, 133, 137, 139, 142, 145, 150, 152, 160
Concreteness, 238, 239
Concurrent endowment of the sects, 80, 94, 103
Congregational Board of Education, 85, 86, 344
—— tracts, 85, 86
—— Union, the, 85
Connection of Religion with Popular Education, The, 86
Conscience clause, 58, 83, 105, 106, 118, 119, 121, 125, 126, 143
——, rights of, 107, 164
Considerations on the increase of the Poor-rates in Kingston-upon-Hull, 12

Consultative Committee on Attendance at Continuation Schools, Report, 156
Continuation schools, 155-6, 160, 174
Contributions to the Cause of Education, 213
Correlation and concentration, 309-310
Corston, William, 48
Cost of education per child, 14-5, 45, 51, 129, 130, 143, 149, 170, 180
Council schools, 172, 175, 176, 177
County and County Borough Councils, establishment of, 162
—— —— as local education authorities, 167, 169, 171
Cowper-Temple clause, 126-7, 173, 175, 176
Crabbe, 5, 183, 211, 232
Crosby Hall Lectures, 85
Cross, Lord, 150
Cross Commission, 144, 150 f., 168, 292, 296, 299, 305, 315
—— —— and payment by results, 154
—— ——, arithmetic, 316
—— ——, buildings, 151
—— ——, curriculum, 153-4
—— ——, English, 316
—— ——, geography, 316-17
—— ——, history, 317
—— ——, majority and minority reports, 151, 154, 155, 158, 159, 361, 363
—— ——, pupil teachers, 359
—— ——, reading and reading-books, 315-16
—— ——, religious instruction, 152
—— —— *Reports,* 108, 116, 117, 155, 156, 291, 315, 348, 371
—— ——, results of, 159
—— ——, school attendance, 152

Cross Commission, staffing, 319-320
—— ——, subjects for investigation, 150
—— ——, training colleges, 152, 361, 363
Crown of Wild Olives, 132
Curiosity, 199, 204, 208
Curriculum at New Lanark, 233, 234
——, building up the primary school, 301 f.
——, Charity school, 14, 185-6, 187-8
——, child and, 309-311
——, " class subjects " in, 148, 302, 304, 305
—— common to all, 134-5, 153
—— determined by Clergy, 59
——, early nineteenth century schools, 29
——, early Sunday schools, 193
——, minimum, 306
——, modernising, 209
——, Mr. Roebuck's, 69
—— previous to 1862, 275, 276
——, Ruskin's, 134-5
——, school of industry, 12, 41, 69, 191, 192
——, " specific subjects " in, 147, 301, 302, 305
——, Whitbread's parochial school, 46
——, widening, 69, 102, 145, 147, 148, 149, 153-4, 250
Cyclopedia of Education, 13
Cygnaeus, 298

" DAILY Routine of the New Lanark Institution, The," 235
Dale, David, 57
—— ——, factory school of, 57
Dame schools, 3, 55, 60, 95
—— ——, description of, 232
Day industrial schools, 143
—— school education unpopular, 12

Day, Thomas, 206
Democracy, enthronement of, 137
Democratisation of education, 33, 130, 157
De Montmorency, J. E. G., 6
Denison's Act, 107
Denominational Education Bill, 105
—— feeling, strength of, 111, 163, 169
—— instruction, facilities for, 59, 75, 83, 102, 164, 170-1, 175, 176, 177
—— management, 103
—— position, 78-9, 164, 170
—— ——, Government recognition of, 126, 164, 175, 176, 177
—— schools, transference of, 121, 176
—— —— and rate aid, 104, 121, 125, 128, 155, 164, 177
—— ——, higher Exchequer, grants to, 128, 149
—— system competing with State system, 64, 122, 151
—— —— defined, 80
Denominationalists, 64, 119, 138, 150
Dessau, 197
Dewey, John, 285, 286, 300, 311-2
Diary of the Education Bill, 1902, 171
Dickens, Charles, and education, 63, 66
Dickens as an Educator, 66
Didactic verse, 241, 243
Digest of Reports (Education) S.B.C.P., 8, 15, 22, 38, 42, 192
Diocesan Boards of Education, 96, 259
Discipline, 212, 215, 227, 242
Discourse concerning Schools and Schoolmasters, 10
—— *on the Education of Children and Youth, A*, 197
Discussions on Education, 287

Disraeli, Mr., and religious education, 77, 127
Dissenters, 60, 63, 74, 81, 82, 83, 84, 87, 104, 105, 140
Diversity in schools between 1833 and 1862, 250
Divine Songs for Children, 10, 197
Dixon, Mr., 120
"Doing," 204, 205, 244, 249, 300, 308
Domestic duties, training in, 134, 155, 185, 192, 256, 276
—— economy, 291, 296, 303, 307
—— (home) education, 3, 5, 198 f., 202
"Draft" lesson, a typical, 242-3
Drawing, 88, 102, 134, 136, 139, 159, 233, 254, 275, 305, 306, 307, 308
Dual system of school organisation, 175
Dunce's pass (certificate), 143, 144
Dunn, Henry, 258, 328, 332, 334

EALING, 264
    Early schooling, importance of, 112
—— Sunday schools, 18, 192-3
Early Discipline, 56, 237
—— *Lessons*, 206
Ecclesiastical control of education, 126 (*see* Church)
Edgeworth family, 43
——, Maria, 198, 200, 201, 206, 208-9, 234
——, R. L., 49, 198 f.
—— ——, conception of a true education, 207-8
—— ——, practice of, defects in, 207
—— —— and his son, 199-200
Edinburgh, 104
—— Sessional School, 229
Edinburgh Review, 47
Education a civil function, 36, 66, 68, 74, 103 (*see* Civic ideal)

Education an ecclesiastical affair, 6, 74, 103
—— and philanthropy (charity), 1, 3, 12, 28 f., 62, 184
—— a parental duty, 143
—— a right, 1, 30, 32, 68
—— a science, 63, 200
—— as police, 23, 37, 46, 61, 80, 93
——, class system of, 2, 6, 27, 183
——, fear of popular, 12-13, 22, 26, 29
—— for all, 9, 23, 24, 26, 30, 46, 65, 107, 124, 133
—— for citizenship, 67, 130-3, 137
——, importance of, 1, 32, 37, 42, 45, 66, 68, 107, 133, 200, 251, 288
—— ladder, 131, 166, 174,
—— of the people, 1, 2, 5, 6, 9, 20, 22, 33, 37, 42, 60, 63, 65, 90, 102, 103, 129, 252
—— of the poor, 1, 2, 9, 29, 38-39, 41, 46, 50, 58, 59, 62, 68-9, 71, 116, 184, 235
—— through bodily activities (play), 196, 204-5, 298
Education Act 1870, 107, 119, 130, 137, 138, 140, 149, 150, 155, 157, 161
—— —— 1876, 143-5
—— —— 1902, 130, 131, 163, 169 f., 174 f., 176
—— (Administrative Provisions) Act 1907, 179
—— (Blind and Deaf Children) Act, Elementary, 161
—— (Defective and Epileptic Children) Act, Elementary, 162
—— ("Free Schooling," 1891) Act, 161
—— (London) Act 1903, 173
—— (Provision of Meals) Act, 178-9
Education Acts—Commonwealth Parliament, 6

Education Acts: England, 65, 128, 142, 146, 162, 166, 173, 178, 179
—— ——, Massachusetts, 6
—— ——, Scotland, 6, 15
Education Bills, 45, 59, 104, 105-6, 107, 119, 122, 124 f., 165, 166, 169, 171 f., 175, 176, 177
—— Department, 113, 147, 153, 154, 163, 167, 168, 280, 291, 302, 304, 313
Education, article on (Mill), 30, 32, 210
Education, Intellectual, Moral, and Physical, 288
Education Crisis, The, 166, 171
Education et Instruction — Enseignement Primaire, 213
Education Magazine, 255, 256, 328, 338, 340
Education of the Poor in the Eighteenth Century, The, 14, 185, 188
Education of the Young, The (Wilderspin), 237
Educational doctrine of early Radicals, 32
—— finance, problems connected with, 180-2
—— forces, early nineteenth-century, 31, 62
—— free trade, 62, 85
—— ideal of eighteenth century, 26-7
—— ideal of early nineteenth century, 29
—— position of the Church, 78-9
—— Settlement Committee, 177
—— teaching of Ruskin, 132 f.
Educational Record, 47, 224, 254, 258
Educational Systems of Great Britain and Ireland, The, 173
Educative process, rival views of, 32, 37, 210-211
Educator, The, 85

Elementary and higher education, relation of, 151, 156 f., 167, 168, 174
—— science, 69, 294-5, 305, 306, 307; (experimental), 205, 295
—— ——, method of teaching, 206, 265, 291, 292, 293
—— school, definition of, 124-5, 157, 173
—— school standards, 278, 302, 304
Elementary Education, 14, 75, 165, 171
Elementary School Manager, The, 284
Emile, 1, 7, 198, 199
Emilie, 235
Emulation, use of, 215, 227, 230
Encyclopaedia Britannica Supplement, 210
English, 194, 303, 305, 306, 308
—— language in Wales, 93, 94, 95
Enquête historique sur l'enseignement manuel, 299
Enquiry concerning Political Justice, 25
Epistle to the Galatians, 103
Epsom, 265
Equality of educational opportunity, 2, 25, 27, 36, 65, 67, 130, 133, 137, 265
"Erudition is not education," 134
Essai d'éducation nationale, 20
Essay on the Evils of Popular Ignorance, 29, 30, 42.
Essay on the French Revolution, 24
Essay on Population, 25
Essay towards the Encouragement of Charity Schools, 12, 14, 186
Essays on the Formation of the Human Character, 34, 35
Evangelical movement, 19
Evans, D., 9

Evening schools, 3, 5, 112, 116, 147, 155, 156, 160, 194
Evenings at Home, 196, 265
Excursion, The, 37
Exeter Hall lectures for teachers, 270
Experiment in Education made at the Male Asylum at Madras, An, 44
Exposition in schools, 185, 186, 187, 194, 230, 239

FABLE of the Bees, 7
Factory Acts, 56, 82, 84, 121, 142
—— Bill, Sir James Graham's, 82-4, 85
—— children, education of, 56, 57, 82, 84, 142
Fearon, D. R., 123
Feeding of school children, 137, 178-9
Fellenberg, 262-3, 265, 269, 298, 301, 334
Fincham, school of industry at, 191
Findlay, J. J., 311
Firmin, Thomas, 9, 10
——, school in Little Britain, 12
First Catechism (Watts), 197
Fitch, Sir Joshua, 123
Fletcher, Mr. H. M. I., 333
Floor space per child, 111, 147, 151, 182, 216
Fors Clavigera, 135
Forster, Mr., 119, 122, 123
Foster, John, 29, 30, 42
Four Periods of Public Education, 75, 90, 258, 272, 281, 338, 343
Fox, Joseph, 48
Fox's Introduction to Spelling and Reading, 189
Fox Bourne, 12
France, 72
Francke, work at Halle, 16, 329
Frank and Rosamond, 209

Free schooling, 39, 46, 105, 119, 120, 121, 125, 128, 133, 137, 152, 160 f.
—— trade, doctrine of educational, 62, 85
Freeman, Kenneth, 324
Friends, 105
——, Society of, 45
Froebel, 66, 276, 286, 294, 298, 299, 307, 308
Fry, Elizabeth, 45

GALLERY, 88, 239, 241, 242, 243, 272
—— lesson described, 241-2
Games, children's, 237, 297, 308
Gardening, 205, 309
Geography, 55, 88, 102, 134, 135, 148, 192, 195, 196, 197, 207, 231, 233, 275, 276, 277, 282, 301, 302, 303, 306, 309, 313
——, method of teaching, 206, 242, 253, 255, 256, 267
Geography (Mrs. Sherwood), 253
Geometry, 135, 255, 302, 313
——, method of teaching, 240
Germany, 294
Gladstone, Mr., 77, 122, 149
Glamorganshire, 95
Glasgow, 244
Godwin, William, 23, 24-5, 26
Gonograph, 240
Gorst, Sir John, 165; (Bill) 165, 169
"Gospel of getting on," educational, 132
Gouge, Rev. Thomas, 8, 9
Government, first duty of, 66
—— grants for education, 85, 87, 89, 90, 111, 114, 117, 124, 143-4, 145, 146, 147, 148, 149, 155, 159, 161, 173, 176, 306, 307
—— inspectors (*see* Inspectors)
Goyder, G. W., 236; (infant school) 243
Graham, Sir James, 80, 81-2, 83

Grammar, 88, 148, 188, 196, 207, 231, 253, 256, 259, 275, 276, 282, 301, 302, 305
——, method of teaching, 242
Gréard, 213
Greaves, J. P., 339
Green, J. A., 228, 261
——, T. H., 129, 131-2; (Works) 132
Gregory, A., 19
——, Robert (Dean), 14, 75, 165, 171
Grey, Kirkman, 6, 12, 19, 30, 330
Griffiths, Rev. Henry (Brecon), 96
Gymnastics, 307

HALF-TIME System, 14, 112, 145
Half-timers, 116, 143, 144, 146
Halle, 16
Hand and eye training, 298, 300
Handicraft, 134, 205, 275, 297-301
Handwork movement, 137, 297-301
Hansard, 72, 75
Harris, Howell, 19
——, J. H., 19, 214
Harry and Lucy, 196, 205, 208
Has the Church or the State the Power to Educate the Nation? 78
Health and Morals of Apprentices Act, 56, 82
Helvetius, 21
Herbart, 286, 309
Heuristic methods, 204, 206, 242, 290, 293
Higher grade schools, 131, 157-8, 168, 169
Hinton, J. H., 105
Hints to Parents, 236
Histoire critique des doctrines de l'éducation en France, 20
History, 102, 134, 135, 196, 197, 234, 255, 259, 275, 276, 282, 301, 302, 304, 306, 307, 309, 313

History and Present State of the Education Question, The, 75, 92
History of England (Macaulay), 11·
History of Philanthropy, 6, 12, 19, 30, 330
History of Philosophy, A, 33
History of the Elementary School Contest, 75, 104, 120, 139, 140
Hobson, J. A., 133
Holidays, care of children during, 179
Holland, H. W., 121
Holyoake, J., 38, 57
Home and Colonial Infant School Society, 56, 266, 340; (Model School) 266-7
Hook, Dr., 102-3
Hoole, Charles, 43
Horticulture, 307
House of Convocation conference on education, 170
Household Words, 66
Housewifery, 307, 309
Hughes, J. L., 66
Hull, 12
Hullah, John, 270
Humanitarian motive in education, 9, 37 f.
Huxley, T. H., 130, 292
Hygiene, 69, 134, 287, 289, 295, 307, 309
Hygienic condition of school buildings, 147, 151, 296
Hymns in Prose, 197

IMPROVEMENT of the Mind (Watts), 197
Improvements in Education, 41, 45, 216, 226, 228, 324, 326
Individual examination, system of, 111, 113, 278, 307
Industrial influence in education, 136
—— schools, 264

Industrial training in schools, 5,
    11, 12, 13, 31, 38, 40, 41,
    184, 191, 263-5, 275, 276
    (*see* Schools of Industry)
Infant education, 54, 232, 236 f.,
    307-8, 340
—— school movement, 37
—— School Society, 339
—— schools, 3, 29, 52, 54, 55,
    56, 68, 71, 112, 151, 230 f.
—— ——, Rev. W. Wilson's,
    56, 339
—— ——, Robert Owen's, 55,
    233
—— ——, Wilderspin's, 56, 239,
    339
Infant Education, 237, 242
—— *Education from Two to
    Six Years of Age* (Cham-
    bers), 242
—— *System, The*, 237, 241
Initiative, development of, 201,
    203
Initiatory schools, 54, 232, 246
    (*see* Dame schools)
Inspected schools, superiority
    of, 109
Inspection, right of, 83
——, school, 88, 119, 124, 147,
    169
Inspectors of schools, Govern-
    ment, 75, 82, 88, 90, 114,
    143, 147, 150, 152, 275,
    292, 302, 313, 349
Inspectors' Reports, 137, 215
Instruction, modes of, 213
——, rational grading of, 287
Instructions to inspectors, 88,
    145, 147, 281, 307, 314
Intellectual education, aim and
    method of, 203 f.
Intellectual system of John
    Wood, 229-231
Intellectual Education (Wyse),
    262
Inter-departmental Committee
    on Partial Exemption
    from School Attendance,
    145

International Exhibition 1851,
    136
Inter-School Athletic League,
    296
Inventiveness, 23, 199, 201, 204,
    207, 208
Ireland, 71, 81
Irish Commissioners of National
    Education, 71, 264

JAMES, William, 300
    James Mill, A Biography,
    32
Jews and education, 72, 79, 105 ;
    (Schools) 182
John Ruskin, Social Reformer, 133
Jolly, W., 135
Jones, David, 17
Jones, Rev. Griffith, of Lland-
    dowror, 10, 16, 19, 184,
    186, 187
Joseph Lancaster, 47
Judgment, business of education
    to ripen, 203

KAY - SHUTTLEWORTH,
    Sir James (Dr. Kay),
    64, 75, 90, 101, 104, 105,
    258, 264, 265, 267
—— as Assistant Poor Law
    Commissioner, 77, 264,
    269, 341
——, experiment in training
    teachers, 341-3
——, "Gathercoal Scuttle-
    worth," 101
——, ideal of school staffing, 271
——, Minutes on method, 269
—— on teachers' salaries, 328-9
——, plan of school organisation,
    272
—— on pupil teachers, 272, 341 f.
——, view of the educative pro-
    cess, 269-270.
Keeling, Frederic, 142, 180
Kempe Committee on Local
    Taxation, 181-2

Kendal schools, 44, 54, 192, 325
Kenyon-Slaney clause, 173
Kerry, Lord, Parliamentary Return, 71
Kildare Place Society, 71
Kindergarten, 298
Kingsley. Charles, 296
Kneller Hall, 343

LA CHALOTAIS, 20, 21
Lancashire, 109, 145
Lancashire Public School Association, 103
Lancaster, Joseph, 5, 43, 44, 45-6, 47, 52, 54, 214, 216, 225, 226, 228, 271, 324, 326, 327
——, educational aim, 215, 226
——, " improvements," 218-9
——, lecturing tours, 49
——, method ot spelling, reading, and writing, 222
—— on industrial training, 41
—— supporters, 48
Lancasterian Plan, 217 f., 234
—— school, arithmetic syllabus in a, 224
—— schools, 53, 54, 243, 254, 255, 256 ; (Secondary) 53 (see British Schools)
Languages in elementary schools, 302, 303
Lansdowne, Marquis of, 74, 75, 79
La Salle, 16
Laundry work, 307, 309
Lay management of schools, 91
Leeds, 73, 84, 85, 104, 120, 123, 124
Leeds Mercury, 84
Leek, 220
Lessons on common objects, 275, 396
Lessons for Children, 195, 205
—— on Objects, 265
Letter to the Welsh People on day schools, 96
Letter to the Marquis of Lansdowne, A, 85

Letters on Elementary Education, 230
Letters on the Educational Institutes of De Fellenberg, 263, 328
Letters to Lord John Russell, 85
—— —— on Education in Wales, 86
Lewisham, 192
Life and Letters of Sir James Graham, 81
—— and Struggles of William Lovett, The, 65
—— and Times of Griffith Jones of Llanddowror, The, 17
—— and Work .of Pestalozzi, 228, 261
—— and Writings of Turgot, 21
—— of Francis Place, 32, 52
—— of Gladstone, 128
—— of John Locke, 12
—— of Sir Hugh Owen, 98
Lingen, Mr. (Lord), 98, 280, 281
Liverpool, state of education in, 123, 124
Living voice in the schools, 248-9
Local education authority, 171-2, 175, 176, 178, 179
—— —— rates, 181-2
—— Government Act, 162
—— —— Board, 169
—— Taxation (Customs and Excise) Act, 162, 167
Locke, John, 11, 198, 287
London, 14, 28, 53, 55, 179, 295
—— Infant School Society, 55, 339
—— School Board, 131, 293, 296
Lord Sandon's Education Act, 143
Lovett, William, 39, 63, 65, 66, 181, 250, 264-5, 336
Lowe, Robert, 113, 115, 118, 122, 123, 147, 356, 373
Lowell, 285
Lucian, 324

MACAULAY, Lord, 11, 87, 326 ; (*Speeches*) 87, 326
MacCunn, 32, 68, 132
Macnab, Henry Grey, 235
Madras plan of school organisation, 216 f., 274
Madras School, The, 41, 215, 226
Maiden Bradley, 330
Malthus, 22, 25, 26
Management clauses, 90-92
Manchester, 34, 103, 104, 105, 120, 121, 123, 139, 157, 158, 259, 287, 295, 299
—— and Salford Committee on Education, 105, 106
—— Church Education Society, 259
—— Education Aid Society, 119
—— —— Bill Committee, 119
—— Literary and Philosophical Society, 56
Mandeville, 7
Manual activities, 249-50
—— instruction, 136, 155, 159, 162, 298, 299, 307 (*see* industrial training)
Manual of the System of Instruction, Meadow St., Bristol, 243
Marsh, Dr., 50
Marvin, F. S., 114
Mathematics, 102, 134, 259, 307, 313
Maurice, Frederick Denison, 78
Mayo, Dr. and Miss, 265, 266
McKenna, Mr., 176 ; (Bill) 176, 180
Mechanical spirit of eighteenth and early nineteenth centuries, 30, 32, 37, 260
Mechanics, 291, 294, 303
Medical inspection of schools, 137, 179
Meiklejohn, Prof., 47, 293
Melbourne, Lord, 74
Memoir of Elizabeth Fry, 28
—— *of Joshua Watson,* 50
Memoirs of R. L. Edgeworth, 200, 201, 202, 207, 208

" Merit " grant, 148-9, 314
Methodist movement, 10, 19
Metropolitan Church Union, 75, 92
Miall, Edward, 85
Mill, James, 30, 31, 32, 49, 53, 55, 210, 211
Mill, John Stuart, 32, 43, 65, 67-8, 131, 160, 225
Mines Acts, 142
Mitchell, Mr., H.M.I., 276
"Mixed method" of school organisation, 272
Monitorial schools, 38, 232, 249
—— ——, books and apparatus in, 254, 256, 257
—— ——, criticism of, 251 f.
—— ——, method of teaching arithmetic in, 224-6
—— ——, method of teaching reading in, 221-4
—— ——, moral training in, 226-8
—— ——, practice in later, 252-5, 268
—— systems, 30, 31, 42, 45, 214 f., 230, 271, 345
—— theory, 215
"Monitorial Schools and their Successors " (by W.), 224
Monitors, 43, 44, 49, 101, 192, 217, 218-9, 230, 239, 246, 247, 256, 272
Monmouth, 95, 96
Moral Tales, 209
Moral training, 134, 150, 153, 209, 245, 309, 313
" Moral Training System," 245
Morley, J. (Lord), 128
Moseley, Mr., H.M.I., 268, 273
Mother's Book, The, 236
Mulcaster, Richard, 329
Mulhaüser method of writing, 270
Mundella, Mr., 144, 292
Mundella, Mr. A. J., 150
Municipalisation of education, 130, 169
Munro, Paul, 13

Music, 69, 102, 134, 135, 254
Mutual instruction, method of, 43, 215, 274

NATIONAL Education Association, 150, 166, 178
National Education Union, 121, 122, 125
National Public School Association, 103, 104
National schools, 15, 51, 52, 92, 149, 170, 252, 256, 268, 274
National Society, 38, 51, 70, 73, 76, 91, 115, 138, 149, 216, 228, 337
———— ——, Committee of Inquiry and Correspondence, 258, 337
———— —— District Societies, 50
———— —— Middle Schools' scheme, 258-9
———— —— principles, 50
National Society Directory, 52
National Union of the Working Classes, 63, 65
Natural history, 55, 69, 196, 233, 234, 255, 277, 304
—— philosophy, 255, 277, 302
Nature, 199
—— study, coming of, 293-4
—— work, 291, 294-5, 309, 313
Needham Marchamont, 7, 10
Needlework, 148, 278, 297, 301, 302, 306 ; time spent on, 277
Nekuomanteia, 324
Nelson, Robert, 8, 330
New Discovery of the Old Art of Teaching Schools, A, 43
New Lanark, 33, 34, 55, 57, 236, 295 ; (New Institution) 233
New View of Society, A, 34
New Views of Mr. Owen of Lanark impartially examined, The, 235
Newcastle Commission, 108-113, 278

Newcastle Commission Report, 112, 355
Newport, Chartist riot at, 93, 96
Nonconformists, 83, 84, 93, 103, 120, 122, 138, 143, 164, 171, 175
Non-provided schools, 172, 174, 175, 176
Normal schools, 68, 87, 96 (see Training colleges)
Number of children in school (see Children at school)

OAKHAM School of Industry, 42, 192
Object lessons, 233, 295 ; (specimen) 265-6
—— teaching, 242-3, 262
Observation lessons, 292, 295, 309
Œconomy of Charity, 40, 330
On Liberty, 67
Open-air teaching, 180, 229, 243, 246, 296, 297
Oral class teaching, value of, 246
Organised Science Schools, 157-8
Owen, Robert, 26, 31, 33, 55, 233, 236, 243
——, infant and elementary schools described, 233-4
——, influence, 235
——, scheme of social and educational reform, 36-7
——, teaching of, 33 f.
Owen, Sir Hugh, efforts on behalf of Welsh education, 96-8

PAIDOMETER, 221
Paine, Thomas, 1, 22, 24, 26
Pakington, Sir John, 106, 108
Palmerston, Lord, 118
Panthier, A., 299
Parent's Assistant, The, 209
Paris Exhibition, 1867, 136
Parker, C. S., 81

Parliamentary grant, first, 61, 62, 63, 69-70, 250
—— Returns, 39, 41, 71
Parliamentary Debates: Elementary Education Bill, 1870, 122, 124, 127
Parliamentary Papers, 79, 113
Parochial Charity School movement, 9, 13 f., 15
—— Schools Bill, 45
Partition of education, 65, 67-8, 129, 130 f., 174
Paternalism in education, 36-7, 65, 133
Pauperism and education, 8, 10-13, 24, 25, 37, 40, 41
Payment by results, 52, 111, 115, 149, 153, 154, 169, 307, 313 f.
Peel, Sir Robert, 81
Peripatetic science instructors, 292
Personality v. mechanism in education, 327
Pestalozzi, 56, 210, 228, 236, 238, 243, 245, 260-1, 265, 269, 286, 288, 290, 298, 299, 326, 327, 334, 342
Pestalozzi's Intellectual or Intuitive Arithmetic, 236
Pestalozzian influence, examples of, 234, 236-7, 261-2, 265, 266, 269, 270, 276
Philanthropy and education, 28 f., 37, 184
Phillips, Sir Thomas, 9, 96
Philosophy of Education (Tate), 276
Physical Deterioration Committee, 178
—— geography, 291, 302, 303, 305
—— training, 88, 134, 159, 199, 237, 239, 242, 255, 275, 287, 296, 307, 309
—— Training Commission (Scotland), 178
Physiocrats, 21
Physiology, 289, 291, 296

"Picturing out," 247-8
Pietas Hallensis, 16
Pietism, 16
Pillans, Prof., 213, 230, 258, 324
Pitt, 40
Place, Francis, 31, 53, 258
Play, 196, 203, 204-5, 267, 291
Playfair, Dr. Lyon, 136
Playground, 55, 88, 151, 232, 237, 239, 245
Pleasant Pages, 276
Pleasure and pain, 201-2
Podmore, Frank, 233
Poetical Nautical Trip round the Island of Great Britain, 196
Political economy in the school, 26, 69, 277, 302
Poor, education of the (see Education)
Poor Girl's Primer, The, 8
Poor Law Reform, 11, 40 ; (Bill) 26
Popular education (see Education of the people)
—— —— divided between State and Voluntary associations, 129
—— —— handed over to Voluntary agencies, 90
Portsmouth, 212
Position of the Catholic Church in England and Wales, 150
Positions (Mulcaster), 329
Pounds, John, 212-3
Practical education, 137, 199, 204, 205, 291, 298
Practical Education, 200, 201, 203, 204, 205, 206, 208
—— *Remarks on Infant Education*, 266
Primary Education, Proposed National Arrangements for, 121
Principality, the 93, 94, 98, 100, 101
Private schools, 3-5, 58, 109, 184

Provided schools, 175, 176
Public Education, 64, 104, 105, 271
Pullen, P. H., 236
Punishment, 215, 227, 230, 290-1
Pupil Teacher Centres, 358, 365, 370, 372
Pupil Teacher System established, 346 ; decline of, 364-5, 368-370
Pupil Teachers, 87, 90, 110, 118, 148, 152, 272
—— ——, Cross Commission on, 359
—— ——, first experiments with, 340-1
—— ——, Matthew Arnold on, 355
—— ——, statistics, 357, 359, 371

QUARTERLY *Journal of Education,* 42, 301
Quarterly Review, 47
Queen's Scholarships, 87, 346, 352, 357, 360
Questioning, value of, 230, 247
Quintilian, 215

RACE parallelism and education, 287-8
Ragged schools, 213, 264
Raikes, Robert, 18, 43, 214
Rate aid for education, 6, 12, 45, 57, 59, 64, 66, 73, 82, 102, 103, 104, 105, 119, 120, 129, 155, 157, 169, 172, 177, 179, 180, 181-2
Rational Primer, The, 205
Reading books, 187, 189-191, 194, 195, 205-6, 218, 304, 315
——, method of teaching, 185, 187, 189, 195, 205, 221f., 231, 255, 270, 283, 315
—— sheets, 218, 242
Rebecca Riots, 93

Reflections upon the Education of Children in Charity Schools, 188
Reform Bills, 61, 68, 121, 137
Reformatory schools, 264
Religion as a "subject," 76, 90
Religious basis of education, 11, 13, 50, 78, 81, 89, 152, 164
—— character of education in charity schools, 184-5
—— influence in education, 6-7, 8f., 12, 14, 29, 31, 37f., 48, 50
—— instruction, 50, 72, 83, 102-3, 105, 106-7, 111, 121, 124, 126, 127, 151, 173, 234, 240, 252, 255, 256
"Religious difficulty," the, 47-8, 64, 77 f., 81, 175, 176, 177
Report on the National Sunday School at Stockport, 252
Reports on Elementary Schools (Matthew Arnold), 114, 118, 130, 284
Reports of the Church Sunday Schools, 229
Reports of the Sunday Schools at Stockport, 13, 193
Representative local management of schools, 83, 91, 103, 106 (see *Ad hoc* bodies)
Revised Code (*see* Code)
Revolutionary thought, influence of, 20-22
Rights of Man, 1, 24
Rise of Democracy, 32, 128
Robert Owen, a Biography, 233
Robert Raikes, a History of the Origin of Sunday Schools, 19
Robert Raikes, the Man and his Work, 19, 194, 214
Roebuck, Mr., 33, 68, 75, 80
Rolland, 21
Roman Catholic Poor School Committee, 90, 344
—— —— schools, 91, 92, 182

Roman Catholics, 60, 72, 79, 91, 103, 104, 105

Rose, J. Holland, 32, 128

Rousseau, 1, 7, 21, 198-199, 200, 202, 210, 326

Rowlands, Daniel, 19

Royal Commission on Educational Charities, 58

—— —— on Secondary Education, Report of, 167, 168

—— —— on Technical Instruction, 136, 162, 299

Royal Lancasterian Institution (Association), 38, 48, 49, 52

Rudimentary subjects, 278, 282

Runciman's Bill, Mr., 177

Ruskin, John, 129, 132, 133, 134, 135

Ruskin on Education, 135

Russell, Lord John, 72, 74, 76, 79, 89, 106, 107

SADLER, Mr. Michael, 169
Salaries of teachers, 59, 89, 97, 99, 104, 152, 257, 325, 327, 338, 347

Salford, 105

Salisbury, Lord, 150, 164

Salmon, Principal (David), 14, 47, 185, 188

Salomon, Otto, 298, 299

Sandford and Merton, 206

Scarborough, 366

Scholarships from elementary schools, 131, 167, 168, 174

School attendance (*see* Attendance)

—— Attendance Committees, 143, 144, 152, 162, 171, 172

—— Boards, 63, 104, 106, 124, 125, 126, 129, 131, 138, 139, 144, 149, 151-2, 162, 163, 165, 166, 169, 171, 172, 250, 274

—— buildings, 88, 99, 135, 145, 151, 155, 180, 322-3 (*see* Building Grants)

School Canteen Committees, 178, 179

—— exemption certificates, 143, 144

—— fees, 3, 12, 24, 39, 51, 54, 59, 69, 84, 89, 95, 105, 112, 120, 121, 125, 126, 139, 142, 146, 176, 192

—— games, 296

—— gardens, 275, 294 (*see* gardening)

—— leaving age, 100, 109, 112, 144, 145

—— library, 135, 254

—— life, duration of, 51, 54, 60, 68, 73, 108, 109

—— masters described, 4, 324-5, 326

—— meals, 12, 14, 42, 133, 137, 178-9, 192

—— organisation, types of, 271 f.

—— staffing, 89, 90, 111, 114, 145, 148, 152, 247, 250, 318 f., 345, 357

—— studies challenged, 287

School and Society, 285

School and the Child, The, 311

Schools Inquiry (Taunton) Commission, 157

—— to equip for life, 260

——, ward, 5

——, workhouse, 5, 12

——, writing, 5

Schools of Industry, 5, 12, 13, 31, 38, 40, 41-2, 48, 54, 68, 69, 87, 183, 188, 264

—— ——, children's earnings at, 12, 40, 41-2, 191-2

—— ——, description of, 191-2, cf. 69

—— —— popularity of, 12, 13, 40

Schools of Hellas, 324

Schoolmistress, The, 3

Science, 136, 155, 159, 196 (*see* Elementary Science)

—— and Art Department, 136, 157, 167, 168

Science of Education (Felkin's translation), 310
Scientific movement, 287, 291, 295
Scotland, 6, 15, 42, 81, 92
Scott, Sir Walter, 208
Scriptural alphabet, 254
—— arithmetic, 253
—— geography, 253, 254
Secondary education, 53, 131, 156, 157, 158, 166, 167, 168
Secular instruction, 22, 48, 74, 83, 89, 92, 102, 103, 120, 121, 126, 129, 139, 146, 153, 255
—— schools, 124, 127, 287, 295
Secularism, distrust of, 74, 121
Secularist Bills, 104, 105, 107
—— party, 64, 101, 104, 105, 107, 119
Select Committees, 42, 51, 58, 71, 73, 105, 328
—— ——, Reports of, 51, 58, 73, 256, 324, 327, 332, 333, 334, 335, 337, 341
Self-Help a Hundred Years Ago, 38, 57
Sesame and Lilies, 136
Sewing, 14, 46, 52, 54, 57, 114, 185, 192, 215, 217, 234, 256 (*see* Needlework)
Shackleton, Mr., 145
Sheffield, 4, 5, 8, 120, 157, 158, 190, 299
Shelley, Godwin, and their Circle, 25
Shenstone, 3
Sherwood, Mrs., 253
Simultaneous method of instruction, 213, 274
Sinclair, Ven. Archdeacon, 90
Singing, 69, 88, 148, 233, 234, 275, 308 (*see* Music)
Single school parishes, 176, 177
Six Radical Thinkers, 32, 68, 132
Slaney, Mr., 72, 80
Slöjd, 298-9

Small Manual for the Use of Village Schools, A, 220
Smith, Adam, 1, 22, 23-4, 26, 160, 296
——, Sydney, 32
Socialistic influences in education, 31, 33-7
Society for Bettering the Condition of the Poor, 31, 38-39, 192
—— for Diffusing Useful Knowledge, 33, 61, 287
—— for Promoting Christian Knowledge, 9, 13 f., 16, 50, 51, 185, 187
—— for the Establishment and Support of Sunday Schools, 19
—— of Industry at Caistor, 40 ; *Reports*, 40
South Kensington, 157, 168, 299
Southwark, 53
"Specific subjects," 147, 301, 302, 305
Spelling, 196, 206, 221, 241, 315
"Spelling off Book," 223
"Spelling on Book," 223, cf. 187
Spencer, Herbert, 36, 131, 286 f.
Spitalfields, infant school at, 56
Spontaneity, 233, 260
Standard Seven, 147, 304
State and education, 6, 20 f., 36, 40, 64, 65, 66, 67, 70, 74, 84, 87, 92, 101, 103, 129, 133, 161, 174 f.
—— cannot educate, 76-7, 78-9, 85-6
—— system, struggle for, 68 f., 103 f., 122
—— training college, 36, 339 ; (controversy) 75 f.
State Intervention in English Education, 6
Statistical methods, use of, 30
—— societies, 71, 72, 73, 82
Stephens, W. W., 21
Stipendiary monitors, 346
Stock, Rev. Thomas, 18
Stockport, 13, 193, 228, 229, 252

Stockport, Minutes of National school at, 257, 325
Stow, David, 228, 243, 244 f., 271, 295, 334, 336
Sunday School movement, 9, 18 f., 40
Sunday School Union, 38, 40
Sunday schools, 5, 10, 13, 18, 31, 38, 40, 43, 71, 85, 94, 96, 184, 189, 192-3, 228
Sunday Schools of Wales, The, 9, 18
Sunderland Lancasterian school, 224
Swedish drill, 296, 307
Swimming, 134, 307
Swiss Family Robinson, 196
Syllabus of Standards, 279-280
"Sympathy of numbers," 246

TATE, T., 276
Teacher's Handbook of Slöjd, The, 299
Teachers, a new sacerdotal class, 117
—— as Civil Servants, 111, 114, 345-6
——, registration of, 167
—— should be the first care of the State, 338
——, social inferiority of, 324-5, 327, 328
Teachers' certificates, 102, 114, 147, 336, 337, 347
—— improvement societies, 328
—— National Society, scheme for, 337
—— pensions, 337, 347-8
Teaching profession, efforts to make an attractive, 90, 104, 346-7
Technical Instruction Act, 162, 167
—— training, demand for, 136, 162, 297, 298
Temple, Archbishop, 353
Test Acts, 63

The Enlightenment and popular education, 7
The Stones of Venice, 133, 134
Theophrastus, 326
Three R's., 11, 48, 54, 67, 68, 69, 111, 114, 143, 147, 148, 155, 232, 251, 259, 275, 278, 281, 282, 298, 301, 315.
Tillotson, Archbishop, 9
Time charts, 197, 234
Time-tables, 147, 215, 284, 309 f.
Tooting, Lancaster's boarding school at, 52
Towards Educational Peace, 178
Toys in education, 196, 205
"Training," meaning of, 245
Training College, age of entry to, 332, 336, 340, 349, 370
—— ——, a London men's, 362-3
—— ——, Borough Road, 97, 330, 344, 348
—— ——, Brecon, 96, 344
—— ——, Carmarthen, 96
—— ——, Chester, 344, 351
—— —— curriculum, 342, 349, 351, 352, 356, 367-8
—— ——, Diocesan, 344
—— ——, Durham, 332
—— ——, effect of Revised Code on, 356
—— ——, Exeter, 344
—— ——, Homerton, 85, 344
—— ——, more variety in, 361, 369
—— ——, Municipal, 172, 366
—— ——, need for demonstration and practising schools, 353
—— ——, Norwich, 332
—— ——, Oxford, 344
—— ——, Rotherhithe, 344
—— ——, St. Mark's, 344, 348, 349, 351
—— ——, St. Mary's, Hammersmith, 344
—— ——, Salisbury, 344
—— ——, Vehrli's, 342
—— ——, Westminster, 344

Training College, Whitelands, 344
—— ——, York, 351, 332
Training Colleges, statistics of, 354, 357, 360, 364, 366, 367
—— ——, Temple's Report on, 353 f.
—— ——, undenominational, 152, 363
—— ——, University Day, 152, 159, 363-4, 366, 368
—— ——, women's, Sir Joshua Fitch's description ⟨ 362
Training of Teachers at th Barrington School, 181〈 331
—— —— at the Borough ⟩ad, 1834, 333-4
—— —— at the Glasgow N⟨ -mal Seminary, 335-6
—— —— by the Home and Colonial Society, 340
—— —— by Wilderspin, 339-40
—— —— entrusted to voluntary agencies, 76, 344
—— —— for Charity schools, 14, 329
—— —— for Infants schools, 56, 339 f.
—— —— for Monitorial schools, 330-1
—— —— in Central schools, 50, 51, 52, 332, 333, 334
—— ——, Kay - Shuttleworth, experiment at Battersea, 341-3, 369
—— ——, period needed for, 332, 335, 336, 340
Training System, The, 228, 245
Treason of the Blue Books, The, 100
Tremenheere, Mr., Report on South Wales, 95 f.
Trimmer, James, 42
Trimmer, Mrs.. 40, 47, 187, 188, 191, 223
—— Charity School Spelling Book, 189, 223
Truant schools, 152
Turgot, 21

Two Hundred Years : a History of the S.P.C.K., 14
Typical schools : a "bad" school, 277-8
—— ——, a "fair" school, 277
—— ——, a "good" school, 276, 306
—— ——, a "poor" school, 306
—— ——, an "average" school, 250, 275
—— ——, an "excellent" school, 314

"UNCOVERED school-room," the, 246
Undenominationalists, 64, 138
University Day Training Colleges, 152
Unorganised school, 213
Unpopularity of day school education, 12
Unsectarian education, 67, 83, 89, 119, 120, 140, 151, 153, 177
Useful knowledge v. developing capacity, 260
Utilitarian movement, 32, 287

VACATION schools, 179
Value of school inspection, 109
Variety in education, plea for, 164
Vehrli, 342
Village school on the Madras plan, 219-220
Virtue the result of education, 200-1
Vocational training, 137, 154, 157, 264, 297
Voluntary denominational teaching, 83, 152
Voluntary schools, 123, 125, 140, 155, 159, 163, 165, 172, 175
—— ——, capital value of, 163-4

Voluntary schools, financial difficulties, 129, 149-150, 163f., 170, 256-7
—— ——, management of, 90-92, 170, 172-3
—— ——, proportion of places provided by, 141, 170, 182
—— ——, transference of, 124, 175, 176, 182
"Voluntaryism," mistake of extreme, 87
——, results, 94, 97, 98
——, resources of inadequate, 102
"Voluntaryists," 64, 84, 104, 105
——, educational position of, 85-6, 170

WALES, 5, 6, 9, 13, 16, 19, 40, 86, 93 f., 144, 168, 181, 306, 323.
Wales, North, education in, 97
——, progress of education in, 93 f.
——, Report of the Commissioners of Inquiry, 1848, 94, 95, 99, 100-1
——, scholarship system in, 168
——, South, education in, 95-6, 97
——, Sunday schools in, 9, 18
Wales (Phillips), 96, 99
Wallas, Graham, 32, 53
Walthamstow, Infant school at, 56
Ward schools, 5
Watson, Joshua, 50
Watts, Dr. Isaac, 10, 13, 14, 186, 197
Wealth of Nations, 1, 24
Welch Piety, 16, 17, 184, 186, 187
Wells, Algernon, 86
Welsh Circulating schools, 16 f., 184
—— Code, 323
—— Education Alliance, 121
—— —— Department, 323

Welsh Education Commission, 1846. 98-101
—— —— Committee, 96
—— Intermediate School Act, 168
—— language, facilities for, 306, 323
—— —— v. English, 9, 16, 93, 94-95, 101
Wesley, 19
Wesleyans, 76, 79, 91, 104
West London Lancasterian Association, 28, 53
Westminster Central Training School, 52, 256-344
Westminster Review, 289
Whiskey Money, 162
Whitbread, Mr., 26, 45, 49, 58
Whitechapel Charity School, 49
Whitefield, George, 19
Whitehall, 168
Whole Duty of Man, 185, 188, 189
Wigram, Rev. J. C., 253, 256
Wilderspin, 55, 56, 236 f., 243, 245, 248, 295, 339
Wilhem's method of teaching singing, 270
William Cobbett, a Biography, 3
William of Wykeham, 43
Williams, Mr., M.P., 98
Wilson, Joseph, 55-56
——, Rev. Wm., 56
Windleband, 33
Wood, John, 229, 245, 334
Wordsworth, 30, 37, 62
Workhouse schools, 82
Working class movement and education, 27, 30, 57, 63, 65, 130
—— Classes, National Union of, 63, 65
—— schools, 11. 12
Wyse, Mr., 68, 72, 74, 262

YORK, Middle School at, 259
Young, Molly, 232
Yverdun, 265

PRINTED AT THE BURLINGTON PRESS, CAMBRIDGE.

A complete Catalogue of Text-Books published by the University Tutorial Press, and separate Sectional Catalogues in English Language and Literature, French, Mathematics, and Science, may be had on application to the Publisher.

SELECTED TEXT-BOOKS

IN

PHILOSOPHY, EDUCATION, ART AND MUSIC

PUBLISHED BY THE

University Tutorial Press Ld.,

25 HIGH ST., NEW OXFORD ST., W.C.

Philosophy.

Ethics, A Manual of. By J. S. MACKENZIE, Litt.D., M.A., Professor of Logic and Philosophy in the University College of South Wales and Monmouthshire, formerly Fellow of Trinity College, Cambridge, Examiner in the Universities of Cambridge and Aberdeen. *Fourth Edition, Enlarged.* **6s. 6d.**

Logic, A Manual of. By J. WELTON, M.A., Professor of Education in the University of Leeds. 2 vols.

Volume I. *Second Edition.* **8s. 6d.**

Volume II. **6s. 6d.**

Vol. I. contains the whole of Deductive Logic, except Fallacies, which are treated, with Inductive Fallacies, in Vol. II.

Logic, Intermediate. By JAMES WELTON, M.A., Professor of Education in the University of Leeds, and A. J. MONAHAN, M.A. With Questions and Exercises. **7s. 6d.**

This book is based upon the *Manual of Logic*; it is a simpler and briefer treatment adapted to the Intermediate University examinations.

Philosophy—*continued.*

Logic, Exercises in. By F. C. Bartlett, M.A. 2s. 6d.

Logic, Questions on, with Illustrative Examples. By H. Holman, M.A., H.M.I., and M. C. W. Irvine, M.A. 2s. 6d.

Psychology, The Groundwork of. By G. F. Stout, M.A., LL.D., Fellow of the British Academy. 4s. 6d.

The work is not an abridgment of the *Manual of Psychology.* Even where the matter presented is substantially the same, the mode of presentation is different.

Psychology, A Manual of. By G. F. Stout, M.A., LL.D. *Third Edition, Revised and Enlarged.* 8s. 6d.

The present work contains an exposition of Psychology from a genetic point of view. The phases through which the ideal construction of self and the world has passed are illustrated by reference to the mental condition of the lower races of mankind. The third edition has been substantially rewritten.

Education.

Principles and Methods of Teaching. By James Welton, M.A., Professor of Education in the University of Leeds. *Second Edition, Revised and Enlarged.* 5s. 6d.

The purpose of this book is to help teachers in their daily work, and to assist them when they offer themselves for examination in that work.

The Teaching of Modern Subjects (from *Principles and Methods of Teaching*).

(1) The Teaching of English (Reading, Language, and Literature). 1s. (2) The Teaching of Geography. 1s. (3) The Teaching of History. 1s. (4) The Teaching of Mathematics and Science. 1s. 6d. (5) The Teaching of Music. 6d. (6) The Teaching of Foreign Languages. 1s.

Principles and Methods of Moral Training with Special Reference to School Discipline. By Professor James Welton, M.A., and F. G. Blandford, M.A., Lecturer in Education in the Cambridge University Training College. 3s. 6d.

Education—*continued.*

Principles and Methods of Physical Education and Hygiene. By W. P. WELPTON, B.Sc., Master of Method in the University of Leeds. With a Sketch of the History of Physical Education by Professor JAMES WELTON, M.A. **4s. 6d.**

Throughout this work the standpoint from which physical education is regarded is such that the physical and the mental aspects of education are brought into harmony.

This book is also issued without the chapters on Hygiene, under the title *Physical Education.* **3s. 6d.**

Psychology, Fundamentals of. A brief account of the Nature and Development of Mental Processes for Teachers. By B. DUMVILLE, M.A., F.C.P. **4s. 6d.**

Child Mind. An Introduction to Psychology for Teachers. By BENJAMIN DUMVILLE, M.A., F.C.P. **2s. 6d.**

Text-Book of Hygiene for Teachers. By R. A. LYSTER, M.D., B.Sc., D.P.H., Medical Officer of Health for Hampshire, and Chief Medical Officer to the Education Committee. **4s. 6d.**

School Hygiene. By R. A. LYSTER, M.D., B.Sc., D.P.H. *Second Edition.* **3s. 6d.**

School Organisation. By S. E. BRAY, M.A., Inspector of Schools to the London County Council. With a Chapter on "The Place of the Elementary School in a National System of Education," by Sir J. H. YOXALL. *Second Edition.* **3s.**

School Training. By R. E. HUGHES, M.A. **2s.**

This work is concerned primarily with the *aim*, and secondarily with the *means*, of school training, and with the relations of school and home, actual and ideal.

The Life and Work of Pestalozzi. By J. A. GREEN, M.A., Professor of Education in the University of Sheffield. **4s. 6d.**

The Educational Ideas of Pestalozzi. By J. A. GREEN, M.A. **2s. 6d.**

The Educational Ideas of Froebel. By J. WHITE, D.Sc. **1s.**

University Tutorial Press Ld., London, W.C.

Education—*continued*.

Synthesis of Froebel and Herbart. By R. D. CHALKE, M.A., LL.D. **3s. 6d.**

The chief aim of the book is to trace the relation of Pestalozzi, Froebel, and Herbart to each other and to the progress of modern education.

Nature Study, the Aims and Methods of. A Guide for Teachers. By JOHN RENNIE, D.Sc., F.R.S.E. With an Introduction by Professor J. Arthur Thomson. **3s. 6d.**

The greater part of the book is devoted to model courses and model lessons dealing with typical studies and designed for all grades in the school. All branches of nature study are included.

Nature Study, the Aims and Methods of (South African Edition). By JOHN RENNIE, D.Sc., F.R.S.E., and GEORGE RATTRAY, M.A., D.Sc. **3s. 6d.**

School Lessons in Plant and Animal Life. By JOHN RENNIE, D.Sc., F.R.S.E. **4s. 6d.**

A course of eighty lessons in Nature Study, with full guidance to the teacher as to how to learn and how to teach the subject.

School Gardening, with a Guide to Horticulture. By A. HOSKING, Lecturer in Horticulture and Chief Supervisor of School Gardens, West of Scotland Agricultural College. With numerous illustrations and plans. **3s. 6d.**

The Teaching of Drawing: its Aims and Methods. By S. POLAK and H. C. QUILTER. **2s. 6d.**

The scheme of the work falls under three heads as follows:— (1) the aims to be kept in view in the teaching of Drawing, (2) the methods by which a teacher should try to realise these aims, and (3) the use of Drawing to illustrate lessons on drawing and on other subjects.

The Teaching of Needlework: its Aims and Methods. By Miss H. M. BRADLEY, B.A. **1s. 6d.**

Voice Training in Speech and Song. By H. H. HULBERT, M.A., M.R.C.S., L.R.C.P. **1s. 6d.**

The Science of Speech: an Elementary Manual of Phonetics for Teachers. By B. DUMVILLE, M.A., F.C.P. **2s. 6d.**

Manual Training. By A. H. JENKINS. [*In preparation.*

University Tutorial Press Ld., London, W.C.

Lightning Source UK Ltd.
Milton Keynes UK
UKHW041207260219
338006UK00012B/917/P